KANT AND THE PLATYPUS

ALSO BY UMBERTO ECO

A Theory of Semiotics
The Role of the Reader
The Name of the Rose
Semiotics and the Philosophy of Language
Travels in Hyperreality: Essays
How to Travel with a Salmon
Art and Beauty in the Middle Ages
The Aesthetics of Aquinas
The Open Work
The Aesthetics of Chaosmos
Foucault's Pendulum
Misreadings
The Island of the Day Before

FOR CHILDREN, WITH EUGENIO CARMI

The Bomb and the General
The Three Astronauts

UMBERTO ECO

KANT AND THE PLATYPUS

Essays on Language and Cognition

Translated from the Italian by
Alastair McEwen

SECKER & WARBURG
London

Published by Secker & Warburg 1999

2 4 6 8 10 9 7 5 3 1

Copyright © 1997 R. C. S. Libri S.p.A
English translation © Alastair McEwen 1999

This is a translation of *Kant e l'ornitorinco*

First published in Italy in 1997 by Bompiani
R. C. S. Libri S.p.A., Milan

First published in Great Britain in 1999 by
Secker & Warburg
Random House, 20 Vauxhall Bridge Road,
London SW1V 2SA

Random House Australia (Pty) Limited
20 Alfred Street, Milsons Point, Sydney,
New South Wales 2061, Australia

Random House New Zealand Limited
18 Poland Road, Glenfield,
Auckland 10, New Zealand

Random House South Africa (Pty) Limited
Endulini, 5A Jubilee Road,
Parktown 2193, South Africa

Random House UK Limited Reg. No. 954009

A CIP catalogue record for this book is available from the British Library

ISBN 0 436 41057 5

Papers used by Random House UK Limited are natural,
recyclable products made from wood grown in sustainable forests.
The manufacturing processes conform to the environmental
regulations of the country of origin.

Printed and bound in Great Britain by
Biddles Ltd, Guildford and King's Lynn

CONTENTS

KANT AND THE PLATYPUS

INTRODUCTION

What has Kant got to do with the platypus? Nothing. As we shall see from the dates, he couldn't have had anything to do with it. And this should suffice to justify the title and its use of an incongruous set that sounds like a tribute to Borges's ancient Chinese encyclopedia.

So what is this book about? Apart from the platypus, it's about cats, dogs, mice, and horses, but also chairs, plates, trees, mountains, and other things we see every day, and it's about the reasons why we can tell an elephant from an armadillo (as well as why we don't normally mistake our wife for a hat). This is a formidable philosophical problem that has obsessed human thought from Plato to present-day cognitivists, and it is one that even Kant (as we shall see) not only failed to solve but didn't even manage to express in satisfactory terms. So you can imagine how much chance I've got.

This is why the essays making up this book (written over twelve months, picking up the themes I have been dealing with—including some unpublished material—over these last few years) spring from a nucleus of interconnected theoretical concerns, and while they are interreferential, they are not to be read as "chapters" of a work with systematic ambitions. Although the various paragraphs are sometimes scrupulously numbered into sections and subsections, this is only to enable rapid cross-referencing between one essay and another, without this artifice necessarily suggesting an underlying architecture. And while I say many things in these pages, there are many more that I don't say, simply because my ideas are not clear in that regard. In fact, I should like to take as my motto a quotation from Boscoe Pertwee, an eighteenth-century author (unknown to me), which I found in Gregory (1981: 558): "I used to be indecisive but now I'm not so sure."

Written therefore in a spirit of indecision and beset by numerous doubts, these essays spring from my feeling of not having honored certain debts incurred when I published *A Theory of Semiotics* in 1976 (in which I took up and developed various lines of research begun in the latter half of the sixties). The debts concerned the problems of reference, iconism, truth, perception, and what in those days I used to call the lower threshold of semiotics. In the course of these twenty-two years, many people have posed me some most pressing problems, orally or in writing, while an even greater number have asked me if and when I was going to write an updated version of *A Theory of Semiotics*. These essays were written also to explain, perhaps to myself rather than to others, why I did not do so.

Basically, there are two reasons. The first is that, while in the sixties it was possible to think of linking up the scattered members of many semiotic research projects in order to attempt a *summa* of them, today the area covered has become so wide (overlapping that of the various cognitive sciences) that any new systematization would seem rash. What we are now faced with is an expanding galaxy and no longer a planetary system for which fundamental equations can be supplied, a situation that strikes me as a sign of success and health. Questioning about semiosis has become central to a great number of disciplines, even on the part of those who did not think they were practicing semiotics, or were practicing it unwittingly, or simply did not wish to practice it. This was already true when I was writing *A Theory of Semiotics* (just to make one example, it was not because biologists had been reading books on semiotics that they began talking about genetic "codes"), but the phenomenon has grown so widespread as to suggest that, no matter how selective their theoretical criteria, those interested in the argument would be well advised to apply a kind of ecumenical tolerance, in the same sense in which the broadminded missionary decides that even the infidel, whatever the idol or superior principle he worships, is *naturaliter* a Christian and shall therefore be saved.

Nevertheless everyone, no matter how tolerant he may be of other people's opinions, must also enunciate his own, at least with regard to fundamental questions. With a view to integrating and correcting *A Theory of Semiotics*, then, here I am ready to explain my most recent ideas regarding some points that that book left in abeyance.

As a matter of fact (and here we come to the second reason), in the first part of *A Theory of Semiotics* I began with a problem: If, in a Peircean sense, there is such a thing as a Dynamical Object, we know it only through an Immediate Object. By manipulating signs, we refer to the Dynamical Object as a *terminus ad quem* of semiosis. In the second part of the book, devoted to the ways in which signs are produced, I presupposed (even though I did not spell it out) that if we speak (or emit signs, of whatever type they may be), it is because Something urges us to speak. And this ushered in the problem of the Dynamical Object as a *terminus a quo*.

The decision to state the problem of the Dynamical Object first in terms of its being a *terminus ad quem* was to determine my successive interests, following the development of semiosis as a sequence of interpretants—interpretants being a collective, public, observable product laid down in the course of cultural processes, even though one does not presume the existence of a mind that admits of, uses, or develops them. This led to what I have written on the problem of signification, the text and intertextuality, narrativity, and the elaboration and limits of interpretation. But it is precisely the problem of the limits of interpretation that set me to wondering whether those limits are only cultural and textual or something that lies concealed at greater depths. And this explains why the first of these essays deals with Being. It's not a matter of delusions of grandeur but of professional duty. As will be seen, I speak of Being only inasmuch as I feel that what *is* sets limits on our freedom of speech.

When we presume a subject that tries to understand what it experiences (and the object—that is to say, the Thing-in-Itself—becomes the *terminus a quo*), then, even before the formation of the chain of interpretants, there comes into play a process of interpreting the world that, especially in the case of novel or unknown objects (such as the platypus at the end of the eighteenth century), assumes an "auroral" form, made up through trial and error; but this is already semiosis in progress, which calls pre-established cultural systems into question.

And so, every time I thought of putting my hand to *A Theory of Semiotics* again, I wondered if I shouldn't have restructured it starting from the second part. The reasons why I wondered this ought to become evident on reading the following essays. The fact that they are presented in essay form, explorations that are vagabond from diverse standpoints, says how I realized—gripped by the impulse to overturn everything systematically—I was unable to structure it (and perhaps no one can do this alone). Out of prudence I decided to shift from the architecture of gardens to gardening, so instead of designing Versailles, I limited myself to digging over some flower beds barely connected by beaten earth paths—and this with the lingering suspicion that all around there was still a romantic park in the English manner.

By deciding where to locate my flower beds, I have decided to take issue with myself (instead of taking issue with thousands of others), and that's to say with various things I had written before, correcting myself when this struck me as the right thing to do, but without denying myself in toto, because one changes one's ideas the way an animal sheds its coat, in patches: it's never a wholesale change from one day to the next. If I had to sum up the nucleus of problems around which I have been circling, I would talk in terms of the characteristics of a cognitive semantics (which certainly has little to do with the truth-functional or the structural-lexical varieties, even though it tries to draw themes and ideas from both) based on a *contractual* notion both of our cognitive schemata and of signification and reference—a position consistent with my previous attempts to elaborate a theory of content featuring a blend of semantics and pragmatics. In doing this, I try to temper an eminently "cultural" view of semiosic processes with the fact that, whatever the weight of our cultural systems, there is something in the *continuum* of experience that sets a limit on our interpretations, and so— if I weren't afraid of sounding pretentious—I would say that the dispute between *internal realism* and *external realism* would tend to compose itself in a notion of *contractual realism*.

THE READER WILL notice that, starting from the second essay and more and more as I go on, these theoretical discussions of mine are interwoven with "stories." Perhaps some readers will know that, when I feel the urge to tell stories, I satisfy it elsewhere, and therefore my decision to tell stories here is not dictated by a need to realize a suppressed vocation (a temptation for many contemporary thinkers who substitute philosophy with pages of *bellelettrisme*). It could be said that there is a profound philosophical reason behind my decision: if, as they say, the era of the "great narrative" has passed, it might be useful to proceed by parables, which let us see something in textual mode—as Lotman would have put it, and as Bruner invites us to do—without wanting to draw grammars from them.

But there is a second reason. In adopting a questioning approach to the way in which we perceive (but also name) cats, mice, or elephants, it struck me as useful not so much to analyze expressions like *There is a cat on the mat* in terms of models, or to go see what our neurons do when we see a cat on the mat (not to mention what the cat's neurons do when it sees us sitting on the mat—as I shall explain, I try not to stick my nose into the "black box," preferring to leave this difficult profession to the experts), as to bring an oft neglected character back to the stage, namely, common sense. And in order to understand how common sense works, there is nothing better than imagining "stories" in which people behave according to its dictates. In this way we discover that normality is narratively surprising.

But perhaps the presence of all these cats and dogs and mice in my discourse has brought me back to the cognitive function of the moralizing bestiaries and fables. In attempting at least to update the bestiary, I have introduced the platypus as the hero of my book. I am grateful to Stephen Jay Gould and Giorgio Celli (as well as to Gianni Piccini, via the Internet) for having aided and abetted me in my hunt for this imponderable little animal (which years ago I also encountered in person). The platypus accompanied me step by step, even where I don't mention it, and I took the trouble to supply it with philosophical credentials by immediately finding it a relation with the unicorn, which, like bachelors, can never be absent from any reflections on language.

In debt as I am to Borges for many ideas in the course of my previous activities, I had been consoling myself for the fact that Borges had talked of everything, except the platypus, therefore I was overjoyed at having escaped the anxiety of influence, but just as I was about to hand these essays over to the printers, Stefano Bartezzaghi pointed out to me that Borges, at least orally, in a conversation with Domenico Porzio, in explaining why (perhaps) he had never gone to Australia, had spoken of the platypus: "Apart from the kangaroo and the platypus, which is a horrible animal, made from the pieces of other animals, now there are camels too."[1] I had already dealt with the camel, when working on the Aristotelian classifications. In this book I explain why the platypus is not horrible, but prodigious and providential, if we are to put a theory of knowledge to the test. By the way, given the platypus's very early appearance in the development of the species, I insinuate that it was not made from the pieces of other animals, but that the other animals were made from pieces of the platypus.

I TALK OF cats and platypuses, but also of Kant—otherwise the title would be unjustifiable. As a matter of fact I talk of cats precisely because Kant brought in empirical concepts (and while he didn't talk about cats, he talked about dogs), after which he didn't know where to put them. I started from Kant to honor another debt I had incurred with myself, back in my university days, when I began to take down lots of little notes on that "devastating" concept (the suggestion came from Peirce) known as the schema. The problem of schematism has cropped up again today, right in the middle of the debate on cognitive processes. But many of these lines of research suffer from insufficient historical background. Some people talk about neoconstructivism, for example, others make explicit references to Kant, but many others again indulge in neo-Kantism all unawares. I still remember an American book, a very good one, what's more (but, as the saying goes, no names, no pack drill), in which at a certain point there is a note that says something like "It seems that Kant said something similar regarding this point (cf. Brown 1988)."

If it seems that Kant said something similar, the task of a philosophical discourse is to take another look at Kant's point of departure and to see what group of problems he had been wrestling with, because his experience can teach us something too. We might still be the unwitting children of his errors (just as we are of his truths), and knowing this might help us avoid making analogous errors or thinking that we have just discovered something that he suggested two hundred years ago. Let's put it this way: Kant knew nothing about the platypus, and that should not worry us, but if the platypus is to solve its own identity crisis, it ought to know something about Kant.

I'M NOT GOING to attempt an exhaustive table of acknowledgments, because it would be pure name dropping, starting with Parmenides. The bibliographical references at the end of this book do not make up a bibliography, they are only a legal device aimed at avoiding accusations of having omitted the names of persons from whom I took direct quotations. And so many important names—those of authors to whom I owe much but whom I have not cited directly—are absent.

I should like to thank the Italian Academy for Advanced Studies in America at Columbia University for giving me the opportunity to devote myself for two months to the first drafts of essays 3, 4, and 5.

Apart from this, in recent years I have been stimulated on these themes by the people who worked with me (and who have introjected the sound principle that you must speak of your friends without mincing words, because elaborate ceremonial is reserved for adversaries only). My debts in this sense, having been accumulated in the course of many debates, are infinite. It will be seen that I have quoted some dissertations produced in recent years, which have directly influenced many of these essays, but goodness knows how many names I have not had occasion to mention, from among all those with whom I debated in the course of workshops held at the Center for Semiotic and Cognitive Studies of the University of San Marino and in the innumerable seminars held at the University of Bologna.

Nor can I omit the various comments and ideas, not to mention the stubborn resistance, offered by the contributors to the anthology *Semiotica Storia Interpretazione: Saggi intorno a Umberto Eco* (Milan: Bompiani, 1992).[2] Finally, the decision to put my hand to these essays after collecting and re-elaborating my various notebooks perhaps came to me following the discussions, diagnoses, and prognoses (still uncertain) offered me by the participants in the *Decade* at Cerisy-la-Salle in the summer of 1996. At the time, those present must have thought that I appreciated the musical evenings enlivened by generous doses of calvados more than anything else, but I didn't miss a word of what was said, and I was in difficulty on several occasions.[3]

My thanks to all of them (especially the youngest of them) for having awakened me from some of my dogmatic slumbers—if not like Hume, at least like old Lampe.

Chapter One

⸺◈⸺

On Being

The history of research into the philosophy of language is full of *men* (who are rational and mortal animals), *bachelors* (who are unmarried adult males), and *tigers* (though it is not clear whether we should define them as feline mammals or big cats with a yellow coat and black stripes). Analyses of prepositions and adverbs (what do *beside, by,* or *when* mean?) are less common (but the few we have are very important), while there are some excellent analyses of emotions (such as *anger* in Greimas), and some fairly frequent analyses of verbs, such as *to go, to clean, to praise, to kill.* On the other hand no semantic study seems to have provided a satisfactory analysis of the verb *to be,* despite the fact that we use it in everyday speech, in all its forms, with a certain regularity.

This was more than evident to Pascal (in a fragment from 1655): "One cannot begin to define being without falling victim to this absurdity: one cannot define a word without beginning with the term *is,* be it expressly stated or merely understood. To define being, therefore, you have to say *is,* thus using the term to be defined in the definition." Which is not the same as saying, as Gorgias said, that we cannot speak of being: we speak about it all the time, too often perhaps; the problem is that this magic word helps us define almost everything but is defined by nothing. In semantics we would speak of a primitive, the most primitive of all.

When Aristotle (*Metaphysics* IV, 1.1) says there is a science that studies being as being, he uses the present participle *to on*. In Italian this is translated by some as *ente,* by others as *essere*. In point of fact this *to on* can be understood as that which is, as the existing being,[1] and finally as what the Schoolmen called the *ens,* whose plural is *entia,* the things that are. But if Aristotle had been thinking only of the things of the real world around us, he would not have spoken of a special science: entities are studied, according to the sector of reality, by zoology, physics, and even by politics. Aristotle says *to on e on,* the *being as such*. When we speak of an entity (be it a panther or a pyramid) as an entity (and not as a panther or a pyramid), then the *to on* becomes that which is common to all beings, and that which is common to all entities is the fact that they are, the fact of their being. In this sense, as Peirce said, Being is that abstract aspect that belongs to all objects expressed in concrete terms: it has an unlimited *extension* and null *intension* (or *comprehension*).[2] Which is like saying that it refers to everything but has no meaning. For this reason it seems clear why in philosophical language the substantive use of the present participle, normal for the Greeks, gradually shifted to the infinitive, if not in Greek, certainly in the Scholastic *esse*. This ambiguity is already to be found in Parmenides, who talks of *t'eon,* but then affirms that *esti gar einai* (DK 6), and it is hard not to take an infinitive (*to be*) that becomes the subject of an *is* as a substantive. In Aristotle being as an object of knowledge is *to on,* but the essence is *to ti en einai* (*Met*. IV, 1028b, 33.36), what being was, but in the sense of that which being stably is (which was later to be translated as *quod quid erat esse*). Nevertheless, it cannot be denied that *to be* is also a verb, which expresses not only the act of being something (and hence we say that a cat is a feline) but also the activity (and hence we say that it's good to be in sound health, or to be on vacation), to the point that often (when one is said to be glad to be in the world) it is used as a synonym for *to exist,* even though the equation leaves room for a great many reservations, because originally *ex-istere* meant "to leave-from," "to manifest one-self," and therefore "to come into being."[3]

Therefore, we have (i) a substantive, the *ens,* let's call it the existing entity, (ii) another substantive, being, and (iii) a verb, *to be.* The perplexity is such that different languages react in different ways to it. Italian and German have a term for (i), *ente* and *Seiende,* but only one term for both (ii) and (iii), *essere* and *Sein.* It was on the basis of this distinction that Heidegger founded the difference between the ontic and the ontological. While French has only one term, *être,* it's true that the philosophical neologism *étant* has been in use since the seventeenth century, but Gilson himself (in the first edition of *L'être et l'essence*) had difficulty in accepting it, and opted to use it only in subsequent editions. Scholastic Latin had adopted *ens* for (i), but in a spirit of tormented casualness it also toyed with (ii), sometimes using *ens* and other times using *esse.*[4] In current English there are only two terms, *to be* and *being,* the second usually covering both senses (i) and (ii): for instance, the current translations of Aquinas's *De ente et essentia* read *On Being and Essence.* Some of Heidegger's translators (see for instance Ralph Manheim's translation *An Introduction to Metaphysics,* New Haven: Yale University Press, 1959) use *essent* for (i) but others (see *Being and Time,* translated by J. Macquarrie and E. Robinson, New York: Harper, 1962) translate "Was ist das Seiende, das Seiende in seinen Sein?" as "What is being, what is beingness in its Being?" Peirce proposed to use *ens* (or *entity*) for all the things that may be spoken of,[5] including not only material entities but also entities of reason, like the laws of mathematics; and that is how *ens* came to be the equivalent of *being,* in the sense that it is a totality that includes not only what is physically around us but also what is below, or inside, or around or before or after, and founds it and/or justifies it.

But in that case, if we are talking about everything that can be spoken of, we need to include the possible too. Not only and not so much in the sense in which it has been maintained that even possible worlds really exist somewhere (Lewis 1973), but at least in Wolff's sense (*Philosophia prima sive ontologia methodo scientifico pertractata,* 134), according to which an ontology regards the entity *quatenus ens est,* regardless of all questions of existence, and so *quod possibile est, ens est.* A fortiori, therefore, not only speculations but also past events would come within the sphere of being: what is, is in all the conjugations and tenses of the verb *to be.*

By this point, however, temporality (both of the *Dasein* and of the galaxies) has inserted itself into being, and there is no need for us to be Parmenideans at all costs: If Being (with a capital B) is everything that can be spoken of, why shouldn't the future also be a part of it? The future looks like a flaw in a vision of being as a compact and immutable Sphere: but at this point we still cannot know if being is not so much inconstant as mutable, metamorphic, metempsychotic, a compulsive recycler, an inveterate *bricoleur*....

In any case, the languages we speak are what they are, and if they contain ambiguities, or even confusion regarding the use of this primitive (ambiguities that philosophical reflection does not clear up), may it not be that this perplexity expresses a *fundamental condition?*

In order to respect this perplexity, in the pages that follow we shall use *Being* in its widest and most open sense. But what sense can be held by a term that Peirce defined as being of null intension? Could it have the sense suggested by Leibniz's dramatic question "Why is there something rather than nothing?"

Here is what we mean by the word *Being:* Something.

1.1 SEMIOTICS AND THE SOMETHING

Why should semiotics deal with this something? Because one of the problems of semiotics is to say whether and how we use signs to refer to something, and a great deal has been written on this. But I do not think that semiotics can avoid another problem: What is that something that induces us to produce signs?

Every philosophy of language finds itself faced not only with a *terminus ad quem* but also with a *terminus a quo.* It must ask itself not only "To what do we refer when we talk, and with what degree of reliability?" (a problem certainly worthy of consideration) but also "What makes us talk?"

Put phylogenetically, this was the fundamental problem—which modernity has prohibited—of the origins of language, at least from Epicurus onward. But while it can be avoided phylogenetically (by pointing to the lack of archaeological evidence), it cannot be avoided ontogenetically. Our own day-to-day experience provides us with the elements, perhaps imprecise but in a certain sense tangible, with which to answer the question "But why have I been induced to say something?"

Structural semiotics has never addressed the problem (with the exception of Hjelmslev, as we shall see): the various languages are considered as systems that are already constituted (and synchronically analyzable) the moment users express themselves, state, indicate, ask, or command. The rest appertains to the production of words, but the reasons why we talk are psychological and not linguistic. Analytical philosophy has contented itself with its own concept of truth (which deals not with how things really are but with the conclusions that should be drawn if a proposition is understood as true), but it has not considered our prelinguistic relation with things. In other words, the statement *Snow is white* is true if the snow is white, but how we realize (and are sure) that snow is white is delegated to a theory of perception or to optics.

Beyond a doubt the only person who made this problem the very foundation of his theory—semiotic, cognitive, and metaphysical all at the same time—was Peirce. A Dynamical Object drives us to produce a *representamen,* in a quasi-mind this produces an Immediate Object, which in turn is translatable into a potentially infinite series of interpretants and sometimes, through the habit formed in the course of the interpretative process, we come back to the Dynamical Object, and we make something of it.

It might be observed that, as soon as we get back to the Dynamical Object and start speaking about it again, we are once more at the point of departure, and so we have to rename it using another *representamen,* so that in a certain sense the Dynamical Object always remains a Thing-in-Itself, always present and impossible to capture, if not through semiosis.

Yet the Dynamical Object is what drives us to produce semiosis. We produce signs because there is something that demands to be said. To use an expression that is efficacious albeit not very philosophical, the Dynamical Object is Something-that-sets-to-kicking-us[6] and says "Talk!" to us—or "Talk about me!" or again, "Take me into consideration!"

We are familiar with the indexical signs, *this* or *that* in verbal language, a pointing finger, an arrow in the language of images (cf. Eco 1978, 3.6); but there is a phenomenon we must understand as presemiotic, or protosemiotic (in the sense that it constitutes the signal that gets the semiosic process under way), which we will call *primary indexicality* or *attentionality* (Peirce spoke of *attention* as the capacity to direct the mind toward an object, and to pay attention to one element while ignoring another).[7] Primary indexicality occurs when, amid the thick stuff of the sensations that bombard us, we suddenly select something that we set against that general background and decide we want to speak about it (when, in other words, while we live surrounded by luminous, thermic, tactile, and interoceptive sensations, only one of these attracts our attention, and *only afterward* we say that it is cold, or we have a sore foot); primary indexicality occurs when we attract someone's attention, not necessarily to speak to him but just to show him something that will have to become a sign or an example, and we tug his jacket, we turn-his-head-toward.

In the most elementary of semiosic relations, the radical translation illustrated by Quine (1960: 2), before knowing what name the native has assigned to a passing rabbit (or to whatever he sees where I see and understand a passing rabbit), and before I ask him, "What is that thing?"—with an interrogative gesture while, in a way he perhaps finds incomprehensible, I point my finger at the spatiotemporal event that interests me—to ensure that he replies with the celebrated and enigmatic *gavagai,* there is a moment in which I fix his attention on that spatiotemporal event. I may cry out, I may grasp him by the shoulders, but I shall do something so that he notices what I have decided to notice.

This fixing of my own or someone else's attention on something is the condition of every semiosis to come; it even precedes that act of attention (already semiosic, already an effect of thought) by which I decide that something is pertinent, curious, or intriguing, and must be explained by a hypothesis. This fixing comes before curiosity itself, before the perception of the object as an object. It is the as yet blind decision whereby I identify something amid the magma of experience that I have to reckon with.

The whole problem of whether, once a theory of consciousness has been worked out, this object becomes a Dynamical Object, noumenon, or the still raw material of an intuition not yet illuminated by the categorical comes afterward. First there is something, even if it is only my reawakened attention; but not even that, it is my attention as it sleeps, lies in wait, or dozes. It is not the primary act of attention that defines the something, it is the something that arouses the attention, indeed the attention lying in wait is already part (is evidence) of this something.

These are the reasons why semiotics cannot avoid reflecting on this something that (to link us with all those who throughout the centuries have tormented themselves over it) we decide to call Being.

1.2 AN UNNATURAL PROBLEM

It has been said that the problem of being (the answer, that is, to the question "What is being?") is the least natural of all problems, the one that common sense never poses (Aubenque 1962: 13–14). "Being as such is so far from constituting a problem that apparently it is as if such a datum 'didn't exist' " (Heidegger 1973: 1969). To the point that the post-Aristotelian tradition ignored the question and, as it were, removed it, which perhaps explains the legendary fact that the text of *Metaphysics* disappeared, to resurface only in the first century B.C. On the other hand Aristotle himself, and with him the entire Greek philosophical tradition, never posed the question that Leibniz was to put to himself in his *Principes de la nature et de la grace:* "Pourquoi il y a plutôt quelque chose que rien?"—adding that, at bottom, nothingness would have been simpler and less complex than something. As a matter of fact this question also represents the distress of the nonphilosopher who sometimes finds it too difficult to think of God in His inconceivable eternity, or worse still, of the eternity of the world, while it would be much simpler and more reassuring if nothing existed or had ever existed, so that there would never have been even one mind prepared to rack its brains over why there is nothing rather than being. But if we aspire to nothingness, by this act of aspiration we are already in being, albeit in the form of frailty and sin, as Valéry suggests in *Ebauche d'un serpent:*

> Soleil, soleil!... Faute éclatante!
> Toi qui masques la mort, Soleil...
> Par d'impénétrables délices,
> Toi le plus fier de mes complices,
> Et de mes pièges le plus haut,
> Tu gardes les coeurs de connaître
> Que l'univers n'est qu'un défaut
> Dans la pureté du Non-être.

Incidentally, if the normal condition were nothingness, and we were only a luckless transitory excrescence, the ontological argument would also collapse. It would not be worth arguing that, if it is possible to think *id cujus nihil majus cogitari possit* (that is, possessed of all perfections), since part of this being's due should also be the perfection that is existence, the very fact that God is thinkable demonstrates that He exists. Of all the confutations of the ontological argument, the most energetic seems to be expressed by the question "Who says that existence is a perfection?" Once it is admitted that absolute purity consists of Nonbeing, the greatest perfection of God would consist of His nonexistence. Thinking of Him (being able to think of Him) as existing would be the effect of our shortcomings, capable of sullying with the attribution of being what has the supreme right and incredible good fortune not to exist. It would have been interesting had there been a debate not between Anselm of Canterbury and Gaunilon but between Anselm and Cioran.

But even if being were a flaw in the purity of nonbeing, we would be ensnared in this flaw. And therefore we might as well try to talk about it. Let us return therefore to the fundamental question posed by metaphysics: Why is there something (whether it is being as such, or the plurality of entities that may be experienced or thought of, and the totality of the immense flaw that has deprived us of the divine tranquillity of nonbeing) rather than nothing? I repeat, in Aristotle (and in the Aristotelian scholastic tradition) this question does not appear. Why? Because the question was avoided by means of the implicit answer that we shall now try to give.

1.3 WHY IS THERE BEING?

Why is there being rather than nothing? *Because there is.*[8]

This is an answer to be taken with the maximum seriousness; it is not a bon mot. The very fact that we can pose the question (which we could not pose if there were nothing, not even the posers of the question) means that the condition of every question is that being exists. Being is not a problem for common sense (or, rather, common sense does not see it as a problem), because it is the condition for common sense itself. At the beginning of *De Veritate* (1.1) Aquinas says: "Illud autem quod primum intellectus concipit quasi notissimum, et in quo omnes conceptiones resolvit, est ens."* That there is something is the first, most obvious, and best known thing conceived by our intellect, and all the rest follows. That is, we could not think if not by starting from the (implicit) principle that we are thinking something. Being is the horizon, or the amniotic

---

* And the *ens* is that which the intellect conceives as first and best known, from which and in which it [the intellect] resolves all rational conceptions.

fluid, in which our thought naturally moves—or, rather, since in Aquinas's view the intellect presides over the first apprehension of things, it is that in which our first perceptual efforts move.

There would be being even if we found ourselves in a Berkeleyan situation, if we were nothing other than a screen upon which God projects a world that does not exist in reality. Even in that case there would be our act, even if it were fallacious, of perceiving that which *is* not (or which *is* only insofar as it is perceived by us), and there would be we as perceiving subjects (and, according to Berkeley's hypothesis, there would be a God that tells us what is not). There would therefore be enough being to satisfy even the most anxious of ontologists. There is always something, since there is someone capable of wondering why there is something instead of nothing.

All this should immediately make clear that the problem of being cannot be reduced to the problem of the reality of the world. Whether what we call the outside World, or the Universe, is or is not, or whether it is the effect of a malign spirit, does not in any way affect the primary evidence that there is "something" somewhere (even if it were no more than a *res cogitans* that realized it was cogitating).

But there's no need to wait for Descartes. There is a fine page in Avicenna who—after having said on many occasions that an entity is that which is conceived first of all, and that it may not be commented upon except through its name, because it is the first principle of every other comment, and that reason recognizes it without having to fall back on a definition, because entity has no definition, genus, or *differentia,* and that nothing is more known than it is—invites us to make an experiment that suggests he was not unfamiliar with certain Oriental drugs:

Let us suppose that one of us has suddenly been created, and is perfect. But he is blindfolded and cannot see external things. He has been created gliding through the air, or, better, in the void, so that he might not suffer the shock of air resistance. His limbs are separated, they neither meet nor touch. He meditates and wonders if his existence is proved. Without any doubt, he would state that he existed: despite the fact that this does not prove the existence of either his hands or his feet, or his insides, or his heart, or brain, or any other external thing, he would say he existed, without establishing whether he had a length, a breadth, or a depth... (Philippe 1975: 1–9)

Therefore there is being because we can pose the question of being, and this being comes before every question, and therefore before every answer and every definition. It is known that the modern objection that Western metaphysics—with its obsession about being—springs only from within a discourse based on the syntactic structures of Indo-European, and that is to say on a language that requires the subject-copula-predicate structure for all judgments (insofar as, as the eighteenth-century constructors of perfect languages did their utmost to propose, even sentences like *God is* or *The horse gallops* can always be resolved as *God is existent* and *The horse is galloping*). But the experience of being is implicit in the first cry emitted by a baby that has just emerged from its mother's womb, to greet or take account of the something that manifests itself to it as the horizon, and in the baby's seeking the breast with its lips. The phenomenon of primary indexicality shows us reaching out toward something (and it is irrelevant whether this something is really there or whether we posit that it is through our reaching out; it is even irrelevant whether it is we who are reaching out—there would be a reaching out in any case).

Being is *id quod primum intellectus concipit quasi notissimum,* as if we had always been on that horizon, and perhaps the fetus is aware of being while it still floats in the uterus. Obscurely, it senses being as *quasi notissimum* (or, better, as the only known thing).

There is no need to wonder why there is being; it is a luminous evidence. Which does not mean that it cannot seem dazzling, terrible, unbearable, lethal—and as a matter of fact it seems that way to many people. Asking questions about its foundations is illusion or weakness and reminds one of the person who, asked if she believed in God, replied, "No, I believe in something much greater."

Being is its own fundamental principle, and we run into this inescapable fact every time we ask ourselves questions about it. Asking questions about the foundations of being is like asking questions about the foundations of the foundations, and then about the foundations of the foundations of the foundations, in an infinite regression: when, exhausted, we stop, we are once more and already at the very foundations of our question.[9]

If anything, the question why is there being rather than nothing conceals another source of disquiet, which regards the existence of God. But first comes the proof of being, then the question of God. The question "Who has made all this, who keeps it in being?" follows the act of recognizing the evidence that there is something, an evidence so well known that it strikes us as being already organized within the cohort of the entities. It seems undeniable that even animals possess evidence of being despite the fact they are incapable of asking themselves the question that follows from it, *an Deus sit*. Aquinas was to reply to this in a *summa* appropriately called "Theologica." But first comes the discussion on the *De ente et essentia*.

1.4 HOW WE TALK ABOUT BEING

Being is even before it is talked about. But we can take it from irrepressible evidence and transform it into a problem (which awaits an answer) only insofar as we talk about it. The first opening to being is a sort of ecstatic experience, albeit in the most materialistic sense of the term, but as long as we remain in this initial, mute evidence, being is not a philosophical problem, any more than water is a philosophical problem for fish. The moment we talk about being, we are still not talking about it in its all-embracing form, because, as we have said, the problem of being (the most immediate and natural of experiences) is the least natural of all problems, the one that common sense never poses: we begin to grope our way through being by carving entities out of it and gradually constructing ourselves a World.

Therefore, since common sense is incapable of thinking of being before having organized it within the system, or the uncoordinated series, of entities, entities are the way in which being makes its rendezvous with us, and it is from there that we must begin.

And so we come to the central question of Aristotle's *Metaphysics*. This question is posed in the form of an observation from which Aristotle does not begin but very nearly arrives at after a succession of steps—stumbling over it, so to speak, as he gradually moves from the first book to the fourth, where, after having said that there is a science that studies being as such, at the point where one would expect the first tentative definition of the object of this science, Aristotle repeats as the sole possible definition what in the first book (992b 19) had appeared only as a parenthetical observation: being can be said in many ways (*leghetai men pollachos*) and in several senses (1001a 33).

What Aquinas thought the intellect *percipit quasi notissimum*, the horizon of our thinking and talking, Aristotle thought (but Aquinas agreed) was by nature (if it had a nature, but we know that it is neither genus nor species) ambiguous and polysemic.

For some authors this statement consigns the problem of being to a fundamental aporia, which the post-Aristotelian tradition has only attempted to reduce, without destroying its dramatic potential. Indeed, Aristotle was the first to try to reduce it to acceptable dimensions, and he did so by playing on the adverb "in many ways."

The many ways might be reduced to four. Being can be said (i) as accidental being (it is the being predicated of the copula, and so we say *The man is white* or *is standing*); (ii) as true, and so it may be true or false that a certain man is white, or that man is an animal; (iii) as potentiality and actuality, and so if it is not true that this healthy man is ill at present, he could fall ill, and today we might say that we could think of a possible world in which it is true that this man is ill; and (iv) being can be said *ens per se,* in other words as *substance*. In Aristotle's view, the polysemy of being subsides in the degree to which, however we speak of being, we say it "with reference to one principle" (1003b 5–6), i.e., to substances. Substances are individual existing beings, and we have perceptual evidence of them. Aristotle never doubted the existence of some individual substances (Aristotle never had doubts about the reality of the world as it appears in our everyday experience), substances in which and only in which the Platonic forms themselves are actualized, without their existing before or afterward in some pale Space beyond the heavens, and this security enables him to master the many senses of being. "The primary meaning of being is the essence that signifies (*semainei*) the substance (*ousia*)" (1028a 4–6).

The problem of Aristotelian being lay not in the *pollachos* but in the *leghetai*. Whether it is said in one or many ways, being is something that is said. It may well be the horizon of every other evidence, but it becomes a philosophical problem only when we begin to talk about it, and it is precisely our talking about it that makes it ambiguous and polyvocal. The fact that this ambiguity can be reduced does not alter the fact that we become aware of it only through speech. As it is thinkable, being manifests itself to us right from the outset as *an effect of language*.

The moment it appears before us, being arouses interpretation; the moment we can speak of it, it is already interpreted. There is no help for it. Not even Parmenides escaped this circle, despite his having labeled the *onomata* unreliable. But the *onomata* were fallacious names that we are led, prior to philosophical reflection, to give to that which becomes. But Parmenides was the first to express *in words* the invitation to recognize (and interpret) the many signs (*semata*) through which being arouses our discourse. And for being to exist, it is necessary to say as well as to think (DK 6).

A fortiori, in Aristotle's view, without words being neither is nor is not: it is there, we are within it, but we don't *think* we are. Aristotle's ontology, and this has been widely commented on, has verbal roots. In the *Metaphysics* every mention of being, every question and answer on being lies within the context of a *verbum dicendi* (be it *leghein, semainein,* or others). When we read (1005b 25–26) that "it is impossible for anyone to suppose that the same thing is and is not," we come across the verb *ypolambanein,* which is indeed "to believe," "to grasp with the mind," but—given that the mind is *logos*—it also means "to take the word."

It might be objected that we say without contradiction that which appertains to the substance, a substance independent of our speaking about it. But up to what point? How do we talk about the substance? How can we say without contradiction that man is a rational animal, whereas saying that he is white or that he runs indicates only a transient accident and cannot therefore be the object of science? In the act of perception the active intellect abstracts the essence from the *synolon* (matter + form), and therefore it seems that in the cognitive moment we immediately and effortlessly grasp the *to ti en einai* (1028b 33.36), what being was and therefore stably is. But what can we say of the essence? All we can do is give its definition: "And definition results from the necessity of its meaning something. Definition is the notion (*logos*) whose name (*onoma*) is the sign (*semeion*)" (1012a 22–24).

Alas! We have irrepressible proof of the existence of individuals, but we can say nothing about them, except by naming them through their essence, that is to say by genus and *differentia* (not therefore "this man" but "man"). The moment we enter the universe of essences, we enter the universe of definitions, that is to say the universe of language that defines.[10]

We have few names and few definitions for an infinity of single things. Therefore recourse to the universal is not strength of thought but *weakness of discourse*. The problem is that man always talks in general while things are singular. Language names by blurring the irrepressible proof of the existing individual. And all attempted remedies will be vain: the *reflexio ad phantasmata,* reducing the concept to *flatus vocis* with respect to the individual as the sole intuitive datum, entrenching oneself behind the indexicals, proper names, and rigid designators...all panaceas. With the exception of a few cases (in which we might not even speak, but point a finger, whistle, seize by an arm—but in those cases we are simply being and not talking about being), we are invariably already situated in the universal when we talk.

And therefore the anchorage of substances, which should make up for the many senses of being, owing to the language that says it, brings us back to language as the condition of what we know about the substances themselves. As has been shown (Eco 1984: 2.4), in order to define, it is necessary to construct a tree of predicables, of genera, of species, and of differences; and Aristotle, who in fact suggested such a tree to Porphyry, never managed (in the natural works in which he really intends to define essences) to apply it in a homogeneous and rigorous fashion (see Eco 1990: 4.2.1.1).

1.5 THE APORIA OF BEING IN ARISTOTLE

But the trouble with being is not that it is just an effect of language. It is that not even language defines it. There is no definition for being. Being is not a genus, not even the most general of them all, and it therefore eludes all definition, if it is necessary to use the genus and the *differentia* in order to make a definition. Being is that which enables all subsequent definitions to be made. But all definitions are the effect of the logical and therefore semiosical organization of the world. Every time we tried to warrant this organization by turning to that safe parameter that is being, we would revert to saying, i.e., to that language for which we are supposed to be seeking a guarantee. As Aubenque observed, "Not only can we say nothing about being, but being tells us nothing about those things we attribute it to" (1962: 232). And this is natural: if being is the horizon of departure, saying that something "is" adds nothing to what was already self-evident by the very fact of naming that something as the object of our discourse. Being underpins all discourses except the one we hold about it (which tells us nothing we did not already know the very moment we began to talk about it).

Some solutions have been put forward to offer a way around this aporia. We could place being elsewhere, in an area where it should not and could not be conditioned by language. This was what Neoplatonism attempted to do, right to its extreme consequences. In order to elude our definitions, the One, the foundation of being, is collocated before being itself and made ineffable: "That being may be, the One may not be being" (*Enneads*, V, 2.1). But in order to place the One beyond the reach of being itself, language becomes negative theology; it circumscribes the unsayable by means of exclusions, metaphors, and negations, as if negation were not itself a motor of semiosis, a principle of identification by opposition.

Or it was possible, as the Schoolmen did, to identify the foundation of being with God as *ipsum esse*. It was as theology that philosophy first filled the empty spaces left by metaphysics as the science of being. But philosophically this is an *escamotage*: it is thus for the philosopher with religious convictions, who must accept that faith will act as a stand-in where reason can say nothing; it is thus for the nonbelieving philosopher, who sees theology constructing the ghost of God in reaction to philosophy's incapacity to control what, while it is more evident than any other thing, is still a mere ghost as far as he is concerned. Besides, just to be able to talk of the *ipsum esse,* which is supposed to be the foundation of our very power of speech, it is necessary to elaborate a language. Since this cannot be the same language that names the entities univocally, and in accordance with the laws of argumentation, it must be the language of analogy. But it is imprecise to say that the principle of analogy allows us to talk of being. It is not that the analogy comes first and then the possibility of applying it to the *ens* or even to the *ipsum esse*. We can talk of God precisely because we admit right from the start that an *analogia entis* exists: of being, not of language. But who says that being is analogous? Language. It is a circle.

And therefore it is not analogy that enables us to speak of being; it is being that, through the way in which it is expressible in words, allows us to speak of God by analogy. Locating being in the *ipsum esse,* which is its own foundation and makes being a part of the worldly entities, does not exempt theology from *talking about* it (otherwise it is a pure beatific vision, and we know that even "a l'alta fantasia qui mancò possa").*

Other solutions? There is one, philosophically sublime and *almost* impregnable: to reabsorb language completely within being. Being is talked of and defines itself within the all-embracing bosom of a Substance where order and the connection of ideas are the

---

* "High phantasy lost power and here broke off"—Dante, *Paradiso*, 33: 142; English trans. Sayers and Reynolds.

same as order and the connection of things. There is no longer a discontinuity between being and its foundations, there is no longer a hiatus between being and the entities (the modes that constitute its flesh), there is no longer a fracture between substance and its definition, there is no longer a gap between thinking and that which is thought. And yet even in an architecture as unyielding and perfect as that of Spinoza, language worms its way in and constitutes a problem. Language seems perfectly suited to the object, which uses it to name itself, as long as it is talking in an abstract way about the substance, its attributes and its modes; but it appears very weak, tentative, perspective, and contingent when it has to reckon, yet again, with the names of worldly entities—*man,* for example. Indeed,

> those who have most often contemplated man's erect posture, by the name *man* understand an animal with an erect posture; those who, on the other hand, have been accustomed to observing other things, will form a common image of men, i.e., that man is an animal who laughs, a biped, without feathers, rational; and so each will form universal images of other things, according to the dispositions of his own body. (*Ethics* XI, scholium 1)

Isn't this a reproposal of the poverty of language and thought, that *penuria nominum* and that abundance of homonyms that used to torment theoreticians of the universals, complicated by the fact that language is now subject to the "dispositions of the body"? And how will we be able to have complete trust in this somatotypic language, when it claims to speak (in terms of *geometric order!*) of being?

This left one last possibility: as being had been separated from the essence and the essence from existence centuries before, all that remained was *to divorce being from itself.*

1.6 THE DUPLICATION OF BEING

When Heidegger, in *What is Metaphysics?*, wonders, "Why is there being rather than nothing?," he uses *Seiende*, not *Sein*. Heidegger thought that the trouble with metaphysics was that it was always taken up with the entity but not with its foundation, that is to say, being and the truth of being. By questioning the entity as an entity, metaphysics has avoided turning to being as being. It has never concentrated on its own foundation: it was part of metaphysics' destiny that being would elude it. Metaphysics has referred to the entity in its totality in the belief that it was talking about being as such; it dealt with the entity as entity while being manifests itself only in and for the *Dasein*. And so we cannot talk about being if not in reference to us, insofar as we are thrown into the world. To think being as being (to think of the truth of being as the foundation of metaphysics) means abandoning metaphysics. The problem of being and the unveiling of it is not a problem for metaphysics as the science of the entity, it is the central problem of existence.

And so enter the idea of Nothingness, which "comes together" with the idea of the entity. It springs from feelings of dread, or angst. This angst makes us feel out of place in the entity and "robs us of speech." Without speech there is no more entity: as the entity flees, there arises the nonentity, in other words, nothingness. Angst reveals Nothingness to us. But this nothingness is identified with being (*Sein*), as the being of the entity, its foundation and truth, and in this sense Heidegger can fall in with Hegel's remark to the effect that pure being and pure nothingness are the same thing. From this experience of Nothingness arises the need to consider being as the essence of the foundations of the entity.

And yet, *non sunt multiplicanda entia sine necessitate,* especially notions as primitive as the entity, being, and nothingness. It is hard to separate Heidegger's thought from the language in which he expresses himself, and he was well aware of this: proud as he was of the philosophical nature of his German, what would he have thought had he been born in Oklahoma, with an extremely vague *to be* and a single *Being* for *Seiende* and *Sein*? If there were still any need to repeat that being appears to us only as an effect of language, the way in which these two words (*Seiende* and *Sein*) are hypostatized into two Somethings ought to suffice. The two entities are created because there is a language, and they can be maintained only if the aporia of being as described in Aristotle is not wholly accepted.

While for Heidegger the entity (*ens, Seiende*) corresponds to substances, of which Aristotle had no doubt (nor does Heidegger have any, because, despite all his yarn-spinning about nothingness, like Aristotle and Kant he never doubted that things are and offer themselves spontaneously to our sensible intuition), there certainly might be something vaguer and more original that lingers on beneath the illusory idea of naming substances univocally. But up to this point we would still be at Parmenides's diffidence with regard to the *onomata*. It would be enough to say that the way in which until now we have segmented the Something surrounding us does not account for it at all, it does not account for its unfathomable complexity, or absolute simplicity, or uncontrollable confusion. If being is really said in many ways, the *Sein* would still be the viscous totality of the entities, before they are subdivided by the language that says them.

But then the problem of the *Dasein,* inasmuch as it is the only one of the entities able to ask itself the question of being, would be precisely this: to realize its circular relation with the totality of the entities it names—a realization sufficient to arouse angst and a sense of not-belonging, but one which in no way would help us get out of the circle into which being-there finds itself thrown.

To say there is something that metaphysics has not yet interpreted, i.e., that still has not been segmented by interpretation, implies that that something is already the object of segmentation, in that it is defined as the whole of that which is yet to be segmented.

If being-there is the entity that fully recognizes the semiosical nature of its relation with the entities, it is not necessary to duplicate *Seiende* and *Sein*.

It is useless to say that the discourse of metaphysics has built us a world of entities in which we live in an inauthentic fashion. This would induce us at most to reformulate a discourse that is fallacious. But this could still be done by starting from that horizon of the entity into which we are thrown. If the set of the entities is not identified solely with the set of the utilizable objects, but also involves the ideas and the emotions, then angst and the feeling of not-belonging are also a constituent part of the ontic universe they ought to dissolve.

Being's awareness of death, angst, and the feeling of nothingness open our minds to nothing that is not already the horizon into which we have been thrown. The entities that come toward us are not only "utilizable" objects; they are also the keyboard of the passions we know so well, because they are the way in which others have apprised us of our being involved in the world. The feelings that seem to open our minds to the *Sein* are already part of the immense territory of the entities. Again, if Nothingness were the epiphany of an obscure force that opposes the entities, in this inexpressible ontological "black hole" we might perhaps meet that traveler through a negative universe which is *das Sein*. But no, Heidegger is not so naïve as to hypostatize a mechanism of thought (negation), or the feeling that reality is vacillating, and to transform it into the ontological "reality" of Nothingness. He knows very well, as did Parmenides, that being really exists, but Nothingness does not exist (DK 6). What could he make of a term that has not only null intension but also null extension? The sensation of nothingness is not a simple tonality of passion, a contingent, chance depression, a mood, but a "fundamental affective situation" (Heidegger 1973: 204). Not the appearance of another Something, but passion.

And so what is it that not-belonging arouses, if not the awareness that our being-there consists of having to talk (to chat) about the entity? Once divorced from the entity of which we are talking, being flees. But this is not an ontological or metaphysical statement, it is more a lexical observation: no meaning corresponds to this word, *das Sein,* as opposed to *das Seiende*. Both terms have the same extension (unlimited) and the same intension (null). "The entity is known to us—but being? When we try to determine, or even just to grasp such a notion, are we not seized by vertigo?" (Heidegger 1973: IV, B, 41). It is exactly the same vertigo that seizes us when we want to say what the entity is *as an entity*. Terms of equal intension and extension (the only instance of absolute synonymy!), *Seiende* and *Sein* both indicate the same Something.

The *Sein* always appears in Heidegger's discourse as an intruder, as the substantivized hypostasis of a verbal usage typical of ordinary discourse. Being-there finds itself again, becomes aware of itself insofar as it is assigned to the entity, and therein discovers its real essence (which is not quiddity but *decision*) as being prepared to meet death. It is a sort of transcendental apperception without "I" and without "I think," in which being-there discovers itself as thought, emotion, desire, and corporeality (otherwise it would not have to die). In relating himself to the entity that he is not, man finds himself already before the entity as that which sustains him, that to which he finds assigned to him, that which, with all his culture and all his technology, he can never fully master (Heidegger 1973: 196). In this horizon the *Dasein* recognizes itself as such: in every state of mind, for which each of us "is" in this or that disposition, our being-there is manifest. Agreed. But why does Heidegger go on to say that we therefore understand being but nevertheless lack the concept (Heidegger 1973, IV, B, 41)? Why is the *Sein* discovered in this state of mind or disposition? It is natural for the concept to be lacking, if its intension is null, as is the case with the entity as such. But why do we need this concept?

As Heidegger says in *Being and Time* (§490), angst constitutes the opening of being-there to its existence as being thrown for its own end; agreed, and the (grammatical) subject of this thrown being is the *Dasein*. But then why is it said immediately afterward that "because of it [angst], being opens to being-there" and "the being of being-there is totally at stake"? The being of being-there is pure tautology. Being-there cannot be based on something, given that it is "thrown" (why? *because it is*). Whence comes this *das Sein* that opens itself to being-there, if the being-there that opens itself is an entity among the entities?

When Heidegger says that the problem of the founding of metaphysics is rooted in man's questioning of being, or, better, in its most intimate foundation "the understanding of being as really existing finiteness" (Heidegger 1973: 198), the *Sein* is none other than the existential understanding of our finite way of being assigned to the horizon of the entities. The *Sein* is nothing, except our understanding that we are finite entities.

And so it could be said that, at most, being's experience of being-there is an efficacious metaphor for the obscure sphere in which an ethical decision is formed: to assume genuinely our destiny to be for death, and at this point silently to sacrifice what metaphysics would have said—at length—about the legion of entities over which it has established its illusory dominion.

But then comes (a philosophically influential event) the *Kehre,* or Turning Point. And in the Turning Point this so intensionally slippery being becomes a massive subject, albeit in the form of an obscure borborygmus wandering about in the bowels of the entities. It wants to *speak* and *reveal itself.* If it speaks, it will speak through us, given that, like *Sein,* it emerges only in its connection with *Dasein.* It is necessary therefore, as was the case with the ontic/ontological duplication by which being was divorced from itself, to have language also divorced from itself. On the one hand, there will be the language of metaphysics, which by this time has had its day, senescent in its stubborn forgetfulness of being, anxious to deal with objects, and, on the other hand, a language capable—shall we say—of giving "un sens plus pur aux mots de la tribu." With the result that, rather than conceal being, it reveals it.

An immense power is therefore conferred upon language, and some maintain that there is a form of language so strong, so consubstantial with the very foundations of being, that it "shows" us being (that is, the indissoluble plexus of being-language) so that the self-revelation of being is actuated within the language. The last verse of Höderlin's *Andenken* is emblematic of this: "But what remains will be intuited by the poets."

1.7 THE QUESTIONING OF THE POETS

The idea is an ancient one and manifests itself in all its glory in the Neoplatonism of the Pseudo-Dionysius. Given a divine One—which is neither body, figure, nor form; which has no quantity or quality or weight; which is in no place; does not see or hear; is neither soul, nor intelligence, nor number, order, or size; is neither substance, nor eternity, nor time; is not shadow and is not light; nor error nor truth (*Theologia mistica*), because no definition may circumscribe it—it can be named only with an oxymoron such as "most luminous soot," or by other obscure dissimilarities, such as Lightning, Jealousy, Bear, or Panther, precisely to underline its ineffability (*De coelesti hierarchia*). This so-called symbolic way— which is abundantly metaphorical in point of fact, and which was to have an influence upon the Thomist and post-Thomist concepts of analogy—is an example of how being can be talked of only through poetry.

So it is the most ancient mystical tradition that has given to the modern world the idea that there exists, on the one hand, a discourse capable of naming the entities univocally, and, on the other, a discourse of negative theology that allows us to talk of the unknowable. This leaves the way clear for the persuasion that the only people who can talk of the unknowable are the poets, the masters of metaphor (which always talks of something else) and of oxymoron (which always talks of the presence of opposites)—an idea to the liking of poets and mystics but even more to that of positivist scientists, prepared to rationalize about prudent limits of knowledge by day and to organize spiritualist séances by night.

This solution could find a place within a highly complex relation with the definitions provided over the course of centuries by poetic—and, generally speaking, artistic—discourse. But let us employ Poetry and Poet as synecdoches for Art and Artist. From Plato to Baumgarten, we have a sort of devaluation of artistic as opposed to theoretical knowledge, from the idea of imitation of an imitation to the idea of a *gnoseologia inferior*. With this, having equated the perfection of knowledge with an understanding of the universal, we reduce poetic knowledge to a kind of halfway house between the perfection of a generalizing knowledge, revealed through the discovery of laws, and the perfection of a knowledge that was predominantly individualizing: the poet conveys to us the nuances of color in a leaf, but he doesn't tell us what Color is. Now, in historical terms, it was precisely with the advent of an era of science, from the Age of Enlightenment to the Century of Positivism, that scientific knowledge and its limits were put to the test. As the validity of this knowledge was gradually questioned, and limited to highly circumscribed universes of discourse, there gradually emerged the possibility of an area of certainty that would definitely come very close to the Universal but through a quasi-numinous revelation of the particular (which is none other than the modern notion of epiphany).

In this way the *gnoseologia inferior* becomes the instrument of privileged knowledge. But *faute de mieux*. The revelatory power attributed to the Poets is not so much the effect of a reevaluation of Poetry as a slump affecting Philosophy. The Poets have not won; the Philosophers have surrendered.

Now, even granted that the Poets speak to us of the otherwise unknowable, before we entrust to them the exclusive task of speaking about being, we must accept as a postulate that the unknowable exists. But this is precisely one of the "four incapacities" listed by Peirce in his *Some Consequences of Four Incapacities*, in which it is argued, in order, that (i) we have no power of introspection, but all knowledge of the internal world is derived by hypothetical reasoning from our knowledge of external facts; (ii) we have no power of intuition, but every cognition is determined logically by previous cognitions; (iii) we have no power of thinking without signs; (iv) we have no conception of the absolutely incognizable.

It is not necessary to agree with the first three propositions in order to accept the fourth. Peirce's argument strikes me as beyond criticism:

Every unidealistic philosophy supposes some absolutely inexplicable, unanalyzable ultimate; in short, something resulting from mediation itself not susceptible of mediation. Now that anything *is* that inexplicable can only be known by reasoning from signs. But the only justification of an inference from signs is that the conclusion explains the fact. To suppose the fact absolutely inexplicable is not to explain it, and hence this supposition is never allowable. (WR2: 213)

By this Peirce does not mean to say that we can or must exclude a priori that the incognizable exists; he says that in order to state this, it is necessary to have tried to know it through chains of inferences. Therefore, if philosophical questioning is to be kept open, we ought not to presuppose or postulate the incognizable from the start. By way of a conclusion (ours), if this presupposition is not allowed, right from the outset we ought not to delegate the power of speaking about the incognizable to those who do not intend to follow the path of hypothesis but go straight for the path of revelation.

What do the Poets reveal to us? It is not that they *say* Being, they are simply trying to emulate it: *ars imitatur naturam in sua operatione*. The Poets assume as their own task the substantial ambiguity of language, and try to exploit it to extract a *surplus of interpretation* from it rather than a surplus of being. The substantial polyvocity of being usually obliges us to make an effort to give form to the formless. The poet emulates being by reproposing its viscosity; he tries to reconstruct the formless original, to persuade us to reckon with being. But he offers us an ersatz and does not tell us anything more about being than being has already told us or than we have had it say, in other words, very little.

We have to decide what the Poets say when they intuit what remains. In *Holzwege* (Heidegger 1950), we notice an oscillation between two very different aesthetics.

For the first, it is stated that when Van Gogh portrays a pair of clogs, the work of art has let us know what shoes really are, and this entity manifests itself in the nonconcealment of its being—in other words, in this representation the being of the entity attains the stability of its appearance. Therefore there is a truth, and there is a being (*Sein*) that says it by appearing, and by using as a vehicle that *Dasein* called Vincent—just as for certain heretics Christ was allegedly incarnated passing through the Virgin *quasi per tubum,* but it was the Word that took the initiative, not its fleshly and accidental go-between.

But a second aesthetic emerges when it is said that a Greek temple appears—and I translate—as an epiphany of the Earth, and through this quasi-numinous experience "the work keeps open the opening on the World." Here the work is not the mediator through which the *Sein* reveals itself; it is (as we were saying) how art makes a tabula rasa of the inauthentic ways in which we encounter the entities, and it invites and provokes us to reinterpret the Something in which we are.

These two aesthetics are irreconcilable. The first affords a glimpse of an *orphic realism* (something outside us that tells us how things really are); the second celebrates the triumph of questioning and hermeneutics. But this second aesthetic does not tell us that being is revealed in the discourse of the Poets.[11] It tells us that the discourse of the Poets does not replace our questioning of being but sustains and encourages it. It tells us that precisely by destroying our consolidated certainties, by reminding us to consider things from an unusual point of view, by inviting us to submit to the encounter with the concrete and to the impact with an individual in which the fragile framework of our universals crumbles. Through this continuous reinvention of language, the Poets are inviting us to take up again the task of questioning and reconstructing the World and of the horizon of the entities in which we calmly and continuously thought we lived, without anxieties, without reservations, without any further reappearance (as Peirce would have put it) of curious facts that cannot be ascribed to known laws.

In this case the experience of art is not something radically different from the experience of talking about Something, in philosophy, in science, in everyday discourse. It is at once a moment and a permanent corrective. As such it repeats to us that there is no divorce between *Seiende* and *Sein*. Here we are still, talking about Something, asking ourselves how we talk about it and if there can be a moment in which the discourse stops. The implicit answer is no, for no discourse stops only because we say to it, "You are beautiful." On the contrary, it is precisely at this point that that discourse asks us to be taken up again in the work of interpretation.

1.8 A MODEL OF WORLD KNOWLEDGE

Let us start off again from the strong assumption that being is said in many ways. Not in four, ascribable to the parameter of substance, not by analogy, but in radically different ways. Being is such that diverse interpretations of it may be given.

But who talks of being? We do, and often as if being were outside us. But evidently, if there is Something, we are part of it. The result is that by opening ourselves to being, we also open ourselves to ourselves. We categorize the entity, and at the same time we realize ourselves in the *I think*. In saying how we can think of being, we already fall victim, for linguistic reasons—at least in the Indo-European languages—to a dangerous dualism: a subject thinks an object (as if the subject were not part of the object of which it is thinking). But since the risk is implicit in the language, let us run it. Then we shall make the necessary corrections.

Let us attempt therefore a mental experiment and construct an elementary model that contains a World and a Mind that knows and names it. The World is a whole composed of elements (for the sake of convenience, let us call them atoms, without any reference to the scientific sense of the term, but rather in the sense of *stoicheia*) structured in accordance with reciprocal relations. As for the Mind, it is not necessary to conceive of it as human, as a brain, as any *res cogitans;* it is simply a device for organizing propositions that serve as a description of the world. This device has elements that we might call neurons or bytes, or *stoicheia,* but again for the sake of convenience let us call them *symbols.*

A word of warning, which is fundamental if we are to have a guarantee against the schematic nature of the model: if the World were a *continuum* and not a series of discrete states (and therefore segmentable but not segmented), it would not be possible to talk of *stoicheia*. If anything, it would be the Mind that, because of its own limitations, would not be able to think of the *continuum* except by segmenting it into *stoicheia*—thereby rendering it homologous with the discrete nature of the Mind's system of symbols. Let us say then that the *stoicheia,* rather than real states of the World, are possibilities, tendencies on the part of the World to be represented through discrete sequences of symbols. But in any case it shall be seen that this rigidity on the model's part will already be called automatically into question by the second hypothesis.

By World we mean the universe, in its "maximal" version: it contains both that which we hold to be the present universe and the infinity of possible universes—we do not know whether unrealized or realized beyond the extreme limits of the known galaxies, in Giordano Bruno's space of an infinity of worlds, perhaps all simultaneously present in different dimensions—the whole that encompasses both physical entities and ideal objects or laws, from Pythagoras's theorem to Odin and Thumbelina. In the light of what we have said about the precedence of the experience of being with regard to the question of its origin, our universe can therefore include God too, or any other original principle.

In a reduced version of the experiment, we could also think of the simple material universe, the one known to physicists, historians, archaeologists, and paleontologists: the things that are in being now, plus their history. If we prefer to understand our model as maximal, it is to elude the dualistic impression that it may give. In the experiment, both the atoms and the symbols can be conceived as ontologically homologous entities, *stoicheia* made of the same stuff, as if in order to represent three spheres, atoms of the world, a mind were capable of arranging a sequence of three cubes, which in their own turn are simply atoms of the same World.

The Mind is only a device that (upon demand, or through spontaneous activity) assigns a symbol to every atom, so that every one of the Mind's sequences of symbols may stand for (it does not matter to whom) a procedure of interpretation of the World. In this sense we overcome the objection that in our experiment a Mind is put in opposition to a World, as if a Mind, whatever it may be, could not in its turn belong to the World. We can conceive of a World capable of interpreting itself, which delegates a part of itself to this purpose, so that among its infinite or indefinite atoms some stand for symbols that represent all the other atoms, exactly in the sense in which we, human beings, when we talk of phonology or phonetics, delegate some sounds (which we emit as actuated phonations) to talk of all phonations that may be actuated. To make the situation more visible and to eliminate the misleading image of a Mind that disposes of symbols that are not atoms of the world, we can think of a Mind that, confronted with a series of ten lightbulbs, wants to explain all their possible combinations to us. This Mind only has to light up various sequences of lightbulbs in series, the switching on of the lightbulbs standing for symbols of those real or possible combinations that the bulbs as atoms could realize.

In that case the system would be, as Hjelmslev would have put it, monoplanar: operations carried out on the *continuum* of the universe, by digitally activating some of its states, would be at the same time "linguistic" operations that describe possible states of the *continuum* (activating states would be the same as "saying" that those states are possible).

Put another way, being is something that, at its own periphery (or at its own center, or here and there in its mesh), secretes a part of itself that tends to interpret itself. According to our inveterate beliefs, this is the task or the function of human beings, but this is presumption. Being could interpret itself in other ways, certainly through animal organisms, but perhaps vegetable and (why not?) mineral ones too, in the silicon epiphany of the computer.[12]

In a more complex model the Mind could therefore be represented not as if put *before* the World but as if *contained* by the World, and it could have a structure that enabled it to talk not only of the world (which is opposed to it) but also of itself as a part of the world, and of the same process whereby it, a part of what is interpreted, could serve as interpreter. At this point, however, we would no longer have a model but precisely what the model was clumsily trying to describe. And if we possessed this knowledge, we would be God, or in a Fichtian sense we would have constructed Him. In any case, even if we succeeded in elaborating such a model, it would be didactically less efficacious than the one (still dualistic) we are proposing. Let us therefore accept all the limitations, and the apparently dualistic nature, of the model, and continue.

First hypothesis. Let us imagine that the World is composed of three atoms (1, 2, 3) and that the Mind has three symbols (A, B, C). The three worldly atoms could combine in six different ways, but if we limited ourselves to considering the World in its present state (including its history), we could suppose that it is equipped with a stable structure given by the sequence 123.

If knowledge were specular, and the truth *adaequatio rei et intellectus,* there would be no problem. The Mind assigns (not arbitrarily) to atom 1 the symbol A, to atom 2 the symbol B, to atom 3 the symbol C, and with the ordered triplet ABC it represents the structure of the World. It should be noted that in this case there would be no need to say that the Mind "interprets" the World: it *would represent it specularly*.

The problems arise if the assignation of the symbols to atoms is arbitrary: for example, the Mind could also assign A to 3, B to 1, and C to 2, and by combinatorial analysis it would have six possibilities of providing a faithful representation of the same 123 structure. It would be as if the Mind had six different languages at its disposal to describe a World that was always the same one, in such a way that different triplets of symbols always stated the same proposition. If we admit the possibility of total synonymy, the six descriptions would still be six different specular representations. But the metaphor of six different mirror images of the same object allows us to think that either the object or the mirror has moved every time, providing six different aspects. At this point it would be better to go back to talking about six interpretations.

Second hypothesis. The symbols used by the Mind are less numerous than the atoms of the World. The symbols used by the Mind are still three, but the atoms of the World are ten (1, 2, 3,...10). If the World were always structured by triplets of atoms, by factorial calculation it could group its ten atoms into 720 different ternary structures. The Mind would then have six triplets of symbols (ABC, BCA, CAB, ACB, BAC, CBA) to account for 720 triplets of atoms. Different worldly events, from different perspectives, could be interpreted by the same symbols. Which amounts to saying, for example, that we would always be obliged to use the ABC triplet of symbols to represent 123, or 345, or 547. We would have a bewildering superabundance of homonyms, and we would find ourselves exactly in the situation described by Aristotle: on the one hand, a single abstract concept such as "man" would serve to name the multiplicity of individuals; on the other hand, being could be said in many ways because the same symbol would stand both for the *is* in "A man is an animal" (being according to substance) and for the *is* in "That man is sitting" (being according to accident).

The problem would not change—except for ulterior complications—if the World were organized not in a stable manner but chaotically (and if it were capricious, evolutionary, bent on restructuring itself in time). By continually changing the structure of the triplets, the language of the Mind would have to adapt itself continually, always because of an excess of homonyms, to the different situations. Which likewise would happen if the world were an infinitely segmentable *continuum,* an epiphany of fractals. The Mind, rather than adapt itself to the changes in the world, would continuously change its image, gradually causing it to gel into systems of different *stoicheia,* depending on how it projects (as copies or schemata) its triplets of symbols onto it.

But it would be worse if the World were hyperstructured, that is to say, if it were organized in accordance with a sole structure given by a particular sequence of ten atoms. By combinatorial analysis, the World could organize itself into 3,628,800 different decuplets or combinations (let us not even think of a World that readjusts itself through successive hyperstructuring, that is, one that changes the arrangement of sequences at every moment, or every ten thousand years). Even in the event of the World's having a fixed structure (that is, if it were organized in a single decuplet), the Mind would still have only six triplets of symbols with which to describe it. It could try to describe it only a piece at a time, as if it were looking at it through a keyhole, unable ever to describe it in its entirety. Which seems very like what happens to us now and what has been happening to us over the course of the millennia.

Third hypothesis. The Mind has more elements than the World. The mind possesses ten symbols (A, B, C, D, E, F, G, H, I, J), and the World has only three atoms (1, 2 , and 3). And that is not all: the Mind can combine these ten symbols in duplets, triplets, quadruplets, and so on. As if to say that the cerebral structure had more neurons and more possible combinations among them than the

number of the atoms and their combinations identifiable in the
World. It is clear that this hypothesis should be immediately abandoned, because it clashes with the initial assumption that the Mind
is also part of the World. If it were part of the World, such a complex Mind should also consider its own ten symbols as worldly
stoicheia. To permit the hypothesis, the Mind would have to leave
the World: it would be a kind of highly rational divinity that has to
account for an extremely poor world, which moreover it does not
know, because the World has been cobbled together by a Demiurge
devoid of imagination. However, we could also think of a World
that in some way secretes more *res cogitans* than *res extensa,* that is,
one that has produced an extremely small number of material
structures, using few atoms, keeping others in reserve for use only
as symbols of the Mind. In any case, it is worth entertaining this
third hypothesis, because it serves to throw a certain light on the
fourth.

It follows from this that the Mind would have an astronomical
number of combinations of symbols to represent the worldly structure 123 (or at most its six possible combinations), each from a different point of view. The Mind could for example represent 123
through 3,628,800 decuplets, each of which accounts not only for
123 but also for the hour and the day on which 123 is represented,
the internal state of the Mind itself in that moment, the ends and
intentions according to which the Mind represents it (assuming
that a Mind as rich as this one also has ends and intentions). There
would be an excess of thought in relation to the simplicity of the
world, we would have an abundance of *synonyms,* or else the stock
of possible representations would exceed the number of the possible existing structures. And perhaps this is the way it happens,
given that we can lie and construct fantastic worlds, imagine and
foresee alternative states of things. The Mind could very well represent even the various ways in which it is in the World. Such
a Mind could write the *Divine Comedy* even if the infundibular
structure of the inferno did not exist in the World, or it could construct geometries with no counterpart in the material order of the
World. It could even set itself the problem of the definition of

being, duplicate entities and being, formulate the question why there is something rather than nothing—given that it could talk in many ways of this something—without ever being sure it was saying it the right way.

Fourth hypothesis. The Mind has ten symbols, as many as there are atoms in the world, and both Mind and World can combine their elements, as in the third hypothesis, into duplets, triplets, quadruplets...decuplets. The Mind would then have an astronomical number of propositions at its disposal to describe an astronomical number of worldly structures, with all the possible synonymies that derive from them. But that is not all; the Mind could also (given the abundance of worldly combinations not yet realized) design modifications of the World, just as it could be taken continuously by surprise by worldly combinations that it had not yet foreseen; moreover, the Mind would be hard put to explain in different ways how the World works.

There would be not an excess of thought with respect to the simplicity of the World, as in the third hypothesis, but a sort of continuous challenge among contenders fighting each other on a potentially equal footing but in reality changing weapons for every attack and thereby putting their adversaries in difficulty. The Mind would confront the World with an excess of perspectives, and the World would avoid the Mind's traps by continuously changing the rules (including the rules of the Mind itself).

Yet again, all this seems very similar to something that has happened to us before and is happening to us now.

1.9 On the possibility that being might abscond

Let us abandon our model now, since it has transformed itself into the (realistic) portrait of our being thrown into being, and it has confirmed to us that being can be nothing other than what is said in many ways. We have understood that, whichever way things stand (but even the very idea that things stand in some way might be called into question), every proposition regarding that which is, and that which could be, implies a choice, a perspective, a point of view. Every attempt to say something about that which is would be subject to revision, to new conjectures on the suitability of using one or the other image, or schema. Many of our claimed representations would be perhaps incompatible with one another, but they could all tell a truth of their own.

I would not say that we cannot have any real knowledge; if anything, I would maintain that we have *an excess* of real knowledge. Some are prepared to object that there is no difference between saying there is no truth and saying there are many truths (even if it were only a very simple double truth). But we might likewise object that this excess of truth is transitory; it is an effect of our groping our way along, between trial and error; it indicates a limit beyond which these different perspectives (all partly true) could one day be combined in a system. And that at bottom our continuous renewal of the question of truth depends precisely on this excess...

It may be that, in our language, there is a superabundance of being. Perhaps when scientists say that hypotheses should not be verified but above all falsified, they mean to say that in order to know, we need to prune away the excess of being that can be stated by language.

In any case, the idea that our descriptions of the world are always perspectival, bound up with the way we are biologically, ethnically, psychologically, and culturally rooted in the horizon of being, would be more than acceptable. These characteristics would not hinder our discourses from corresponding to the world, at least from a certain standpoint, without this leading to our feeling satisfied by the degree of correspondence, with the result that we are never persuaded to maintain that our answers, even when they seem basically "good," must be considered definitive.

But the problem is not how to come to terms with the fact that being may be talked of in many ways. It is that, having identified the deep mechanism of the plurality of answers, we come to the final question, which is central in what has become known as the postmodern world: If the perspectives on being are infinite, or at least astronomically indefinite, does this mean that one equals the other, that all are equally good, that every statement on that which is says something true? Does this mean that—as Feyerabend said about scientific theories—anything goes?

In other words, the final truth would lie beyond the limits of the Western logocentric model; would elude the principles of identity, of noncontradiction, and the excluded middle; would coincide precisely with the kaleidoscope of truth that we formulate by attempting to name it. There would be no transcendental meaning; being would be the same process of continuous deconstruction that is made ever more fluid, malleable, and elusive by our speaking of it, or—as Gianni Vattimo once said—being would be moth-eaten and friable; in other words, rhyzomatic, a network of jumping-off points that could be traveled along according to an infinity of different options, a labyrinth.

But there's no need to go as far as Feyerabend, or the loss of transcendental meaning, or Vattimo's "weak thought." Let us listen to Nietzsche, still not yet thirty, in *Über Wahrheit und Lüge im aussermoralischen Sinne* (Nietzsche 1873: 355–72). Since nature has thrown away the key, the intellect plays on fictions that it calls truth, or systems of concepts, based on the legislation of language. Nietzsche's first reaction owes, I would say, a debt to Hume, the second is more decidedly skeptical (why do we designate things on the basis of an arbitrary selection of properties?), the third is a prelude to the Sapir-Whorf hypothesis (different languages organize experience in different ways), the fourth is Kantian (the Thing-in-Itself may not be grasped by the constructor of the language): we think we talk about (and know) trees, colors, snow, and flowers, but they are metaphors that do not correspond to the original essences. Every word becomes concept as its pallid universality takes the color out of the differences between fundamentally unequal things: thus we think that in correspondence with the multiplicity of individual leaves there exists a primordial "leaf" on "the model of which all leaves have supposedly been woven, drawn, circumscribed, colored, wrinkled, and painted—but by a clumsy hand—in such a way that no exemplar would seem to be correct and reliable as a faithful copy of the original shape" (360). It costs us an effort to admit that birds or insects perceive the world differently from us, nor is there any sense in saying which of the perceptions is more correct, because we would need that criterion of "exact perception" that does not exist (365), because "nature instead knows no form and no concept, and therefore no genus either but only an *x,* for us unattainable and indefinable" (361). A Kantism therefore, but without a transcendental foundation and without even a critique of judgment. At most, after having stated that our antithesis between individual and genus is only an anthropomorphic effect and one that does not spring from the essence of things, the correction, more skeptical than the skepticism it attempts to correct, says: "We dare not say that this antithesis corresponds to this essence. This would be in fact a dogmatic assertion, and as such as indemonstrable as its opposite" (361).

It has to be decided, therefore, what truth is. And it is said—metaphorically, agreed, but precisely—by someone who is telling us that something is known only through free and inventive metaphor. In fact, the truth is a poetically elaborated "mobile army of metaphors, metonymies, and anthropomorphisms" that subsequently gel into knowledge, "illusions whose illusory nature has been forgotten," coins whose image has been worn away and are taken into consideration only as metal; so we become accustomed to lying according to convention, in a style that is binding for everyone, placing our actions under the control of abstractions, and having reduced the metaphors to *schemata* and *concepts*. Thence a pyramidal order of castes and ranks, laws and delimitations, constructed entirely by language, an immense "Roman columbarium," the graveyard of intuition.

That this is an excellent portrait of how the edifice of language regiments the landscape of the entities, or perhaps of a being that refuses to become set within categorial systems, is undeniable. But, even from the passages that follow, two questions are missing: whether by adapting to the constrictions of this columbarium we can manage to reckon with the world in some way (which would be no insignificant observation); and whether it doesn't happen that every so often the world obliges us to restructure the columbarium, or even to choose an alternative form to the columbarium (which is, at the end of the day, the problem of the revolution of cognitive paradigms). Nietzsche, who after all supplies us with the image of *one* of the ways of explaining the world that I outlined in the preceding paragraph, does not seem to ask himself whether or not the world has many possible forms. His is a portrait of a holistic system where no new factual judgment can intervene to throw the system into confusion.

In other words, to tell the (textual) truth, he recognizes the existence of natural constrictions and knows a way of change. The constrictions appear to him as "terrible forces" that put continuous pressure on us, opposing "scientific" truths with other truths of a different nature. But evidently he refuses to recognize those other truths by conceptualizing them in their turn, since it was to escape from them that we forged ourselves a protective suit of conceptual armor. The change is possible, not as a restructuring but as a permanent poetic revolution:

> If each of us, for himself, had a different sensation, if we ourselves could perceive now as birds, now as worms, now as plants, or if one of us saw the same stimulus as red and another saw it as blue, and if a third were even to hear this stimulus as a sound, then no one could talk of such regularity in nature. (366–67)

What a coincidence that these lines were written two years after Rimbaud, in a letter to Demeny, proclaimed, "Le Poète se fait *voyant* par un long, immense et raisonné *dérèglement* de *tous les sens*" and in the same period saw "A noir, corset velu des mouches éclatantes" and "O suprême Clairon plein des strideurs étranges."

And thus in Nietzsche's view, art (and with it myth)

> continuously muddles the rubrics and the compartments of concepts, presenting new transcriptions, metaphors, and metonymies; it continuously reveals the desire to give the subsisting world of waking man a figure so multicolored, irregular, devoid of consequences, incoherent, exciting and eternally new, which is that provided by the world of dreams. (369)

A dream of trees that conceal nymphs, and of gods in the form of bulls dragging along virgins.

But here the final decision is missing. Either we accept that what surrounds us, and the way in which we have tried to order it, cannot be lived in, and so we deny it and opt for dreams as an escape from reality (which is reminiscent of Pascal, for whom dreaming of being king really *every night* was sufficient grounds for happiness)—but Nietzsche himself admits (370) that this would be a deception, albeit a supremely light-hearted one that does no harm, and that this would be the dominion of art over life. Or, and this is what Nietzsche's followers have taken as the real lesson, art can say what it says because it is being itself, in its languid weakness and generosity, that accepts this definition too and takes pleasure from seeing itself seen as changeable, a dreamer, extenuatingly vigorous and victoriously weak. However, at the same time, no longer as "fullness, presence, foundation, but thought instead as fracture, absence of foundation, in definitive travail and suffering" (Vattimo 1980: 84). Being can therefore be said only insofar as it is in decline, as it does not impose itself but absconds. This brings us to an "ontology supported by 'weak' categories" (Vattimo 1980: 9). Nietzsche's announcement of the death of God is nothing more than the proclamation of the end of the stable structure of being (Vattimo 1983: 21). Being exists only "as suspension and as shirking" (Vattimo 1994: 18).

In other words: once the principle is accepted that being can be spoken of only in many ways, what is it that prevents us from believing that all perspectives are good, and that therefore not only does being strike us as an effect of language but that it is radically the effect of language and nothing else but the effect of language, and specifically of the form of language that can permit itself the greatest unruliness: the language of myth and of poetry? Being, therefore, would be not only moth-eaten, malleable, and weak but also pure *flatus vocis*. At this point it really would be the work of the Poets, understood as dreamers, liars, imitators of nothing, capable of irresponsibly putting an equine head on a human body, and turning every entity into a chimera.

Not at all a comforting decision, given that once we have reckoned with being, we find ourselves having to reckon with the subject that emits this *flatus vocis* (which is moreover the limit of every magic idealism). And that is not all. While it is a principle of hermeneutics that there are no facts, only interpretations, this does not prevent us from asking if there might not perchance be "bad" interpretations. Because to say that there are no facts, only interpretations, certainly means saying that what appears to us as fact is the effect of interpretation but not that every possible interpretation produces something that, in the light of subsequent interpretations, we are obliged to consider as if it were a fact. In other words, the fact that every winning poker hand is constructed by a choice (maybe encouraged by chance) on the part of the player does not mean that every hand the player lays down is a winning one. It would be sufficient if my opponent played a royal flush to my three of a kind, and my bet would be shown to be a bluff. Does our game with being begin as soon as Something replies with a royal flush to our three aces?

The real problem with every "deconstructive" argumentation of the classic concept of truth is not to demonstrate that the paradigm by which we reason might be fallacious. It looks as if everybody is in agreement about this, by now. The world as we represent it to ourselves is an effect of interpretation. The problem has more to do with the nature of the guarantees that authorize us to attempt a new paradigm that others must not recognize as delirium, pure imagination of the impossible. What is the criterion that allows us to distinguish between dream, poetic invention, and an "acid trip" (because there are people who, after having taken the drug, throw themselves out of windows convinced they can fly, only to wind up splattered all over the ground; an end, mark you, in sharp contrast with their hopes and intentions) from acceptable statements on the things of the physical or historical world around us?

We can even posit, as Vattimo does (1994: 100), a difference between epistemology, which is "the construction of rigorous bodies of knowledge and the solution of problems in the light of paradigms that dictate the rules for the verification of propositions" (and that seems to correspond to Nietzsche's portrait of the conceptual universe of a given culture), and hermeneutics as "the activity that takes place during the encounter with different paradigmatic horizons, which do not allow themselves to be assessed on the basis of some kind of conformity (to rules or, in the final analysis, to the thing), but exist as 'poetic' proposals of other worlds, of the establishment of new rules." What new rule should the Community prefer, and what others condemn as folly? There are and will always be those who wish to demonstrate that the world is square, or that we do not live on the exterior but on the interior of its crust, that statues weep, that you can bend forks on television, or that apes descend from men—and to be flexibly honest and not dogmatic we likewise need to find a public criterion with which to judge whether their ideas are in some way acceptable.

In a debate held in 1990 (now in Eco 1992) with regard to the existence or otherwise of textual criteria of interpretation, Richard Rorty—broadening the discourse to include criteria of interpretation of things that are in the world—denied that the use made of a screwdriver to tighten screws is imposed by the object itself, while the use made of it to open a parcel is imposed by our subjectivity (he was discussing my distinction between the interpretation and use of a text; see Eco 1979).

In the oral debate, Rorty also alluded to the right we would have to interpret a screwdriver as something useful to scratch our ears with. This explains my reply, which also remained in the printed version of the debate, without my knowing that in the speech sent by Rorty to the publisher the allusion to ear scratching had disappeared. Evidently Rorty had interpreted it as a simple *boutade,* an off-the-cuff remark made in the course of the conversation, and therefore I refrain from attributing this no longer documented example to him. But if Rorty does not use it, someone else might, and therefore my counterobjection is still valid. Indeed, I reconfirm it in the light of that notion of pertinence, of the perceptual *affordances* I talk of in this volume (3.4.7). A screwdriver can serve also to open a parcel (given that it is an instrument with a cutting point, easy to use in order to exert force on something resistant); but it is inadvisable to use it for rummaging about in your ear, precisely be-cause it is sharp and too long to allow the hand to control the action required for such a delicate operation; and so it would be better to use not a screwdriver but a light stick with a wad of cotton at its tip.

It suffices to imagine a possible world in which there is only a hand, a screwdriver, an ear (or at most a parcel and a screw) for the argument to acquire all its ontological value: there is something in the conformation both of my body and the screwdriver that pre-vents me from interpreting the latter at my whim.

Now, so we might get out of this tangle: Does there exist *a hard core of being,* of such a nature that some things we say about it and for it cannot and must not be taken as holding good (and if they are said by the Poets, let them be held good only insofar as they refer to a possible world but not to a world of real facts)?

1.10 THE RESISTANCES OF BEING

As usual, metaphors are efficacious but risky. By talking of a "hard core" I do not think of something tangible and solid, as if it were a "kernel" that, by biting into being, we might one day reveal. What I am talking about is not the Law of Laws. Let us try rather to identify some *lines of resistance,* perhaps mobile, vagabond, that cause the discourse to seize up, so that even in the absence of any previous rule there arises, within the discourse, a phantasm, the hint of an anacoluthon, or the block of an aphasia.

That being places limits on the discourse through which we es-tablish ourselves in its horizon is not the negation of hermeneutic activity: instead it is the condition for it. If we were to assume that everything can be said of being, the adventure of continuously questioning it would no longer have any sense. It would suffice to talk about it randomly. Continuous questioning appears reasonable and human precisely because it is assumed that there is a Limit.

One can only agree with Heidegger: the problem of being is posed only to those thrown into Being-there, into the *Dasein,* of which our disposition both to notice that something is there and to

talk about it is a part. And in our Being-there we have the fundamental experience of a Limit that language can say in advance (and
therefore only predict), in one way only, beyond which it fades into
silence: it is the experience of Death.

We are induced to postulate that being, at least for us, sets limits
because we live, in the horizon of the entities and also in the horizon of that limit that is being-for-death. Either we do not talk of
being because its presence overwhelms us, or, as soon as we talk of
it, among the first statements that we are accustomed to considering a model of all certain premises, we find "All men are mortal."
Our elders inform us of this very soon when, once we learn to
speak, we formulate the first whys.

Since we talk of being in the knowledge that there is at least one
limit, all we can do is continue with our questioning to see whether,
by chance, there are others. Just as we don't trust those who have
lied to us at least once, we don't believe the promise of the unlimited made by those who have introduced themselves to us by immediately setting a limit.

And, as we pursue the discourse, we very soon discover other
limits in the horizon of the entities we have named. We learn by
experience that nature seems to manifest stable tendencies. It is not
necessary to think of obscure and complex laws, like those of universal gravitation, but of simpler, more immediate experiences,
such as the rising and setting of the sun, gravity, the objective existence of the species. The universals may well be a figment and in-
firmity of thought, but once dog and cat have been identified as
species, we learn immediately that if we mate a dog with a dog, another dog is born of it, but if we mate a dog with a cat, nothing is
born of it—and even if something were born, it would not be able
to reproduce itself. This still does not mean that there is a certain (I
would like to say "Darwinian") reality of the genera and species. It
is only intended to suggest that even though speaking in *generalia*
may be an effect of our *penuria nominum;* nonetheless, *something* resistant has driven us to invent general terms (whose extension we
can always review and correct). The objection that one day some
biotechnology might make this grain obsolete is invalid: the fact

that any breach of the grain would require a technology (which by definition alters natural limits) means that natural limits exist.

The Possible Worlds are part of another region of being. In the ambiguous horizon of being, things might have gone differently, and there is nothing to exclude that there might be a world in which these confines between the species might not exist, where the confines are other or even absent—that is, a world in which there are no natural genera, and in which the crossing of a camel with a locomotive might produce a square root. Nevertheless, if I can think of a possible world in which only non-Euclidean geometries are valid, the only way I can think of a non-Euclidean geometry is to establish its rules, and therefore its limits.

1.11 THE SENSE OF THE *CONTINUUM*

It is also possible that there are regions of being about which we are unable to talk. It seems odd, seeing that being always manifests itself in language only, but let us grant this—since there is no reason why one day humanity might not invent languages different from the known ones. But let us keep to those "regions" of being we usually talk about and tackle this talk of ours in the light not of a metaphysics but of a semiotics, that of Hjelmslev. We use signs to express a content, and this content is carved out and organized in different forms by different cultures (and languages). What is it made from? From an amorphous stuff, amorphous before language has carried out its vivisection of it, which we will call the *continuum* of the content, all that may be experienced, said, and thought: the infinite horizon, if you will, of that which is, has been, and will be, out of both necessity and contingency. It would seem that before a culture has organized it linguistically in the form of content, this *continuum* is everything and nothing and therefore eludes all determination. Nonetheless, scholars and translators have always been perplexed by the fact that Hjelmslev called it *mening* in Danish and in the English translation of 1943 (which the author cosigned with his translator) "purport."

At a certain point Hjelmslev makes it clear that the fact that different expressions such as *Jeg véd det ikke, I do not know, Je ne sais pas, Naluvara* "have a factor in common, namely the purport, the thought itself," even though this purport still exists as an amorphous mass and receives a particular form only in and from a particular language (1943: 50–52). The same could not be said of expressions such as *Piove, Il pleut, It is raining*.

What does it mean to say there is "purport" before any sensate articulation effected by human cognition? I would prefer to translate Hjelmslev's *mening* as "sense," a term that can suggest both *meaning* (but there is no meaning or content before a given language has segmented and organized the *continuum*) and *direction* or *tendency*. As if to say that in the magma of the *continuum* there are lines of resistance and possibilities of flow, as in the grain of wood or marble, which make it easier to cut in one direction than in another. It is like beef or veal: in different cultures the cuts vary, and so the names of certain dishes are not always easy to translate from one language to another. And yet it would be very difficult to conceive of a cut that offered at the same moment the tip of the nose and the tail.

If the *continuum* has a grain, unexpected and mysterious as it may be, then we cannot say all we want to say. Being may not be comparable to a one-way street but to a network of multilane freeways along which one can travel in *more than one direction;* but despite this some roads will nevertheless remain dead ends. There are things that cannot be done (or said).

The fact that these things were said once upon a time does not matter. Afterward we ran up against some evidence that convinced us that it was no longer possible to say what had been said before.

Here we should avoid a misunderstanding. When we talk of the experience of something that obliges us to recognize the grain and lines of resistance, and to formulate laws, by no means are we claiming that these laws adequately represent the lines of resistance. If along the path that leads through the wood, I find a boulder blocking the way, I must certainly turn right or left (or decide to turn back), but this gives me absolutely no assurance that the decision taken will help me know the wood better. The incident simply interrupts a project of mine and persuades me to think up another one. To state that there are lines of resistance does not yet mean, as Peirce would have said, that there are universal laws at work in nature. The hypothesis of universal laws (or the hypothesis of a specific law) is only one of the ways in which we react to the onset of a resistance. But Habermas, in his search for the kernel of Peirce's criticism of the Kantian Thing in Itself, emphasizes that the Peircean problem is not that something (concealed behind the appearances that would mirror it) has, like a mirror, a rear side that eludes reflection, a side that we are almost sure we will one day discover, as long as we manage to get around the figure we see; it is that reality imposes restrictions on our cognition only in the sense that it refuses false interpretations (Habermas 1995: 251).

To state that there are lines of resistance merely means to say that being, even if it appears only as an effect of language, is not an effect of language in the sense that language freely constructs it. Even those who state that being is pure Chaos, and therefore susceptible to all discourse, would at least have to exclude that it is Order. Language does not construct being *ex novo:* it questions it, in some way always finding something already given (even though being *already given* does not mean being already finished and completed). Even if being were moth-eaten, there would always be a fabric whose warp and web, confused by the infinite holes that have eaten into it, still subsist in some stubborn way.

This *already given* is in fact what we have called the lines of resistance. The appearance of these Resistances is the nearest thing that can be found, before any First Philosophy or Theology, to the idea of God or Law. Certainly it is a God who manifests Himself (if and when He manifests Himself) as pure Negativity, pure Limit, pure No, that of which language cannot or must not talk. Which is something very different from the God of the revealed religions, or it assumes only His severest traits, those of the exclusive Lord of Interdiction, incapable of saying so much as "Go forth and multiply" but only intent on repeating "Thou shalt not eat from this tree."

On the other hand, something resists even the God of the revealed religions. Even God prescribes limits for Himself. This brings to mind the *Quaestio Quodlibetalis* in which Aquinas asks himself *utrum Deus possit reparare virginis ruinam,* that is, whether God can remedy the fact that a virgin has lost her virginity. Aquinas's reply is clear: If the question concerns spiritual matters, God can certainly remedy the sin committed and restore the state of grace to the sinner; if it concerns physical matters, with a miracle God can restore the girl's physical integrity; but if the question is logical and cosmological, well, not even God can ordain that what has been has not been. Let us leave it open as to whether this necessity was freely laid down by God or whether it is part of divine nature itself. In any case, from the moment He is, even the God of Aquinas is limited by it.

1.12 Positive conclusions

After having said that nothingness and negation are pure effects of language and that being always manifests itself in the positive, one might wonder whether it is not contradictory to speak of its limits and its capacity to refuse. Let us therefore correct another metaphor, which struck us as so handy for rhetorical reasons, to make clear what we wanted to suggest. Being says no to us in the same way a tortoise would say no if we asked it to fly. It is not that the tortoise realizes it *cannot* fly. It is the bird who flies; in its own way it knows it can fly and does not conceive of not being able to fly. The tortoise proceeds on its earthbound path, positively, and does not know the condition of not being a tortoise.

Of course, the animal also encounters obstacles that it senses as limits, and it seems to struggle to remove them; just think of the dog who scratches and barks at the door while biting the handle. But in such cases the animal is getting closer to a condition similar to our own; it manifests desires and intentions, and it is with respect to them that the limit is set. A closed door is not in itself a no; on the contrary, it could be a yes for those who, inside, seek privacy and protection. It becomes a no only for the dog planning to cross the threshold.

It is we, given that the Mind can provide imaginary representations of impossible worlds, who ask things to be what they are not. And, when they carry on being what they are, we think they are telling us no, and setting limits for us. We are the ones who think that our leg (in articulating at the knee) can describe some angles, from 180 to 45 degrees, but it *cannot* describe an angle of 360 degrees. The leg—for what little a leg can be said to "know"—is unaware of any limits and is aware only of possibilities. To us who capriciously would like to live on, death appears as a limit, but for the organism it arrives when things go exactly as they must.

Being never tells us no, except in our metaphor. Simply, faced with a demanding question on our part, it does not give the answer we would have wished. But the limit is in our desire, in our reaching out for absolute freedom.

Of course, in the light of these resistances, the language of the Poets seems to occupy a free zone. Liars by vocation, they are not those who say what being is but seem to be those who instead often permit themselves (and us) to deny its resistances—because for them tortoises can fly, and there can even be creatures that elude death. But their discourse, in telling us sometimes that even the *impossibilia* are possible, brings us face to face with the immoderate nature of our desire: by letting us glimpse what could be beyond the limit, on the one hand they console us for our finiteness and on the other they remind us how often we are a "useless passion." Even when they refuse to accept the resistances in being, in denying them they remind us of them. Even when they suffer on discovering them, they let us think that perhaps we have identified them (and hypostatized them into laws) too soon—that perhaps the resistances could still be got around.

What the Poets are really saying to us is that we need to encounter being with gaiety (and hopefully with science too), to question it, test its resistances, grasp its openings and its hints, which are never too explicit.

The rest is conjecture.

Chapter Two

—◉—

KANT, PEIRCE, AND THE PLATYPUS

2.1 MARCO POLO AND THE UNICORN

Often, when faced with an unknown phenomenon, we react by approximation: we seek that scrap of content, already present in our encyclopedia, which for better or worse seems to account for the new fact. A classic example of this process is to be found in Marco Polo, who saw what we now realize were rhinoceroses on Java. Although he had never seen such animals before, by analogy with other known animals he was able to distinguish the body, the four feet, and the horn. Since his culture provided him with the notion of a unicorn—a quadruped with a horn on its forehead, to be precise—he designated those animals as unicorns. Then, as he was an honest and meticulous chronicler, he hastened to tell us that these unicorns were rather strange—not very good examples of the species, we might say—given that they were not white and slender but had "the hair of the buffalo" and feet "like the feet of an elephant." He went on to give even more detail:

> It has one horn in the middle of the forehead very thick and large
> and black. And I tell you that it does no harm to men and beasts

with its horn, but only with the tongue and knee, for on its tongue it has very long spines and sharp...

It has the top of the head made like a wild boar... It is a very ugly beast to see and unclean. And they are not so as we here say and describe, who say that it lets itself be caught in the lap by a virgin girl: but I tell you that it is quite the contrary of that which we believe that it was. (Polo, *The Description of the World*, ed. and trans. A. Moule and P. Pelliot, London: Routledge, 1938)

Marco Polo seems to have made a decision: rather than resegment the content by adding a new animal to the universe of the living, he has corrected the contemporary description of unicorns, so that, if they existed, they would be as he saw them and not as the legend described them. He has modified the intension and left the extension unchanged. Or at least that is what it seems he wanted to do, or in fact did, without bothering his head overmuch regarding taxonomy.[1]

What would have happened if Polo had arrived in Australia rather than in China and spotted a platypus along some riverbank?

The platypus is a strange animal. It seems to have been conceived to foil all classification, be it scientific or popular. On the average about fifty centimeters long and roughly two kilos in weight, its flat body is covered with a dark-brown coat; it has no neck and a tail like a beaver's; it has a duck's beak, bluish on top and pink or variegated beneath; it has no outer ears, and the four feet have five webbed toes, but with claws; it stays underwater (and eats there) enough to be considered a fish or an amphibian. The female lays eggs but "breast-feeds" her young, even though no nipples can be seen (the male's testicles cannot be seen either, as they are internal).

We are not wondering whether Marco Polo would have recognized the animal as a mammal or an amphibian, but he certainly would have had to ask himself if what he was seeing (presuming it was an animal and not an illusion of the senses, or a creature from hell) was a beaver, a duck, or a fish, and in any case if it was a bird, sea animal, or land animal. A nice quandary, from which he could not escape by using the notion of the unicorn; at best he could have fallen back on the idea of the Chimera.

The first Australian colonists to see the platypus found themselves in the same quandary: they saw it as a mole, and in fact they called it the "water mole," but this mole had a beak, and therefore it was not a mole. Something perceptible outside the "mold" supplied by the idea of mole made the mold unsuitable—because to recognize a beak as a beak we would have to presume that the colonists had a "template" for the beak.

2.2 PEIRCE AND THE BLACK INK

Had he come across one, Peirce too would have had problems with the platypus, many more than he had with lithium or apple pie.

While it can be maintained that semiosic processes are involved in the recognition of the known, because it is precisely a matter of relating sense data to a (conceptual and semantic) model, the problem, which has been debated for a long time now, is to what extent a semiosic process plays a part in the understanding of an unknown phenomenon. Any semiotician of the Peircean school is convinced that semiosis lies hidden in the perceptual processes, and not so much because we still have to reckon with the fact that a good part of the psychological-philosophical tradition talks of perceptual "meaning" as because Peirce repeatedly stresses the inferential character of perceptual processes. Once again it should suffice to quote *Some Consequences of Four Incapacities* and the polemic against Cartesian intuitionism: we have no introspective or intuitive powers, but all knowledge derives by hypothetical reasoning from the knowledge of external facts and previous knowledge (WR 2: 213).

Peirce's proposal seems almost to describe Marco Polo's clumsy attempts with the rhinoceros. Polo had no "Platonic" intuition of the unknown animal, nor did he try to construct its image and notion *ex novo,* but cobbled together previous notions, thus creating a new entity starting from some ideas about entities already known. All things considered, the recognition of the rhinoceros appears to be a far more complex abduction than the canonical ones: first of all, faced with a curious and inexplicable result, Polo guessed that it might constitute the case of a rule and concluded that the animal was a unicorn; then, on the basis of successive experiences, he proceeded to reformulate the rule (the list of properties that characterizes unicorns was changed). I should call this an interrupted abduction.

What did Marco Polo *see* before *saying* he saw unicorns? Did he see something that nonetheless had to be an animal? Note that we are opposing a primary "see" to a "say." Of course, "to see" is a rhetorical figure, it stands for any other tactile, thermic, or auditory response. But the problem is that, on the one hand, it seems that the fullness of the perception (as the assignation of meaning to the unknown) has been attained by starting from a sketch, a skeleton plan, an outline, an "idea," if you like; on the other hand, after having brought into play the idea of the unicorn, Marco Polo had to admit that that unicorn was not white but black. This obliged him to correct his first hypothesis. What happened when he said *this* is *black*? And did he say it before or after hypothesizing that the animal was a unicorn? And if he said it before, why did he nevertheless insist on the hypothesis that it was a unicorn? And when he realized that the animal did not coincide with his idea of the unicorn, did he simply admit that what he saw was not a unicorn, or did he correct his idea of unicorns, deciding that the world also contained ill-favored black unicorns?

Marco Polo was not a philosopher. And so let us get back to Peirce. In passing from the contact with the Dynamical Object, through the *representamen,* to the formation of an Immediate Object (which then becomes the starting point of the chain of interpretants), Peirce posits the Ground as an instance that seems to constitute the initial moment of the cognitive process. The Ground makes its first appearances in Peirce's youthful writings, where the interest is eminently logical.[2] Between the concept of *substance* (the present in general, a subject still devoid of intension, to which properties will later be attributed, pure Something on which our attention fixes, a yet-to-be-determined "it") and the concept of *be-*

ing (pure conjunction of subject and predicate) we find (as accidents) the reference to the Ground, the reference to a correlate, and the reference to an interpretant.

The Ground, insofar as it is a Quality, is a predicate. And while the reference to the correlate regards denotation and extension, reference to the Ground regards comprehension and connotation (in the logical sense of the term): the Ground has to do with "internal" qualities, the properties of the object. In *The ink is black* the quality "black" or, rather, blackness, embodied by the ink, is abstracted from it, through a process of abstraction, or prescision. Nonetheless, even from a logical standpoint, the Ground is not the totality of markers that make up the intension of a term (such a totality can be ideally realized only in the process of interpretation): in *prescinding,* attention is paid to one element by neglecting another. In the Ground the object is seen *in a certain respect,* the attention isolates one feature. In purely logical terms, it is evident that if I predicate the blackness of ink, I do not predicate its liquidity. But if we were to cleave to the logical value of the Ground, we would not get very far. At most we would find ourselves once more among examples that seem to confuse our ideas rather than clarify them, prisoners of compulsive Peircean triadism.[3] Moreover, the choice of the term *Ground* is not one of the happiest: it suggests a background against which something is set, while Peirce's view was that it was probably a something set against a background that was still indistinct.

But we must not underestimate the fact that these youthful writings were explicitly influenced by Kant. In them Peirce basically wanted to explain how our concepts serve to unify the manifold of sense impressions. He makes it clear that the first impressions on our senses are not representations of certain things unknown in themselves, but that these very first impressions are something unknown until the mind manages to wrap them up in predicates. Like the post-Kantian he was on his way to becoming, Peirce was later to say that this process of conceptualization proceeds only *by hypothetical inferences* therefore: it happens not only in the process of conceptualization but even in the recognition of sensations. In a certain sense (in fact, in all of them) Peirce does not give a satisfactory explanation of the shift from impression to concept, seeing that for both he proposes, by way of example, the hypothetical workings of one who recognizes, from a series of sounds, a sonata by Beethoven and recognizes it as beautiful. But all things considered, Peirce distinguishes the two moments: both are identified with *the naming of* that which is experienced, and to name is always to make a hypothesis (just think of Marco Polo's efforts in this regard). But the names given to recognize sensations (such as the sensation of redness) are casual, not truly motivated; they serve only to distinguish (as if by sticking a label on them) a certain sensation from others: I say that I sense redness to exclude other possible chromatic sensations, but the sensation is still subjective, temporary, and contingent, and the name is attributed to it as a signifier whose meaning is still unknown. Instead, with the concept we move on to the signified.

It might be said that here Peirce is thinking of the Kantian distinction between perceptual judgments and judgments on the basis of experience (see 2.4 below), even though, like Kant, he does not manage to give a precise definition of the former. As a matter of fact, naming the quality "black" no longer characterizes the moment of an impression, otherwise the Ground would not be a category, and Peirce insists that the blackness predicated is already pure *species* or abstraction.

Nonetheless he sees the name given to the Ground as a term, not as a proposition or as an argument. The term still precedes every assertion of existence or truth, and, even before referring to something still to be identified, it refers inferentially to an aspect of that something.

This takes us from a logical problem to an epistemological one. The Ground is Firstness not by virtue of triadic symmetry but because it lies at the roots of the origin of conceptual understanding. It is an "initial" way of considering the object from a certain point of view. I could consider ink as a liquid, but in the example put forward I consider it immediately *under the profile* of blackness. As if to say: I don't know yet that the something I am confronted with is ink, but I grasp it as something black, I grasp it from the point of view of blackness.

My use of the word *profile* is not only metaphorical. Insofar as it is a Quality, the Ground is a Firstness and therefore an Icon or a Likeness.

After that, it appears that Peirce abandoned the idea of the Ground for about thirty years, and we shall see in 2.8 how he picked it up again. Even thirty years afterward, he was talking about it as "a sort of idea," in the "Platonic" sense, in which it is said that someone grasps another's idea, just as by remembering what one was thinking of before one recollects the same idea (CP 2.228). In the meantime, he had better elaborated what he meant by perceptual judgment, which in 1903 is defined as "a judgment asserting in propositional form what a character of a percept directly present to the mind is. The percept of course is not itself a judgment, nor can a judgment in any degree resemble a percept. It is as unlike it as the printed letters in a book, where a Madonna of Murillo is described, are unlike the picture itself" (CP 5.54).

Perceptual judgment already appears as an inference, a hypothesis starting from those sense data that appear to be "percepts," and it already belongs to Thirdness, at least as the premise of a subsequent chain of interpretations (CP 5.116). At this point where should the Ground be? On the side of the percept that is not yet judgment?

On the one hand, Peirce tells us that perceptual judgment already contains or prefigures general elements, that universal propositions are deducible from perceptual judgments, that abductive inference shades off into perceptual judgment, without a clear line of demarcation between them, so that, as Proni observes, logical principles are apprehended in the amalgam of perceptual cognition itself (1990: 331). On the other hand, and in the same text, Peirce tells us that "perceptual judgments are to be regarded as an extreme case of abductive inferences, from which they differ in being absolutely beyond criticism" (CP 5.181). Which means (as we see in CP 5.116) that insofar as first premises of all our reasonin, "our perceptual judgments...cannot be called into question."

A curious position: if there is inference in the perception itself, then there is fallibilism, and in fact Peirce also deals with perceptual illusions (CP 5.183); and yet it seems that at the same time these perceptual inferences are not hypothetical but "apodictic." A fine and explicit affirmation of realism, were it not uttered by one who never ceased saying that perception is also semiosis and therefore already abduction. And finally, if perceptual judgment could not be called into question, we would have an intuition of the singular, an idea Peirce always rebelled against, right from his anti-Cartesian writings. Moreover, if that which cannot be called into question, and is singular, is the "percept" (and the percept is identified with the Ground), it cannot set off inferential processes that have to do only with general terms (CP 5.298). If there is an abstractive moment in perception, then there is interpretation, even if rapid and unwitting (see Proni 1990: 1.5.2.4), and if there is interpretation, there is "possible criticism."

If we were to forget these subtleties (and the inevitable contradictions found in writings from different periods), we might be able to cut a long story short this way: agreed, there is an unclear blend in that space lying between Firstness (Ground or non-Ground) and fully realized Thirdness; there is a first moment of reaction of the senses that is unquestionable; the moment in which the quality presents itself to me as the quality of something (Secondness), this something becomes the premise of every other inference, in the sense that I know that in any case there is a Dynamical Object that is triggering the chain of my responses. At this point the work of interpretation begins, and, when perceptual judgment establishes itself and takes shape, it resolves itself into the formation of the Immediate Object.

Some aspects of the Ground converge in the Immediate Object (it has the nature of an icon, of Likeness) as well as all the aspects of perceptual judgment (it presents itself as the point of departure of every subsequent interpretation). At most we can say that there are also Immediate Objects of something we do not know through perception (there must certainly be two Immediate Objects that correspond to the terms *president* and *Alpha Centauri*). But it should not trouble us too much if we think that an icon is not necessarily an image in the visual sense of the term, because also the melody we whistle, perhaps tunelessly, may be an icon of Beethoven's *Fifth*; and because even a graph has an iconic nature—though it perhaps does not betray any morphological similarity with the situation represented.

We could therefore gain a breathing space by recognizing that, while the notion of the Ground and the very nature of perceptual judgment are still obscure, the same cannot be said of the notion of the Immediate Object. It is the object as it is represented (CP 8.343), in the respect in which it is thought (CP 5.286), it is the *type* of which the Dynamical Object that triggered the sequence of responses was the *token* (Prodi 1990: 265).[4] To some extent it eludes the individuality of perception, because insofar as it is interpretable, it is already public and intersubjective; it does not tell us all about the object, but it is only by coming to it that finally we know and can say something about the object.

Now, in this process and in the moment of its first fulfillment, it appears to me that a problem arises that Peirce had already come across in Kant. Peirce is trying to reformulate, without deducing it transcendentally, the Kantian notion of *schema*.

Is Peirce really thinking of Kantian schematism? Is it by trying to distinguish the categories (but which, his or Kant's?) from the schema and the categories from the manifold of the sensible intuition that an apparently inextricable knot between the Ground and the Immediate Object is created?

Peirce always returns, almost parenthetically, to the Kantian notion of schema. In CP 2.385 he says without hesitation that the Kantian schema is a *diagram;* but he speaks of it in an abstract fashion, in reference to the postulates of empirical thought in general, and within a framework of modal logic. However, in 1885, he said that the doctrine of schemata must have come to Kant's mind only late, when the system of the first *Critique* had already been laid down: "[F]or if the schemata had been considered early enough they would have overgrown his whole work" (WR 5: 258–59). It seems like a research program, the identification of a breach through which it should be possible to arrive at a nontranscendental Kantism. But what had Peirce understood of schematism, of which even Kant, as we shall see, had understood something only step by step?

2.3 KANT, TREES, STONES, AND HORSES

Is there a reason why Peirce, the future theoretician of semiotics, started by reading and rereading Kant, considering Kant's table of judgments and categories as if they had been handed down to him from Sinai?[5]

Kant has been reproached for a radical lack of attention to the problem of semiotics. But as Kelemen (1991) notes, since Hamann's and Herder's day this lack has been attributed to the fact that Kant considered a very close nexus between language and thought to be implicit, and it has been suggested that this nexus presents itself precisely in the doctrine of schematism, so much so as to suggest that the schema was concept-word (*Wortbegriff*). On the other hand, it cannot be denied that there is an implicit semiotics in the distinction between analytic and synthetic judgments, that there is explicit discussion of the theory of signs in the *Anthropology*,[6] and that it is possible to read the entire *Logic* in semiotic terms (see Apel 1972). Moreover, the nexus between knowing and communicating has been repeatedly underlined, a nexus of which Kant speaks in numerous passages, even though he does not dwell on the subject overmuch, as if he considered the question obvious (Kelemen 1991: 37). Finally, and we shall be coming back to this, there are the semiotic pages of the third *Critique*.

In any case it should suffice to consider the purely verbal origin of Kant's categorial apparatus as much as Aristotle's and quote a celebrated remark of Heidegger's:

[B]eings equipped with an intuitive capacity must always be able to mingle in the intuition of the entity, but finite intuition, insofar as it is intuition, always remains in the first place anchored to the singular intuited from time to time. The entity intuited is known only if everyone can make it comprehensible to himself and to others, and succeeding in this way in communicating it. (1973, I, 2)

To talk of that which is means rendering what we know communicable. But to know it, and to communicate it, implies recourse to the generic, which is already an effect of semiosis, and depends on a segmentation of the content in which the Kantian system of categories, bound fast to a venerable philosophical tradition, is a cultural product that is already established, culturally rooted, and linguistically anchored. When the manifold of the intuition is ascribed to the unity of the concept, the *percipienda* are by that time perceived as culture has taught us to talk about them.

That a semiosic foundation is implied by the general framework of Kantian doctrine is one thing, but whether Kant ever elaborated a theory of how we assign names to the things we perceive, be they trees, dogs, stones, or horses, is another matter.

Given the question "How do we assign names to things?," in the way that Kant had received the problem of a theory of knowledge, the answers were in brief two. One was provided by the tradition we will call Scholastic (but begins with Plato and Aristotle): Things present themselves to the world already ontologically defined in their essence, raw material modeled by a form. It is of no importance to decide whether this form (universal) is *ante rem* or *in re:* it offers itself to us, splendid in its individual substance, is grasped by the intellect, is thought and defined (and therefore *named*) as a quiddity. The work of our mind amounts to what the active intellect (wherever it may work) *does* in the blink of an eye.

The second answer was provided by the British Empiricists: We do not know substances, and if there were any, they would not reveal anything to us. What we do have, according to Locke, are sensations, which propose simple ideas, both primary and secondary, but still disconnected: a rhapsody of weights, measures, dimensions, and then colors, sounds, tastes, and reverberations, which change with the time of day and the state of the subject. Here the intellect is active, in the sense that it *works:* it combines, correlates, and abstracts, in a way that is certainly spontaneous and natural, but only thus does it coordinate simple ideas into those compound ideas to which we give the name of man, horse, tree, and then triangle, beauty, cause, and effect. To know is to put a name to these compositions of simple ideas. The task of the recognition of things was even simpler for Hume (we work directly on impressions, of which ideas are faint images). If anything, the problem arises in establishing relations among ideas of things, as happens in affirmations of causality. And here we would say that there is work, but carried out gently, by force of habit and a natural tendency to believe, even if we are asked to consider the contiguity, priority, or constancy in the succession of our impressions.

Kant certainly did not think it possible to repropound the Scholastic solution; on the contrary, if there is a genuinely Copernican aspect to his revolution, it lies in the fact that he suspends all judgment on form *in re* and assigns a synthetic-productive, and not merely abstractive, function to the old active intellect. As for the British Empiricists, Kant's goal was to establish a transcendental foundation for the process that they basically accepted as a reasonable way of moving in the world, a process whose legitimacy was confirmed by the fact that, all things considered, it worked.

But in doing this, Kant considerably shifted the focus of interest within a theory of knowledge. It is rash to say, as Heidegger did, that the *Critique of Pure Reason* has nothing to do with a theory of knowledge but is, rather, ontology questioning itself regarding its own intrinsic possibility; but it is also true that, to use Heidegger's words again, it has little to do with a theory of ontic knowledge, that is, of experience (1973: 24).

Yet Kant believed in the evidence of phenomena; he believed that our sensible intuitions came from somewhere; he took the trouble to articulate a confutation of idealism. Apparently it was Hume who awoke him from his dogmatic slumbers, by posing the problem of the causal relation between things, and not Locke, who had also tabled the problem of an activity of the intellect in the naming of things.

To say why, after having received an impression of something, I decide I am confronted with a tree or a stone was a fundamental

problem for the Empiricists, but it seems that it became a secondary problem for Kant, overly concerned with guaranteeing our
knowledge of celestial mechanics.

The first *Critique* constitutes not so much a theory of everyday
knowledge as a theory of scientific knowledge. Kant was not interested in *knowledge of* but *knowledge that;* in other words, interested
not in the conditions of knowledge (and therefore of naming) of
objects as much as in the possibility of founding the truth of our
propositions about objects.[7] His primary interest is how it is possible to have a pure mathematics and a pure physics, or how it is possible to make mathematics and physics two theoretical bodies of
knowledge that must determine their objects a priori. The nucleus
of the first *Critique* concerns the search for a warrant for a legislation of the intellect regarding those *propositions* that have their
model in the Newtonian laws—and that out of necessity are sometimes exemplified by more understandable and venerable propositions such as *All bodies have weight.* Kant is concerned with
guaranteeing the knowledge of those laws that underpin nature
understood as *the set of the objects of experience;* he never doubts that
these objects of experience are also the same objects that exercised
the Empiricists so much: dogs, horses, stones, trees, or houses. But
(at least until the *Critique of Judgment*) he seems extraordinarily uninterested in clarifying how we know the objects of everyday experience, at least those objects that today we customarily call *natural
kinds,* such as camel, beech, and coleopteran. This was realized
with evident disappointment by a philosopher interested in *knowledge of,* like Husserl.[8] But the disappointment was converted into
satisfaction for those who instead maintained that the problem of
knowledge (both *of* and *that*) could be resolved only in linguistic
terms, that is to say, in terms of coherency among propositions.

Rorty (1979: 3.3) takes issue with the idea that knowledge must
be "a mirror of nature," and he even wonders how it was possible
for Kant to assert that intuition offers us the manifold, when this
manifold is known only after it has already been unified in the synthesis of the intellect. In this sense Kant would have made a step
forward with respect to the epistemological tradition that runs

from Aristotle to Locke, a tradition for which attempts were made to model knowledge on perception. Kant would have liquidated the problem of perception by stating that knowledge hinges on propositions and not objects. Rorty is satisfied for evident reasons: even though his idea is to overturn the very paradigm of analytic philosophy, this is nonetheless his point of departure, even in terms of his personal history, and therefore Kant strikes him as the first to have suggested to the analytic tradition that it was necessary not so much to wonder what a dog is as to wonder if the proposition *Dogs are animals* is true or not.

This does not eliminate Rorty's problems, not even if he intended to reduce knowledge to a purely linguistic problem, because it prevents him from tackling the problem of the relations among perception, language, and knowledge. That is to say, if the opposition is (if, like Rorty, we may pick up the thread of an opposition proposed by Sellars) between "knowing how X is" and "knowing what type of thing X is," we would still have to ask ourselves whether in order to answer the second question it is not necessary also to have answered the first.[9]

This does even less to eliminate the problems of Kant, who not only seems uninterested in explaining how it happens that we understand *how X is* but also is unable to explain how we decide *what type of thing X is*. In other words, the first *Critique* fails to deal with the problem of how we understand that a dog is a dog, and it does not even explain how we are able to say that a dog is a mammal. There is nothing extraordinary about this if we reflect upon the cultural climate in which Kant was writing. By way of examples of rigorous knowledge that might be founded a priori, he had at his disposal mathematical science and physical science as they had already been established for centuries, and he knew very well how to define weight, extension, force, mass, triangle, or circle. But he did not have a science of dogs, just as he did not have a science of beech or lime trees, or of coleopterans. Let us not forget that when he was writing the first *Critique*, only a little more than twenty years had passed since the publication of Linnaeus's *Systema Naturae*, the first tentative monument to the establishment of a classification of "natural kinds." The dictionaries of the preceding century defined dog as a "known animal"; attempts at universal classification such as those of Dalgarno or Wilkins (seventeenth century) employed taxonomies that today we would define as approximative.[10] One understands why Kant could define the concept of dog as an empirical one; and, as he was to repeat on several occasions, we shall never be able to know all the notes of empirical concepts. That is why the first *Critique* begins (Introduction vii) with the declaration that in transcendental philosophy concepts containing anything empirical must not appear: the object of the a priori synthesis cannot be the nature of things, which is in itself "inexhaustible."

Therefore, even if he realized that he was reducing knowledge to the knowledge of propositions (and therefore to linguistic knowledge), Kant could not have posed himself the problem, which Peirce was to set himself, that the nature of knowledge was not linguistic but *semiosic*. It is true that, while Kant could not do this in the first *Critique*, he was to move in this direction in the third, but in order to take that path he had to reckon with the difficulties encountered in the first *Critique* by bringing into play the notion of the schema, of which more will be said in 2.5.

According to a Kantian example (P §23),[11] I can move from an uncoordinated succession of phenomena (there is a stone, it is struck by the sun's rays, it is hot—and, as we shall see, this is an example of perceptual judgment) to the proposition *The sun heats the stone*. If we suppose that the sun is A, the stone B, and the being hot C, we can say that A is the cause whereby B is C.

According to the table of categories, of transcendental schemata and of the principles of pure intellect (see fig. 2.1) the axioms of intuition tell me that all intuitions are extensive quantities and, through the schema of the number, I apply the category of the singularity to A and B; through the anticipations of perception, by applying the Schema of Degree, I state the reality (in an existential sense, *Realität*) of the phenomenon given me by intuition. Through the analogies with experience, I see A and B as substances, permanent in time, into which I insert accidents; and I establish that the

	Judgments	Categories	Schemata	Principles of Pure Intellect
Quantity	Universal Particular Singular	Unity Plurality Totality	Number	*Axioms of intuition*: all intuitions are extensive quantities
Quality	Affirmative Negative Infinite	Reality Negation Limitation	Degree	*Anticipations of perception*: in all appearances, the real possesses an intensive quality, a degree
Relation	Categorical	Subsistence and inherence (substance/accident)	Permanence of the real in time	*Analogies with experience*: permanence of the substance
	Hypothetical	Causality (cause/effect)	Succession of the manifold	Temporal succession according to causality
	Disjunctive	Community (reciprocal action)	Simultaneity of the determinations	Simultaneity according to the reciprocal law
Modality	Problematic	Possibility/impossibility	Agreement between the synthesis of different representations	*Postulates of empirical thought in general*: that which agrees with the formal conditions of experience is possible
	Assertive	Existence/nonexistence	Existence in a determined time	That which is connected with the material conditions of experience is real
	Apodictic	Necessity/contingency	Existence in all times	Things whose connection with the real is determined by universal conditions of experience necessarily exist

Figure 2.1 - Table of Categories

accident C of B is caused by A. Finally I decide that what is linked to the material conditions of experience is real (reality in the modal sense, *Wirklichkeit*) and, for the schema of existence in a set time, I assert that the phenomenon is effectively occurring. Equally, if the proposition were *By natural law it always and of necessity occurs that the sun's light heats (all) stones,* I should have to apply in the first instance the category of unity and in the last instance that of necessity. If we take the transcendental foundation of a priori synthetic judgments as good (but this is not the matter in dispute), the Kantian theoretical apparatus would have explained to me why I can say with certainty that A necessarily causes the fact that B is C.

But at this point Kant has still not said how he can bind the variables: why do I perceive A as sun and B as stone? How do the concepts of pure intellect intervene to make me understand a stone as such, distinct from all the other stones in the heap, from the sunlight that heats it, and from the rest of the universe? Those concepts of the pure intellect that are the categories are too vast and far too general to enable me to recognize the stone, the sun, and the heat. It is true that Kant assures us (CPR/B: 94) that once a list of primitive pure concepts has been drawn up, it is "easy" to add the derived and subaltern ones, but, since his task was to deal with the principles of the system rather than with the completeness of the system, he saved this integration for another work. In any case all we need do is consult the manuals of ontology and thereby nimbly subordinate the predicables of force, action, and passion to the category of causality, or the predicables of birth, death, and change to the category of modality. But even then we should still be on such a high level of abstraction that we could not say *This B is a stone*.

Therefore the table of categories does not allow us to say how we perceive a stone as such. Concepts of the pure intellect are only logical functions, not concepts of objects (P §39). But, if I am unable to say not only that this A is the sun and this B is a stone but also that this B is at least a body, all the universal and necessary laws that the concepts of the pure intellect guarantee me are worth nothing, because they could refer to any datum of experience. Perhaps I could say that there is an A that heats everything, whatever empirical concept I may assign to B, but I wouldn't know what this heating entity is, because I would not have assigned any empirical concept to A. Concepts of the pure intellect have need not only of sensible intuition but also of concepts of objects to which they may be applied.

The concepts of sun, stone, and air (and Kant is clear about this) are *empirical concepts,* and in that sense they are not very different from those that the Empiricists called "ideas" of genera and species. Kant sometimes talks of generic concepts, which are concepts, but not in the sense in which he often calls concepts the categories, which are indeed concepts, but of the pure intellect. The categories—as we have seen—are most abstract concepts, such as unity, reality, causality, possibility, necessity. The concept of horse is not determined through the application of the pure concepts of the intellect. An empirical concept derives from the sensations, through comparison with the objects of experience.

Which science studies the formation of empirical concepts? Certainly not general logic, which, according to Kant, must not investigate "the *source* of concepts, or the way in which concepts have their *origin,* insofar as they are representations..." (LI §5); however, it seems that Kant also thought that not even critical philosophy is entitled to undertake this task, since it should examine not how experience takes place (a task more for empirical psychology) but what experience contains. This point of view would be admissible only if the production of empirical concepts had nothing to do with the legislative activity of the intellect. We would have to know horses and houses either through manifest quiddity (as the Aristotelian-Scholastic school had it) or through a simple process of combination, correlation, and abstraction, which was Locke's view.

There is a passage in the *Logic* that might confirm this interpretation:

[T]o form concepts from representations it is therefore necessary to be able to *compare, reflect,* and *abstract;* these three logical operations of the intellect, in fact, are the essential and universal conditions for the production of any concept in general. I see, for example, a willow and a linden tree. By comparing these objects, first of all, I note they are different from each other with regard to the trunk, branches, leaves, etc.; but then, on reflecting only upon what they have in common: the trunk, branches and the leaves themselves, and by abstracting from their size, their shape, etc., I obtain the concept of a tree. (LI §6)

Are we really, still, at Locke? The passage would be Lockian if words such as "intellect" retained the weak (all things considered) meaning of "Humane Understanding." Which could not be the case for the older Kant, who had already published the three *Critiques*. Whatever work the intellect does to understand that a willow and a linden are trees, it does not find this "arboreality" in the sensible intuition. Without a legislative activity of the intellect, the material of intuition remains "blind." And in any case Kant has not told us why, on having a given intuition, I understand that it is the intuition of linden tree.

On the other hand, even "abstracting" in Kant does not signify to take from, to make arise from (which would still be the scholastic perspective), and not even to construct through (which would be the empiricist position): it is pure considering-separately, it is a negative condition, it is the supreme maneuver of the intellect, which knows that the opposite of abstraction is the *conceptus omnimode determinatus,* the concept of an individual, which in Kant's system is impossible: the sensible intuition must be elaborated by the intellect and illuminated by general or generic determinations.

And as a matter of fact the passage was perhaps a response to exigencies of didactic simplification—in a text that is a collection of notes taken and then certainly reelaborated by others in the course of his lessons—because it is in clear contrast with what is said two pages before (I, 3): "[T]he empirical concept derives from the senses by comparison of the objects of experience and thanks to the intellect it receives only the form of universality."

Only?

2.4 PERCEPTUAL JUDGMENTS

When Kant dealt with empirical psychology in the decade prior to the first *Critique* (and here too the reference is to lessons given out of necessity and transcribed by others),[12] he already knew that information provided by the senses was insufficient, because you need the intellect that reflects on what the senses have put before it. The fact we think we know things on the sole basis of the testimony of the senses depends on a *vitium subreptionis:* from infancy we are so used to grasping things as if they appeared to us already given in the intuition, that we have never considered the role played by the intellect in this process. Being unaware that the intellect is in action does not mean that it is not working: and so in the *Logic* (Intr. I) many automatisms of this kind are mentioned, as for example when we talk and therefore show we know the rules of language, but if someone asked us which rules, we would be unable to reply, and perhaps we would not even be able to say they exist.

Today we would say that to obtain an empirical concept we must be able to produce a perceptual judgment. But by perception we intend a complex act, an interpretation of sensible data that involves memory and culture and that ultimately results in the understanding of the nature of the object. On the other hand, Kant talks of *perceptio* or *Wahrnehmung* only as a "representation with consciousness." Such perceptions can be subdivided into sensations, which simply modify the state of the subject, and forms of objective knowledge. As such they can be empirical intuitions, which through the sensation refer to the singular object, and they are still appearances, devoid of concept, blind. Or they are imbued with concept, through a distinctive sign common to many things, a *note* (CPR/B: 249).

For Kant, then, what is a perceptual judgment (*Wahrnehmungsurteil*) and how is it distinguishable from a judgment on the basis of experience (*Ehrfahrungsurteil*)? Perceptual judgments are a lower-order logical activity (LI §57) that creates the subjective world of personal consciousness; they are judgments such as *When*

sunlight bathes a stone, the stone is heated; they can also be mistaken
and are in any event contingent (P §20, §23). Judgments based on
experience instead establish a necessary connection (e.g., they in
fact assert, *The sun heats the stone*).[13] It seems therefore that the categories intervene only in judgments based on experience.

But then why are perceptual judgments "judgments"? Judgment is not immediate but mediated knowledge of an object, and
in all judgments we find a concept that holds good for a plurality of
representations (CPR/B: 85). It cannot be denied that having the
representation of the stone and its heating already represents a uni-
fication actuated in the manifold of the sensible: to unify representations in the consciousness is already "to think" and "to judge"
(P §22), and judgments are a priori rules (P §23). If we were not
satisfied, "all synthesis, without which even perception would be
impossible, is subject to the categories" (CRP/B: 125). It cannot
be that (as is said in the P §21) the a priori principles of the possibility of every experience are propositions (*Sätze*) that subordinate all perception to intellectual concepts (*Verstandesbegriffe*). A
Wahrnehmungsurteil is already deeply imbued with *Verstandesbegriffe*. There's no way around it, recognizing a stone as such is already a perceptual judgment, a perceptual judgment is a judgment,
and therefore it too depends on the legislation of the intellect. The
manifold is given in the sensible intuition, but the conjunction of a
manifold in general can come to us only through an act of synthesis
on the part of the intellect.[14]

In short, Kant postulates a notion of empirical concept and of
perceptual judgment (a crucial problem for the Empiricists), but he
does not manage to pull either of them out of the mire, from that
muddy ground between sensible intuition and the legislatory activity of the intellect. But for his critical theory this no-man's-land
cannot exist.

The various phases of knowledge, in Kant, could be represented
by a series of verbalizations in this sequence:

1. This stone.
2. This is a stone (or Here there is a stone).

3a. This stone is white.
3b. This stone is hard.
 4. This stone is a mineral and a body.
 5. If I throw this stone, it will fall back to earth.
 6. All stones (insofar as they are minerals and therefore bodies)
    have weight.

The first *Critique* certainly deals with propositions like (5) and (6), it is debatable whether it really deals with propositions like (4), and it certainly is vague about the legitimacy of propositions like (1) and (3b). It is legitimate to wonder if (1) and (2) express different locutionary acts. With the exception of infantile holophrastic language, it is impossible to conceive of someone who, when confronted with a stone, utters (1)—if anything, this syntagm could occur only in (3a) or (3b). But no one has ever said that there must be a verbalization in correspondence with every phase of understanding, and the same freedom holds good even for acts of self-consciousness. Someone could walk along a road at whose sides stand heaps of stones, without paying any attention to them; but if he were asked what there was along the road, he could very well reply that there were only stones.[15] Therefore, if the fullness of perception is in fact already a perceptual judgment—and if we wanted to verbalize it at all costs, we would have (1) which is not a proposition and therefore does not imply judgment—by the time we get to the point of verbalizing it, we are immediately at (2).

Therefore, when questioned with regard to what he has seen or is presently looking at, someone who has seen a stone will either answer (2) or there will be no guarantee of his having perceived anything. As for (3a) and (3b), the subject can have all the possible sensations of whiteness or hardness, but the moment he predicates whiteness or hardness, he has already entered the categorial, and the quality he predicates is applied to a substance, precisely to determine it at least from one respect or capacity. Perhaps he might start from something expressible, such as *This white thing* or *This hard thing,* but even so he would already have begun the work of hypothesis—and it is worth observing that this would be the situation typical of a person who sees a platypus for the first time, a swimming thing with fur and a beak.

It remains for us to decide what happens when our subject says that that stone is a mineral and a body. Peirce would have said that we have already entered the moment of interpretation, whereas for Kant we have constructed a generic concept (but as we have seen, he is very vague about this). The real Kantian problem, however, concerns (1–3).

There is a difference between (3a) and (3b). For Locke, while the first expresses a simple secondary idea (color), the second expresses a simple primary idea. Primary and secondary are qualifications of objectivity, not of the certainty of perception. One by no means irrelevant problem is whether, on seeing a red apple or a white stone, I can also understand that the apple is white and juicy inside, and that the stone is hard inside and has weight. We might say that the difference lies in whether the object perceived is already an effect of the segmentation of the *continuum* or whether it is an unknown object. If we see a stone, we "know," in the very act of understanding that it is a stone, what it is like inside. Someone who sees a fossil of coralline origin for the first time (in the form of a stone, but red in color) still does not know what it is like inside.

But also in the case of the known object, what does it mean to say "we know" that the stone, white on the outside, is hard inside? Were someone to ask us such an irritating question, we might reply: "That's the way I imagine it, stones are usually like that."

It seems curious to put an imagining at the foundation of a generic concept. What does "imagine" mean? There is a difference between "to imagine$_1$," in the sense of calling up an image (we are now in the realm of fancy, the delineation of possible worlds, as when my desire portrays a stone I would like to find to crack a nut with—and this process does not call for the experience of the senses) and "to imagine$_2$," in the sense that, on seeing a stone as such, precisely on account of and in concomitance with the sensible impressions that have stimulated my visual organs, I *know* (but I do not *see*) that it is hard. What interests us is this second kind of "imagining." The first sense, as Kant would have put it, might as well be left to empirical psychology; but the second sense is crucial for a theory of understanding, of the perception of things, or—in Kantian terms—in the construction of empirical concepts (not to mention the fact that, even imagining in the first sense, wishing for a stone with which to crack a nut, is possible because, when I imagine$_1$ a stone, I imagine$_2$ that it is hard).

Wilfrid Sellars (1978) proposes using the term *imagining* for to imagine$_1$ and *imaging* for to imagine$_2$. For reasons that shall soon be clear, I propose to translate *imaging* with "to figure" (both in the sense of constructing a figure, of delineating a structural framework, and in the sense in which we say, on seeing the stone, "I figure" it is hard inside).

In this act of figuring some properties of the stone, we make a choice, we figure it in a certain respect or capacity: if on seeing or imagining the stone, I did not intend to crack a nut but to drive off a bothersome animal, I would also see the stone in terms of its dynamic possibilities, as an object that can be projected and that, insofar as it has weight, has the property of falling toward the target rather than rising in the air.

This figuring in order to understand and understanding by figuring is crucial to the Kantian system: it reveals itself as essential both for the transcendental grounding of empirical concepts and for permitting perceptual judgments (implicit and nonverbalized) such as *This stone*.

2.5 THE SCHEMA

In Kantian theory it is necessary to explain why categories that are so astrally abstract can be applied to the concreteness of the sensible intuition. I see the sun and the stone, and I must be able to think *that* star (in a singular judgment) or *all* stones (in a universal judgment, even more complex, because in point of fact I have seen only one stone, or a few, heated by the sun). Now, "Special laws, therefore, as they refer to phenomena which are empirically determined, cannot be completely derived from the categories, […] Experience must be superadded" (CPR/B: 127). But, since the pure concepts of the intellect are heterogeneous with respect to sensible intuitions, "in comprehending any object under a concept" (CPR/B: 133, but in reality one should say "in every subsumption of the subject of the intuition under a concept, so that an object may arise"), we need a third mediating element that, so to speak, makes it possible for the concept to wrap itself around the intuition and renders the concept applicable to the intuition. In this way the need for a *transcendental schema* comes into being.

The transcendental schema is a product of the imagination. Let us leave aside the discrepancy between the first and second edition of the *Critique of Pure Reason*, whereby in the first edition the Imagination is one of the three faculties of the soul, together with Sense (which empirically represents appearances in perception) and Apperception, while in the second edition Imagination becomes only a capacity of the intellect, an effect produced by the intellect on the sensibility. In the view of many interpreters, including Heidegger, this transformation is enormously relevant, to such a degree that one is obliged to go back to the first edition and over-look the second thoughts found in its successor. From our point of view this issue is secondary. Let us grant therefore that the Imagination, whatever faculty or activity it may be, provides the intellect with a schema, so that it can apply it to the intuition. Imagination is the capacity to represent an object even without its being present in the intuition (it is "reproductive" in the sense that we have called to imagine$_1$), or it is *synthesis speciosa,* productive imagination of a species, figure.

This synthesis is that whereby the empirical concept of plate can be thought by means of the pure geometric concept of the circle, because "the roundness which is conceived in the first" forms an intuition in the second (CPR/B: 134). Despite this example, the schema is not an image; and therefore it becomes clear here why I preferred "figure" to "imagine." For example, the schema of num-ber is not a quantitative image, as if I imagined the number 5 in the form of five dots lined up one after the other, like this: • • • • •. It is evident that in such a way I could never imagine the number 1,000, not to mention greater numbers. The schema of number is "rather the representation of a method of representing in one image a certain quantity...according to a certain concept" (CPR/B: 135), so that one could understand Peano's five axioms as the elements of a schema for the representation of numbers: zero is a number; the successor of every number is a number; there are no numbers with the same successor; zero is not the successor of any number; every property of the zero, and the successor of any number with those properties, belongs to all numbers—so that any series x0, x1, x2, x3...xn, which is infinite, contains no repetitions, has a beginning, and does not contain terms that cannot be reached starting from the first, in a finite number of passages, is a series of numbers.

In the preface to the second edition of the first *Critique*, Kant mentions Thales, who from the figure of one isosceles triangle, in order to discover the properties of all isosceles triangles, did not follow step by step what he saw, but had to produce, to *construct* the isosceles triangle in general.

The schema is not an image, because the image is a product of the reproductive imagination, while the schema of sensible concepts (also of figures in space) is a product of the pure a priori capacity to imagine "a monogram, so to say" (CPR/B: 136). If anything one should say that the Kantian schema, more than what is commonly understood as a "mental image" (which evokes the idea of a photograph), is like Wittgenstein's *Bild*, a proposition that has the same form as the fact it represents, in the same sense in which we talk of an "iconic" relation for an algebraic formula, or of a "model" in the technical-scientific sense.

In order to gain a better understanding of the concept of schema, perhaps we need to consider what computer operators call a *flow-chart*. The machine is capable of "thinking" in terms of IF... THEN GOTO, but this is an overly abstract logical device, given that it can serve us both for making a calculation and for drawing a geometrical figure. The flowchart shows us the steps that the machine must perform and that we must order it to perform. Given one operation, at a certain juncture in the process a possible alternative is produced, and, depending on the answer that appears, a choice needs to be made; depending on the new answer, it is necessary to return to a higher node of the chart, or proceed beyond, and so on. The chart has something that can be intuited in spatial terms, but at the same time it is substantially based on a temporal course (the flow), in the same way as Kant observes that the schemata are based fundamentally on time.

This idea of the flowchart seems to explain rather well what Kant meant by the schematic rule that governs the conceptual construction of geometrical figures. No image of a triangle, which I find in experience—the face of a pyramid, for example—can ever provide adequate cover for the concept of triangle in general, which must hold good for all triangles, be they right-angled, isosceles, or scalene (CPR/B: 136, 1–10). The schema is proposed as a rule for the construction in any situation of a figure having the general properties of triangles (let us say, even without talking in strictly mathematical terms, that one of the prescribed steps the schema obliges me to take is that, if I have arranged three toothpicks on the table, I must not seek a fourth but must for the time being close the figure with the three toothpicks available).[16]

Kant reminds us that we cannot think of a line without tracing it in our thoughts; we cannot think of a circle without describing it (I believe that in order to describe it I must have a rule that tells me that all the points of the circle must be equidistant from the center). We cannot represent the three spatial dimensions without putting three lines perpendicular to one another. We cannot even represent time without tracing a straight line (CPR/B: 120, 21 ff.). Note that at this point we have radically modified what we defined at the beginning as Kant's implicit semiotics, because thinking is not just the application of pure concepts deriving from a previous verbalization, it is also the entertaining of diagrammatic representations.

As well as time, memory comes into the construction of these diagrammatic representations: in the first edition of the *Critique* (CPR/A: 78–79), Kant says that if while counting I forget that the units now present to my senses have been added gradually, I cannot know the production of pluralities through successive addition, and therefore I cannot even know the number. If in thought I were to trace a line, or if I wished to think of the time between one noon and the next, but in the process of addition I always lost the preceding representations (the first parts of the line, the preceding parts in time), I would never have a complete representation.

We can see how schematism works in the anticipations of perception, a really fundamental principle because it implies that observable reality is a segmentable *continuum*. How can we anticipate what we have not yet sensibly intuited? We must work as if degrees might be inserted into experience (as if one could digitize the continuous) without this causing our digitization to exclude infinite other intermediate degrees. Cassirer points out that if we were to admit that in the instant a a body manifests itself in the state x and in the instant b it manifests itself in the state x, without having passed through the intermediate values between these two, then we would conclude that we were not dealing with the "same" body: we would assert that the body that was in the state x in the moment a, had disappeared, and that in the moment b another body appeared in the state x. The upshot is that the assumption of the continuity of physical changes is not a singular result of observation but a presupposition of knowledge of nature in general, and therefore it is one of those principles that govern the construction of the schemata (Cassirer 1918, III, 3).

2.6 AND THE DOG?

So much for the schemata of the pure concepts of the intellect. But it so happens that it is precisely in the chapter on schematism that Kant introduces examples concerning empirical concepts. It is not only a matter of seeing how the schema allows us to homogenize the concepts of unity and reality, inherence and subsistence, possibility and so on with the manifold of the intuition. There is also the schema of the dog: "[T]he concept of dog means a rule, according to which my imagination can always draw a general outline of the figure of a four-footed animal, without being restricted to any particular figure supplied by experience or to any possible image which I may draw in the concrete" (CPR/B: 136).

It is no accident that after this example, a few lines later, Kant wrote the renowned phrase according to which this schematism of our intellect, which also concerns the simple *form* of appearances, is an art concealed in the depths of the human soul. It is an art, a procedure, a task, a *construction,* but we know very little of how it works. Because it is clear that our nice little analogy with the flowchart, which might help us understand how the schematic construction of the triangle proceeds, works far less well in the case of the dog.

A computer can certainly construct the image of a dog, provided it is given suitable algorithms: but it is not by examining the flowchart for the construction of the dog that a person who has never seen a dog can have a mental image (whatever a mental image may be) of one. Once more we find ourselves faced with a lack of homogeneity between categories and intuition, and the fact that the schema of the dog can be verbalized as "quadruped animal" brings us back only to the extreme abstractness of every predication by genus and *differentia,* but it does not allow us to distinguish a dog from a horse.

Deleuze (1963) observes that the schema consists not of an image but of *spatiotemporal relations that embody or realize some purely conceptual relations,* and this seems exact as far as the schemata of concepts of pure intellect are concerned. But it does not seem to be sufficient when it comes to empirical concepts, since Kant was the first to tell us that in order to think of a plate, I must resort to the image of the circle. While the schema of the circle is not an image but a rule for constructing the image if necessary, the empirical concept of the plate should nonetheless include the notion that its *form* may be constructed in some way—in a visual sense, to be exact.

One must conclude that when Kant thinks of the schema of the dog, he is thinking of something very similar to that which, in the sphere of the present-day cognitive sciences, Marr and Nishishara (1978) call a "3-D Model," which they represent as in figure 2.2.

In perceptual judgment the 3-D model is applied to the manifold of experience, and we distinguish an *x* as a man and not as a

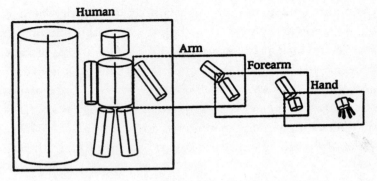

Figure 2.2

dog. Which ought to demonstrate how a perceptual judgment does not necessarily boil down to a verbal assertion. In fact it is based on the application of a structural diagram to the manifold of sensation. The fact that other judgments are necessary to determine the concept of man in all its possible properties (and, as happens with all empirical concepts, the task seems infinite, never fully realized) is another matter. With a 3-D model I could even confuse a man with a primate and vice versa—but it would be difficult for me to mistake him for a snake. The fact is that in some way one starts off from a schema of this kind, even before knowing or asserting that man has a soul, that he talks, or even that he has an opposable thumb.

At this point we might say that the schema of the empirical concept comes to coincide with the concept of the object: in fact, we might say that around the schema a kind of trinity comes to be constructed, whose three "persons" are in the final analysis one and one alone (even though they can be considered the three points of view): *schema, concept,* and *meaning.* Producing the schema of the dog means having at least one essential concept of it. Does a 3-D model of man correspond to a concept of "man"? Certainly not as far as the classic definition (mortal rational animal) is concerned; but as far as the possibility of recognizing a human being is concerned, and then of being able to add the determinations that derive from this first identification, it certainly does. Which explains why in the *Logic* (II, 103) Kant noted that a synthesis of empirical concepts can never come to an end, because in the course of experience it will still be possible to identify other notes of the object dog or man. But unfortunately, using an overly strong expression, Kant said that therefore empirical concepts "cannot even be defined." They cannot be defined once and for all, like mathematical concepts, but admit of a first nucleus around which successive definitions will gel (or arrange themselves harmoniously).

Can we say that this first conceptual nucleus is also the meaning that corresponds to the term with which we express it? Kant does not use the word meaning (*Bedeutung*) very often, but, fancy that, he uses it precisely when talking of the schema: concepts are wholly impossible, nor can they have any meaning, unless an object is given either to them or at least to the elements of which they consist (CPR/B: 135). Kant is suggesting in a less explicit way that coincidence of *linguistic meaning* and *perceptual meaning* that was later to be energetically asserted by Husserl: a red object is recognized as red and denominated as *red* as the result of a single act. "All things considered to *denominate as red*—in the sense of present denomination, which presupposes the underlying intuition of the denominated—and to *recognize as red* are expressions whose meanings are identical" (*Logical Investigations* vi, 7: 327).

But if this is so, not only the notion of empirical concept but also the notion of the meaning of terms that refer to perceivable objects (e.g., names of natural kinds) introduces a new problem. And this is that the first nucleus of meaning, the one identified with the conceptual schema, may not be reduced to a mere classificatory datum: a dog is not understood and identified (and recognized) because it is a mammalian animal but because it has a certain *form* (and for the time being let us allow this term to keep all its Aristotelian connotations, despite their being highly dangerous in this context).

As we have just seen, the concept of plate must also have a correspondence with that of circularity, and Kant tells us that the schema of dog includes its having legs and that there are four of them. A man (in the sense of a member of the human race) is nonetheless still something that moves in accordance with the articulations provided for by the 3-D model.

Where does this schema come from? While in the case of the schema of geometrical figures, it sufficed to reflect on the pure intuition of space, and therefore the schema could be drawn from the very constitution of our intellect, this is certainly not the case with the schema (and therefore the concept) of dog. Otherwise we would have a repertoire, if not of innate ideas, of innate schemata: a repertoire including the schema of doghood, horsehood, and so on, until we had exhausted the inventory of the entire universe. And in that case we should also be equipped with an innate schema of the platypus, even before ever having seen one, otherwise we would not be able to think of one if we saw one. It is eminently clear that Kant could not endorse a Platonism of this sort (and whether Plato did or not is a matter for debate).

So, the Empiricists would have said, the schema is drawn from experience: the schema of the dog is none other than the Lockian *idea* of dog. But this statement is unacceptable in Kant's view, seeing that experience occurs precisely by applying the schemata. I cannot abstract the schema of dog from intuitive data, because the data become thinkable precisely as a consequence of the application of the schema. And therefore we are in a vicious circle, which the first *Critique* (and I think this can be said with some confidence) does nothing to get us out of.

Which leaves only one solution: by reflecting upon the data from the sensible intuition, by comparing them, assessing them, by using an innate and secret art hidden in the deepest profundities of the human soul (and therefore of our own transcendental apparatus), we do not abstract but *construct* the schemata. While we have been taught the schema of dog—and we don't even realize when we apply it, since by *vitium subreptionis* we are led to believe that we are seeing a dog because we are receiving sensations—Kant (as we have seen) saw it as a side effect of the quasi-unconscious way in which we put the transcendental apparatus to work.

That Kantian schematism implies—in the sense that it cannot but bring us to think about it—a constructivism is not an original idea, especially in the return to Kant discernible in many contemporary cognitive sciences. But that the schema can and must be a construction should not emerge so much from the fact that previously constructed schemata (e.g., that of the dog) apply; the real problem is *What happens when we must construct the schema of an object that is as yet unknown?*

2.7 THE PLATYPUS

The choice of the platypus as an example of an unknown object does not spring from mere whimsy. The platypus was discovered in Australia at the end of the eighteenth century and was first named "water mole," "duck mole," or "duck-billed platypus." In 1799, a stuffed specimen was examined in England, and the naturalists could not believe their eyes, with the result that some insinuated it was a practical joke on the part of a taxidermist. In 4.5.1, I shall come to the story of how it was studied and defined. When the platypus made its appearance in the Western world, Kant had already written his works (the last work published was *Anthropology from a Pragmatic Point of View*, 1798). By the time people began talking about the platypus, Kant was already senile; it may be that someone had mentioned it to him, but the information would have been inaccurate in any case. By the time it was finally decided that the platypus was an egg-laying mammal, Kant had been dead for eighty years. We are therefore free to conduct our mental experiment and to decide what Kant would have done had he come across a platypus.

It would have been a matter of figuring the schema, starting from sense impressions, but these sense impressions are not suited to any previous schema. How could one reconcile the beak and the webbed feet with the fur and the beaver tail, or the idea of beaver with the idea of an oviparous animal; how could one see a bird where there was a quadruped? Kant would have found himself in the same situation as Aristotle when, after drawing up all possible rules for distinguishing ruminants from the other animals, no matter which way he turned, he never managed to find a place for the camel, which eluded all definition by genus and *differentia*. Had Aristotle tried to make one fit, he would have had to chase another ruminant, the ox, out of its own definitory space.[17]

Some would be tempted to say that Aristotle would have found himself in an even more awkward position, because, since he would have been convinced that a platypus had to have an essence independent of our intellect, the impossibility of finding a definition for it would have disquieted him all the more. Kant, the confuter of idealism, would also have known very well that if the platypus offered him a sensible intuition, then it *was* and therefore could necessarily be thought; and no matter where the form that he conferred upon it sprang from, it had to be possible to construct it.

What problem would Kant have faced if he had encountered a platypus? The terms of the problem became clear to him only in the *Critique of Judgment*. Judgment is the faculty of thinking of the particular as part of the general, and if the general (the rule, the law) is already given, judgment is *determinant*. But if *only the particular is given and the general must be sought for,* judgment is *reflective.*

By introducing schematism to the first version of the system, as Peirce suggested, Kant found himself with an explosive concept that obliged him to go further: in the direction of the *Critique of Judgment*, in fact. But, we might say, once we arrive at reflective judgment from the schema, the very nature of determinant judgment enters a crisis. Because the capacity of determinant judgment (we finally find this clearly spelled out in the chapter of the *Critique of Judgment* on the dialectic of the capacity of teleological judgment) "does not have in itself principles that found *concepts of objects,*" determinant judgment limits itself to subsuming objects under given laws or concepts such as principles. "Thus the capacity of transcendental judgment, which contained the conditions for subsumption under categories, was not in itself *nomothetic,* but simply indicated the conditions of the sensible intuition under which a given concept may be given reality (application)." Therefore any concept of an object, if it is to be founded, must be fixed by the reflective judgment, which "must subsume under a law that is yet to be given" (CJ §69).

As far as Kant is concerned, nature is before our eyes, and his native realism prevents him from thinking that the objects of nature are not there, functioning in a certain way, given that they develop by themselves. One tree produces another tree—of the same species—and at the same time grows and therefore also produces itself as an individual; and the bud of one tree leaf grafted onto the branch of another tree produces yet another plant of the same species; the tree lives as a whole at which the parts converge, since the leaves are produced by the tree, but defoliation would have an effect on the growth of the trunk. Therefore the tree lives and grows by following its own internal organic law (CJ §64).

But what this law is cannot be known from the tree, given that the phenomenal teaches us nothing about the noumenal. Nor do the a priori forms of the pure intellect teach us anything, because the entities of nature obey a plethora of particular laws. And yet they should be considered necessary according to the principle of the unity of the manifold, which is moreover unknown to us.

These objects of nature are (apart from those highly general laws that allow us to think of the phenomena of physics) dogs, horses, stones—and platypuses. We must be able to say how these objects are organized into genera and species, but—and mark this—genera and species are not only a classificatory judgment of ours: "[I]n nature there is a subordination of genera and species that we can grasp; in their turn the genera approximate themselves to one another according to a common principle, so that it is possible to move from one to the other, and with that, to a higher genus" (CJ Intr. V).

And so we try to construct the concept of tree (we assume it) *as if* the trees were as we can think them. We imagine something as possible according to the concept (we try for an agreement between the form and the possibility of the thing itself, even though we have no concept of it), and we can think of it as an organism that obeys certain ends.

To interpret something *as if* it were in a certain way means proposing a hypothesis, because the reflective judgment must subsume under a law not yet given "and therefore in fact it is only a principle of reflection on objects for which objectively there is absolutely no law or a concept of the object sufficient for the cases that arise" (CJ §69). And it must be a very adventurous type of hypothesis, because from the particular (from a Result) it is necessary to infer a Rule as yet unknown; and in order to find the Rule somewhere or other it is necessary to presume that that Result is a Case of the Rule to be constructed. Of course Kant did not express himself in these terms, but Peirce the Kantian did: it is clear that reflective judgment is none other than an *abduction*.

In this abductive process, as we have said, the genera and species are not merely arbitrary classifications—and if they were such, they could become established only after abduction has taken place, in an advanced phase of conceptual elaboration. In the light of the third *Critique* it has to be admitted that, insofar as it is teleological, the reflective judgment assigns a character of "animality" (or of "living being") to the object already in the course of schematic structure. Let us reflect on what would have happened to Kant if he had seen a platypus. He would have had the intuition of a multiplicity of characteristics that obliged him to construct the schema of an autonomous being, not moved by external forces, that could manifestly coordinate its own movements, an organic and functional relation between beak (which permits it to take food), feet (which permit it to swim), head, trunk, and tail. The animality of the object would have suggested itself as the fundamental element of the perceptual schema, not as a successive abstract attribution (which would only have ratified conceptually what the schema already contained).[18]

Had Kant been able to observe the platypus (its morphology, usage, and customs) as was done gradually over the two centuries that followed, he would probably have come to the same conclusion as Gould (1991: 227): this animal, which was already present during the Mesozoic, before the other mammals of the Tertiary period, and whose evolution never went any further, does not represent a clumsy attempt on nature's part to produce something better but is a masterpiece of design, a fantastic example of environmental adaptation, which permitted a mammal to survive and flourish in rivers. Its fur seems to have been created specifically to protect it from cold water; it can regulate its own body heat; all its morphology makes it suited to diving into water to find food with eyes and ears closed; its front limbs enable it to swim; the rear limbs and the tail serve as a rudder; the renowned rear spurs equip the male to compete with other males in the mating season. The platypus has, in short, a most original structure, perfectly designed for the purposes to which it is intended. But probably Gould could not have given this "teleological" reading of the platypus, if Kant had not suggested to us that "an organized product of nature is one in which all is end and, reciprocally, means too" (CJ §66) and that the products of nature manifest themselves (unlike machines, moved by a mere driving force, *bewegende Kraft*) as organisms moved internally by a *bildende Kraft*, a capacity, a formative force.

And yet Gould, in his attempt to define this *bildende Kraft,* found nothing better to do than fall back on the metaphor of design, which is a way of modeling nonnatural entities. I don't think that Kant could have said Gould was wrong; if he had, he would have found himself in a felicitous contradiction. The fact is that the Capacity of Judgment, once it has emerged as reflective and teleological, overwhelms and dominates the entire universe of the cognizable and informs all thinkable objects, even a chair. It is true that a chair, as an art object, could be judged only insofar as it is beautiful, a pure example of an end without a purpose and universality without a concept, a source of pleasure without interest, the result of a free play of the imagination and the intellect. But at this point it does not take much to add a rule and a purpose whence we sought to abstract them, and the chair will be seen in accordance with the intention of the person who conceived it as a functional object, whose end is intended for its function, organically structured so that all its parts sustain the whole.

It is Kant who passes with a certain nonchalance from teleological judgments on natural entities to teleological judgments on products of artifice:

> If someone were to perceive, in a seemingly uninhabited land, a geometric figure, drawn on the sand, a regular hexagon let us say, then his reflection, by elaborating a concept of that figure, would realize through the reason, albeit obscurely, the unity of the principle of generation of this hexagon, and so, in conformity with reason, he would deem that neither the sand, not the sea nearby, nor the winds, nor even the animals with their tracks, which he knows, nor any other cause devoid of reason are the foundations of the possibility of this figure: because a coincidence with this concept, which is possible only in the reason, would seem to him so infinitely contingent that there might as well be no natural law in that regard; and it would seem to him as a consequence that there is not even a cause in nature (which produces effects in a merely mechanical manner) able to contain the causality for this effect, but that only the concept of this object can, as a concept that only the reason can provide and with which it can compare the object, and that as a consequence that object can certainly be considered as an end, but not as a natural end: therefore, as a product of art (*vestigium hominis video*). (CJ §64)

Kant is certainly among those who have convinced philosophers that it is legitimate to construct a sentence that in the Academy edition runs to twenty-two lines before the full stop finally arrives, but he makes a good job of telling us how to develop an abduction worthy of Robinson Crusoe. And if someone were to observe that in this case art has nonetheless imitated a regular figure, which is not invented by art but produced by pure mathematical intuition, it should suffice to mention an example given shortly before the one quoted here: where, by way of an example of empirical ends (as opposed to the pure one of the circle, which seems to have been conceived with a view to highlighting all the demonstrations that can be deduced from it), he proposes a fine garden, and certainly a fine garden in the French style, in which nature bows before art, with its well-ordered flower beds and avenues; and talks of ends, empirical ones, agreed, and real, insofar as we are well aware that the garden has been arranged in accordance with a purpose and a function. It can be said that seeing the garden or the chair as organisms with ends calls for a less adventurous hypothesis, because I already know that artificial objects obey the intentions of the creator, while for nature judgment postulates the end (and indirectly a creative constructiveness, a sort of *natura naturans*) as the only possibility of understanding it. But in any case even the artificial object cannot but be informed by reflective judgment.

It would be optimistic to say that this teleological version of the schema is exposed with absolute clarity in the third *Critique* too. See, for example, the celebrated §59, which has caused rivers of ink to flow on the part of those who have sought to rediscover in Kant the elements of a philosophy of language. Above all he delineates therein a difference between *schemata,* proper to the pure concepts of the intellect, and examples (*Beispiele*) that hold good for empirical concepts. In itself the idea is not devoid of charm: in the schema of the dog or the tree "prototypical" ideas come into play, as if ·through the *ostension* of *one* dog (or of the image of a single dog) one could represent all dogs. Nonetheless, we would still have to decide how this image, which must mediate between the manifold of the intuition and the concept, may not already be interwoven with concepts—to be the image of a dog *in general* and not of *that* dog. And, once again, which "example" of dog would mediate between intuition and concept, seeing that for empirical concepts it really seems that the schema comes to coincide precisely with the possibility of figuring a generic concept?

Immediately afterward it is said that the sensible exhibition of something ("hypotyposis") can be *schematic* when a concept grasped by the intellect is given a corresponding intuition (and this holds good for the schema of the circle, indispensable for understanding the concept of "plate"); but it is *symbolic* when a concept that only the reason can think of, there being no corresponding intuition, is supplied by analogy: as would happen if I wanted to represent the monarchical state as a human body. Here Kant is certainly talking not only of symbols in the logical-formal sense but also of phenomena such as metaphor or allegory.

Therefore a gap still remains between schemata and symbols. While for the platypus I can say that the first impact was metaphorical ("water mole"), the same cannot be said of the dog.

There is a gap, which I believe Kant tried to bridge in the *Opus Postumum*. Of which, without going into its labyrinthine complexities, one can say that Kant was trying even harder to determine the various particular laws of physics that cannot be deduced from the categories only. In order to ground physics, Kant had to postulate the ether as a material that, diffused throughout cosmic space, is found in and permeates all objects.

External perceptions, as the stuff of a possible experience, which lack only the form of their connection, are the effect of the moving (or driving) forces of matter. Now, to mediate the application of these motive forces to the relations that present themselves to experience, it is necessary to identify empirical laws. They are not given a priori but need concepts *constructed* by us (*selbstgemachte*). These are not concepts given by reason or experience but *factitious* concepts. They are *problematic* (and we should remember that a problematic judgment depends on the Postulate of Empirical Thought in General, whereby that which agrees with the formal conditions of experience is possible).

These concepts must be thought of as the foundation of natural inquiry. We must therefore postulate (in the case of the factitious concept of ether) an absolute whole subsisting in matter.

Kant repeats on various occasions that this concept is not a hypothesis but a postulate of reason, but his distrust of the term *hypothesis* has Newtonian roots: in fact a concept (built, so to speak, on nothing) that makes possible the totality of experience is an abduction that appeals, in order to explain some Results, to a Rule constructed *ex novo*.[19] Nor should we let ourselves be distracted by the fact that the postulate of ether was subsequently proved erroneous: it worked well enough for a long time, and good abductions (just think of the theories of epicycles and deferents) endure for long periods, until a more suitable, more economical, and more powerful abduction comes onto the scene.

As Vittorio Mathieu observes with regard to Kant's last work, "The intellect makes experience by designing the structure according to which the driving forces of the object can act." Rather than observe (and thence produce schemata), the reflective judgment produces schemata to be able to observe, and to experiment. And "such doctrine goes beyond that of the first *Critique* for the freedom that it assigns to the intellectual designing of the object."[20]

With this late schematism the intellect does not construct the simple determination of a possible object but *makes* the object, *constructs* it, and in the course of this activity (problematic in itself) it proceeds by trial and error.[21]

At this point the notion of trial and error becomes crucial. If the schema of empirical concepts is a construct that tries to make the objects of nature thinkable, and if a complete synthesis of empirical concepts can never be given, because new notes of the concept (LI §103) can always be discovered through experience, then the schemata themselves can only be revisable, fallible, and destined to evolve in time. If the pure concepts of the intellect could constitute a sort of atemporal repertoire, empirical concepts could only become "historic," or cultural, if you will.[22]

Kant did not "say" this, but it seems hard not to say it if the doctrine of schematism is carried to its logical conclusions. In any case this was the understanding of Peirce, who put the entire cognitive process down to hypothetical inference, whereby sensations appear as the interpretations of stimuli; the perceptions as interpretations of sensations; perceptual judgments as the interpretation of perceptions; particular and general propositions as interpretations of perceptual judgments; and scientific theories as interpretations of series of propositions (see Bonfantini and Grazia 1976: 13).

In the light of the infinite segmentability of the *continuum*, both perceptual schemata and propositions regarding the laws of nature (what a rhinoceros is like, whether the dolphin is a fish, whether it is possible to conceive of the cosmic ether) carve out objects or relations that—albeit to different degrees—always remain hypothetical or subject to the possibility of fallibilism.

Naturally at this point transcendentalism will also undergo its Copernican revolution. The guarantee that our hypotheses are "right" (or at least acceptable as such until proved otherwise) will no longer be sought for in the a priori of the pure intellect (even though the intellect's most abstract logical forms will be saved) but in the historic, progressive, and temporal consensus of the Community.[23] Faced with the risk of fallibilism, the transcendental is also historicized; it becomes an accumulation of interpretations that are accepted, and accepted after a process of discussion, selection, and repudiation.[24] This foundation is unstable, based on the pseudo-transcendental of the Community (an optative idea rather than a sociological category); and yet it is the consensus of the Community that today makes us favor Kepler's abduction rather than Tycho Brahe's. Naturally the Community has supplied what are called proofs, but it is not the authoritativeness of the proof in itself that convinces us or prevents us from falsifying it; it is, rather, the difficulty of calling a proof into question without upsetting the entire system, the paradigm that supports it.

This detranscendentalization of knowledge crops up again, through an explicitly Peircean influence, in Dewey's notion of "warranted assertion," or, as people now prefer to say, of *warranted assertibility*, and it is still present in the various holistic concepts of knowledge. But, even though in that sense an acceptable concept of truth depends on the structural pressure of a body of interdependent knowledge, within this body facts nonetheless are always emerging, which show themselves gradually and which seem "recalcitrant to experience." And so in this way within a unitary and unanimous paradigm there reappears what in Peirce's view was always one of the fundamental problems (and tasks) of the Community: how to recognize—after having collectively and at length run up against the nos, the opposition and refusals—the grain of the *continuum*. But I'll be coming back to this in 2.9.

2.8 PEIRCE REINTERPRETED

In 2.2, we said that Peirce, in feeling his way through Ground, perceptual judgment, and Immediate Object, was trying to solve the problem of schematism from the standpoint of an inferential view of knowledge. I do not think that, on the various occasions in which he again took up the theme that runs through all his work, Peirce gives us one definitive answer. He attempted lots. He needed a concept of schema, but he could not find one with its modalities already founded and he could not deduce them. He had to find them "in action," in the middle of an incessant activity of interpretation. And so I don't think it is enough to trust in philology, at least I have no intention of doing so here. What I shall do is try to say how I think Peirce should be read (or reconstructed, if you will); in other words, I shall try to make him say what I wish he had said, because only in that case will I manage to understand what he meant to say.

Fumagalli (1995: 3) points out that in 1885 there was a change in Peirce's thinking. From that date the categories of the youthful "New List" were no longer deduced from an analysis of the proposition but concern three areas of experience. There is a sort of shift, I would say, from logic to epistemology: the Ground, for example, is no longer a predicate but a sensation. Likewise, the second moment (that of indexicality) becomes a type of experience that has the form of a shock; it is an impact with an individual, with a *haecceitas* that "strikes" the subject without being a representation yet. Fumagalli observes that we have a Kantian return here to the immediacy of intuition, prior to all inferential activity. Nevertheless, since this intuition, as we shall see, remains the pure sentiment that I am confronted with something, the intuition would still be devoid of all intellectual content, and therefore (it seems to me) it could withstand the young Peirce's anti-Cartesian polemic.

The Ground is a Firstness. As we have seen, the term can mean "background" (and this would be a misleading interpretation) or "basis" or "foundation." It is a "foundation" in the sense of the cognitive process, which is nonmetaphysical, otherwise the Ground would be the substance, something that obscurely proposes itself as the *subjectum* of predications. Instead, the Ground itself seems a possible predicate, more like an "It is red" than a "*This* is red." We are still before the encounter with something that resists us; we are about to enter Secondness, but we are not there yet. At a certain point Peirce tells us that it is "pure species," but I don't think one can understand the term in its scholastic sense; it should be understood in its current sense, as appearance, as semblance (Fabbrichesi 1981: 471). Why does Peirce call it icon, and likeness, and say that it has the nature of an idea? I think this is because Peirce was brought up in the Graeco-Occidental tradition, in which knowledge is always transmitted by a vision. If Peirce had been brought up in the Jewish tradition, perhaps he would have talked of a sound, of a voice.

2.8.1 The Ground, *qualia,* and primary iconism

What is visual about the immediate sensation of heat, which is every bit as much Firstness as a sensation of red? In both cases we still have something elusive, so much so that Peirce uses an extremely delicate term to express the idea of Firstness, which is "so tender that you cannot touch it without spoiling it" (CP 1.358).

But this is the way the Ground should be seen, from the standpoint both of Peirce's realism and from that of his theory of the icon. From the point of view of Peircean realism, Firstness is a presence "such as it is," no more than a positive characteristic (CP 5.44). It is a "quality of feeling," like a purple color noticed without any sense of the beginning or the end of the experience, without any awareness other than the feeling of color; it is not an object, nor is it initially inherent to any recognizable object; it has no generality (CP 7.530). It *is*, and it induces us to pass on to Secondness, to take account of several qualities, which already reciprocally oppose one another before opposing *us* (7.533), and also because at that point we do have to say that something is there. From that moment interpretation may begin, but forward, not backward. However, by appearing, it is still "mere may-be"

(CP 1.304), potentiality without existence (CP 1.328), mere possibility (CP 8.329), and in any case a possibility of a perceptual process that is "not rational, yet capable of rationalization" (CP 5.119). "It cannot be articulately thought: assert it, and it has already lost its characteristic innocence; for assertion always implies a denial of something else...Only, remember that every description of it may be false" (CP 1.357).[25]

Peirce is not a Kantian here: he is not at all concerned with discovering a manifold in intuition. If primary intuition exists, it is absolutely simple. I imagine that other attributes, after the first red, the first heat, the first sense of hardness, may later be added, in the inferential process that follows as a consequence; but the beginning is an absolute point. I think that, when Peirce says the Ground is a quality, he means to say what philosophy still defines today as the phenomenon of *qualia* (see Dennet 1991).

The Ground shows all the antinomies of the dramatic problem posed by *qualia:* How can it be pure possibility, prior to any conceptualization, and yet become a predicate, a *general* predicable of many different objects; in other words, how can a sensation of white be a pure *album* that precedes even the recognition of the object to which it is inherent, and still be not only nameable but predicable as *albedo* of different objects? And, a further problem for Peirce, how is it possible that this pure quality and possibility (as we mentioned in 2.2) can be neither criticized nor called into question?

Let us start with the last problem. With regard to a quality Peirce is still not talking about perceptual judgment; he is talking about a mere "tone" of cognition, and it is this tone that he defines as being resistant to all possible criticism. Peirce is telling us not that the sensation of red is "infallible" but that, once it has been, even if we then realize that we were wrong, it is still beyond doubt that it has been (see Proni 1992, 3.16.1). In an example in CP 5.412, there is mention of something that in the first instance strikes one as perfectly white and then, after a series of successive comparisons, strikes one as off-white. Peirce could have developed the example to tell me of a housewife who in a first moment perceives of her freshly washed sheet as extremely white but then, after comparing it with another, admits that the second is whiter than the first. There is nothing casual or roguish about this reference to the canonical schema of detergent commercials: Peirce's intention was to talk about exactly this problem.

Faced with the television commercial, Peirce would have told us that the housewife initially perceived the whiteness of the first sheet (pure "tone" of awareness); then, once she had moved on to the recognition of the object (Secondness) and had begun a comparison full of inferences (Thirdness), discovering that whiteness is manifested by *degrees*, she could state that the second sheet is whiter than the first, but at the same time she could not cancel the preceding impression, which as a pure quality *has been*; and therefore she says, "I thought (*before*) that my sheet was white, but *now* that I have seen yours, et cetera."

But—and now we come to the first problem—in the course of this process, by comparing diverse gradations of the *album* that was at first pure possibility of awareness, in other words by reacting to the *album* of at least two different sheets, the housewife has moved on to the predicate of the *albedo,* i.e., to a *general,* which can be named and for which there is an Immediate Object. We might say that it is one thing to perceive an object as red, without having become aware as yet that we are dealing with something external to our awareness, and it is another thing to perform the prescission whereby one predicates of that object the quality of being red.

But having said this, we still have not answered a series of questions. We have made clear *what* Peirce wanted to talk about but not *how* he might have explained the process he was talking about. How is it that a pure quality (Firstness), which should be the immediate and unrelated point of departure of all subsequent perceptions, can function as a predicate, and therefore already has been named, if semiosis is established only in Thirdness? And how is it, all knowledge being inference, that we have a point of departure that cannot be inferential, since it manifests itself immediately without even having been discussed or denied?

For example, the Ground should not even be an icon, if the icon is likeness, because it cannot have a relation of likeness with anything if not with itself. Here Peirce is swinging between two notions: in one sense, as we have seen, the Ground is an idea, a skeleton plan, but if it is such, it is already an Immediate Object, a full realization of Thirdness; in another sense it is a Likeness that does not resemble anything. All it says to me is that the sensation I feel is in some way emanated by the Dynamical Object.

In this case we must liberate (even if this means going against Peirce, who, by changing the term every time, confuses our ideas) the concept of likeness from the concept of comparison. Comparison occurs in relations of *similitude*, when on the basis of a given proportion we say—of a graph, for example—that it expresses certain relations that we must suppose in the object. Similitude (already riddled with laws) explains the workings of *hypoicons*, such as diagrams, drawings, pictures, musical scores, and algebraic formulae. But the icon is not explained by saying that it is a similitude, nor even by saying that it is a likeness. The icon is a phenomenon that founds all possible judgments of likeness, but it cannot be founded on likeness itself.

Therefore it would be misleading to think of the icon as a mental "image" that reproduces the qualities of the object, because in that case it would be easy to abstract a general image from many particular images, just as one abstracts (however this happens) a general idea of bird or tree from many birds or many trees. I do not wish to say that mental images must not be admitted or that in certain moments Peirce did not think of the icon in terms of a mental image. I am saying that in order to conceive the concept of primary iconism, the one that establishes itself in the moment of the Ground, we have to abandon even the notion of mental image.[26]

Let us try to eliminate the mental facts and make a mental experiment instead. I have just got up and, still half asleep, I put the coffee percolator on the gas. Probably I have put the gas on too high, or I haven't put the percolator in the right place, but the fact remains that the handle has got too hot, and when I pick up the percolator to pour the coffee, I burn myself. Standard expletives emitted (and deleted), I protect my fingers and pour the coffee.

End of story. But the next morning, I make the same mistake. If I were to verbalize the second experience, I would say that I put the *same* percolator on the gas and that I had the *same* painful sensation. But the two types of recognition are different. Establishing that the percolator is the same is the effect of a complex system of inferences (full Thirdness): I could have (as I do have) two percolators of the same type, one older and one newer, and establishing which of the two I picked up implies a series of recognitions and conjectures regarding some morphological characteristics of the object, and even the memory of where I put it the day before.

But "feeling" that what I feel today is *the same* (with some negligible variations in thermic intensity) as what I felt yesterday is quite another kettle of fish. I am pretty sure I have *the same* impression of burning, or, rather, I feel a painful thermic sensation that in some way I *recognize* as *similar* to that of the previous day.

I don't think many inferences are required to activate this recognition. The handiest solution would be that the previous experience has left a "trace" in my neural circuits. But there is the risk of already considering this trace as a schema, a prototype of the feeling, a rule for recognizing similar feelings. Let us accept, if we wish, an idea current in neoconnectionist circles, whereby it is not necessary for the neural network to construct a prototype of the category, and there is no distinction between rule and data (i.e., the memory of the stimulus and the memory of the rule would have the same configuration, the same neural pattern). Even more modestly, we can assume that, the moment I feel the sensation of pain, a point in my nervous apparatus is activated that is the same one activated the day before and that this point, in activating itself, in some way makes me feel, along with the sensation of heat, a feeling of "again." I am not even sure if one must presuppose a memory, if not in the sense that if on one occasion we have suffered an injury in one part of the body, the body has retained a "memory" of the injury and, when a new injury occurs, it reacts in a different way than if it were hurt in a part still undamaged. It is as if the first time I noticed a sensation of "$heat_1$," and the second time a sensation of "$heat_2$."

Gibson (1966: 278), while maintaining that the idea that feelings leave a trace is fairly reasonable and, all things considered, handy, and that the input present must in some way reactivate the trace left by the previous experience, nevertheless observes that an alternative explanation would be that the judgment of likeness between stimuli reflects a concordance between the perceptual system and the invariants of the informative stimulus. No trace, no preliminary "schema," simply something that we cannot but call *conformity*.

It is not that we have plunged back into a theory of knowledge (or at least of its sensory anteroom) as *adaequatio*. We are dealing with a matter of simple correspondence between stimulus and response. Therefore, we do not have to tackle all the paradoxes in a theory of correspondence at higher cognitive levels: if, on perceiving a dog, we find it corresponds to our schema of dog, we must ask ourselves on what basis the judgment of correspondence is founded, and in seeking the model of correspondence, we enter the spiral of the Third Man. On the contrary, identity, the statistical correspondence between stimulus and response, tells us that the response is exactly that caused by the stimulus.

What does correspondence mean in this case? Let us suppose that somebody managed to record the process that comes about in our nervous system every time we receive the same stimulus, and that the record always has the configuration x. We should say therefore that x corresponds adequately to the stimulus and is the icon of it. Let us say, then, that the icon evinces a *likeness* with the stimulus.

This correspondence we have decided to call likeness has nothing to do (yet) with an "image" that corresponds point by point with the characteristics of the object or the field of stimulus. As Maturana (1970: 10) reminds us, two states of activity in a given nerve cell can be considered the same (i.e., as *equivalents*) if "they belong to the same class" and are defined by the same *pattern* of activity, without their having to possess the nature of a map with one-to-one correspondences. For example, let us accept as good Fechner's Law, whereby the intensity of a sensation is proportional to the logarithm of the excitatory influence. If this were the case, and if the proportion were constant, the intensity of excitation would be the icon of the excitatory influence (in the formula $S = K \log R$, the equals sign would express the relation of iconic similarity).

I think that for Peirce primary iconism lies in the correspondence whereby the stimulus is *adequately* "represented" by that sensation and not by another. This correspondence is not to be explained but only recognized. That is why it is the icon that becomes a parameter of similarity and not vice versa. If from that moment we mean to talk of other and more complex relations of similarity, or of calculated relations of similitude, it is on the basis of the model of that primary likeness, the icon, that we establish what it means, evidently in a sense that is less immediate, rapid, beyond dispute, to be *similar to*.[27]

In 6.11 we shall see that a relation of this kind, nonmediated, beyond dispute (provided there is no interference from elements capable of "fooling" the senses), occurs in mirror images. But here I prefer to avoid recourse to an image of any nature, precisely to free the notion of iconism of its historic ties with visual images.

2.8.2 The lower threshold of primary iconism

If it is possible to define primary iconism in nonmental terms, it is because within Peirce's thinking there is an encounter between two different but mutually dependent perspectives: the metaphysical-cosmological standpoint and the cognitive standpoint. Unless they are read from a semiotical point of view, Peirce's metaphysics and cosmology are certainly incomprehensible; but the same thing ought to be said of his semiotics with regard to his cosmology. Categories such as Firstness, Secondness, and Thirdness, and the concept of interpretation itself, not only define *modi significandi*—that is, the ways in which the world can be known—they are also *modi essendi,* ways in which the world *behaves,* the procedures through which the world, in the course of evolution, interprets itself.[28]

From the cognitive standpoint the icon, seen in its nature as pure quality, state of awareness, absolutely unrelated, is a Likeness, because it corresponds to what called it into being (the icon is thus, even though it has not yet been compared to its own model, even though it is not yet seen in connection with any object external to the senses). From the cosmological standpoint the icon is the natural willingness of something to *correspond to* something else. If Peirce had come to know about the theory of the genetic code, he would certainly have said that the relation that permits chains of nitrogenous bases to produce successions of amino acids, or permits triplets of DNA to be replaced by triplets of RNA, was an iconic one.

I am referring to what in *A Theory of Semiotics* (0.7) I had defined as "the lower threshold of semiotics," excluding it from a discussion in which an attempt was made to work out a semiotics of cultural relations, the only one that made any sense if the Dynamical Object was considered a *terminus ad quem* of the processes of signification and reference. But we are now considering the Dynamical Object as a *terminus a quo*, and therefore this natural semiosis (*a parte objecti*) must be taken into consideration.

With all due caution: in no way am I repudiating the distinction (which remains fundamental) between signal and sign, between dyadic processes of stimulus-response and triadic processes of interpretation, so that only in the full expansion of this last do phenomena such as signification, intentionality, and interpretation (however you wish to consider them) emerge. I am admitting with Prodi (1977) that to understand the higher cultural phenomena, which clearly do not spring from nothing, it is necessary to assume that certain "material bases of signification" exist, and that these bases lie precisely in this disposition to meet and interact that we can see as the first manifestation (not yet cognitive and certainly not mental) of primary iconism.

In this sense the elementary condition of semiosis would be a physical state whereby one structure is willing to interact with another (Prodi would have said: "Is willing to be *read* by"). In a debate between immunologists and semioticians in which the immunologists maintained that phenomena of "communication" occurred on a cellular level (Sercarz et al. 1988), what was at stake was to decide if some phenomena of "recognition" on the part of lymphocytes in the immune system could be dealt with in terms of "sign," "meaning," and "interpretation" (see the same problem in Edelman 1992, III, 8). I am still wary of extending beyond the lower threshold of semiosis terms that indicate higher cognitive phenomena; but it is certain that we need to postulate what I am presently calling primary iconism to explain why and how "T lymphocytes have the capacity to distinguish infected from normal macrophages because they *recognize* as signs of abnormality small bacterial fragments on the macrophage surface" (Eichmann 1988: 163). Let us eliminate from this context the word "signs" and allow terms such as "to recognize" a metaphorical value (by rejecting the notion that a lymphocyte recognizes something in the same way that we recognize the faces of our parents); let us also refrain from commenting upon the fact that many immunologists think that the lymphocyte also makes some "choices" with regard to alternative situations. The fact remains that, in the situation cited, two some-things meet because they *correspond to* each other, *as a screw corresponds to the female thread.*

In the course of the same debate, Prodi (1988: 55) commented:

> An enzyme...selects its substrate from among a number of mean-ingless molecules with which it can collide: it reacts and forms a complex only with its partner molecule. This substrate is a *sign* for the enzyme (for *its* enzyme). The enzyme explores reality and finds what corresponds to its own shape: it is a lock that seeks and finds its own key. In philosophical terms, an enzyme is a reader that "cat-egorizes" reality by determining the set of all the molecules that can react with it factually...This semiotics (or proto-semiotics) is the basic feature of the entire biological organization (protein synthesis, metabolism, hormonal activity, the transmission of nervous im-pulses, and so on).

Yet again I would refrain from using terms such as "sign," but it is beyond doubt that when we come up against this lock that seeks its

own key, we come up against a protosemiotics, and it is to this protosemiotic disposition that I would tend to give the name of natural
primary iconism.

Every time I wondered how I would have reorganized *A Theory
of Semiotics* if I had to write it again now, I would say to myself that
I would have begun at the end, i.e., by putting the part on modes of
sign production at the beginning. It would have been interesting to
begin instead by starting with what happens when, subjected to the
pressure of the Dynamical Object, one decides to consider it a *terminus a quo*. Had I begun from the end, I would have to return to
the pages of the book where (taking my cue from Volli 1972) I
identified *congruencies* (i.e., casts) as being among the first modalities of the production (and recognition) of signs (Eco 1976, 3.6.9).

On that occasion I was interested in how, starting from a cast,
where at each point in the physical space of the expression there is a
corresponding point in the physical space of an impresser, "by reverse transformation" one could infer the nature of the impresser. I
started from the example of a death mask, because I was interested
in the object as a *terminus ad quem* of an already conscious process
of the interpretation and recognition of a sign. I was so interested
in the relation of construction of a possible *content* of the sign that I
was prepared to consider also cases of interpretation of a death
mask that was not such but, rather, the simulation of a nonexistent
impresser. Now all we have to do is take up the example again and
focus the attention not on the moment in which the cast is "read"
but on the moment in which it produces itself (and it produces itself by itself, without the action of a conscious being who intends to
produce a sign destined for interpretation, an expression that must
then be correlated with a content).

We would then be at a beginning, still presemiotic, where something is pressed onto something else. Only afterward could anyone,
finding the *concavity* that something *convex* had produced, begin to
project backward, in an attempt to infer what could have been
there before from what is there now, with regard to which what is
there now can be assumed as an impression, and therefore an icon.

But at this point an objection would arise.

If primary iconism is to be considered this way, how can we define the moment of Firstness using the metaphor of the cast or the impression, which calls for an impressing agent, and therefore an original contact, a comparison, a de facto correspondence between two elements? By virtue of that very fact we would already be in Secondness. Let us think of the process of the transmission of genetic inheritance, which we were talking about earlier: therein we have an occurrence of *steric* phenomena, a series of correspondences, and therefore we would have a stimulus-response process that already has to do, from a Peircean standpoint, with Secondness. Peirce would probably have been the first to agree: he said on many occasions that Firstness can be *prescinded* (logically) from Secondness but cannot *occur* in its absence (see Ransdell 1979: 59). Therefore, in talking of primary iconism as a cast, we are talking not of actuated correspondence but of a *predisposition to correspond,* of "likeness" through the complementary nature of one element with respect to another *to come*. Natural primary iconism would be the quality proper to impressions that still have not found (necessarily) their impresser but that are ready to "recognize it." But if we know that that impression is ready to receive its own impresser, and if we know the ways of the impression to come (the natural law whereby only this screw can be screwed into this screw thread), then we can infer (if the impression is theoretically seen as a sign) the form of the impresser from the impression. Exactly the same way in which (as we shall be saying later) in the course of the perceptual process we can—from that unrelated sensation elsewhere called the Ground—construct the Immediate Object of something that should possess, among other qualities, that quality as well.

It may seem paradoxical to talk of the icon, which Peirce held was the first moment of an absolute evidence, as pure disposition-to, of pure absence in some way, an image of a thing that is not there yet. It would seem that this primary icon is like a *hole*, given that we have everyday experience of it but nonetheless have difficulty defining it, and given that 152 can be recognized only as an absence within something that is present (see Casati and Varzi

1994). And yet it is precisely from that nonbeing that one can infer the shape of the "plug" that could stop it up. But since by talking of holes we already enter the realm of metaphysics (and we have said that primary iconism cannot be understood if not in initially metaphysical terms), I should like to mention another page of metaphysics, the text in which Leibniz talks of one and zero (*De organo sive arte magna cogitandi*) and identifies two fundamental concepts: "God himself, and also nothingness, that is to say privation: which is demonstrated by an admirable similitude." The similitude was the binary calculus where "with admirable method all the numbers between Unity and Nothingness are expressed in this way."

It is singular that, in discussing the nature of the icon (which has always been enlisted in the army of the analogical), one must have recourse to the text that laid the foundations of the future digital calculus, and find oneself translating the concept of the icon in Boolean terms. But in terms of the dialectic between presence and absence the possibility of all steric phenomena can be defined, including the admirable correspondence between a hole and its plug. In defining the least "structured" of experiences, iconic Firstness, we find the structural principle whereby an element can be identified insofar as it is not the other, which, by evoking it, it excludes (see Eco 1968, 2nd ed.: xii).

Naturally, once this presupposition is accepted, we can tackle those situations halfway between natural primary iconism and nonhuman cognitive systems, such as cases of recognition and camouflage among animals, a regular bee in the bonnet—if I may put it that way—for many zoosemioticians.[29] All these phenomena, which I was personally reluctant to consider semiosic because they seem to me to belong more to the *dyadic* reaction (stimulus and response) than to the *triadic* one (stimulus, series of interpretations, and possible final logic interpretant), now acquire all their importance the moment we need (on seeing the Dynamical Object as a *terminus a quo*) to find a basis (and a prehistory) for that initial iconic moment of the cognitive process that Peirce is telling us about.

Otherwise we could not even explain in what sense this primary iconism, in Peirce's view, is connected with the "giveness" of the manifold of the Kantian intuition, which constitutes the "hard core" of the cognitive process; nor could we explain the unswerving confidence that prompted Kant to confirm his "confutation of idealism."

2.8.3 Perceptual judgment

Once primary iconism has been recognized, we must ask ourselves how, in Peirce's view, in the shift from Ground to Immediate Object it is reelaborated and transformed at higher cognitive levels. Having entered the symbolic universe, Peirce's incontrovertible basic "realism" is called into question, i.e., it is subjected to the activity of interpretation.

The iconic moment establishes that everything starts from an evidence, albeit imprecise, which we have to take account of; and this evidence is the pure Quality that in some way emanates from the object. But the fact that the Quality emanates from the object does not provide any guarantee of its "truth." Insofar as it is an icon, it is neither true nor false: the "torch of truth" must still pass through many hands. It is the condition whereby we set off on our way to saying something.

On the way, and right from its first instants, even that primary iconism can be subjected to scrutiny, because I could have received the stimulus under conditions (external or internal) capable of "fooling" my nerve ends. But we are already in an advanced phase of elaboration; we no longer have only one Ground to answer to, we have many of them to keep together, and therefore to interpret, one in the light of the other.

In Peirce's thinking, this primary iconism is still a postulate of his fundamental realism rather than a realistic proof of the existence of the object. Since he denies that intuition possesses any power and asserts that all cognition springs from previous cognitions, not even an unrelated sensation, be it thermic, tactile, or visual, can be recognized without bringing into play an inferential process that, no matter how instantaneous and unconscious, verifies the sensation's reliability. This is why such a point of departure, which precedes even what Kant would have said was the intuition of the manifold, can be defined in logical terms but not clearly identified in epistemological terms.

The certainty supplied by the Ground is not even proof that we are faced with something real (because it is still pure may-be), but it tells us under what conditions we could accept the assumption that we are faced with something real, and that this something is this and that (see Oehler 1979: 69). In fact, in the *New List* Peirce had already said that "the *Ground* is the self abstracted from the concreteness which implies the possibility of an other" (WR 2: 55), and while everybody is free to interpret Peirce's dreadful English as he sees fit, we should reflect on this point. Firstness lets us know that *it is possible* that something is there. In order to say that it is, to say that something is resisting me, we must already have entered Secondness. It is in Secondness that *we really run into* something. Finally, in moving on to Thirdness, which implies generalization, one arrives at the Immediate Object. But since it has opened the gateway to the universal for me, it no longer offers me any guarantee that the something is there, or that it is not a construction of mine.[30] And yet the Ground will remain in the Immediate Object (whose iconic aspect is emphasized by Peirce on several occasions) as a "memory" of that warrant supplied by primary iconism— which is moreover still a Kantian concept, except that in Peirce's case the guarantee, granted by something that precedes the intuition of the manifold, is nonetheless warranted only by perceptual inference.

And so, in a vague and swampy region between Firstness, Secondness, and Thirdness, the perceptual process begins. I say *process* (something in movement), not judgment, which suggests conclusion and rest. Insofar as it is a process, if we are to account for it, we can no longer content ourselves with a stimulus-response schema. It will be necessary to bring into play those mental facts that I had excluded from the attempt to define primary iconism in some way. The fact that for Peirce these can be "quasi mental" facts—in the sense that a theory of interpretation can be established in a formal fashion, without taking account of a mind in which this happens—is another argument. At this point the "contrivance" of something that functions as a mind emerges as indispensable. What explains the perceptual process to us is that by the time I arrive to calm the process, to stop it for a moment, having ascertained that the something I am faced with is a hot (or white, or circular) plate, I shall already have delivered a perceptual judgment.

There is a series of texts from the early twentieth century, in which Peirce reaffirms what he meant by perceptual judgment (CP 7: 615–88). Feeling, pure Firstness, is the awareness of a moment of absolute and atemporal singularity; but from this first moment we already enter Secondness, we attribute the first icon to an object (or at least to something we are faced with), and we have the sensation, an intermediate moment between Firstness and Secondness, between icon and index. The first stimulus, which I am "working" to integrate into a perceptual judgment, is an index of the fact that there is something to perceive. Perhaps something catches my eye, without my being moved by any intention, and something impinges upon my perception. I see a yellow chair with a green cushion: but mark this, I am already beyond Firstness, I am opposing two qualities, I am moving on to a moment of greater concreteness. What is taking shape before me is what Peirce calls a *percept*, which is not yet a full perception. Peirce notes that one might call what I see an "image," but this would be a misnomer, because the word would make me think of a sign that stands for something else, while the percept stands for itself, it simply "knocks at the portal of my soul and stands there in the doorway" (CP 7.619).

I am forced to admit that something appears, but this something is still, precisely, obtuse appearance, it does not make any appeal to reason. It is pure individuality, in itself "dumb."

Only at this point does perceptual judgment come on the scene, and we are in Thirdness.[31] When I say *That is a yellow chair*, I have already used a hypothesis to construct a judgment of the percept present. This judgment does not "represent" the percept, just as the percept was not even its premise, because the percept was not even a proposition. Any statement regarding the character of the percept is already the responsibility of the perceptual judgment; it is the judgment that warrants the percept, not vice versa. Perceptual judgment is not a copy of the percept (at most, according to Peirce, it is a symptom of it, an *index*). Perceptual judgment no longer moves on that threshold where the line between Firstness and Secondness is blurred; it is already asserting that what I see is true. Perceptual judgment has an inferential freedom that the percept, stupid and inane, has not.

But that's not all. It is clear that for Peirce, when I state that the chair is yellow, my perceptual judgment retains a trace of primary iconicity. And yet it *desingularizes* it:

> The perceptual judgment pronounces quite carelessly the chair yellow. What the particular shade, hue, and purity of the yellow may be it does not consider. The percept, on the other hand, is so scrupulously specific that it makes this chair different from any other in the world; or rather, it would do so, if it indulged in any comparisons. (CP 7.633)

It is dramatic to see how already in the perceptual judgment (for which yellow was *that* yellow) primary iconism shades off into a generic equality (*that* yellow is like *all* the other yellows I have seen). The individual sensation has already transformed itself into a class of "similar" sensations (but the similarity of these sensations is no longer the same quality of similarity between stimulus and Ground). By this point, if we can say that the predicate "yellow" resembles the sensation, it is only because a new judgment would predicate the same predicate of the same percept. And here Peirce does not seem particularly interested in saying how and why this happens: he seems to endorse the interpretation I gave to the Ground in 2.8.2: two stimuli are respectively the icon (the Likeness) of each other, because they are both the icon of my response pattern.

And in fact Peirce says that the same percept arouses in the mind an "imagination" that involves "elements of the senses." Therefore "it is clear that the perceptual judgment is not a copy, icon, or diagram of the percept, no matter how crude" (CP 7. 637).

This is puzzling. Because we might be tempted to say that this perceptual judgment so permeated by Thirdness is identified with the Immediate Object. And yet Peirce has repeatedly emphasized the iconic character of the Immediate Object. But the iconism of the Immediate Object certainly cannot be the primary iconism of Feeling; it is already dominated by calculations of similarity, by ratios of proportion, it is already diagrammatic or *hypoiconic*.

Therefore must we suppose that when Peirce talks of the Immediate Object, he is not talking about perceptual judgment, and when he is talking about perceptual judgment, he is not talking about the Immediate Object? But it is equally clear that the second should be none other than the completed fulfillment of the first.

I think we have to distinguish the function of the Immediate Object, and its relation with perceptual judgment, according to whether it is constructed, so to speak, *ex novo* (but not in the absence of previous cognitions) when faced with a new experience (e.g., the platypus) or in the process of recognizing something already known (e.g., the plate). In the first case, the Immediate Object will still be imperfect, tentative, *in fieri*; it will come to coincide with the first hypothetical perceptual judgment (perhaps this thing is like this or like that). In the second case, I have recourse to an Immediate Object, which has already deposited itself in my memory, as if to a preformed schema that orients the formation of the perceptual judgment, and is a parameter of it at the same time. Having perceived the plate therefore means having recognized it as a token of an already known type, and at that point the Immediate Object would perform the same function that—in the cognitive process—is performed by the Kantian schema. The upshot is that in that phase I shall not only know that what I have perceived is a white plate but also know (before having touched it) that it should have a certain weight, because the schema already formed also contained that information.

The perceptual process was tentative, still private, while the Immediate Object, insofar as it is interpretable (and therefore transmissible), is on its way to becoming *public*. It can even, as a cognitive schema already consigned to me by the community, act not to encourage but to block the process of perceiving something new (as was the case with Marco Polo and the rhinoceros). Indeed it too must be subjected to continuous scrutiny, revision, and reconstruction.[32]

This is why it has been possible to maintain (see, e.g., Eco 1979: 2.3) that, from a certain point of view, Ground, Immediate Object, and *Meaning* are the same thing. From the point of view of the knowledge that has provisionally subsided into a first outline, the original iconic elements, the information I already possessed, and the first attempts at inference have composed themselves into a single schema. On the other hand, it is certain that if we consider the *temporal scansion* of the perceptual process (even though the process is sometimes almost instantaneous—but for Kant, too, temporality was a constituent of the schema), the Ground and the Immediate Object are respectively the point of departure and the first stop on a journey that could continue for a long time as it runs along the tracks of potentially infinite interpretation.

Only in this sense can the Ground, the moment it is consciously inserted into the process of interpretation, be considered as a "filter," a selector, on the part of the perceptual signal, of those properties of the Dynamical Object destined to be made pertinent by the Immediate Object. And the hitherto uninterpreted Ground represents the presemiosic moment, pure possibility of segmentation traced out in the hitherto unsegmented *continuum*.[33]

In this phase one could also reintroduce icons to the Immediate Object, as a phenomenon of visual correspondence. After all, Kant too used to say that in order to perceive the plate, I have to bring the concept of the circle into play. But I should like to keep this Peircean reading out of the extremely lively debate, within modern cognitive sciences, between *iconophiles* and *iconophobes* (Dennett 1978: 10). It could always be said that the schema that is the Immediate Object does not necessarily have to be a "photo in your head," it might be more like the description of a scene than its "portrayal" (see, e.g., Pylyshin 1973). Without involving Peirce in the debate regarding a "computational" theory of knowledge, we could always

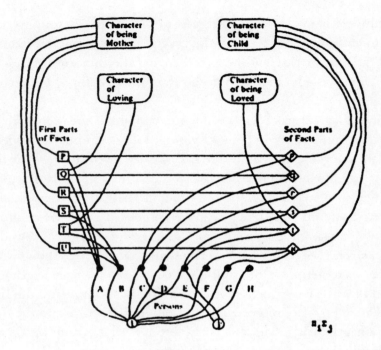

Figure 2.3

say that the circle by which a plate is perceived is not a visible geometrical form but the precept, the rule for drawing the circle. As far as the dog is concerned, seeing that in order to identify its morphological characteristics (coat, four legs, the shape of the nose) I have not so much pure geometrical concepts at my disposal but (as we have said) a 3-D model, it is hard to think of the dog's Immediate Object without having to presume mental images. I am not sure how Peirce would have taken part in current debates within the cognitive sciences.

Also because there can be an Immediate Object that corresponds to a term that is not intended to take account of a perceivable object, such as *cousin* or *square root*.

When Peirce conceives a diagram (which he says is a "pure icon") not for objects but for propositions—since like Kant he is thinking of a schema that also mediates between categories and sense data through experientially based judgments that assume proportional form, and also through propositions that assert something about objects not known through perceptions—the diagram assumes the aspect of a "program" that is only occasionally represented visually. I am thinking in general of the theory of graphs, and in particular of a diagram that appears in the *Grand Logic*, where Peirce wonders how to "put into shape" the proposition that "every mother loves some child of hers."[34] I am surprised by the analogies between this "program" and some present-day representations of cognitive processes, and, even without following the long and detailed reading that Peirce gives of it, I feel it is enough to reproduce it (see fig. 2.3).

Peirce makes it clear that the diagram, precisely because it is a pure icon, shows a state of things and nothing else: it does not assert in a distinct fashion that which is understood by the proposition, but limits itself to showing some relations of inherence. It is in fact a schema and a prelude to subsequent interpretations. But it is clear that this schema could today be supplied to a machine as an instruction expressed in nonvisual language, and the relations it expresses would be retained. Independently of whether one presumes, as its container or active producer, a mind.

This schema, abundantly imbued with symbolic (and therefore conceptual) elements—which does not tend to account for any perceptual experience—is the Immediate Object that regulates the understanding of the situation in question. It is also a schema of its meaning.

Therefore, from a primary iconism and through a perceptual process already imbued with inferences, we come to an identity (if not final, at least temporarily established) between perceptual judgment and Immediate Object, and between Immediate Object and the first nucleus of meaning associated with a *representamen*. And the complete meaning as an all-inclusive set of markers, definitions, and interpretants? It vanishes, in a certain sense, and one can agree with Nesher (1984), that it cannot be collocated in any of the phases of the cognitive process but that it distributes itself through every phase (including the most advanced ones, but certainly starting from the most elementary ones) of the process.

In this case the Immediate Object is something more than the

Kantian schema: it is less "empty"; it does not mediate between concept and intuition but is in itself the first conceptual nucleus and at the same time (insofar as its iconic nature is always reiterated) does not only put into shape, does not translate, but reelaborates by conserving, and in a certain sense it "captures" and "memorizes" something of the sensations from which it started. Or, at least, when it is the Immediate Object that realizes perceptual situations and not abstract terms. Unlike the schema—or at least the version of it given in the first *Critique*—it is tentative, revisable, ready to grow by virtue of interpretation. And yet it certainly represents the way in which Peirce settles the inheritance of schematism in a non-transcendental vein.

But Peirce had already said as much: if Kant had had to deduce all the consequences of the advent of the schemata, his system would have been thrown into confusion.

2.9 THE GRAIN

The time has come, in bringing this double rereading of Kant and Peirce to a conclusion, to say why and in what way it is connected to the reflections I made in 1.10. And I shall do this by continuing for the time being to use the concept of schema, which even at the end of this rereading still emerges as being rather vague. But it is handy to let it fluctuate like this, between the Immediate Object and a "cognitive model" whose physiognomy I shall try to fix better in 3.3.

Even though cognitive schemata are constructs, imbued with "as if," that in Kant's view start from a still blind material of the intuition, and in Peirce's view start from a primary icon that does not yet provide us with any guarantee of "objectivity," there must have been something in the platypus that prevented the explorer from defining it as a quail or a beaver. This does not guarantee us that it was right to classify it among the monotremes. Tomorrow a new taxonomy could radically change the rules. And nonetheless right from the start, in order to construct a schema of the platypus, attempts were made to respect the grain possessed by that manifestation of the still unsegmented *continuum*.

Even granting that the schema is a construct, we can never assume that the segmentation of which it is the effect is completely arbitrary, because (in Kant as in Peirce) it tries to make sense of something that *is there,* of forces that act externally on our sensory apparatus by exhibiting, at the least, some resistances.

Therefore there is probably a "truth" of the schema, a point of view, a profile, an *Abschattung* that always shows us something from a certain perspective. The 3-D model of a human being still depends on the fact that man cannot be interpreted as a quadruped, and no matter how many joints he has in his body, the ones that articulate the arm at the elbow and the leg at the knee will always exhibit a pertinence that would be hard to revoke (it can be abstracted but not denied).

There was also a truth in the schema that depicted the whale as a fish (i.e., with the schematic traits proper to fish). It was wrong (as we now say) from the taxonomic standpoint, but it was not (and still is not, even for us) from the standpoint of the construction of a stereotype. But in any case it *would never have been possible* to schematize the whale as a bird.

Even if the schema were a construct in a state of perpetual inferential becoming, it would still have to take account of experience and allow us a return to it by acting according to habits. This does not exempt us from supposing that perhaps there might be better ways of organizing experience (otherwise the principle of fallibilism would make no sense), but at the same time it must guarantee us that, according to the schema, experience can be reckoned with in some way. The schema of something cannot be constructed arbitrarily, even though it is possible to have different schematic representations of one and the same thing. In Kant's view, that the sun rises, that it illuminates the stone, and that the stone is gradually heated come from the perceptual judgment; that between the rising of the sun and the heating of the stone there is a lapse of time comes from pure intuition; that the sun is the cause of the heat of the stone comes from the marshaling of the entire categorial apparatus. Everything depends on the legislative activity of the intellect.

But that it does not happen that the heat of the stone comes *before* and the sunrise *after* depends on the very stuff of the sensible intuition. I cannot think of the causal nexus that runs from the sun to the heated stone without the forms of the intellect, but no form of the intellect can ever allow me to establish that it is the heating up of the stone that causes the sun to rise.

The schemata can also be considered unnatural, in the sense that they do not preexist in nature, but this does not change the fact that they are *motivated*.[35] It is in this hint of motivation that the grain of the *continuum* is revealed.

Chapter Three

Cognitive Types and
Nuclear Content

3.1 From Kant to cognitivism

If Kant had considered schemata early enough, Peirce said, they would have overgrown his whole work (WR 5: 258–59). In the previous chapter, I suggested that it was precisely the problem of schematism that obliged Kant to undertake a change of direction in the third *Critique*. But we might say something more: if we were to reconsider the problem of Kantian schematism, much of the semantics of this century, from the truth-functional to the structural variety, would find itself in difficulty. And this is what has happened in the area usually referred to as "cognitive studies."

In point of fact, a hint of various forms of Kantian schematism (connected to a constructivist idea of knowledge) is present in the contemporary cognitive sciences, even though their practitioners are sometimes unaware of this connection.[1] Nevertheless today, when we come across notions such as schema, prototype, model, and stereotype, they are certainly not comparable to the Kantian notion (they do not imply transcendentalism, for example), nor can these terms be understood as synonyms.

Moreover these cognitive "schemata" are usually intended to account for phenomena such as perception and the recognition of objects or situations, while we have seen that Kantian schematism, created to explain how judgments such as *All bodies have weight* are possible, fell short of the mark precisely when it had to explain how we manage to have empirical concepts. Cognitivism drew attention back to empirical concepts and recommended wondering about the same things Locke (and Husserl too, basically) had wondered about: What happens when we talk about dogs, cats, apples, and chairs?[2]

But to say that cognitivism asks questions about cats and chairs does not mean to say that the conclusions it comes to (which are many and discordant) are satisfactory. The ghost of schematism haunts much contemporary research, but the mystery of this secret art has not yet been revealed.

Nor have I any pretensions to revealing it in these pages, also because, as we shall see, I would rather not poke my nose into the black box of our mind or brain processes. I shall ask myself only a few questions regarding the relations between a possible neo-schematism and semiotic notions of meaning, dictionary and encyclopedia, and interpretation.[3]

Given the erratic character I should like these reflections to have, I shall not always try to identify positions, theories, research, or the schools of thought within contemporary cognitivism. Instead I shall recount, as will be seen, lots of "stories" (mental experiments in narrative form) that exemplify some of the problems.

Most of my stories are about something *fairly similar* to what Kant held to be empirical concepts: I mean to say that I intend to deal with the way in which we speak (i) of objects or situations of which we have or might have direct experience (such as dog, chair, walking, eating out, climbing a mountain); (ii) of objects and situations of which we have no experience but could have (such as armadillo, or performing an appendectomy); (iii) of objects and situations of which someone has certainly had experience but we can no longer have, and regarding which the Community nevertheless transmits us sufficient instructions to speak of as if we had had experience of them (such as dinosaur and Australopithecine).

Dealing with such elementary phenomena from a semiotic standpoint poses first and foremost a preliminary question: whether there is any sense in talking of perceptual semiosis, that is, of a semiotic aspect of perception.

3.2 Perception and semiosis

The problem of perception as a semiosic process has already made its appearance in 2. Of course, those unfamiliar with the Peircean standpoint will find this concept difficult (or quasi "imperialist"), because if we accept that even perception is a semiosic phenomenon, discriminating between perception and signification gets a little tricky.[4] We have seen that Husserl also thought that perceiving something as red and naming something as *red* ought to be the same process, but this process might have diverse phases. Between perceiving a cat as a cat and naming it *cat,* or indicating it as an ostensive sign for all cats, is there not a jump, a gap (at least that shift from *terminus a quo* to *terminus ad quem*)?

Can we detach the phenomenon of semiosis from the idea of sign? There is no doubt that when we say that smoke is a sign of fire, the smoke we notice is not yet a sign; even if we accept the Stoic standpoint, smoke becomes a sign of fire not in the moment in which it is perceived but when we decide that it *stands for* something else. In order to pass on to that moment, we must leave the immediacy of perception and translate our experience into propositional terms so that the observation of smoke becomes the antecedent of a semiosic inference: (i) there is smoke, (ii) if there is smoke, (iii) then there is fire. The passage from (ii) to (iii) is a matter of inference expressed propositionally; while (i) is a matter of perception.

On the contrary, we speak of perceptual semiosis not when *something stands for something else* but when from something, by an inferential process, we come to pronounce a perceptual judgment *on that same something* and not on anything else.[5]

Let us suppose that someone with almost no knowledge of English but nonetheless accustomed to seeing English titles, names, or phrases on record sleeves, postcards, or various tinned goods receives a fax that, as often happens, has superimposed or distorted lines and illegible letters. Let us suppose (by transcribing the illegible letters as *X*) that he attempts to read *Xappy neX Xear.* Even without understanding the meaning of the words, he remembers seeing expressions such as *happy, new,* and *year* and presumes that these were the words the fax was intended to transmit. He will therefore have made inferences solely on the basis of the graphic form of the terms, from what was there on the sheet of paper (the expression plane) and not from what the words stood for (and so he would have to consult a dictionary).

Therefore any phenomenon, for it to be understood as a sign of something else and from a certain point of view, must first of all be perceived. The fact that the perception may be successful precisely because we are guided by the notion that the phenomenon is hypothetically understood as a sign (otherwise we would pay no attention to certain stimuli) does not eliminate the problem of how we perceive it.[6]

When the phenomenological tradition speaks of "perceptual meaning" it refers to something that legitimately precedes the constitution of meaning as the content of an expression; and yet (see *A Theory of Semiotics* 3.3) if I descry an indistinct animal form in the darkness, the success of the perception (the judgment *That is a dog*) is governed by a cognitive schema, something that I already know about the dog and that can legitimately be considered as a part of the content I usually assign to the word *dog*. In such a case I have made an *inference:* I have surmised that the indistinct form I descried in the darkness was a *token* of the type *dog*.

In the example of the fax, the letters *-ear* stand, in the inferential process, for the *y* they make it possible to hypothesize. The subject of our example possesses the (purely graphical) knowledge of at least one English word that could end with those letters and therefore guesses that *-ear* is an (incomplete) *token* of the lexical *type* denominated *year*. If on the other hand he has a good knowledge of English, he will also have the right to assume that the missing letter could be chosen from among *b, d, f, g, h, n, p, r, t,* and *w* (with each of which one can form an English word that makes sense), without being able to assume *c, i, o, q,* or *u.* But if he extends the inference to the whole syntagm *Xappy neX Xear,* he notices that one solution is more probable than the others, because he assumes that the whole string (incomplete in three places) is none other than *Happy New Year* (a stock phrase and a highly codified expression of good wishes).

We could then say that even in such an elementary process the token *stands for* its type. But what happens in the perception of un-known objects (such as the platypus)? The process is certainly more adventurous, that *to stand for* is contracted through processes of trial and error, but the relation of mutual referral from type to to-ken is fixed once a perceptual judgment has been established.[7]

If (as is reiterated in Eco 1984) the basic characteristic of semiosis is inference, while the equivalence established by a code (a = b) is only a scleroticized form of semiosis, fully found only in *ciphers* (i.e., in the equivalences between one expression and the other, as in Morse code—see Eco 1984: 172–73), then the perceptual inference may be considered a process of primary semiosis.[8]

Naturally it might be decided that the question is wholly nomi-nalistic. If it were established that semiosis occurred only when in-stitutionalized sign functions appeared, then any talk of semiosis in the case of perception would be purely metaphorical—and in such a case we would have to say that so-called primary semiosis is only a precondition of semiosis. If this makes it possible to do away with pointless discussion, I have no problems in speaking of perceptual presemiosis.[9] But things would not change that much, because, as we shall see in the following story, the relation between this pri-mary phase and the successive development of full-fledged semiosis presents no evident fractures; rather, it constitutes a sequence of phases in which the preceding one determines the following one.

3.3 MONTEZUMA AND THE HORSES

The first Aztecs to hasten to the coast witnessed the landing of the conquistadors.[10] Although only a very few traces of their first reac-tions remain and the best information we have depends on Spanish reports and indigenous chronicles written after the event, we know for sure that various things must have completely amazed them: the ships; the Spaniards' awesome and majestic beards; the protective coverings that lent those fully armored "aliens" with their unnaturally white skins such a frightening air; the muskets and the cannons; and finally, apart from the ferocious dogs, those unheard-of monsters, the horses, in terrifying symbiosis with their riders.

The horses must have been no less perceptually puzzling than a platypus. At first (maybe also because they did not distinguish the animals from the pennants and armor that covered them), the Aztecs thought that the invaders were riding deer (and in so thinking they behaved just like Marco Polo). Oriented therefore by a system of previous knowledge but trying to coordinate it with what they were seeing, they must have soon worked out a perceptual judgment. *An animal has appeared before us that seems like a deer but isn't.* Likewise they must not have thought that each Spaniard was riding an animal of a different species, even though the horses brought by the men of Cortès had diverse coats. They must therefore have got a certain idea of that animal, which at first they called *maçatl,* which is the word they used not only for deer but for all quadrupeds in general. Later, since they began adopting and adapting the foreign names for the objects brought by the invaders, their Nahuatl language transformed the Spanish *caballo* into *cauayo* or *kawayo.*

At a certain point they decided to send messengers to Montezuma to tell him of the landing and of the terrifying marvels they were witnessing. We have posterior evidence of the first message they sent to their lord: one scribe gave the news in pictograms, and he explained that the invaders were riding deer (*maçaoa,* the plural of *maçatl*) as high as the roofs of the houses.

I don't know whether Montezuma, confronted with such incredible news (men dressed in iron with iron weapons, perhaps of divine origin, equipped with prodigious instruments that hurled stone balls capable of destroying all things), understood what those "deer" were. I imagine that the messengers (worried about the fact that in their neck of the woods, if the news was not to the hearer's liking, there was a tendency to punish the bearer of it) screwed up their courage and integrated the report with more than just words, since it seems that Montezuma was wont to require his informers to provide him with all the possible expressions for one and the same thing. And so they must have used their bodies to hint at the movements of the *maçatl,* imitating its whinnying, trying to show how it had long hair along its neck, adding that it was most terrifying and ferocious, capable in the course of the fray of overwhelming anyone who tried to withstand it.

Montezuma received some descriptions, on the basis of which he tried to get some idea of that as yet unknown animal, and goodness knows how he imagined it. That depended both on the skill of the messengers and on his agility of wit. But he certainly understood that it was an animal, and a worrisome one too. In fact, still according to the chronicles, at first Montezuma did not ask other questions but withdrew into a distressing silence, with head bowed and wearing an absent, sorrowful air.

Finally the encounter between Montezuma and the Spaniards came to pass, and I would say that, no matter how confused the messengers' description may have been, Montezuma must have easily identified those things called *maçaoa.* Simply, faced with the direct experience of the *maçatl,* he must have adjusted the tentative idea he had conceived of them. Now, like his men, every time he saw a *maçatl,* he too would recognize it as such, and every time he heard talk of *maçaoa,* he would understand what his interlocutors were talking about.

Then, as he gradually got to know the Spaniards, he would learn many things about horses, he would begin to call them *cauayo,* he would learn where they came from, how they reproduced, what they ate, how they were reared and trained, what other uses they could be put to, and to his regret he would very soon understand how useful they could be in battle. But according to the chronicles, he must also have harbored a suspicion regarding the invaders' divine origins, because he was told that his men had managed to kill two horses.

At a certain point the learning process whereby Montezuma was gradually increasing his knowledge of horses stopped, not because he could not learn any more but because he was killed. And therefore I will leave him (and the great number of those who were massacred along with him for having had the revelation of Horsehood) in order to observe that in this story a great number of different semiotic phenomena come into play.

3.3.1 The Cognitive Type (CT)

At the close of their first perceptual process, the Aztecs elaborated what we shall call a Cognitive Type (CT) of the horse. If they had lived in a Kantian universe, we should say that this CT was the schema that allowed them to mediate between the concept and the manifold of the intuition. But for an Aztec where was the concept of horse, given that he did not have one before the Spaniards landed? Of course, after having seen some horses, the Aztecs must have constructed a morphological schema not that dissimilar to a 3-D model, and it is on this basis that the coherence of their perceptual acts must have been established. But by speaking of a CT, I do not mean just a sort of image, a series of morphological or motor characteristics (the animal trots, gallops, rears); they had perceived the characteristic neigh, and perhaps the smell, of horses. Apart from the appearance, the Aztecs must have immediately attributed a characteristic of "animality" to the horse, given that the term *maçatl* was immediately applied, as well as the capacity to inspire terror and the functional characteristic of being "rideable," since it was usually seen with human beings on its back. In short, let's say that the CT of the horse was of a *multimedial* nature right from the start.

3.3.1.1 The recognition of tokens

On the basis of the CT thus elaborated, the Aztecs must have been immediately able to recognize as horses other exemplars that they had never seen before (and this apart from variations in color, size, and vantage point). It is precisely the phenomenon of recognition that induces us to talk of *type,* in fact, as a parameter for the comparison of tokens. This type has nothing to do with an Aristotelian-Scholastic "essence," and we have no interest in knowing what the Aztecs grasped of the horse (perhaps wholly superficial features of a kind that left them unable to discriminate between horses and mules or donkeys). But it is certain that by talking of type in this sense, we conjure up the ghost of a Lockian type of "general ideas," and some might object that we have no need of these to explain the phenomenon of recognition. All we need say is that the Aztecs applied the same name to diverse individuals because they found them similar to one another. But this notion of similarity between individuals is no less confusing than that of similarity between a token and a type. Even to express a judgment according to which a token X is similar to a token Y requires the elaboration of criteria of similarity (two things are similar in some aspects and dissimilar in others) and therefore the ghost of a type reappears that can be referred to as a parameter.

On the other hand, some contemporary cognitive theories tell us that recognition occurs on the basis of *prototypes,* whereby an object elected as a paradigm is deposited in the memory and then others are recognized in relation to the prototype. But to say that an eagle is a bird because it is similar to the prototype of the sparrow signifies having chosen some features of the sparrow that are more pertinent than others (at the expense of dimensions, for example). And so, if things were like this, our prototype would have become a type.

If we were to reutilize the Kantian notion of schema here, the CT could be a rule, a procedure for constructing the image of the horse rather than a sort of multimedial image. In any case, whatever this CT may be, it is something that permits recognition. At this point, having postulated the existence (somewhere or other) of this type (schema or multimedial image, as it may be), we have if nothing else cleared the field of a venerable presence, which beyond a doubt still inhabited the Kantian universe: if we postulate a CT, we no longer have any need to bring *concepts* into play. Especially for our Aztecs, the CT does not mediate between the concept of horse (which they could not have had anywhere, unless we postulate a Platonism that is *very* transcultural) and the manifold of the intuition. The CT is that which allowed them to unify the manifold of the intuition, and if this was good enough for them, it ought to be good enough for us too.

3.3.1.2 Naming and felicitous reference

And should someone come along and say that the concept of horse is far richer than anything the Aztecs knew, this proves nothing. There are plenty of people around who have a CT of the horse that is no more elaborate than the one the Aztecs had, and that does not prevent them from saying they know what horses are, given that they can recognize them. In this phase of our story, there are a great number of things that the Aztecs still do not know about the horse (whence it comes, how it eats, how it reproduces, how it nurtures its young, how many breeds there are in the world, and even whether it is a dumb animal or a rational being). But on the basis of what they know, they manage not only to recognize it but also to agree on a name for it, and in so doing, they realize that each one of them reacts to the name by applying it to the same animals that the others do. Naming is the first social act that convinces them that they all recognize various individuals, at different times, as tokens of the same type.

It was not necessary to name the object-horse to recognize it, just as one day I may become aware of an internal sensation that is unpleasant but indefinable and recognize only that it is the same one I felt the day before. However, "that thing I felt yesterday" is already a name for the feeling I have; it would be even more a name if I were to mention this feeling—an extremely private one, moreover—to others. The passage to a generic term springs from the social need to be able to detach the name from the *hic et nunc* of the situation, and then to bind it to the type.

But how did the Aztecs know they were applying the name *maçatl* to the same CT? A Spanish observer (let's call him José Gavagai) might have wondered whether, when an Aztec indicated a generic point in space-time by saying *maçatl,* he meant by that name the animal that every Spaniard recognized; or else the still inseparable unit made up of horse-horseman, the animal's shining trappings, the fact that an unknown thing was coming toward him; or whether he wanted to express the proposition "Behold as out of the sea come those divine beings promised by our prophets and that one day Gulliver will call Houyhnhnms!"

The certainty that everybody shares a common CT, corresponding to the name, comes about only in cases of felicitous reference (i.e., of reference crowned by success). In 5, I shall be dealing with how problematic the notion of reference is. But experience tells us that there are cases in which we refer to something and others have shown that they understand very well what we wanted to refer to—for example, when we ask someone to bring us the book that is on the table, and this someone brings us the book and not a pen. Given that the Spaniards rapidly allied themselves with some local populations, if someone had asked a native to bring him a horse, and the native returned bringing a horse (and not a basket, a flower, a bird, or a portion of horse), we would have the proof that with that name both parties identified tokens of the same CT.

On this basis it is possible to suggest the existence of CTs without being obliged to wonder what and where they are. While in times of violent antimentalism it was forbidden even to hypothesize the existence of any mental event whatsoever, in a period in which cognitive studies are flourishing it is legitimate to wonder whether the CT of the horse in the "mind" of the Aztecs was made up of mental images, diagrams, definite descriptions expressed propositionally; or whether it consisted of a set of semantic markers and abstract relations that constituted the innate alphabet of their "mentalese," and they processed strings of discrete signals in pure Boolean terms. A problem of maximum import in the world of the cognitive sciences, but, in my view, wholly irrelevant from the standpoint I have chosen to adopt: to take into account only the data of a folk psychology or, rather, to revive a venerable philosophical concept that I hold to be still of maximum usefulness, that is, to consider things from a standpoint of *common sense*. It is on the basis of common sense that we find evidence of the two phenomena of recognition and *felicitous reference*.[11]

3.3.1.3 The CT and the black box

What happens in our "black box" when we perceive something is a problem that cognitive scientists debate by discussing, for example, (i) whether the environment provides us with all the necessary information without a constructive contribution on the part of our mental or neural apparatus, or whether there is a selection, interpretation, and reorganization of the stimulating field; (ii) whether in the black box there is something that may be designated as "mind" or pure neural processes, or whether, as happens in the field of neoconnectivism, we can assert an identity between rule and data; (iii) where cognitive types or schemata of any kind are (if there are any); and (iv) how they are configured mentally or cerebrally. All these are problems I do *not* intend to deal with.

CTs may be in the mind, in the brain, in the liver, in the pineal gland (were the pineal gland not already occupied, these days, by melatonin); they could even belong to an impersonal warehouse, packed into some universal active intellect, whence a miserly divinity takes them and doles them out to me, out of occasionalism, every time I need them (and the cognitive scientists who spend their lives questioning subjects that cannot tell a glass from a plate will have to decide why some of those subjects' cerebral areas are no longer in tune with the divine wavelength). But we must start from the principle that, if there are felicitous acts of reference, it is because, both in recognizing a second time something perceived previously and in deciding that object A and object B can satisfy the requisite of being a glass, a horse, or a building—or that two forms are both definable as right-angled triangles—we relate *tokens* to a *type* (whether it be a psychic phenomenon, a physically existing prototype, or one of those Third World entities that philosophy has always tried to account for, from Plato to Frege, from Peirce to Popper).

Postulating CTs does not even oblige us to decide beforehand whether they assume, wholly or in part, the configuration of a mental image or are simply computable and processable in terms of discrete symbols. It is well known how this debate between *iconophiles* and *iconophobes* is today a central issue for cognitive psychologists. We might restrict ourselves to a summary of the Kosslyn-Pylyshyn polemic:[12] on the one hand, forms of mental representation of the iconic type seem indispensable if we are to explain a whole series of cognitive processes with respect to which propositional explanations emerge as insufficient, and this hypothesis would also seem confirmed by computer simulations; on the other hand, mental imagination would seem to be a simple *epiphenomenon*, explicable as an elaboration of information accessible only in digital terms. From this standpoint, therefore, mental images are not incorporated into our hardware but are only secondary output.

Now, it could be said that love does not exist on a neural level and that falling in love is an epiphenomenon based fundamentally on complex physiological interactions, which might one day be expressible through an algorithm. This does not stop the epiphenomenon "falling in love" from being central to our personal and social life, to art and literature, to morals, and often even to politics. The result is that a semiotics of the passions does not wonder about what happens in our hardware when we feel hate or fear, anger or love (even though something worth investigating certainly does happen), but about how it happens that we recognize them, express them, and interpret them—so that we understand perfectly well what it means when Orlando is described as *furioso* rather than *innamorato*.

Semiosic experience tells us that we have the impression that we retain mental images (even if a mind does not exist), and above all that we interpret many terms publicly and intersubjectively through visual representations. And so the iconic component of knowledge must be postulated as well as the existence of the CT, if we are to account for what common sense proposes to us. Images are as much systems of instructions as they are verbal devices, and if I have to tell someone how to get to Main Street, I can supply him with lengthy verbal indications regarding the streets he must take as well as show him a map (which is not an image of Main

Street but a diagrammatic procedure that makes it possible to find it). Which of the two procedures is the better depends on the capacities and disposition of my interlocutor.[13]

My refusal to stick my nose into the black box might be interpreted as a confession that philosophy (and in this specific case general semiotics as a philosophy) is an "inferior" form of knowledge with respect to science. But this is not the case. We can postulate the CTs in the black box precisely because we can have an intersubjective check on what constitutes their output. We have the instruments with which to talk about this output—and this is perhaps the contribution that semiotics can make to the cognitive sciences, that is to say, to the semiotic aspect of the cognitive processes.

3.3.2 From CT toward Nuclear Content (NC)

Whereas at first the Aztecs might have felt that their CT was private, as soon as they all began indicating the same animals by pronouncing the name *maçatl,* they must have realized that, on the contrary, the CT had established an area of consensus. At first the area of consensus could be postulated only to explain the fact that they understood one another by using the same word. But bit by bit they must have proceeded to *collective interpretations* of what they understood by that word. They associated a "content" with the expression *maçatl*. These interpretations were as similar as we can imagine to a definition, but we certainly cannot think that our Aztecs had said to one another that by *maçatl* they meant, as an encyclopedia might put it, "a browsing herbivorous mammal of the family Equidae, order Perissodactyla, with a highly developed middle toe of the foot enveloped by a protective nail (hoof)."

At first this agreement must have taken place as a disordered exchange of experiences (some would have pointed out that the animal had hair along its neck, some that the hair in question swirled in the wind when the animal was galloping, while someone must have been the first to note that the trappings were extraneous to the creature's body, and so on). In other words, the Aztecs gradually interpreted the features of their CT, in order to homologate it as much as possible. While their CT (or CTs) could have been private, these interpretations were *public:* if they had written them down, or had used pictograms, or if someone had tape-recorded what they said to one another, we would have a verifiable series of *interpretants.* As a matter of fact we have them, in the sense that indigenous testimony is still extant, and while we do not know exactly what went through the heads of the first Aztecs when they first saw horses, it is only because we have reason to suspect that the testimony is decidedly tardy, interpretations of the interpretations that the conquistadors had made of the Aztecs' first behavioral responses. But if these interpretants were available integrally, as is the case with the scientists who saw a platypus for the first time, the Aztecs would not only make clear what their CT was but also circumscribe the meaning they assigned to the expression *maçatl.*

We shall call this set of interpretants the Nuclear Content (NC).

I prefer to speak of Nuclear Content rather than Meaning, because by time-honored tradition one tends to associate meaning with a mental experience. In certain languages the confusion is greater than in others, and we need think only of the English word *meaning,* which can stand for "that which exists in the mind" but also for an intention, for what is recognized as being, for what is denoted or understood, for sense, signification, and so on. Nor should we forget that *meaning* can also appear as a form of the verb *to mean,* which is variously defined as to have in mind, to intend, to stand for, and only in a few cases does it come to denote a socially recorded synonymy (the example given in Webster is "the word *ja* in German *means* yes"). The same variations of sense are found also in the German verb *meinen.* As far as Italian is concerned, even though the term *significato* is more often understood as "a concept expressed by a sign," the pair *significato* and *significare* can be used for the expression of thoughts or sentiments, for the emotional effect caused by an expression, for the importance or value that something assumes for us, and so on.

On the other hand, the term *content*—in Hjelmslev's sense, as the correlate of an expression—is less compromised and may be used, as I shall use it, in a public sense and not a mental one. Once this has been made clear, when the requirements of argument of some current theory may encourage me to do so, I shall use the word *meaning,* but only as a synonym of *content*.

In certain cases CT and NC can practically coincide, when the CT wholly determines the interpretants expressed by the NC and the NC makes it possible to conceive an adequate CT. Nevertheless I wish to make clear yet again that *the CT is private, while the NC is public*. We are not talking about one and the same phenomenon (which some might call generically "the Aztecs' competence regarding horses"): on the one hand, we are talking about a phenomenon of perceptual semiosis (CT) and, on the other, about a phenomenon of communicative consensus (NC). The CT—which cannot be seen and cannot be touched—may be postulated only on the basis of the phenomena of recognition, identification, and felicitous reference; the NC represents the way in which we try intersubjectively to make clear which features go to make up a CT. The NC, which we recognize in the form of interpretants, *can be seen and touched*—and this is not just a metaphor, given that the interpretants of the term *horse* include a great many horses sculpted in bronze or stone.

If Montezuma had collected all the pictograms drawn by his messengers, filmed their gestures, tape-recorded their words, and then locked up all this testimony in a chest before having the messengers put to death and then committing suicide, what remained in that chest would be the content of the expression *maçatl* for the Aztecs. It would then be up to the archaeologist who found that chest to interpret those interpretants in his turn, and only through the interpretation of that content would the archaeologist be able, afterward, to conjecture what the Aztecs' CT of a horse had been.

A CT does not necessarily spring from a perceptual experience; it can be transmitted culturally (in the form of an NC) and lead to the success of a future perceptual experience. Such was the NC of *maçatl* that the messengers communicated to Montezuma by means of images, gestures, sounds, and words. On the basis of these interpretations Montezuma must have tried to get an "idea" of horses. This "idea" is the nucleus of the CT that he temporarily constructed on the basis of the NC received in the form of interpretations.[14]

The way in which NCs are expressed also helps to loosen the knot regarding the question as to whether we have mental images or not.[15] An NC is expressed sometimes in words, sometimes with gestures, sometimes through images or diagrams. Basically, the drawing of Marr's 3-D model, insofar as it is public, is an element of the NC that interprets a procedural modality of our CT. In our brain, what corresponds to that presumed image? Neuronal activation, let's say. Now, even if the pattern of that activation did not correspond to what we intuitively call an image, those cerebral phenomena would represent the cause or the equivalent of our ability both to conceive and to interpret our type of the horse. We postulate a CT as a disposition to produce an NC, and we treat an NC as proof that there is a CT around somewhere.

3.3.2.1 Instructions for identification

The NC of the term also supplies criteria or instructions for the identification of one of the tokens of the type (or rather, as they say, for the identification of the referent).[16] I use "identification" instead of "recognition" because I should like to reserve the latter term for cognitive phenomena strictly dependent on a previous perceptual experience, and the former term for the capacity to identify perceptually something about which we still have no experience. I identified an alligator, the first time I saw one on the banks of the Mississippi, on the basis of the instructions that had been supplied to me previously through words and images. That is, the NC of the word *alligator* had been communicated to me.

By supplying instructions with which to identify a token of the type, the NC orients one toward the formation of a tentative CT. If the messengers supplied Montezuma with good interpretations, his tentative CT would have been so rich and precise as to permit immediate identification, with few readjustments on the basis of direct perception. But sometimes the instructions supplied by the NC are insufficient. The messengers might have insisted to such a point on the analogy with deer that Montezuma was led to construct a tentative CT so imperfect, it rendered easy identification of horses impossible at the first encounter, so that he confused horses with the oxen in the train of the soldiers.[17]

3.3.2.2 Instructions for retrieval

There is another possibility: that the messengers did not successfully express the properties of the horse to Montezuma. They might have restricted themselves to telling him that some strange and terrible animals had appeared at a point on the coast, and that if he went to that place, he would see white men who wore iron trappings and moved by sitting with legs astride something; and this something was what the messengers were referring to. In this way they would have supplied Montezuma with instructions not for the identification but for the *retrieval* of the object.

The cases I am about to cite concern the CTs of individuals, of which I shall have more to say in 3.7.6, but in any event they serve to distinguish identification from retrieval. *First case:* Every evening I bump into a man in the bar; I recognize him every time, but I don't know his name, and if I were to correlate an NC to the generic name *man,* it would simply be the description "the man I see every evening in the bar." One day I see this man robbing the bank across the road. On my being questioned by the police, by means of verbal interpretations I help the specialized artist make a fairly accurate sketch of him. I have supplied instructions for the identification of this person, and the police can elaborate a CT of him (albeit a vague one—with the result that there is a risk of their erroneously identifying someone else). *Second case:* Every evening I recognize a man in the bar, even though I have never observed him closely, but one day I hear him saying over the telephone that his name is George Brown and that he lives at number 15 London Road. One day this man argues with the bartender, whom he kills by smashing a bottle over his head, then he flees. The police question me as a witness, but I am quite unable to give the artist instructions for a sketch (at most I can say that the man in question is tall, with ordinary features and an unpleasant look), but I *can* supply his name and address. On the basis of my private CT, I cannot supply instructions for identification; but on the basis of the NC that I associate with the name George Brown (a being of the male sex who lives at 15 London Road), I am able to provide the police with instructions for his retrieval.

3.3.3 Molar Content (MC)

When, having seen horses in the flesh and having talked with the Spaniards, Montezuma acquired other information about horses, he could have reached the point where he knew what a Spaniard knew about them (though not as much as a zoologist knows today). In this case he would have had what is called a *complex* knowledge of them. Note that I am talking not about an "encyclopedic" knowledge, in the sense of a difference between Dictionary and Encyclopedia (to which I shall return in 4.1), but about "broadened knowledge," which includes notions that are not indispensable for perceptual recognition (e.g., that horses are reared in such and such a way or that they are mammals). With regard to this broadened competence I shall talk of Molar Content (MC). The format of Montezuma's MC might be different from that of his first messengers or his priests, and it would be in continuous expansion. We cannot be sure how it evolved—we need only think of the fact that in our times the MC of *horse* includes the information that this animal flourishes in the American continent (something that certainly could not have been said in Montezuma's day). I would not identify the MC with knowledge exclusively expressible in propositional form, because it could include images of horses of various breeds or of different ages.

A zoologist has an MC of *horse,* and so does a jockey, even though the two areas of competence are not coextensive. It is on the level of MC that Putnam's division of linguistic labor occurs, something I would prefer to define as a division of cultural labor. On the level of MC there ought to be generalized consensus, albeit with some fraying and gray areas (see 3.5.2). And since it is this area of consensus that constitutes the nucleus of the present discourse, I would tend to avoid considering the MC, which can assume different forms depending on the subject and represents portions of sectorial competence. Let us say that the sum of the MCs coincides with the Encyclopedia as a regulative idea and a semiotic postulate, as is said in Eco 1984, 5.2.

3.3.4. NC, MC, and concepts

On reading the first version of these pages, someone asked me the difference among NC, MC, and concept. I would not know how to answer the question before I resolved two cases: (i) What is the difference between the cognitive type of the platypus constructed by its first discoverer and the concept of platypus that he obviously could not have had previously, not even in the case of an overpopulated Platonic universe? (ii) What is the difference between the first Aztecs' concept of the horse and a zoologist's concept of the same animal?

For the first question, it strikes me as evident that, right from the Kantian idea of a schema for empirical concepts, it was clear that, if a concept existed, it ought to have been mediated by the schema. But if we introduce the schema, then there is no need for concept—and let proof of that be the possibility of constructing schemata for concepts we do not have, like that of the platypus. Therefore the idea of concept becomes a perplexing residue.

For the second question, if by "concept" we mean a mental conception, as etymologists would have it, there are two answers: either the concept governs perceptual recognition, and in that case it is the same as the CT and is expressed not by the classic definition but by the NC; or it is a rigorous and scientific definition of the object, and in that case it is the same as a particular sectorial MC.

It seems outrageous to say so, but from the point of view from which I have adopted the word *concept,* it comes to mean only what one has in mind. Owing to my intention not to look into the black box, I cannot say what this might be. I wonder, rather, whether those who do look inside the black box ask themselves what it is. But that's another matter.

3.3.5 On referring

Throughout the story we have been examining, the Aztecs assign an NC to the expression *maçatl,* but when they speak among themselves about what they have seen, *they refer* to individual horses. I shall be talking about that very complex phenomenon, the act of referring, in 5. Here we need to detach not only the content from the reference but also the instructions for the identification of the *referent* from the concrete acts of *referring.* Someone could have received instructions for identifying an armadillo and yet never in his life referred to an armadillo (i.e., he never said *This is an armadillo* or *There is an armadillo in the kitchen*).

The CT provides instructions for identifying the referent, and this undoubtedly constitutes a form of competence. Referring to Something is, instead, a form of performance. It is certainly based on referential competence but, as we shall see in 5, not only on that. The referent of the word *horse* is a thing. Referring to horses is an act, not a thing.

After listening to his messengers' accounts, Montezuma possessed an embryonic competence, but if, as was related, he withdrew for some time into a stubborn silence, then he did not immediately carry out any act of reference to horses. Even before they provided him with instructions for identifying the referent, his messengers were referring to horses when they told him they intended to talk to him about Things they dared not describe. On emerging from his silence, Montezuma could have referred to these as yet unknown Things, for example by asking what and how they were, even before he possessed instructions for their identification. In this way he would have demonstrated that one can understand reference to entities, and one can refer to them, without possessing a CT or even an NC. Montezuma understood that the messengers were carrying out an act of reference, and nevertheless he was unable to understand what the referent of that act was.

3.4. SEMIOSIC PRIMITIVES

3.4.1 Semiosic primitives and interpretation

Let us think of a being placed in an elementary environment, before it comes into contact with others of its kind. However it decides to name them, this being will have to acquire some fundamental "notions" (no matter how it might later decide to organize them into systems of categories, or in any case into units of content). It will have to have a notion of high and low (essential for its corporeal equilibrium); of standing upright or lying down; of some physiological operations, such as swallowing or excreting; of walking, sleeping, seeing, hearing; of perceiving thermic, olfactory, or gustatory sensations; of feeling pain or relief; of clapping hands, thrusting a finger into some soft material, hitting, gathering, rubbing, scratching, and so on. As soon as it comes into contact with other beings, or with the surrounding environment in general, it will have to have notions regarding the presence of something that opposes its body: coitus, struggle, the possession or the loss of an object of desire, probably the cessation of life... However it comes to name these fundamental experiences, they are certainly original.

This means to say that the moment in which we "enter language," there is a disposition toward meaning of a prelinguistic character; in other words, there are "certain classes of meanings about which human beings are in innate agreement."[18] The attribution of animality to a certain object would be an example of this type. It may be that such an attribution will later emerge as erroneous, as would happen in the case of an archaic mentality that saw the clouds as animals, but it is certain that one of the first ways in which we react to what comes toward us in the environment is an attribution of animality or vitality to an object standing before us, and this has nothing to do with "categories" such as Animal: the animality I am talking about is certainly precategorial.

I shall say in 3.4.2 why I consider this use of the terms *category, categorial,* and *precategorial* to be improper. In any case, notions such as Animal, Mineral, and Artifact (which in many compositional semantics are considered as semantic primitives, probably innate, not open to further analysis, and occasionally constituted in hierarchic finite systems of hyponyms and hyperonyms) can make sense as elements of an MC. The possibility of their being primitive, impervious to analysis, and organized into hierarchies and the question of to what extent a finite inventory of them can be conceived have been discussed in Eco (1984, 2). They certainly depend not on perceptual experience but on a segmentation and organization of the *continuum* of the content that presupposes a coordinated system of assumptions. The semiosic primitives I am talking about are not like this, as they depend on the preclassificatory perception of something as either living and animated or devoid of life.

When we feel on the arm or the hand the presence of a foreign body, no matter how small, occasionally without even looking (and sometimes the interval between perceptual hypothesis and motor response is infinitesimal), either we use the other hand to squash something, or we prime the index finger with the thumb to flick something away. Usually we squash when we have assumed (even before having decided, because our safety depends on the speed of our reflexes) that the presence is a mosquito or some other bothersome insect, and we flick the body away when we assume it is vegetable or mineral waste. If it is decided that we must "kill," it is because a feature of animality in the foreign body has been noticed. It is a primary recognition, preconceptual (in any case prescientific), having to do with perception and not with categorial knowledge (if anything, it orients categorial knowledge, it offers itself as a basis for interpretation at higher cognitive levels).

3.4.2 On categories

Cognitive psychology often talks of our capacity for thought as being founded on the possibility of categorial organization. The idea is that the world of which we have experience is made up of such a number of objects and events, that if we were to identify and name them all individually, we would be overwhelmed by the complexity of the environment. And so the only way to avoid becoming a prisoner of the particular lies in our capacity to "categorize," that is, to make different things equivalent, grouping objects and events into classes (e.g., Bruner et al. 1956).

In itself the idea is incontrovertible. But, and this is not to say that the ancients had already thought of everything, if we substitute "categorization" with the term "conceptualization," it will be noticed that yet again we are talking about the problem of how language (and with it our cognitive apparatus) leads us to talk and think in *generalia*—in other words, that we unite individuals in sets.

Grouping manifold tokens under a single type is the way in which language (affected, as they used to say in the Middle Ages, by *penuria nominum*) works. But it is one thing to say that, faced with various individuals, we manage to think of them all as "cat" and another to say that we manage to think of all cats as animals (or felines). These are two different problems. Knowing that a cat is a feline seems to belong more to the competence registered as MC than to that registered as NC, while the quasi immediate perception of cat struck us as a precategorial phenomenon.

The fact is that in contemporary literature on this subject, the term "category" is used in a way very different from the one in which it was used by both Aristotle and Kant, even though we often see authors who, when they tackle the problem, refer back— without specific quotations but and in an almost rhetorical attempt to legitimize their assumptions—to the classical heritage.

Aristotle thought there were ten categories, the Substance and the nine predicates that could be predicated of them, i.e., that something was in a certain time, in a certain place, that it had certain qualities, that it feared something or did something else, et cetera. What a certain subject was (a man, a dog, a tree) was not a problem for Aristotle. One perceived a substance and understood what its essence was (in other words, Aristotle thought that as soon as we see the token of a man, we assign it to the type "man"). In the Aristotelian sense, applying the categories does not go much further than saying that a cat is being perceived, that it is white, that it is running through the Lyceum, etc.). From the standpoint of contemporary cognitive psychology, all this would belong to the precategorial, or it would barely bring into play those things that are called "basic categories," such as "cat," and bring into play also a rather vaguely defined activity that would consist in recognizing that a given object has active or passive properties.

For Kant, categories were something far more abstract than the Aristotelian categories (unity, plurality, reality, negation, substance and accident, causality, etc.), and we saw in 2.3 how difficult it was for him to say what they have to do with empirical concepts such as dog, chair, swallow, or sparrow.

But let us get back to Aristotle. That on seeing a cat running through the Lyceum, one perceived a cat running through the Lyceum was a natural and spontaneous fact for him. Naturally, then, there was the matter of *defining* what the substance "cat" was. As definition was arrived at through genus and difference, the Aristotelian tradition had to identify the *predicables*. The predicables are as close as you can get to the categories as understood by modern taxonomies: they are instruments for definition (in the Aristotelian tradition, the cat is a mortal irrational animal, and I grant that this is not a lot, while for modern taxonomies it is of the species *Felis catus,* genus *Felis,* sub-order *Fissipeda,* and so on, all the way to the class of Mammals).

Is this type of classification—and we could talk of categorization if we took the Aristotelian predicables as subcategories—essential for the recognition of something? Not a bit. Certainly not for Aristotle, who failed to define the camel satisfactorily (see Eco 1983, 4.2.1.1) but who nonetheless continued to identify and name it correctly; and not even for cognitive psychology, because no one has ever denied that someone is capable of perceiving and recognizing a platypus without necessarily knowing whether it is a Mammal, Bird, or Amphibian.

In a certain sense, with regard to this matter, the perplexity would be greater for Aristotle than it would be for Kant or the contemporary cognitivists. The cognitivists would get around the problem, if need be, by assuming that there is something of the precategorial in perception. Kant managed to transfer dogs and cats to the ranks of the empirical concepts, and their classification into genera and species into the territory of reflective judgment. But

Aristotle tells us that when faced with an individual substance, we understand what its essence is (man or cat), and he would have willingly admitted that it was possible for a slave to recognize a cat even if the slave could not express the definition, yet when he must say what the substance is, he can do it only in terms of definition, by appealing to genus and *differentia*. It is as if Aristotle were to admit that in some way we have CTs but we can interpret them only in terms of an MC (since the knowledge of classifications appertains to the MC).

Unless he wanted to say exactly what we are saying: that to perceive (by applying categories—his) is to move precisely in what is today called the precategorial, and that attributions of life, animality, and even rationality are precategorial. At least in the sense that Aquinas tried to explain it.[19] We do not at all perceive differences such as rationality but infer them from perceivable accidents; the result is that we infer that man is rational through exterior manifestations, for example, the fact that he talks or is a biped. And therefore it is the immediate perception of these accidents that comes to be part of the perceptual experience, and the rest is cultivated elaboration.

What contemporary cognitivism calls categories (which would have been the predicables for Aristotle) are, rather, what the natural sciences call *taxa,* which are embedded into one another from species to genus (or from orders to classes, or from classes to kingdoms). What cognitivism calls basic categories are certainly CTs, while what it calls superordinate categories (as Tool, with respect to the basic category of hammer) are *taxa.* *Taxa* belong to a more complex phase of cultural elaboration and are stored in the MC of some particularly gifted speakers (they depend on a coherent system of propositions, or on a given cultural paradigm).

By the way, I would point out that the distinction was already very clear in John Stuart Mill, when he was examining the various naturalistic classifications that in his day were still the subject of heated debate:

There is... a classification of things, which is inseparable from the fact of giving them general names. Every name which connotes an attribute, divides, by that very fact, all things whatever into two classes, those which have the attribute and those which have not... The Classification which requires to be discussed as a separate act of the mind, is altogether different. In the one, the arrangement of objects in groups, and distribution of them into compartments, is a mere incidental effect consequent upon the use of names given for another purpose, namely that of simply expressing some of their qualities. In the other, the arrangement and distribution are the main object, and the naming is secondary to, and purposely conforms itself to, instead of governing, that more important operation.

Since one cannot combat the inertia of language, I too shall adapt myself to calling these classificatory items categories, but let it be clear that they do not contribute immediately to telling us what a thing is. They show how it becomes hierarchically ordered in a system of basic, superordinate, and subordinate concepts.[20]

Another observation is that if categories (in the modern sense of the term) are *taxa,* they have nothing at all to do with those primitives elaborated or identified by "featural semantics"—and that by chance have the same name as many categories or *taxa,* the ones that are usually printed in small capitals, such as ANIMAL, HUMAN, LIVING, ADULT, et cetera. It is a matter for discussion as to whether these primitives are finite in number, whether they function by conjunction or by intersection, but they are not always organized into hierarchies like *taxa,* even though in some authors they are organized by relations of hypo- or hyperonymy (for this argument, see Violi 1997, 2.1 and 4.1). In fact, these semantic primitives are often assimilable to those I have called semiosic primitives (which some would define as precategorial).

If noticing that something is a body, it flies in the sky, it is ananimal, and has weight are semiosic primitives, then, if anything, *taxa* come into being as elaborations of such precategorial

experiences—at least in the sense of "precategorial" that I have resigned myself to respecting.

3.4.3 Semiosic primitives and verbalization

Wierzbicka (1996), who backs up her hypotheses with a vast recognition of different languages, persuasively maintains the existence
of certain *primes* common to all cultures. In her view, these are notions such as I, Someone, Something, This, Other, One, Two,
Many, Much, Think, Want, Feel, Say, Do, Happen, Good, Bad,
Small, Big, When, Before, After, Where, Under, No, Some, Live,
Far, Near, If, and Then (my summarized list is incomplete). The
interesting aspect of this proposal is that it aims at resolving all
other possible definitions in terms of these primitives.

Nevertheless, before going on to utilize some of Wierzbicka's
suggestions, I wish to make it clear that I assume these *primes* with
all due caution. To say that these notions are *original* does not necessarily mean admitting (i) that they are phylogenetically primitive
and therefore innate: they can be primitives only for a single individual, while other individuals start from other, different experiences (for example, seeing will not be a primitive experience for
someone born blind); (ii) that they are universal (even though I see
no obvious reason for denying this; but we have to make a distinction between the theoretical hypothesis of their universality and ascertaining empirically that precise terms for them exist in all
known languages); (iii) that by virtue of their being primitives they
are not interpretable.

Point (iii) represents a weakness in Wierzbicka's argument. This
fallacy springs from the fact that it has traditionally been assumed
that the semantic primitives mentioned in the previous paragraphs—those presumed features such as HUMAN or ADULT that
ought to constitute atoms of meaning that may not be split any further—are noninterpretable. But what Wierzbicka calls *primes* are
not like this—even though the author sometimes tends to treat
them as if they were. They are not meaning postulates; they are elements of a primordial experience. To say that a child has a pri-

mordial experience of milk (and so one presumes that as she grows, she will know exactly what milk is) does not mean at all that the child, upon request, cannot interpret the content of *milk* (see in 3.7.2 what a child does when asked to interpret the word *water*). It may be that those experiences expressed by the words *see* and *hear* are primordial experiences of this sort, but even a child is capable of interpreting them (with reference to different organs).

By not admitting this Wierzbicka reacts emphatically to the opinion held by Goodman (1951: 57), according to which "it is not because a term is indefinable that it is chosen as primitive; rather, it is because a term has been chosen as primitive for a system that it is indefinable ...In general, the terms adopted as primitives of a given system are readily definable in some other system. There is no absolute primitive." Wilkins has already shown us how it is possible, through a spatial and nonpropositional cognitive schema, to interpret and define both high and low, both *toward* and *under,* or *inside* (see Eco 1993, 2.8.3).[21]

Having made this reservation clear, Wierzbicka starts off with an acceptable criticism of the so-called definitions of dictionary and of encyclopedia. Take the example of the mouse (1996: 340 ff.). If the definition of the term *mouse* is also to allow us to be able to identify the referent, or in any event to have a mental representation of a mouse (just as Montezuma must have imagined what a horse was like), it is clear that a strictly dictionary-type definition such as "mammal, murid, rodent" (which goes back to the *taxa* of the naturalistic classifications) is insufficient. This insufficiency seems to extend even to the definition proposed by the *Encyclopedia Britannica*, which starts off with a zoological classification, specifies the areas in which the mouse flourishes, and expatiates on its reproductive processes, its social life, its relations with man and the domestic environment, and so on. Those who have never seen a mouse would never be able to identify one on the basis of this extremely vast and organized collection of data.

In opposition to these two definitions Wierzbicka offers her own *folk* definition, which contains primitive terms only. The definition takes up two pages and is made up of items of this type:

People call them Mice— People think that they are all of the same
kind—because they come from other creatures of the same kind—
People think they live in or near places where people live—Because
they want to eat things that people keep for people to eat— People
don't want them to live there...

A person could hold one easily in one hand—(most people
wouldn't want to hold them). They are grayish or brownish—
One cannot notice them easily—(some creatures of this type are
white)...

They have short legs—because of this when they move you can't
see their legs moving and it seems as if their whole body touches
the ground ...

Their head looks as if it were not a separate part of the body—
The whole body looks like one small thing with a long thin hairless
tail— The front part of the head is pointed— It has a few stiff hairs
sticking out sideways— There are two round ears sticking up one
on each side of the head— They have small sharp teeth that they
bite things with.

This folk definition recalls the Kantian idea that the schema for
dog must contain the instructions for imagining the form of the
dog. If we were to play one of those parlor games in which someone verbally describes a drawing and someone else must manage to
reproduce it (a game measuring at once the verbal capacities of the
former and the capacity for visualization of the latter), the game
might succeed, in that the second person could probably respond to

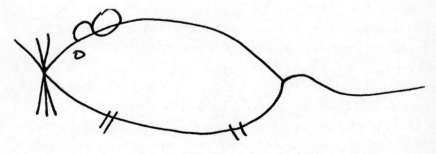

Figure 3.1

the description-stimulus proposed by Wierzbicka by drawing an image like that shown in figure 3.1.

But is the image only the interpretative output of the verbal definition, or is it a primary and constitutive element of that definition? In other words, is this morphological schema also a part of our NC of the mouse? A good encyclopedia should insert, into the long and satisfying scientific definition of the mouse, also a drawing or a photo of a mouse. Wierzbicka does not trouble to tell us whether the encyclopedia she consulted contains an illustration, nor whether it is a bad thing that it does not. This oversight is not fortuitous: the explanation comes on page 332, where it is maintained that language cannot reflect the neural representation of color, because the representation is private, while language "reflects conceptualization." It is for this reason that, while seeking to gain a firm hold on the notion of semiosic primitives that should precede the very processes of categorization, she ends up by recognizing the primitives only insofar as they are expressible in (general) verbal terms, with the result that the semiosic primitive of "something" is deliberately printed as SOMETHING—in other words, as if it were a semantic primitive closely bound to the use of verbal language.[22]

3.4.4 *Qualia* and interpretation

If there were noninterpretable *primes,* we should have to return to the problem of *qualia* (which I thought I had laid aside in the previous chapter) and return to Peirce. Let us pose the problem in its toughest and most provocative form: Do we have CTs for *qualia?* If the answer is no, then *qualia* are "bricks" for the construction of CTs, but in that case we can say neither why we predicate them (this thing is red or boiling) nor why we usually agree about such predications—albeit at the cost of some negotiation. Peirce had said as much: the first feeling that I have of something white is pure possibility, but when I proceed to the comparison of two qualities of white, I can begin a series of inferences and therefore of interpretations; the perceptual judgment desingularizes the quality (CP 7.633). This shift to Thirdness is already a shift to the universal.

It has been a matter of endless discussion as to whether my feeling of red is the same as my interlocutor's feeling, but, except in cases of color blindness, when I tell someone to fetch me the red pen, there is usually a case of felicitous reference, and I do not receive the black pen. Since felicitous reference has been assumed as a proof that the CTs exist (in the black box), then *qualia* too have CTs.

Yet again I limit myself to saying that they *must* be there, and I do not allow myself to say how they are constituted. But a good proof that there is a CT is that it can be interpreted. Can we interpret *qualia?* We can in the sense that I can not only define red in terms of the corresponding wavelength but also say that it is the color of cherries, of the jackets of the Canadian Mounties, and of many national flags. In addition, through various comparisons I can interpret various qualities of red. Finally, experiments on categorial perception (see Petitot 1983) tell us that there are "catastrophe points" on this side of which the subjects perceive red and on the other side of which they perceive another color—and even though the catastrophe point varies depending on the exposure to the stimulus, it varies in a constant fashion for all the subjects.

Sensations of sweet or bitter are private events, and yet wine experts use persuasive metaphors to discern the flavor and consistency of wines, and if they were unable to recognize *qualia* on the basis of a CT, they would be unable to tell a Pinot from a Tokay, nor would they be able to identify the vintage.[23]

One of the usual proofs against the interpretability of colors is that they cannot be interpreted for the sightless. All we need to do is agree on what is meant by interpretation. In Peircean terms, an interpretant is that which lets me know *something more* about the object expressed by the name, but not necessarily that which lets me know *everything* that other interpretants tell me. It is obvious that someone who is blind from birth cannot have any perception of red, a semiosic primitive that may be acquired only through perceptual experience. Nonetheless let us suppose (and the experiment is not all that far from scientific fact, see Dennett 1991, 11.4) that the blind person has been equipped with a video camera inserted in special eyeglasses, capable of identifying colors and communicating them in the form of impulses to some part of the body: faced with a traffic light, the blind person, trained to recognize different impulses, would know whether it was signaling red or green. We would have equipped him with a *prosthesis* capable of supplying him with a datum that would allow him to make up for the missing sensation. I am not deciding whether or not he would "see" something similar to red in his brain, but that his brain would register an *interpretation* of red. In order to characterize an interpretation as such, it is unnecessary for it to appear as perfect; on the contrary, every interpretation is always partial. To say to the blind person that red is the color of incandescent substances is a vague interpretation, but it is not less satisfactory than telling someone that a heart attack is that thing you perhaps have when you feel sharp pains in your chest and left arm. On becoming aware of a pain in the chest, we have as many reasons to say *Maybe this is a heart attack* as a congenitally blind person has to say *Maybe this substance is red* on becoming aware of an intense feeling of heat. The congenitally blind person simply registers red as a "hidden quality," just as we register something that manifests itself in the form of a symptom as a hidden quality.[24]

3.4.5 The CTs and the image as "schema"

If we found something interesting in the Kantian notion of schema, it was not when the schema appeared to us as something extremely abstract such as "number," "degree," or "permanence of the manifold," but precisely when (and it was at this point that the first *Critique* was unable to provide a satisfactory answer) it had to permit the formation of an empirical concept such as that of dog (and mouse). We saw that it was necessary in some way to introduce *the instructions for producing a figure* into the perceptual process. The image of the mouse in figure 3.1 must not be seen as the image of *one* particular mouse (not even if it were a photograph, which could only be of one particular mouse). And in fact when we see images of this kind in an encyclopedia, we do not think they must supply us with visual instructions for the identification of an animal "exactly" the same as the one shown. In point of fact we assume them as images of the mouse in general.

How can we start off from a "picture" (ever fated to be the representation of an individual, even were it the image of a triangle, which can be only the image of a certain triangle and none other) and use it as a general schema with which to identify or recognize tokens of a type? Precisely by understanding it as a (2-D or 3-D) schematic suggestion for the construction of similar images, despite notable differences in the details. Precisely by understanding it as the Kantian schema—and so there is never a (schematic) image of the dog, but a system of instructions for the construction of the image of a dog. The mouse in figure 3.1 is not the image of a certain mouse, nor does it represent the Mouse as Such. It is like a sketch that tells us which salient features we ought to recognize in any thing we can define as a mouse, just as the schematic image of a Doric column (in a manual of architectonic orders) ought to induce us to recognize as Doric those columns that are neither Ionic nor Corinthian, regardless of their details and dimensions.

The very fact that we are led, in terms of ordinary language, to define as "schematic" the image in figure 3.1 tells us that the image can be supplied as an interpretant and mentally retained as a "model" for mice of different colors, sizes, and (were we capable of discriminating them) individual physiognomic features. And note well that this would happen even if the Encyclopedia contained a photograph instead of the schematic drawing: we would start off from it by operating in a way comparable to the process known as solarization, which is simply a form of deprivation or diminution of the individual features in order to arrive at a rule for the construction of the image of any mouse. And the same thing would happen if, as a result of psychological matters that have to do with the mysteries of the black box, we were to react to the word *mouse* by calling up the image of *that* mouse, which we have seen for the first time. The mental representation of that individual would serve us as a cast or model (a schema, in fact), and we would easily be able to transform the experience of an individual mouse into a general rule for the recognition or construction of mice.

However, we can recognize or identify not only natural or artificial objects but also tokens of geometrical figures such as the triangle, and above all of actions and situations (from walking to going out to dinner). If for the type triangle one can think of proto-types or rules for the construction and identification of the figure (not unlike what can happen with regard to the morphological fea-tures of a mouse or a glass), and if even notions such as room or restaurant can presuppose a basic visual structure, on the model of Minsky's frames, then the recognition and identification of actions such as going out to the restaurant, arguing, and scolding, or of sit-uations such as a pitched battle, a meeting, or a sung Mass, require genuine "scripts" (like those proposed in Artificial Intelligence, or representations through Cases and Actants, or more complex nar-rative sequences, such as Greimas's schema for anger).[25]

And that's not all. I maintain that CTs also include pairs of op-positions: not only is it difficult to interpret *husband* in the absence of the notion of *wife* (and we shall be talking about cognitive types by functional genera later) but also in some way a part of our idea of dog derives from the fact that this animal barks or snarls and does not meow or purr (features sufficient for us to decide at night, in the dark, which animal is scratching at the door).

In such cases we undoubtedly possess CTs that do not necessar-ily or particularly take morphological features into consideration. Likewise we can have CTs that take account of temporal se-quences, or logical relations that, while they may be expressed in diagrammatic form (which on the level of expression assumes the form of a visual configuration), still do not regard visual experi-ences.

If there is a "strong" element in the Peircean theory of the inter-pretant, it is that the series of interpretations of a sign can also assume "iconic" forms. But "iconic" does not necessarily mean "vi-sual." Sometimes the CT includes perceptual primitives or even *qualia,* which are not easy to interpret but which must be ac-counted for: part of the CT of the skunk—even for those who have never seen one—should include the powerful smell it can give off, and its NC should include the instruction that the skunk is identifiable mainly through its smell (if there were a Kantian schema for skunk, as Kant presupposed one for dog, it would have the form of a flowchart whose higher nodes contain instructions to proceed immediately to an olfactory check).

Are we sure that our CT of the mosquito is fundamentally made up of morphological features and not (eminently) of the irritating effects it can have on our epidermis? We know very little about the form of the mosquito (unless we have observed one under a microscope or seen one in an encyclopedia), but we perceive it first and foremost through our hearing as a flying creature that produces a characteristic whine as it comes closer, and so we can even recognize one in the dark—indeed it is by referring to these features that we would provide someone with instructions for the identification of mosquitoes.

I maintain that the CT (and the NC) of the mouse also includes "tymic" (see Greimas-Courtés 1979: 396) elements. We have already seen how it is fundamental to perceive the mouse (usually) as a repugnant little creature. Apart from its morphological characteristics, the CT of the mouse also includes a *frame,* a sequence of actions: with the exception of those who have never seen mice outside a cage, the idea of the mouse (and the capacity to recognize a mouse) is based on the fact that it usually appears to us as an indistinct form that moves from one side of a room to the other at high speed, emerging from one hiding place only to slip into another.

This lends particular conviction to the idea proposed by Bruner (1986, 1990) that we use narrative schemata to organize our experience. I think that our CT (and NC) of the tree also includes the (narrative) sequence that it grows from a seed, goes through various phases of development, modifies itself with the changing of the seasons, et cetera. A child soon learns that chairs are not planted but constructed, and that a flower is not constructed but planted. Our cognitive type of the tiger includes not only that it is a big yellow cat with a striped coat but also that if we were to meet one in the jungle, it would behave in a particular fashion toward us (see in this regard also Eco 1990, 4.3.3).

With regard to expressions such as *yesterday* and *tomorrow,* can we really say we have only NCs that may be expressed propositionally and not also a sort of diagram with vectorial pointers, the result being that (even if the disposition varies according to the culture) in one case we configure a sort of mental image of "pointing backward" and in the other of "pointing forward"?

I shall freely adapt a fine mental experiment found in Bickerton (1981). Let us suppose that I have been interacting for a year with a very, very primitive tribe, whose language I understand only very poorly (names of objects and elementary actions, verbs in the infinitive, proper nouns without pronouns, etc.). I accompany Og and Ug on a hunt: they have just wounded a bear, which, bleeding, has taken shelter in its cave. Ug wants to follow the animal into its lair to finish it off. But I remember that a few months before, Ig had injured a bear before following it boldly into its lair, where the animal demonstrated that it was still strong enough to devour him. I should like to remind Ug of that precedent, but to do so I have to be able to say that I recall a past event, and I do not know how to express either verb tenses or doxastic operators such as *I remember that*. And so I restrict myself to saying *Umberto see bear.* Ug and Og obviously believe that I have spotted another bear, and they are frightened. I try to reassure them: *Bear not here.* But the pair only draw the conclusion that I make jokes in the worst possible taste at the worst possible time. I persist: *Bear kill Ig.* But the others reply: *No, Ig dead!* In short, I should have to desist, and Ug would be lost. So I fall back on nonlinguistic interpretants. On saying *Ig* and *bear,* I use a finger to strike my head, or my heart, or my belly (according to where I presume they locate the memory). Then I draw two figures on the ground, and I designate them *Ig* and *bear.* Behind Ig's back I draw images of lunar phases, hoping that they understand the meaning of "many moons ago," and in the end I once more draw the bear that killed Ig. If I try this, it is because I presume that my interlocutors have notions of recalling, and above all a few CTs (that may be interpreted not propositionally but diagrammatically) for activities of "protensity" toward temporal points different from the present. That is to say, I start from the principle that, if I am capable of understanding a sentence in which I am told that something happened yesterday or will happen tomorrow, I should have a CT for these temporal entities. In my experiment I would try to *interpret* visually (vectorially) my CT, and my interpretation might prove incomprehensible to the natives. But the difficulty of the operation does not exclude its being postulated as possible in some way.

We certainly possess cognitive types of sound sequences, if we can usually distinguish the timbre and the rhythm of the telephone bell from those of the doorbell, military calls such as taps and reveille, and often the melodies of two songs we know well.

If we admit that semiosic primitives exist, they are certainly elementary experiences such as walking, jumping, or running. When we skip, we are aware (or could be aware, if we pay attention to what we are doing) whether we use the right foot twice and the left foot twice or always the same foot. Yet it so happens that these last two operations have two distinct terms in English but not in Italian. This table by Nida (1975: 75), figure 3.2, distinguishes between the content of some English terms for motor activities.

	run	walk	hop	skip	jump	dance	crawl
One or another limb always in contact vs. no limb at times in contact	-	+	-	-	-	+/-	+
Order of contact	1,2,1,2	1,2,1,2	1,1,1,1	1,1,2,2	not relevant	variable but rhythmic	1,3,2,4
Number of limbs	2	2	1	2	2	2	4

Figure 3.2

Anyone who wants to translate a text describing these operations from English to Italian must interpret the terms according to this table, which—even though it uses linguistic terms—provides instructions of a motor type (one might very well think of its translation into film footage, or into a series of diagrams that use signs improperly called "iconic").[26]

3.4.6 "Affordances"

The CT ought to include those conditions for perception that Gibson calls "affordances" (and Prieto would have called *pertinency*):[27] the various tokens of the type "chair" are recognized because we are dealing with objects that make it possible for one to sit down, while tokens of the type "bottle" are recognized because they are objects that allow us to hold and pour liquid substances. It is instinctive for us to recognize a tree trunk as a possible seat and not a column (unless someone is a stylite), due to the length of our legs and the fact that we find it comfortable to sit with our feet resting on the ground. On the other hand, in order to categorize a knife, fork, and spoon among Cutlery, or a chair and a cupboard among Furniture, we must leave aside this morphological pertinency and fall back on more generic functions, such as the manipulation of food and the preparation of a habitable environment.

Our capacity to recognize affordances is registered, so to speak, in linguistic usage itself. Violi (1991: 73) wonders why, when faced with a table with a vase standing on it, we are led to interpret verbally what we see as *The vase is on the table* and not *The table is under the vase*. She suggests that "the selection of linguistic expressions seems regulated by complex configurations of the intentional relations between the subject that moves in space and the objects that surround it." But this is equivalent to saying that our CT of the common vase also includes the sequence of actions that it permits, and so a vase is something easily movable that usually stands *on* something. On the other hand, our CT of the table includes not only its morphological features but also the notion (I would say,

nuclear) that it is used for putting something *on* (and never for being inserted *under* something).[28]

But Arnheim (1969: 139) suggests that language can block our
recognition of pertinency. Quoting a remark made by Braque, he
admits that a coffee spoon acquires perceptual saliency that differs
according to whether it is set alongside a coffee cup or inserted between shoe and heel like a shoe horn. But often it is the name with
which we indicate the object that highlights one pertinency at the
expense of others.

In conclusion, we still have imprecise ideas about the extremely
various ways in which our CTs are organized—and how they express themselves in NC. I would tend to follow Johnson-Laird's
(1983: 7) proposal, whereby from time to time different types of
representation gradually offer themselves as options for the codification of different types of information, and in general we move
from real images to mental "models" (like Marr's 3-D representation) and real propositions.[29] Rather than talk of "double coding,"
as is usual in these cases, I think we ought to talk of *multiple coding,*
of our capacity to maneuver the same CT on different occasions by
accentuating either the iconic component, or the propositional one,
or the narrative one regarding our capacity to activate—within the
ambit of a complex situation—more complex nuclear contents and
information.[30]

All this induces us to review, I should like to say with
indulgence, those fairly rigidified semantic representations (compositional analysis models, case grammar, contextual and circumstantial selections; see *A Theory of Semiotics* 2.10–2.12) that seem to
be challenged by a reconsideration of the complex way (certainly
not linear, but like a *network*) in which our cognitive types are organized and of how we interpret them through nuclear content.
These skeletal models are naturally stenographic forms that consider our NCs from a certain standpoint, according to what we
wish to emphasize within the framework of a set theoretical discourse, or according to how we wish to indicate the ways followed
in order to have a certain contextual disambiguation of the terms.
With such models we interpret the quantity of NC we need as the

need arises. They are metalinguistic (or metasemiotic) interpretations of interpretations rooted in perceptual experience.

3.5 EMPIRICAL CASES AND CULTURAL CASES

Until now I have dealt with CTs that concern "natural kinds" such as mice, cats, and trees. But we have said that there are certainly CTs for actions such as walking, climbing, and skipping. The expression "natural kinds" is insufficient: CTs for artificial kinds, such as chair, boat, or house, obviously exist. Let us say, then, that I have considered CTs for all the objects or events we can know through perceptual experience. I cannot manage to identify a suitable term for indicating various objects of perceptual experience, and I choose the expression "empirical cases" (on the model of the Kantian empirical concepts): an empirical case would be the fact that I perceive or recognize a cat, a chair, someone sleeping or walking, and even that a certain place is a church and not a railway station.

It is a different matter with "cultural cases," among which I would put a disparate series of experiences with regard to which we can certainly discuss whether it happens that what I name in a particular way is named correctly and whether I recognize something that others are also supposed to recognize. Nevertheless the definition of these "cases," just as the instructions for their recognition, depend on a system of cultural assumptions. Among the cultural cases, I would put the functional genera (such as cousin, president, archbishop); a series of abstract concepts (such as the square root), which can also objectively "exist" on some Platonic Third World but which are definitely not objects of immediate experience); events, actions, relationships (such as contract, swindling, emphyteusis, or friendship). What is common to all these cases is that, if they are to be recognized as cultural, they require a reference to a framework of cultural rules.

This distinction could correspond to the one Quine made between those *occasion sentences* that are at the same time *observation sentences* and those that are not. One might agree with him. Except that, as we shall see, *This is a bachelor* is not completely nonobservational.

In the case of the bachelor, Lakoff (1987) would talk of Idealized Cognitive Models (ICM): it is hard to say when the term should be applied, but ideally it has a sense. Lakoff is thinking of the last phase of the debate on bachelors, which boasts a long history featuring an admixture of highly sensible observations and mere witticisms.[31] It has been said that it is questionable whether the definition "unmarried adult male" can really circumscribe bachelors, because "unmarried adult males" includes Catholic priests, homosexuals, eunuchs, and even Tarzan (at least in the novel where he does not meet Jane), with the result that we cannot define them as bachelors unless our intentions are humorous or metaphorical. The reply has been made, with a good deal of common sense, that bachelors are definable not only as unmarried adult males but also as adult males who have chosen not to marry (for a period marked by indefinite temporal limits) *even though they are physically or socially able to do so;* which therefore does not apply to the eunuch (unmatched as a result of a life sentence), to Tarzan (quite unable to find a partner, within the time limits), to the priest (celibate by obligation), and to the homosexual (unmarried out of a natural impulse toward other forms of union). In a situation where homosexuals can legally marry persons of the same sex, it would be possible to distinguish homosexual bachelors, who do not live in couples, from married homosexuals. It is evident that, even once these specifications have been made, to be able to talk about bachelors we need other negotiations bound up with the circumstances. For example, a homosexual *could* marry a person of the opposite sex for social convenience (e.g., if he or she were heir to a throne) without ceasing to be a homosexual for all that, while a priest could not marry a person of the opposite sex without rejoining the ranks of the laity and ceasing to be a priest; and so—if we cared to—we could say that a homosexual bachelor is more of a bachelor than a priest. But since a priest who has not been defrocked but has been suspended *a divinis* may get married at a registry office in Reno, is a priest who has been suspended *a divinis* and does not get married *more* of a bachelor than a homosexual who does not cohabit with his or her partner of the opposite sex? As we can see, the negotiations can continue indefinitely, and that is why today, customs having changed, the word *bachelor* is almost never used anymore (also, it has particular connotations of the free and easy life and evokes the complementary notion, equally in desuetude, of the unmarried lady or, even, the "spinster"). And so bachelors are now a part of the hazy archipelago of "singles," which includes unmarried adults of both sexes, homosexuals or heterosexuals, divorcees, widowers, spouses on the rocks, and spouses still madly in love with their partner but obliged to work in New York while their partner has found a job in California. Lakoff's notion of ICM is still valid in the sense that, while an idealized definition of *bachelor* does not always allow us to say whether someone is a bachelor, it certainly does allow us to say that he is not a bachelor if he is the happily married (and cohabiting) father of five children.[32]

Nevertheless the fact that notions of this kind require negotiation on the basis of conventions and behavior bound up with cultures does not allow us to exclude that the occasion sentences they permit have no observational basis.

Consider the difference between killing and murdering. Someone's killing another is directly perceivable: in some way we have a CT of killing, in the form of a fairly elementary scenario; we recognize we are faced with a killing when someone strikes another living being and thereby causes its death. I think the experience of killing is common to different cultures. It's another case with murder: a killing can be defined as homicide in self-defense or culpable or without malice aforethought, as ritual sacrifice, as an act of war recognized by international convention, or finally as murder, depending entirely upon the laws and customs of a given culture.

What is puzzling about this difference between empirical cases and cultural cases is that the first are without a doubt based on the testimony of the senses, but it cannot be said that experiential data are devoid of value in the second. Just for a start, an act cannot be recognized as murder unless there is experience (direct or indirect) of the fact that it was a killing.

Granted therefore that there is a difference between empirical and cultural cases and seeing that there are CTs for empirical cases, do we also have CTs for cultural cases?

One could avoid this perplexing question by saying that CTs concern the objects of perceptual experience and that's all. For other concepts, ones expressed by linguistic terms, there are no CTs, only NCs, which would be the same as saying that some things are known to us on the basis of perceptual experience while others we know only through definitions, duly contracted within the ambit of a culture. Which brings us back to Russell's distinction between object-words and dictionary words (see Russell 1940), except for our broadening of the concept of object-word to include natural genera and *qualia* as well as experiences of other kinds.

But, seeing that the CT has been defined as "something in the head," which allows us to recognize something and name it as such, even though it has not yet been publicly interpreted in terms of NC, can we perhaps say that when we pronounce the word *cousin* or *president,* we have nothing in our heads, and certainly not anything remotely similar to the Kantian schema? Note that the question remains even if it is admitted that we do not think in images but only by processing abstract symbols. In this second case, the question ought simply to be reformulated as follows: Is it possible when we state that something is a cat, that we process something "in the head," while when we state that X is Y's cousin, we process nothing?

When I understand the meaning of *cousin* and *president,* I call up in some way a kinship or an organizational schema, a Peircean graph. What happens when I understand that, in correspondence with the Italian term *nipote,* there are two different positions in the kinship schema, expressed in English by *nephew* and *grandson?* It is true that I can express the difference verbally too (which brings us to the NC), and so there is a *nipote* who is the child of an uncle and a *nipote* who is the child of a child. But the question—which I do not feel like answering, owing to my intention not to stick my nose into the black box—is whether this verbally expressed NC is all I know about the difference, or whether it constitutes the verbal interpretation of a difference grasped and understood via a diagram.

A supporter of the eminently visual nature of thought, such as Arnheim, seems to surrender before an example made by Bühler: asked to respond to the question "Should it be lawful or not to marry the sister of one's own widow?" the subjects asserted they had come to understand that the statement was senseless without the help of images (1969, 6). Of course, and especially in the case of a person with a well-trained mind, the answer to the question can be arrived at propositionally. But on repeating the experiment, I also found someone who came to recognize the contradictory nature of the question by imagining a widow weeping, with her sister beside her, over the grave of her own husband (and intuitive evidence suggests that a husband in the grave is unlikely to get married).

The same holds good for the Italian word *presidente,* and even more so when I have to decide whether the apparent synonymy (in English) is a good translation. As a matter of fact, not only is an American president unlike (in constitutional terms) an Italian president (their relations of power are expressed by two different organization charts), but also in the world of business what Italians call the *Presidente* of a company is the equivalent of the Chairman of the Board in UK English, while the role of President of an American company is very like that of the *Direttore Generale* (Managing Director) in an Italian one. In this case too the difference becomes evident on considering the position of the President in a company organization chart. Naturally the organization chart can be interpreted verbally, by saying that the president is the man or woman who gives orders to X or Y but not to K (who gives orders to him or her), but this would be the same as saying that expressions such as *above* or *below* may be interpreted only verbally (in terms of an NC), while we know very well that we translate them mentally in terms of CTs. And the fact that someone is the *boss* of a group of gangsters that we see in action can be inferred through perceptual experience. Does this mean, therefore, that there is a CT for *boss* while there is none for *president?*

Many people would be incapable of interpreting in words or with other signs the NC of the word *murder,* and yet on seeing someone cracking an old lady's skull and then snatching her handbag before fleeing, they would realize they were witnessing a murder. Is there not a CT (a frame, or narrative sequence) for murder, therefore?

It would be puzzling to say that in order to recognize a triangle or a hypotenuse, or the fact that there are two onlookers rather than three, things are based on perceptual experience (and therefore there is a CT for these empirical cases), while it is not on the basis of a CT that we recognize 5,677 to be an odd number. Identifying an odd number, even a very large one, depends on a rule, and this rule is certainly an instructional schema. If there is a system of instructions for recognizing a dog, why shouldn't there be one for recognizing that 5,677 is an odd number?

But if there is a system of instructions for recognizing 5,677 as an odd number, why shouldn't there be a system of instructions for recognizing whether a certain agreement is a contract? Is there a CT for contracts?

It is agreed that the instructions for recognizing an odd number are of a different kind to those we have introjected in order to recognize a dog. But in the discourse on schematism in 2.5 we acknowledged that to characterize the schema as a system of instructions it is not indispensable for the instructions to be morphological in nature. We have already forsaken the idea of understanding CTs exclusively as visual images, and we have decided that they can also correspond to scripts or flowcharts for the recognition of a sequence of actions.

The quality of being a bachelor does not seem recognizable on the basis of experience. But does that of soccer referee? To be a referee is certainly not to belong to a natural kind: a camel is always a camel, but a referee is a referee only in certain moments or periods of his life. The functions of the referee are indeed expressed by verbal interpretations. But let us suppose we have been suddenly transported to the stands of a football stadium while a football match is in progress, even though no one, players included, is wearing a shirt that permits perceptual recognition. After a little we would be able to say, by inferring from each person's behavior, which of the twenty-three people is the referee, just as we are able to tell someone who is jumping from someone who is running.

Although a vast competence is required to distinguish a referee from a goalkeeper (no vaster, however, than that required to tell a platypus from an echidna), we introject instructions for recognizing a referee in action. Some could be morphological (the referee wears an outfit of a certain type—and for the same reasons we can recognize who the bishop is in a religious ceremony), but they are not strictly necessary. The bishop in an ordination ceremony and the referee (even if in plain clothes) in a football match are recognizable by what *they do,* not by their appearance. And this recognition is also based on perceptual experiences.

Nevertheless perceptual experience must be oriented by a set of cultural instructions: those who do not know what a soccer match is see only a gentleman who, instead of kicking a ball like the other twenty-two gentlemen, runs about among them performing incomprehensible actions. But the person who saw a platypus for the first time saw something incomprehensible too: just as someone who knows nothing about soccer sees men on a field and is not quite sure what they are doing, or at least why they are doing it and in accordance with what rules, this person saw an animal equipped with some fairly original properties without understanding what it was or whether it breathed under the water or out of it. And just as little by little he began to recognize other tokens of the platypus, even without being able to classify it in a reasonable manner, we can perhaps say that the soccer ignoramus, after having been exposed to the experience of several games, manages to infer that it is a matter of an activity probably having to do with play, in which the players try to propel a ball into a net, while the twenty-third gentleman intervenes occasionally to interrupt or regulate their activity. And so, if we admit right from the start that the discoverer of the platypus had elaborated a CT of the still provisionally named animal, why can't the soccer ignoramus produce a CT (God only knows what kind, but probably a functional one) to recognize tokens of the referee?

It seems therefore that the referee is perceptually more recognizable than a cousin or a bachelor, and this is empirically true. But even in the case of natural kinds, we recognize some on a morphological basis (cat and platypus), others on the basis of definitions and a list of their possible behavior patterns, and we need only think of certain chemical elements or certain minerals of which we have never had perceptual experience. Yet no one is saying that we have a CT for cat but not for uranium: as Marconi (1997) suggests, a simple competence regarding the definition of uranium would allow us to recognize perceptually a sample of uranium if we had to choose between it, a butterfly, and an apple. It is not enough to say that we recognize as uranium something that has the evident property of not being a butterfly or an apple: as a matter of fact the simple information that uranium appears in mineral form disposes us to recognize one thing rather than another.

I do not think that the difference between the competence we have of a cat is different from the one we have of a bachelor, on the basis of the difference that according to Greimas-Courtés (1979: 332) lies between *figurative semes* (exteroceptive, which refer to the sensible qualities of the world) and *abstract semes* (interoceptive, dimensions of content that serve to categorize the world). The abstract semes are of the type "object vs. process," not "bachelor vs. married." Where do the bachelors stand according to Greimas? His abstract semes are extremely general categories, and between them and the figurative semes we would still need that mediation that Kant entrusted to the schemata, intermediaries between the abstraction of the categorial apparatus and the concreteness of the manifold of the intuition.

Nor do I think that Marconi's (1997) distinction between *referential competence* and *inferential competence* stands up, or not in this case at least. Ideally speaking, someone who knows what a pangolin is has referential competence regarding it (he possesses the instructions with which to identify a token of it), while someone who knows what a bachelor is has only inferential competence (he knows that bachelors are unmarried adult males). But let us suppose we provide a computer with the necessary instructions for an understanding of English: its competence regarding the world *pangolin* would be no different from its competence regarding the word *bachelor,* and in both cases it would be prepared to make inferences of the type "If pangolin, then animal" and "If bachelor, then unmarried." I could have only inferential and not referential competence of the pangolin, to the point that if one were to appear at my desk while I was writing, I would not know what it was. But it might be objected that, in ideal conditions, I could obtain all the instructions necessary for recognizing a pangolin. Would I have to exclude that, in ideal conditions, I cannot be supplied with all the instructions for recognizing a bachelor? Let us imagine I am a detective, and that I am following day by day, hour by hour, the behavior of an individual. I note that in the evenings he goes back to the apartment where he lives alone, and that he has only transitory contact with members of the opposite sex, changing his partner every day. He could certainly be a false bachelor, a husband who lives separated from his wife, or a compulsive adulterer. But in the same way, could I not fail to recognize a hyperrealistic plastic model of a pangolin or a pangolin-robot, which behaves in every way like a pangolin, rolling itself up into a ball when threatened, or whose scales and sticky tongue are accessible to the sight and touch?

Counterobjection: a pangolin is such by divine (or natural) decree, while a bachelor is such by social decree or linguistic convention. Agreed, it would be sufficient to consider a society that does not recognize the institution of marriage, so that those whom we recognize as bachelors would no longer be so. But what is in question here is not that there is a difference between natural kinds, functional kinds, and goodness knows how many other types of objects, or that there is a difference between empirical and cultural cases (between cat and emphyteusis). The question is whether we can talk about CTs as systems of instructions that allow us to recognize tokens for cultural kinds too.

3.5.1 The story of the Archangel Gabriel

The following story is inspired by the canonical Gospels, but it strays from them in some aspects. Let us say that it is inspired by an apocryphal gospel that, as it is apocryphal, I might have written myself.

The Lord decides to get the business of the Incarnation under way. He has prepared Mary for immaculate conception since her birth, and she is the only human being suited to this purpose. In addition, let us suppose that He has already seen to or is about to see to the miracle of virginal conception. But He must inform Mary of the event, and Joseph of the task that awaits him. He therefore calls for the Archangel Gabriel and gives him his orders, which we might sum up as follows: "You must descend to the Earth, to Nazareth, find a young girl called Mary, the daughter of Anna and Joachim, and tell her this and that. Then you must identify a virtuous and chaste man, called Joseph, of the line of David, and you will tell him what he must do."

All very simple, if an angel were a human being. But angels do not speak, because they understand one another in an ineffable fashion, and what they know they see in the beatific vision. Yet in this vision they do not learn all that God knows, otherwise they would be God; they learn only what God allows them to know, according to their rank in the Heavenly Host. Therefore the Lord must make Gabriel able to carry out his mission by transmitting him certain competences: first of all, the entirely human capacity to perceive and recognize objects, then a knowledge of Hebrew, as well as other cultural notions, without which, as we shall see, the mission could not come to a happy conclusion.

Gabriel descends to Nazareth. Identifying Mary is not hard. He asks around for Joachim's house, enters a fine and gracious colonnade, sees what is beyond doubt a young woman, calls her by name to be sure he is not making a mistake (she reacts by gazing at him in trepidation), and as far as the Annunciation is concerned, that's that.

The serious problems begin now. How to identify Joseph? It's a matter of identifying a member of the male sex, and Gabriel is perfectly able to discern, from dress and facial features, a male from a female. But the rest? After his successful strategy with Mary, he begins calling for Joseph loudly all around the village, but no good comes of it, because many men come running at his call, and he realizes that names may well be rigid designators in certain circumstances (he has read a little modal logic in the Divine Mind), but they are far less so in social life, where Josephs are more abundant than strictly necessary.

Naturally Gabriel knows that Joseph must be a virtuous man, and it is possible that he has received some typological instructions about how to recognize the virtuous: by the serenity of their features, by their generous behavior toward the poor and infirm, and by the pious gestures they make in the Temple. But there is more than one righteous adult male in Nazareth.

From among these virtuous men Gabriel must choose a bachelor, and, having received instructions about the Jewish language and the society of the period, he knows that his candidate must be an adult male and unmarried, even though the man could marry if he wished. And so Gabriel does not think of going to look for a homosexual, a eunuch, or a priest of some religion that requires ecclesiastical celibacy.

All he needs do is pay a visit to the Nazareth registry office. But, alas, as we all know, Caesar Augustus was to announce the famous census only nine months afterward, and at the time there were no public records, or if there were, they were in unspeakable disorder. To establish whether the various Josephs he has spotted are bachelors or not, Gabriel can infer their condition only from their behavior. The Joseph who lives alone in the back of his carpenter's shop could be a bachelor (but he could also be a widower).

In the end, Gabriel remembers that Joseph is of the line of David; he supposes that in the Temple there will be old registers; he subpoenas them, and then, by comparing them with oral testimony, he manages to identify the Joseph he is looking for. End of

Gabriel's mission. Gabriel reascends to heaven to receive the warm congratulations of his fellow angels for a mission well and truly accomplished. With them Gabriel would be able to interpret and therefore to describe step by step the procedures he followed to ascertain that Joseph was a bachelor; then he would supply his fellow angels with the NC of the expression bachelor, which certainly includes the cultural rule that says "an adult male who is unmarried even though he could be otherwise," but also includes a mixture of images, scripts that concern typical behavior, and procedures for the collection of data.[33]

But now let us make our story more complicated. Lucifer, by nature rebellious when it comes to divine decrees, wants to try to prevent the Incarnation. He cannot oppose the miracle of virgin conception, but he can act on events—as he will indeed do later, by instigating Herod to commit the massacre of the innocents. And therefore Lucifer tries to make the encounter between Mary and Joseph fail in such a way that, if the birth must occur, it will seem illegitimate in the eyes of all Palestine. So he orders Belphagor to precede Gabriel to Nazareth and to eliminate Joseph with a dagger.

Fortunately the Prince of Darkness teaches us his tricks but not how to hide them. He forgets that Belphagor—who for millennia has been assigned to the savage peoples of Terra Incognita—is used to the customs of those peoples, among whom virtue is expressed through acts of warlike ferocity and is ostentated (or vaunted) by tattoos and scars that render the face repugnant. And so our poor devil tries to identify the virtuous Joseph and sets his eye, by an understandable error, on the father of the future Barabbas. He does not know what a bachelor is, because he comes from a hirsute tribe where by decree lads of tender years must couple with lascivious old men, only to move on, immediately after initiation, to an unbridled but legitimate polygamy. And Belphagor will have trouble identifying Mary, since he does not know what it means for a young girl to be nubile and chaste; in the place whence he comes women are given, while still children, to the men of another clan, and they procreate by the time they are twelve. Nor does he know what it means for a bachelor or a nubile girl to live alone or with their parents, because in his neck of the woods everybody lives in large huts that house entire families—and the only ones who live alone are those the gods have made mad. As the society from which Belphagor comes from is founded on the avuncular principle, the archdevil does not know what it means to be of the line of David. As a result, Belphagor does not manage to identify Joseph and Mary, and his mission fails.

It fails because Belphagor did not know some things that Gabriel knew. But he was not wholly ignorant. Like Gabriel, Belphagor could tell a male from a female, night from day, the habitat that was little Nazareth from that of great Jerusalem. If he had passed by Joseph's workshop, he would have seen that Joseph busied himself planing wood rather than pouring olives into a press; if he had met Mary, he would surely have said to himself that this was a young woman. In short Belphagor and Gabriel would have shared cognitive types that referred to empirical cases but not cognitive types dependent on the Palestinian cultural system of the first century (just) B.C.

In the light of this story, it would be easy to conclude that (i) there are empirical cases that we know and recognize through perceptual experience; (ii) it can happen that, for objects never before perceived directly, we first receive an NC by interpretation, and it is only on the basis of this that we produce a CT, even though a tentative one; (iii) for empirical cases therefore we go from the CT, founded on experience, to the NC, while for cultural cases the reverse occurs.

But things are not that easy. We have seen that to discriminate between *to hop* and *to skip* we must consider data proceeding from perceptual experience but also need information that I would call "choreographic," without which it is impossible to count the order in which the limbs contact the ground (and it would be impossible to recognize that a certain convulsive movement executed by a dancer is a perfect *entrechât*). Conversely, being a professor is certainly a cultural case, but anyone who enters a (traditional) classroom can immediately tell the teacher from the students, because of their reciprocal spatial positions—and better than an ordinary person, when asked, can distinguish between a weasel and a stoat or even between a frog and a toad. We are able to understand the different cognitive operations that distinguish the recognition of a cat from the recognition of a square root, but between these two extremes there stand a variety of "objects" whose cognitive status is fairly unstable.

By way of a conclusion, my guess is that we must recognize the existence of CTs for cultural cases too, and therefore when necessary I shall take them into consideration, without putting them in question and without even trying to create an exhaustive typology of them. In reality, in this chapter, I am concerned with cognitive types for empirical cases, and I shall continue to deal with them directly.

Naturally this decision does not eliminate another problem: that is, whether there are observation sentences independent of a "corporate" system of assumptions, or whether the difference between a male and a female is not in some way possible only within a system of "warranted assertions." But I shall be dealing with this in section 4.

3.5.2 CT and NC as zones of common competence

I certainly have some notions about a mouse, and I am able to recognize a mouse in the little animal that suddenly flashes across the floor of my house in the country. A zoologist knows many things about the mouse that I don't, perhaps more than those things recorded in the *Encyclopedia Britannica*. But if the zoologist is with me in the lounge of that country house, and if I draw his attention to what I am seeing, under normal conditions he ought to agree with me that there is a mouse in the corner over there.

It is as if, given the system of notions that I have about the mouse (MC_1, which probably also includes personal interpretations due to previous experiences, or many notions about mice in literature and the arts, which are not part of the zoologist's competence) and given the system of notions, or MC_2, of the zoologist, we both agree on an area of knowledge that we have in common (fig. 3.3).

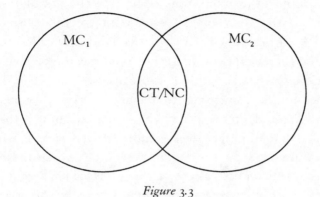

Figure 3.3

This area of knowledge coincides with the CT and NC shared by the zoologist and me; it allows both of us to recognize a mouse and to make some commonsensical observations about mice, probably to distinguish one from a sewer rat (even though this is a controversial point), and to react with some common behavior patterns.

The fact that the zoologist reacted not only with the verbal expression *There's a mouse!* but also with dynamic interpretants that I could foresee, and the fact that, were he asked to draw what he saw, he could supply something very similar to figure 3.1, or that he can always explain what mice are in words to a child by using a series of descriptions not dissimilar to those proposed by Wierzbicka—all this tells me that, somewhere, the zoologist must have a notion not unlike my own. Proof of this lies in the fact that both of us, were we to construct a mousetrap, would build it more or less the same size, and both of us would study the distance between the bars so that a standard-format mouse would not be able to escape, and both of us would use cheese as bait rather than salad or chewing gum. Neither of us would construct a cage for grasshoppers or an immense cage with steel bars like the one used to hold Lecter in *The Silence of the Lambs.*

The moment the zoologist and I agree to recognize a mouse, we have both ascribed the token supplied to us by the stimulating field to the same CT that the zoologist can also interpret in terms of NC. Must this NC be identified with what is habitually called the "literal meaning" of an expression? If the literal meaning is that found in the dictionary, then certainly not, because we have seen that the CT of the mouse also ought to include tymic "connotations," frames, and so on. If, on the other hand, literal meaning is to be understood as what most people are induced to associate with the word *mouse* under ordinary circumstances, i.e., when there is no need to suspect metaphorical use or explicit affective accentuations (such as the diminutive *mousie,* or when we talk of the *mouse* of a computer), then we can answer in the affirmative. Except that this literal meaning is also made of information that is usually recognized as "encyclopedic" and involves experience of the world.

This bears out yet again that the canonical opposition between Dictionary and Encyclopedia is perhaps useful for certain theoretical ends but does not refer in the slightest to the way in which we perceive and name things.

Up to now I have said that the zoologist and I "possess" a zone of common competence, and I have identified this zone with the CT and NC that is elaborated from it. The doubt might arise, since both the zoologist and I share the same CT, that it is *given* to us. A legitimate suspicion, given that it seems to spring from perceptual experiences, both my own (that I have already seen and can recognize mice) and those of the people who transmitted them to me (when they taught me to recognize mice).

But if this zone is given to us, we automatically wonder if we are dealing with an entity deposited somewhere or other, like the species or essences or ideas of days gone by. If this were the case, it would be the same for everybody (and at bottom the problem facing Kant was how to construct a schematic procedure that, in the third *Critique* at least, would become a conjectural labor that was the same for everybody). Instead, we have seen how this zone is bound up with the subject's disposition, experiences, and knowledge, so much so that I have expressed doubts as to whether it includes the notion that mice are different from rats. This common competence is continuously negotiated or contracted (the zoologist agrees to ignore something he knows about the mouse, to accept only what I know about it, or he contributes to the enrichment of my CT of the mouse by making me note something that had escaped me). It can be negotiated, because the cognitive type is not an entity (even though it seems to carry out the function usually assigned to concepts): it is a procedure—as the Kantian schema is a procedure.

3.6 FROM TYPE TO TOKEN OR VICE VERSA?

When we recognize or identify something as a mouse, a token is ascribed to a type. In the process, we pass from the particular to the general. Only under these conditions can I use language and talk about a mouse. It has been seen that in the language of modern cognitive psychology this procedure is indicated (in a historically debatable way) as a phenomenon of categorization, and I have resigned myself *pro bono communicationis* to go along with this usage.

Nevertheless when the zoologist and I agree that we have seen a mouse, we are referring, verbally too, to *that* mouse. While in order to understand that particular token, I have had to bind it to the general, now I will once more bind the general to the particular. As Neisser (1976: 65) observed, discussing this oscillation from a psychological standpoint, on the one hand I generalize the object and on the other I particularize the *schema*.[34]

I do not know if it is a source of comfort or despair that, by so saying, he is merely retabling a debate that began some time ago. Thomas Aquinas would have said that on seeing a mouse one grasps, in the *phantasma* offered by the sensation, a *quidditas,* and therefore not "that mouse" but "the mouse as such" (naturally it would be necessary to recognize, as he did, that the sensation immediately offers us something already organized, as if a retinal image offered us a fully defined object that naturally, spontaneously, referred to the corresponding mouse, without any interpretative mediation). But Aquinas was aware that by so doing we do not explain why we can still go on talking about *that* mouse, the one we are seeing. And so he came up with the *reflexio ad phantasmata,* not to the single mouse, mind you, but to its image. An unsatisfactory solution, all things considered, especially for a realist. Duns Scotus's attempt (first the *haecceitates*—but in that case we have to decide how to form the universal concept) to obviate this problem (catching the single mouse) does not seem definitively persuasive, nor does that proposed by Ockham (first the single individual, and the concept as pure sign—which is a way of saying that CTs are drawn from the individual, without explaining how to solve the universal-particular dialectic when encountering other individuals that may be signified with the same concept).

Basically these were all ways of solving the problem of the black box. To keep out of it, we must focus on only one fact: that something happens. In talking of the mouse, we generalize it, but after having identified the token as a token of a type, we dwell once more on the token: otherwise we could not say, for example, that *that* mouse has lost a bit of its tail, while neither the mouse as such nor the CT of the mouse has a cropped tail.

This brings us back precisely to the Kantian problem of the schema: if the general is too general, perhaps we might manage to compare it to the manifold of experience (which deep down must be that mouse as *Maus an sich*), but it would be difficult to return from the general to the individual manifold. As a procedure for imagining the mouse, the schema mediates, and therefore there must be some correspondence, not of a straight one-to-one sort but at least of a many-to-very-many sort between the features of the type and those that can be found in the token. This means to say that the relation between type and token should not be that which exists between the concept of a geographical map and any geographical map but that which exists between a particular geographical map and the territory it is intended to represent. Peirce would have said that in the moment of Thirdness everything is generalized, but there is no Thirdness that is not impregnated with that *hic et nunc* that arises in Firstness and Secondness.

Throughout the entire history of philosophy it has been said that the individual is *omnimode determinatus,* determined in all respects, and therefore its properties are infinite. With regard to the mouse I am now looking at, I could predicate the number of hairs, its position with respect to Mecca, or the food it ate yesterday. If we always knew only individuals, then every general proposition would derive from an effective knowledge of all individuals in all respects. In order to say that mice are animals, I would not just have to say that for every *x*, if *x* is a mouse, then *x* is an animal; rather, I have really enumerated all the *x*s and have discovered that they all indiscriminately exhibit a property that can be signified by the term *animal.* Or I would have to say that there are some *x*s, the ones I have known, that have the property of being animal (suspending my judgment on the *x*s of which I have no experience). But if there is a function for the CT and the corresponding NC (not to mention the MC), it is that it must also stand for the *x*s I have still not met.

Let us once more refuse all bets regarding what happens inside the black box. Common sense assures us that the zoologist and I recognize *a* mouse, but we know we are dealing with *that* mouse, and if by chance we caught it and marked its back with a pen, on the next occasion we would recognize that we were dealing with the same mouse—which is moreover the way in which, by virtue of characteristic features that are far more complex than the stroke of a pen, we recognize the individuals we normally come into contact with every day (and when we cannot do this, the doctor starts talking about Alzheimer's disease). We recognize individuals because we relate them to a type, but we are able to formulate types because we have experience of individuals. That we are capable of some *reflexio ad phantasmata* (or *ad res*) is a fact that we must take as food for thought, even though, personally, I possess no instruments for explaining it and take as my motto the phrase with which Saul Kripke (1971) ended a conference speech on identity and necessity: "The next topic would be my own solution of the mind-body problem, but that I do not have" (1971: 164).

But there is something we can say, and it is not only that we have some experience of *this* man (token) even when we recognize him as *a* man (type) but also that we assign a proper name to certain individuals and recognize them as those determined individuals and not in general. Therefore if it is assumed that we recognize thanks to a CT, we must admit that there is a CT for men in general (and it might even assume the most schematic form of a 3-D model) and there are different CTs for our fathers, wives, husbands, children, friends, and neighbors. I shall be dealing with this in 3.7.6. but, before getting to that point, we have to venture into that swampy area that lies between the general and the individual.

3.7 THE CT ARCHIPELAGO

3.7.1 Types vs. basic categories

Certainly it is one thing to refer to a CT to recognize a token of a natural kind, such as mouse, and another to refer to a CT to recognize individually a person. Neisser (1976: 55) admits that our schemata can operate on different levels of generality, so that we are ready to recognize "something," "a mouse," "my brother-in-law George," and even a sneer of disdain (not a smile) on George's face. Of the possible existence of individual types (and the oxymoron already obliges us to investigate further), I shall have more to say in 3.7.6., but for now we need to talk of the difference between generic types and specific types, in other words, of the fact that we sometimes want to tell a tabby cat from a Siamese, sometimes a cat from a dog, or sometimes only a quadruped from a biped. Evidently it is a matter of postulating CTs at *different levels of generality,* but the problem immediately arises as to whether we can think of a sort of "tree" for the different CTs or whether we must consider them as an archipelago with no hierarchical order.[35]

The fact that has been and is still widely discussed is that we show different capacities of discrimination for different natural and artificial kinds. As for myself, I am capable of distinguishing a hen from a turkey, a swallow from an eagle, and a sparrow from a canary (and even a barn owl from a little owl), and therefore I have a CT of them; however, I would not be able to distinguish between wrens, redstarts, chaffinches, bullfinches, blackcaps, skylarks, goldfinches, great tits, warblers, starlings, jays, curlews, or wagtails. I would recognize them as birds, and that's all. Naturally a hunter or a bird-watcher would have a competence different from mine, but this is not the problem. The problem is, if that of the swallow is a CT, what is the CT of birds in general? Even if we accept the idea that we know by categorial organization, this organization varies according to diverse areas of experience, according to human groups, and according to the individual.

If our knowledge were really structured according to a homogeneous system of classes and subclasses, we should name and recognize the objects that follow according to the diagram in figure 3.4.

Superordinate categories	Basic categories	Subordinate categories
FURNITURE	Chair	Kitchen chair, living room chair
	Table	Kitchen table, living room table
TREE	Maple	Silver maple, Canadian maple
	Birch	Silver birch, black birch
FRUIT	Apple	Rennet, Golden Delicious
	Grape	Muscatel, Pinot noir

Figure 3.4

When we presuppose a schema of this kind, we likewise presuppose that the *basic categories* are the ones learned first and that therefore they not only play a crucial role in linguistic exchange but also govern the processes of identification or recognition. When subjects are asked to enumerate the features, properties, or attributes of a series of stimulus terms (such as animal, furniture, chair, dog, fruit, apples, and pears) it can be seen that (i) for the superordinate categories, the features are very few in number; (ii) for the basic categories, the features grow remarkably; and (iii) for the subordinate categories, the difference in terms of features as compared to the basic categories, is minimal. For example, only two features are individuated to define clothing (it's something we put on and something that keeps us warm), a great number of features are individuated for trousers (legs, pockets, buttons, they are made of cloth, you put them on in a certain way, etc.), while for a subordinate category such as *jeans* the subjects usually add only the characteristic feature of color (they are usually blue). According to the number of these distinguishing features, it is obvious that it is easier to tell trousers from a jacket than to discriminate between two different kinds of trousers.[36]

All the experiments in this regard have shown that our everyday knowledge does not correspond to this classification. The situation can vary according to the subjects, but while many of them can tell a hen from a turkey, in the case of the curlew and the redstart they recognize only a bird.

Rosch (1978: 169) talks of an unexpected result when, although Tree and Furniture were hypothesized as superordinate categories, it was seen that the subjects could tell a chair from a table much better than they could an oak from a maple, which were both generically recognized as trees. I was not surprised in the least by the result, bearing in mind that for some time Putnam has been telling us that he cannot distinguish between an elm and a beech (and I must join the club), while I imagine he can distinguish very well between a chair and a table or between a banana and an apple. There are two problems here.

We tend to elaborate CTs with reference to perceptual situations in which, as far as our corporeal exigencies are concerned, morphology and pertinency count for more than the function we might call aesthetic and social (and I refer the reader to the paragraph on *affordances* in 3.4.7). To decide that a bookshelf and a chair both belong to the superordinate category of Furniture, we need to have an elaborate notion of what a habitat is, of what we expect from a standard habitation, and of where one goes to purchase the objects that serve to furnish a standard habitation. The category Furniture, therefore, requires a capacity for abstraction. I maintain that a dog may recognize a chair or a divan, and perhaps a table, as objects on which he can curl up and have a nap, while he sees a bookshelf or a (closed) cupboard simply as obstacles, every bit as much as he sees the walls of the room as obstacles.[37]

On the other hand the property of something being a tree is one of those semiosic primitives that we instinctively distinguish in the surrounding environment, and as a result we discriminate between the tree and animals and other objects (and I don't think a dog behaves any differently when he uses trees generally as urinals—except for any repugnance he may feel for some particular olfactory stimulus). We elaborate first and foremost a CT of the tree (while the difference between beech and linden tree belongs only to a more elaborate type of knowledge), because, unless we are primitive forest dwellers who depend on their ability to recognize different species of trees, trees appear to us as furnishings of the environment that, as far as our needs go, all perform the same function (they give shade, mark boundaries, cluster together in woods or forests, etc.).[38]

But we can tell a banana from an apple very well, because the difference counts for our needs and our alimentary preferences, because we often have to choose between them, or because they present different conditions of consumability. Therefore it seems natural that we have distinct CTs for banana and apple and a generic CT for trees.[39]

These statistical rules are subject to noteworthy exceptions depending on personal experience. Unable as I am to tell an elm from a linden tree, I can recognize both banyan trees and mangroves very well. There are three reasons for this: the first is that we are dealing with trees that nourished my childish imagination as a reader of adventure stories (especially Salgari's books, at least as far as the banyan is concerned); the second, which depends on the first, is that in the course of my travels, when I heard it said that something was a banyan and that the clumps of vegetation along the coasts of an island or alongside a swampy canal were mangroves, I hastened to look at them and to commit their morphological features to memory; the third is that both the banyan and the mangroves have highly singular and uncommon features, the former because the trunk branches out toward the roots in a series of star-shaped "blades," and the latter because (by no means fortuitously) they are known in colloquial English as *walking trees,* that is to say, from a distance they look like insects walking on the water.

Naturally, still owing to biographical accidents, by this time I would recognize a platypus with certainty. I can identify an iguana, but I still have only the vaguest ideas about the anaconda. This does not mean that were I obliged to tell an anaconda from a badger and a magpie, I could not identify it, because I know it is a snake, but my idea of snake is "wild" and has nothing to do with the scientific idea of reptile.

3.7.2. Tiny Tim's Story

We know very well that it is only at a certain age that children acquire classificatory competence, which does not prevent them from recognizing many objects perfectly well. The following dialogue is the transcription of a tape recording made without any scientific intention in 1968, in the course of a children's party, with the sole purpose of making them play with the recorder, to tell stories or improvise dialogues. As far as I recall, the subject whose responses are transcribed here, whom we shall call Tiny Tim, was between four and five years old.

I: Listen, Tim, I am a gentleman who has always lived on a desert island on which there are no birds, only dogs, cows, and fish, but no birds. Finally I am about to come here, and I ask you to explain to me what a bird is, so that I can recognize one if by chance I should see one....
TIM: Well, it has a little meat, but it is small in the breast, and it has little feet and a tiny little head and a little breast, and its wings are little too, and a few feathers on its breast and... and then it flies with these feathers and....

(As can be seen, the child has his own idea of birds, he is probably thinking of the only birds he has seen on the balcony at home, sparrows, and this could suggest a few ideas in the discussion that will follow about prototypes; but it does not enter his head to say that a bird is a flying biped.)

I: All right. Now listen. I am a gentleman who has always lived on the top of a mountain, where I quenched my thirst by eating fruit, but I have never seen water. Now could you explain to me what water is like?

TIM: What it's like?

I: Yes.

TIM: I don't know what water is like, because nobody has ever even explained it to me...

I: Have you never seen it?

TIM: Yes, when you put your hands under the water...

I: But I don't know what water is like, so how can I put my hands under it?

TIM: But under the water that wets... first you put your hands under the water, then you take the soap, and you put it on, and then you rinse it away with the water...

I: You have told me what I must do with water, but you haven't told me what water is. Maybe it's that red thing in the stove that burns?

TIM:... Nooo! Water is... is....

I: What do I see when I see water? How can I know it is water?

TIM: You get wet when you put your hands under the water!

I: But what it does it mean that it wets you? If I don't know what water is, then I don't know what wetting means....

TIM: It is transparent....

I: Oh, is it that stuff in the windows that lets you see what's on the other side?

TIM: Nooo!

I: You said it was transparent....

TIM: No, it's not glass, glass doesn't wet you!

I: But what does to get wet mean?

TIM: Getting wet is um… ehm….

ANOTHER ADULT, *breaking in*. That gentleman should know what wet means if he always eats fruit on that mountain….

TIM: It's damp!!

I: Good. Is it damp like fruit?

TIM: A little bit.

I: A little bit. And is it shaped like fruit, I mean, round?….

TIM: Nooo, water is shaped like… it goes around all over the place, round, square, all over the place….

I: It takes all the shapes it wants?

TIM: Uh huh….

I: Then here and there you can see square waters, round waters….

TIM: No, not here and there, only in rivers, in streams, in wash-basins, in baths….

I: So it's a transparent thing, damp, that takes the shape of all the things it goes into?

TIM: Yes.

I: And so it's not a solid thing like bread….

TIM: No!

I: And so if it's not solid, what is it?

TIM: I dunno.

I: What is everything that isn't solid?

TIM: It's water.

I: Is it liquid, perhaps?

TIM: You see, water is a transparent liquid that you can't drink, because the normal stuff has little flies, microbes that you can't see….

I: Good boy, a transparent liquid.

(As can be seen, Tim knows what a liquid is, and after a lot of hints he even arrives at a definition that would delight a dictionary semantician ("transparent liquid"). Apparently he cannot get there on his own, and the first definition he gives is of a functional nature (what water is for: he does not go so much for the "dictionary" or morphological charac-teristics of the object as much as its affordances). *Nevertheless we should recall the question. It was about a man who lived on a moun-*

*taintop and quenched his thirst without knowing what water was. Tim
understood that the man drank fruit juice, and so the idea of liquid
struck him as implicit. He tried to identify other characteristics of water compared to other liquids. This is a typical case in which the formulation of the question can lead to answers that we then consider
deviant or insufficient.)*

I: Listen now, I have never seen a radio. How can I recognize
one?

TIM: (*hesitant mumbling*)

I: Do it the way you did with water before, when you finally told
me the most important thing, that it was a transparent liquid.

TIM: With batteries or plugged in?

I: But I don't know what a radio is, and therefore I don't know
which is better.

TIM: Well, it has electricity that says everything that... that in the
... batteries is (*incomprehensible word*)... and says everything that
has happened....

I: And that's a radio?

TIM: You put in the electricity like there is here (*points to the tape
recorder*) and then it goes.

I: But what is the radio—is it an animal that goes ahead if I put
the electricity inside it?

TIM: No, it's an electrical box that....

I: An electrical box?

TIM: No, it's that inside there is the electricity and the batteries,
with wires... that says everything that has happened.

I: So it's like that box over there, that if I put a record on, it says
what has happened?

TIM: Nooo, it doesn't have a record.

I: Oh, it's a box with electricity, wires, batteries, and without a
record that says everything that has happened.

TIM: Yes.

*(Apart from the fact that an adult would also find it difficult to give a
scientific definition of a radio, and it being evident that Tim could recognize a radio perfectly well, it will be noted that he did not think to*

distinguish it from the water and the bird as an artificial kind or Arti-fact, not even when I suggested the opposition with Animal to him.)

I: Now listen to this. I am a gentleman who has always lived....
TIM: Not on a desert island again!!
I: No, this time in a hospital where the people were ill and each one was missing a part, some an arm, others a leg. I have never seen a foot. What is a foot?
TIM: Ha ha... It's this here.
I: No, you mustn't show me it, you must explain to me what it is, so that when I see one, I can say, oh, this is a foot.
TIM: It's made of meat, it has toes. Don't you know what toes are?
I: So it's a thing made of meat with toes ... Is this it? (*I show him a hand.*)*
TIM: Nooo. Because the foot has the elbow here, and instead the hand has it here.
I: Then it is an ill hand, like this (*I imitate a withered hand*)....
TIM: Nooo! It has the corners and toes straight out in front, it's like this.
I: Then the street where we live is a foot. It has corners, it is straight...
TIM: No, it's smaller, and then it has a thing here.
I: Try to tell me where it is...
TIM: It is where the men that walk... It is the thing that men rest on the ground to walk with... What begins at the hips and goes down and at the end of the leg—which is that thing there—there is the foot.
I: One more: it's the man who lives on the desert island again. And he doesn't know what a hot sausage is.
TIM: It's round.
I: Like a ball?
TIM: No, it's like this, it has corners like this, and it's longer than a ball and is made of meat.
I: Then it's a leg....

---

* Translator's note: In Italian, *finger* and *toe* are expressed by the same word: "dito."

TIM: Without the bones, because a leg has bones.

I: How can I recognize a frankfurter? You told me it was made of meat...

TIM: It's round, it's a half of a ball, but it's only at the corners that it has nothing, that inside that... halfway... that inside is very very thin, and then it's made of meat and is pink.

(The session finished here, because Tim was showing signs of tiredness. As can be seen, he did not think of saying that a foot is a Limb and that a frankfurter is a Food. He must agree with Neisser (1978: 4): categories cannot be a mode of perception.)

3.7.3. Quadruped oysters

I shall say in 4.3 in what sense the scientific categories must be distinguished from the "wild" categories, but for the time being I propose to assume that we have, in line and without any embedding from general to particular, CTs for apple, banana, tree, hen, sparrow, and bird. How is it possible to have two distinct CTs for sparrow and hen and only one for great tits, curlews, and skylarks all together? It is possible largely because it happens (and by time-honored definition all that happens is possible). The CT for birds is so "generous" (or vague, or rough) as to accommodate all animals with wings that fly in the sky and alight on power lines or trees, and if we spot a sparrow from a distance, we can in fact decide, for the moment, to consider it a bird and that's that. The term *bird* has a greater *extension* than terms such as *hen* or *sparrow,* but I would not say that this means we perceive the CT of bird as a superordinate category with respect to that of the hen. That of "animal that flies in the sky with wings" (which is our ingenuous notion of bird) is a semiosic primitive. For some animals we perceive only that property, and we relate them to the rough CT of the bird. For others, on recognizing certain additional properties, we elaborate a CT with a finer grain.

We recognize a CT of the bird on the basis of the features or the procedures *x, y;* we recognize a CT of the sparrow on the basis of the features or the procedures *x,y, z;* and a CT of the swallow on the basis of the property *x,y,k;* and we realize that there are common features not only between sparrow and swallow but also between a sparrow and other animals we recognize as birds. But at first this must have nothing to do with the logical criterion by

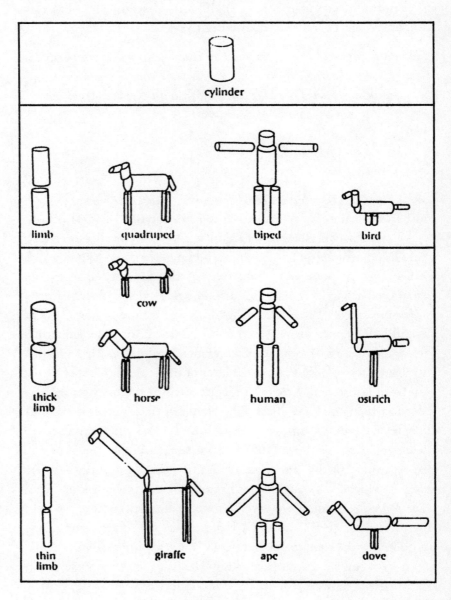

Figure 3.5

which we relate the sparrow to the class of birds, even though it is certainly by starting from similarities that we go on to elaborate taxonomies. We are simply capable of recognizing sparrows, swallows, and birds, and if then someone wishes to devote himself to the study of birds in liberty, he will also have a CT for the curlew and another for the skylark. CTs are generous and disordered; some people have a CT for the cat, some have one both for a tabby and a Siamese, and most of the features of the tabby will certainly be shared by the cat. But even though it seems so evident that it is on this basis that we can go on to state that every tabby is a cat, I insist on reiterating that, on the level of a perceptual process, this is still a suspicion, an intuition of identity of properties, and not yet an inscription in a categorial tree.

If a CT is a procedure for the construction of the conditions of recognizability and identification of an object, see figure 3.5, which shows various 3-D models.

There is a 3-D model for the dog or the horse. Nothing prevents us, owing to more specific needs, from constructing a 3-D model for a Labrador and a pointer, or for a black horse or a Lippizaner, just as nothing prevents Putnam and me from going to work in a nursery one day and learning to distinguish elms from beech trees. But at first, beech, elm, and tree are all CTs that should be put on the same level: and each one of us uses the one or the other according to his own relations with the environment, considering himself more or less satisfied. The observation sentences *I have seen a pointer* and *I have seen a dog* are equally useful and pertinent according to the circumstances, even before it has been decided that the category of pointer is subordinate to that of dog. Perceptually the CT of the dog is cruder than that of the pointer, but it is perfectly adequate in certain circumstances; it does not oblige us to choose between a Great Dane and an Irish wolfhound, and we ask no more than that.

In my view, therefore, the discourse on the CTs still has nothing to do with the discourse on a taxonomic-categorial system. The CTs are only *bricks* for use in the erection of categorial systems.

Nonetheless there are some possible counterexamples. I admit that the experiment I am about to cite could be used both to equate the categories to the CTs and to deny this equation. Humphreys and Riddoch (1995: 34) tell us of a patient affected by cerebral lesions, who, when shown an insect, drew it with not very much realism but certainly in a way that allows us to recognize something very similar to an insect (fig. 3.6). The fact that he drew it tells us he interpreted it and therefore supplied indications for its identification and future recognition; in short, if he did not have one before, he had now constructed a CT. But when the insect was removed and he was asked to draw it, the subject represented it as a kind of bird (fig. 3.7).

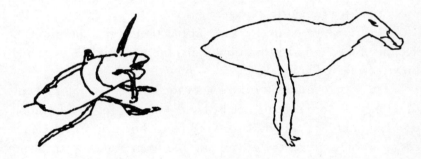

Figures 3.6 and 3.7

When the same patient, capable of recognizing an oyster as such (in the absence of the model), was invited to draw it, he represented it with four legs. The authors note that, for the short-term visual memory, we must postulate deposited mental knowledge, whose degeneration compromises the reconstruction of the remembered object. Could the case be interpreted in terms of a disturbance of categorial competence? In point of fact, in the absence of the insect the patient did not draw a chair and in place of the oyster a pencil. His memory retained a feature of "animality," and therefore it could have worked its way up from the insect or the oyster to the superordinate category of the animals, and thence back down toward the birds or some other unspecified beast. But if we consider the perception of animality as a precategorial experience, then by retaining only one vague attribute of what he had seen, the patient might have gone to fish out any CT that contained it, thus slipping from one CT to another, as if surfing in the archipelago of the CTs, instead of working his way up from species to genus.

I am not maintaining that previous knowledge or categorial suspicions do not play a part in the construction of a CT—and the case of Marco Polo mentioned in 2.1 confirms this. I am merely supposing that CTs (i) can be constructed independently of an organized categorial competence and (ii) can also be activated independently and even in conflict with such a competence (as will be seen when we retell the story of the platypus in 4.5).

3.7.4 CTs and prototypes
3.7.4.1 *Stereotypes and prototypes*
Can we identify CTs with those that Putnam (1975: 295) calls *stereotypes*? If we consider Putnam's representation of the content of the term *water* (fig. 3.8),

Syntactic Markers	Semantic Markers	Stereotype	Extension
Noun	Natural kind	Colorless	H_2O
Concrete	Liquid	Transparent	
Mass noun		Tasteless	

Figure 3.8

we could say that the CT includes both semantic markers and stereotypical information (while naturally the property of being H_2O is part of the MC). In any case the CT has the folk nature of the stereotype, and the random blend of dictionary and encyclopedic elements.

But it is perhaps more interesting to make it clear that stereotypes are not what cognitivist literature has called *prototypes*.

One of the ways in which the prototype is currently understood is that it is a member of a category, which becomes a model for the recognition of other members that share some properties recognized as salient. When invited to define a bird, Tiny Tim thought of the prototype of the sparrow, for the simple reason that this was the bird he was most familiar with. If taken literally, the experiments carried out regarding the identification of prototypes allow one to think that this is the way we all usually behave.

Others are inclined to consider it as more a bundle of features, and in that sense it would be closer to the stereotype. When we think of a dog (unless we live with one on a day-to-day basis), we do not think of a Dalmatian rather than a Labrador but of a *mongrel* type. When we think of a bird, we imagine a winged biped of average size (let's say between a sparrow and a pigeon) and seldom (unless we have come straight from the *Arabian Nights*) something like the roc. This mongrel form varies according to the culture (I imagine that an inhabitant of the South Sea islands might have a CT of the bird that emphasizes the vividness of the plumage more than is the case with us), but it is precisely in the negotiation of a space for common agreement that the CTs happily mongrelize themselves. Let's think of an animal such as the dinosaur, which we do not know by direct experience but through real prototypes offered us by the Encyclopedia. Even in this case I maintain that the most common CT is a cross between a dinosaur, a brontosaurus, a *Tyrannosaurus rex,* and various other extinct giant reptiles. If it were possible to project an average of the mental images that each of us has in this regard, we would find ourselves with an animal out of Walt Disney rather than something we see reconstructed in a natural history museum.[40]

A third version would have the prototypes as something more abstract, a set of requisites that may be expressed propositionally, necessary if we are to predicate something as belonging to a category; and here the ambiguity of "category" crops up again, since in this last case we are already thinking in terms of classification.

3.7.4.2 Some misunderstandings regarding prototypes

Prototypes have enjoyed and still enjoy vast popularity in psychological literature, but their history is fairly complex, partly because the person who has worked most on them, Eleanor Rosch, has successively changed her mind about their nature. The scholar who has reconstructed the matter with the greatest precision is perhaps Lakoff (1987), and I will keep to his synthesis.

The story of prototypes springs from a series of questions, from Wittgenstein to Rosch, that regard family resemblances, centrality (the idea that some members of a category are better examples than others), gradience (the hen is seen by many as *less of a bird* than the sparrow), linguistic economy (the fact that language uses shorter and more easily memorizable words for things that appear as organic wholes rather than a set or class of morphologically different objects). But this, as we have seen in the preceding paragraphs, proves the fact that there are basic categories that depend on the perception of forms, on our motor acts, and on the facility of memorization, and that on this level speakers name things that manifest "an integrity of their own" and are "human-sized" with greater ease (Lakoff 1987: 519).

But this does not show that the categories assume the form of prototypes. To say that the words *cat*, *Katz*, or *chien* are handier and easier to memorize than the words *Felis* or *Mammal* certainly confirms that in everyday experience it is easier for us to identify something as cat rather than as mammal, but it does not tell us whether there is a prototype of the cat or, if there is, what this may be. If anything, the problem of prototypes concerns phenomena such as that of the extensibility of categorial limits (extendible boundaries), so that it is debatable whether certain highly complex irregular polyhedrons are polyhedrons, while there are no doubts about the better known regular polyhedrons, or whether transfinite numbers are numbers or not, while no one doubts that 2 or 100,000,000 are numbers.

But the existence of basic categories is inferred from spontaneous everyday linguistic behavior, whereas an experiment like the one on polyhedrons or numbers requires an interviewer to ask a subject to answer a question that brings complex classifications into play. Therefore the problem is: Can the existence of prototypes be inferred from everyday behavior (not only linguistic but also behavioral, such as felicitous recognition) or from verbal responses to sophisticated questions?

To come to Eleanor Rosch, in a first phase of her experiments (between the sixties and the seventies) prototypes were a matter of perceptual pertinence. In a second phase (the first half of the seventies) the prototypical effects obtainable by experiment were thought to provide a characterization of the internal structure of the category (hence the persuasion that they constituted mental representations). In a third phase (the late seventies) prototypical effects were thought to subdetermine mental representations, but there was no one-to-one correspondence between prototypical effects and mental representations. The effects were not thought to reflect categorial structure. Therefore we might know judgments of prototypicality, but they would tell us nothing about our cognitive processes, and prototypical effects would be superficial.[41]

In point of fact Rosch (1978: 174ff.) makes it clear that the prototype is neither a member of a category nor a precise mental structure but, rather, the result of an experiment that aims at collecting and quantifying judgments on the degree of prototypicality. What does degree of prototypicality mean? We are said to have an identification of prototypicality when a member of a category is assigned the greatest number of attributes that it shares with other members of the category.

Now, the subjects who attribute to vehicles in general only two properties (of moving and of transporting people), tend to identify a motor car as the prototype of vehicle (with about twenty-five characteristic features) and to put the bicycle or boat on lower levels, while reserving the lowest places in the ranking for the lighter-than-air vehicle and finally the elevator. The elevator is attributed with only two properties (of moving and of transporting people).[42] But in that case, the elevator ought to be the prototype of Vehicles, seeing as it presents precisely those properties common to any vehicle and would therefore allow us to relate even the most diverse species and tokens to vehicles. In any categorial order, the superordinate genus must have fewer features than the subordinate species, and the species fewer of the individual tokens that make recognition possible. If the CT for dog provided instructions for "constructing" a Pekinese and nothing else, it would be hard to apply it to an Irish wolfhound. If a prototype (where a classificatory system has already been established) and a CT have anything in common, it would be that both ought to have maximum extension and minimum intension. Instead the prototype has minimum extension and maximum intension.

It seems to me that the notion of prototype has a value for making clear the "borders" of a basic category. If it is decided that the salient features of the superordinate category of birds are beak, feathers, wings, two feet and the ability to fly, it is natural that there be some difficulty over defining the hen fully as a bird, because it does not fly but, at best, flaps about (and yet it is not excluded, because it must be admitted that other birds do not cease being birds when they are not flying). It strikes me that what is more debatable here regards the identification of what the prototype *is,* because I believe that such identification depends on environmental experiences and that judgments of prototypicality have more value for cultural anthropological research than for the determination of cognitive mechanisms in general.[43]

3.7.4.3 The mysterious Dyirbal

In any experiment on classification, it is always the experimenter who proposes a subdivision into classes inspired by a certain cultural model, tending not only to obliterate "wild" forms of classification but also to presuppose a classification in which probably there are only morphological accidents devoid of a semantic counterpart.

A curious case of this kind is to be found in Lakoff (1977: 6), where reference is made (on the basis of other research) to the Dyirbal language (Australia), in which every term must be preceded by one of these words:

Bayi: men, kangaroos, possums, bats, most snakes, most fishes, some birds, most insects, the moon, storms, rainbows, boomerangs, some spears, etc.
Balan: women, bandicoots, dogs, platypuses, echidnas, some snakes, some fishes, most birds, fireflies, scorpions, crickets, the

hairy mary grub, anything connected with water or fire, sun and stars, shields, some spears, some trees, etc.
Balam: all edible fruits and the plants that bear them, tubers, ferns, honey, cigarettes, wine, cake
Bala: parts of the body, meat, bees, wind, yam sticks, some spears, most trees, grass, mud, stones, noise, language, etc.

Lakoff is surprised that such "categorizations" are used by the natives automatically and almost without their being aware of it, and he seeks semantic and symbolic reasons to justify them. He finds, for example, that birds are classified with women, because they are held to be the spirits of dead women, but he does not manage to explain why the platypus is grouped with women, fire, and dangerous things—as you can see, I am not the only one for whom this animal is a source of continuous worry.

However, Lakoff notes that for speakers of the latest generations, who have lost almost all of the tongue of their fathers, there remain only *Bayi* for males and nonhuman living creatures, *Balan* for human females, and *Bala* for all the rest, and, reasonably, he connects the phenomenon with the influence of the English pronominal system (He, She, It). A correct observation, which nonetheless would encourage one to go further—beyond English, I mean to say. Let is suppose that in a Mediterranean peninsula there lives a singular population whose natives have the curious habit of putting one of two words before every noun: *il* (with the variant *lo*) or *la*, with the following "categorial" effects:

> *Il* is applied to men, kangaroos, bats, many snakes (boa, python, cobra), many fish (bass, pike, swordfish, shark), many insects (hornet, ladybird), sun, guardian, storm, rainbow, boomerang, wagon, rifle, machine, pistol, platypus, rhinoceros.

> *La* is applied to women, sentinel, the tiger, locomotive, some snakes (viper, grass snake), some fish (trout, gilthead), many birds (swallow, great tit), insects (wasp, fly), water, moon, star, armor, pistol, spear, some trees (oak, palm), giraffe, skunk.

As we well know, grammatical gender has nothing to do with sexual gender and not even with any classification that on a conceptual level puts *sentinel* on the same side as *locomotive* and *moon*, and the *sun* on the same side as *guardian* and *wagon*. At the end of the day, we could even suppose that to the north of that peninsula, on the other side of a mountain range, there lives another (extremely barbarous) population that, like the young Dyirbal, put one of three words before every term: *der, die,* and *das* (perhaps owing to an effect of "pidginization," under the influence of the English pronominal system), but that in this case the fact that the sun is *die* like woman, the moon *der* like the leopard and the tiger, and that the platypus, the ear, and gold are all *das* is of no categorial importance.

I am not suggesting in the slightest that something occurs in the Dyirbal language that is similar to what occurs in Italian, German, French, and many other languages. I am merely expressing the suspicion that grammatical phenomena are often discussed as phenomena of classification—which casts a shadow over many investigations in which classifications familiar to the experimenter but not shared by the subjects are presumed, or in which the experimenter vainly struggles to deduce classifications where the subjects do not classify at all and merely follow grammatical automatisms.[44]

3.7.5. Other types

I intend to restrict myself to those cases in which objects or events of actual or possible perceptual experience are in question, rather than go further into what happens when we talk of the *Bank of England, government, the majority system, emphyteusis, fate, adversity, metonymy, precision, instinct,* and so on. But up to what scale can we talk of objects of possible perception?

Is the Italian peninsula perceivable? Today it is, just as much as the moon, nor is there any need to look at it from the moon, when we can photograph it from a satellite. And before we had satellites, was there a CT of the Boot? Of course there was, as every Italian schoolboy knows, just as every French schoolboy had a CT of the Hexagon. Yet in those days nobody had *perceived* these territories. However, through successive approximations, by mapping the coasts to a scale that was almost one to one, an image was obtained (certainly variable in time and according to the projections or the imperfection of the measurements, as happened with ancient maps) that transmitted the NC of the geographical expressions *Italy* and *France*.

Are there CTs of historic figures? For some, who have inspired a massive and highly popular iconography (such as Napoleon), the answer is certainly yes. Is there a CT of Roger Bacon? I doubt it; there is only an NC, not known to everybody either ("medieval philosopher") and an MC available for the experts. I think that, beyond a certain limit, some very intricate situations arise. We certainly do not have a CT for some chemical substances, but we have one for others, such as hydrochloric acid, at least as much as we have one for the skunk (see Neubauer and Petöfi 1981); but a chemist might have a more developed competence in this regard. We do not have a cognitive type for diabetes (it is a different matter to say that a doctor has a cognitive type for the symptoms of diabetes), but we have the impression that we can identify at a glance a person suffering from a cold, so much so that people with colds can be caricatured or mimed.

Just how little the archipelago of the CTs has been explored is revealed to us by a very common experience.

3.7.6 If on a Winter's Night a Driver

I am driving at night on a country road, covered with a thin layer of ice to boot. At a certain point I see ahead of me, in the distance, two sources of white light, which gradually get bigger. First there comes Firstness: two white lights. Then, in order to compare a sequence of stimuli distributed temporally (light in $time_2$ greater than light in $time_1$), I must have already begun a perceptual inference. At this point there come into play what Neisser (1976, 4) calls "schemata," forms of expectation and anticipation that orient the selection of elements from the stimulating field (which does not mean that the stimulating field does not offer me some salient features, some preferential directions). I really do not think I could activate a system of expectations if I did not already possess the CT "motor car" plus the script "motor car at night."

The fact that I see two white lights and not two red lights tells me that the motor car is not moving away from me but coming toward me. If I were a rabbit, I would remain dazzled without being able to interpret such a singular phenomenon, and I would be run over. In order to control the situation, I must understand instantly that what is coming toward me is not a pair of bright eyes but a body with certain morphological features, even if those are not in my stimulating field. Even though the lights I see are those lights (a concrete token), as soon as I pass on to perceptual judgment, I have already entered the universal: what I can see is a car, and I'm not much interested in the make, or in who is driving it.

This is by way of a reply to Gibson and his fundamentally realistic and nonconstructivist, "ecological," theory of perception. One might agree with him when he states that

> the function of the brain ... is not to decode signals, nor to interpret messages nor accept images... The function of the brain is not even to *organize* sensory input or *to process* data... The perceptual systems, including the nerve centers at various levels up to the brain, are ways of seeking and extracting information about the environment from the flowing array of ambient energy. (1966: 5)

Let us admit that it is the stimulating field itself that offers me salient features, that it is something *which is there* that provides me with sufficient information to perceive two bright round sources of light, to distinguish the "borders" that separate them from the surrounding environment. I imagine that the rabbit sees something similar, and that its receptors react preferentially to the source of light rather than the surrounding darkness. But only by calling, as Gibson does, this first phase of the process "perception" are we right in saying that it is determined by salient features proposed by

the stimulating field. However, if I wish to keep faith with my terminological premises, perceptual judgment is something far more
complex than this. What makes me different from the rabbit is that
I pass from those stimuli, for all they are determined by the object,
to the perceptual judgment *That is a car,* applying a CT and then
integrating what stimulates me now with what I already knew.

Only when I have formulated the perceptual judgment am I
able to proceed to a further series of inferences. First of all, I relate
the type to the token; the position of the headlights tells me if the
car is keeping to the right side of the road or if it is getting danger-
ously close to the middle, if it is traveling at high or low speed. According to whether I started off by seeing two barely perceptible
light sources in the distance or whether the appearance of the lights
was preceded by a diffuse glow, I understand whether there is a
bend or a dip in the road coming up. Knowing that the road is icy
also persuades me to follow other (learned) rules of prudence. As
Neisser (1976: 65) would have put it, in this oscillation I am generalizing the object on the one hand and particularizing the schema
on the other.

If this is the way things happen, I do not even need to think, as
Kant does, that on the one hand there is the manifold of sensation
and on the other the abstract apparatus of the categories waiting to
be applied with, as a mediatory element, the schema. The schema
would be a device, a system of instructions so flexible as to mediate
itself continuously, so to speak, and to enhance and correct itself on
the basis of the specific experience I am having, impregnated as it is
both with semiosic primitives (an object, a brightness) and categorial elements (a car, a vehicle, a moving object).

As I assess the entire situation, there also come into play what
Neisser calls "cognitive maps." I apply to the situation what I know
about the default characteristics of a country road (and an icy one
at that), and I also assess the width, for example, of the one on
which I am traveling, otherwise I could not establish whether the
car down there is keeping to the right side of the road or whether
there is a risk of its colliding with me. From the way in which my
car reacts to little exploratory dabs on the brake pedal, I estimate

whether the road surface would tolerate sudden, heavier braking (and in such a case I do not perceive with my eyes but with my feet and buttocks, interpreting a quantity of stimuli that come to me proprioceptively).

In short, in the course of this experience I put to work diverse CTs; CTs of objects, situations, and specific competences that would seem to belong more to MC; schemata of cause-and-effect relations, as well as inferences of various types and degrees of complexity. What I see is only a part of what I understand, and what I understand includes a system of rules of the road, of acquired habits, of laws, of a learned case history, and so I already know that in the past a failure to respect those rules has led to a fatal accident....

That most of these competences are public is borne out intersubjectively by the fact that, if I am inattentive or sleepy, someone beside me will be able to warn me that a car is coming straight for us, and to advise me to steer more to my side of the road (note that this someone has arrived at the same perceptual judgment as I even though he or she is receiving the stimuli at a different angle).

Perhaps, in the course of this process, I have assessed only epiphenomena. But if I did not take these epiphenomena seriously, I would be a rabbit on death row.

3.7.7 Physiognomic types by individuals

But let's go back to the census of the various CTs that make up our as yet largely unexplored archipelago. A CT can also regard individuals. Jackendoff (1987: 198–99) suggests that, even though we have recourse to the same 3-D model both for the recognition of individuals and of genera, two distinct processes are involved. In the case in which I categorize George as a male human being, I decide that the token$_i$ is an example of the type$_k$. In the case in which I recognize George as George, I decide that a token$_i$ is identical to the token$_j$. Others would say that in the first case I recognize George as *similar* to other people, in the second as *the same* person. We could say that type and token coincide in individuals. But it does not happen like this in the processes of recognition, because token$_i$ (the individual I see in this instant) really is a token, while token$_j$ is after all retrieved from the memory, be it a mental image or any other form of record, and therefore it is a CT, which we ought to define as an "individual type" but which, since this term borders on oxymoron, I shall call *physiognomic type*.

If we do not postulate physiognomic types, the fact that we are able to recognize the same person over the course of time remains inexplicable. Year after year people change, the face gets fatter or thinner, wrinkles appear, the hair grows white, the shoulders sag, the walk loses its elasticity. It is prodigious that in normal circumstances we can recognize someone after having lost touch for a great many years. If we do not recognize him right away, all we need is a tone of voice, a glance, to push us toward recognition and the ritual "You haven't changed a bit!"

This means that we had constructed a physiognomic type of the subject with only a few salient features of the original, which sometimes have more to do with a way of moving the eyes than the shape of the nose or the quantity and length of hair. We memorize a sort of gestalt of the face (or of the posture, or sometimes the gait) that can even resist changes in each individual property.

The extent to which the physiognomic type is schematic is well known to lovers, prone to having two apparently contradictory experiences. On the one hand, they are always under the impression they have spotted their beloved in the distance, only to realize later that they were wrong: this amounts to saying that desire led them to apply the physiognomic type with generosity, trying to make it applicable to many concrete tokens. On the other hand, when the loved one is absent, lovers try desperately to reconstruct his or her features in the memory and are constantly left disappointed by the fact that they do not have the same intense feeling that occurred when they saw their beloved directly. In this case they find out how the physiognomic type serves for the recognition of tokens but not as a surrogate for direct perception of the token (with the exception of subjects with an eidetic memory, like many artists who can draw a portrait relying on memory alone). In other words, they become aware of the remarkable difference between "recognition" and "recall" (see Evans 1982, 8).

But physiognomic types for individuals possess a characteristic that distinguishes them from generic CTs, which, however private they may be, can usually be made public in the form of an interpreted NC. It certainly happens that someone can easily recognize mice but cannot or has never had occasion to express the morphological features by which he recognizes them, and therefore we have no guarantee that with regard to mice this person has a type like that of other people (for idiosyncratic reasons he may recognize them only by their rapid movement, having no notion of their shape). When we talk about mice to this person, at best he would describe them as "disagreeable rodents that thrive in the home," and since this notion is a part of the common NC, we would come to the mistaken conclusion that this person's CT has the same format as our own and shares with our CT a knowledge of all the morphological features that are part of the area of common knowledge. But the circumstances of communal life make a case of this kind highly improbable, and while this could happen nowadays with mice (very seldom seen by the vast majority of people), it could happen only rarely with a cow and extremely rarely with a chair.

The same thing does not happen with physiognomic types of individuals. Note that the phenomenon occurs not only with humans but also, a fortiori, with individual animals, vegetables, and artifacts. Anyone will agree about what a dog, a bicycle, or a pipe looks like, but it is extremely hard to explain to someone what the dog Tom, my bicycle, or my pipe looks like. In the case of animals and objects, the generic features usually prevail, and we sometimes have trouble recognizing our car from among a large number of cars of the same make in the parking lot (unless our car has distinguishing marks). But the import of the problem is different with regard to human individuals.

I would recognize Johnny among a million individuals, and it would be the same for Mark, and yet the reasons why I recognize Johnny may be enormously different from those that lead Mark to recognize him. Mark and I could spend a lifetime referring to Johnny, and both of us would recognize him when we met him, without ever having had occasion to make public the features through which we identify him. We would notice the difference between our CTs only if one day we were both asked to collaborate on his police sketch: only then would I discover that Mark not only has never paid attention to the shape of Johnny's nose but also has ignored Johnny's abundance of hair or incipient baldness, and perhaps he considers him slim while I see him as robust. If someone were then to ask us who Johnny is, on interpreting the content of the name, we would notice not only that our interpretations fail to coincide but also that the boundaries between NC and MC would be very vague. Perhaps both of us might say that he is a human being, of the male sex, a professor of such and such at the university of such and such, but for me Johnny would be Louis's brother and the author of a renowned book on the Nahuatl language (which was Montezuma's native tongue), while Mark might show that he did not know these details. And yet just one of these details could enable a third party to associate the name Johnny with a very large number of other properties, and even push this third party to disinter, from his own memory, data useful for Johnny's identification. For his part, Mark might be the only one to know that Johnny has the property of being Jack the Ripper, and nobody would dream of saying that this is an insignificant property—even though it strikes me as being a part of the MC and not the NC.

Let us say then that with individuals three phenomena occur: (i) the frequently idiosyncratic nature of the CTs that make it possible to recognize individuals, (ii) the difficulty of interpreting these CTs publicly and therefore of providing instructions for identification, and (iii) the elasticity of the properties that may be expressed in terms of an NC. I think that this is one of the reasons many theoreticians maintain that the proper names of individuals have no content but designate their bearer directly. Clearly this is a foregone conclusion, because much of our life is spent defining (for others) the various individuals that we name by correlating their names to an occasionally vast series of properties, expressed through verbal descriptions and visual representations; but it is certain that such descriptions express features that in certain situations and for some people are *salient,* despite the fact that the features are not always salient for everybody, while there can be a notable gap between one interpretation and another.[45]

In 1970, I grew a beard. Twenty years later, I shaved it off for a few months, and I noticed that some friends did not recognize me at first sight when they met me, while others immediately established a normal interaction, as if they were unaware of the change.

I understood later that the subjects in the first category had known me only in the last twenty years, therefore when I already had a beard, while those in the second category had known me before I grew the beard. We construct physiognomic types of the persons we meet (almost always based on first impressions or, in exceptional cases, on the moment in which the impression was most vivid) and rely on that for the rest of our life—in a certain sense we adapt the features of the "new" token we meet to the initial type, rather than correct the type at every new encounter.[46]

This leads me to think that, just as caricatures emphasize features that are really to be found in the face portrayed, and just as the study of stupidity often serves to gain a better understanding of intelligence, much pathological behavior does little more than emphasize "normal" tendencies, which are usually controlled by and reabsorbed into more complex models of behavior. I am thinking of the studies on prosopagnosia and in particular of the fine analysis made by Sacks (1985) on the man who mistook his wife for a hat. Since not even Sacks knows what really happened inside Mr. P.'s black box, we can content ourselves with considering Mr. P.'s verbal interpretations.

P. does not recognize faces, but he is not just suffering from prosopagnosia, he also has generalized agnosia and does not recognize landscapes, objects, or figures: he focalizes his attention on particular features without managing to compose them in a global image. He gives a minute description of a rose but does not identify it as such until he smells its scent; he supplies a most detailed description of a glove but recognizes it only when he slips it on...

Sacks says (with reference to Kant) that P. was incapable of judgment, but I would say that P. did not possess *schemata* (and in fact in a bibliographical note Sacks admits that P. must have had a "Marr type" deficit and that he did not have a "primal sketch" for objects).

Nevertheless there is something in the way that P. laboriously recognized people that strikes us as being very close to the way in which we recognize them—except for the fact that P.'s behavior is a *caricature* of ours. First of all P. notices the details; he recognizes the photo of Einstein only because of the mustache and hair, and the photo of his brother Paul only because of the large teeth. This was like another patient mentioned by Sacks in the postscript: he did not recognize his wife and children but recognized some friends through certain relevant characteristics: a tic, a mole, extreme thinness.

It seems to me that in elaborating types of individuals, we normally proceed like this. We certainly have the ability to construct schemata and "primal sketches," we can abstract from an infinite number of particulars, we restrain our tendency to dwell on every minimal individual detail: nevertheless we accept a regulated imbalance, we tend to seize on salient aspects and retain them with greater care in our memory. My physiognomic type of Johnny is different from Mark's, because both of us (to a very limited extent) are like Mr. P. Ultimately it is continuous social interaction that obliges us not to be completely like Mr. P., because to be defined *normal,* it suffices (for better or worse) to keep to the *rules* laid down—and if necessary corrected—by the community, step by step.

3.7.8 CTs for formal individuals

Johnny is an individual, unique and unrepeatable, but Mark and I can both recognize him for different reasons. Now let us ask ourselves if there is a CT for Scott's *Ivanhoe* and Beethoven's Fifth. I would say that there is, because on opening the book (or at least on reading the first lines) or at the beginning of the composition, anyone who knows these two works well will recognize them. But what are these works of the intellect (I use this expression not only for literary, pictorial, architectonic, and musical works but also for philosophical and scientific essays)? Let us take another look at what was said in Eco (1976 3.4.6–8).

Johnny is an individual. The phoneme I pronounce is a *replica* of the phoneme type (there are variations in pronunciation, but the pertinent features established by the type are retained). Any first edition of *Ivanhoe* is a *double* of all the other books with the same title printed by the same publisher (in the sense that every copy has, at least on a molar level, all the properties of any other copy). But it is at the same time the clone of a "literary" archetype: the publishing type regards the substance of the expression (paper, font, binding), while the literary archetype regards the form of the content. In this case my paperback copy of *Ivanhoe* (paper and typographic problems excluded) is a clone of the same literary archetype of which the first copy of the 1819 edition is itself a clone. While from an antiquarian standpoint (in which the substance of the expression, the paper, becomes pertinent) a copy of the 1819 edition is more valuable, from a linguistic and literary standpoint (the form of the expression) my copy possesses all the pertinent properties of the archetype as it flowed from the author's pen (with the result that, immaterial of the edition, an actor could declaim passages from the text, producing the same substance of the sound expression and creating the same aesthetic effects).

The archetype of *Ivanhoe* is not a generic type, a form of Peircean Legisign: it looks more individual than Johnny, because Johnny would always be Johnny even if he lost his hair, teeth, and arms, whereas if someone were to change the beginning or the end or replace words here and there, *Ivanhoe* would become something else, a counterfeit, a case of plagiarism in part.

Is *Ivanhoe* as individual as the *Mona Lisa*? We know (Goodman 1968: 99) that there is a difference between *autographic* art, which does not allow of notation and is therefore not replicable (the *Mona Lisa*) and the *allographic* arts, replicable—some in accordance with rigorous criteria, such as books, but others in accordance with interpretative flexibility, such as music. But if one day it were possible to replicate every nuance of color, every brush stroke, and every detail of the canvas of the *Mona Lisa,* the difference between the original and the copy would have antiquarian value (just as in the world of rare books the more valuable copy between two copies of the same edition is the one signed by the author) but not semiotic value.

In short, whether we like it or not, *Ivanhoe* is an individual, even though it has the property of being reproducible (but in such a way that every one of its doubles has the same exquisite individual characteristics as the archetype).[47] That is why I can have a nongeneric physiognomic type of it. Not knowing what to call these strange types of individuals that are works of the intellect, and bearing in mind that their individuality concerns only the form of the expression and the content, not the substance, I would venture to call them *formal individuals*. Once we are on this path, other interesting formal individuals could be identified, but for the time being I shall restrict myself to applying the definition to those works of the intellect that are objects of direct perception.

Naturally, I might open a book I have already read and fail to recognize it from the first pages, but on the other hand if I caught a glimpse of Johnny from a distance and from behind and in the middle of a crowd into the bargain, I might feel just as puzzled. It is worth talking about this puzzlement, because it could upset our ideas on recognition and identification. Since the ploy of *Ivanhoe* or the *Fifth* seems too facile, let us try a mental experiment that involves a more problematic formal individual.

3.7.9 Recognizing SC2

All the electrical appliances at home are out of order following a blackout, except for the radio with the built-in CD player, which is battery-powered. Left in total darkness, all I can do is listen to my favorite composition, Bach's Second Suite for Solo Cello (which henceforward I shall call SC2), in a transcription for the treble recorder. Since it is pitch dark and I cannot read the CD labels, there is nothing for it but to try them all. To make the story more complicated, since I have a plaster cast on one foot but my friend Robert, like me a fan of SC2, is in the room, I ask him to grope his way to the CD player-radio and to do the job in my stead. Therefore I say to him: *Please, go to find me SC2*, precisely as if I were asking him to go meet our mutual friend Johann Sebastian at the railway station. I have started an operation of reference that presumes, on Robert's part, the capacity to identify the referent, or the *designatum* of my linguistic act.[48]

As far as a musical piece is concerned, the notion of individuality seems compromised by the fact that different executions of the same composition can be made by different performers. In such a case, however (and for those sensible of these differences), the individual would be not SC2 but that thing known as SC2/Brüggen, as distinct from SC2/Rampal. In this mental experiment of ours, we shall behave as if there were only one execution of SC2, reproduced on thousands of records. In this case recognizing SC2 is like leafing through various books and recognizing *Ivanhoe*. And in fact this is exactly how it happens with the majority of listeners, who always recognize SC2 in its various executions despite the differences in interpretation.

What are the instructions that Robert possesses in order to identify the individual, and to what extent do they coincide with those at my disposal?

Wittgenstein (*Tractatus*, 4.104) says that "the gramophone record, the musical thought, the score, the waves of sound, all stand to one another in that pictorial internal relation, which holds between language and the world. To all of them the logical structure is common." Let us leave aside the strong assumption of Wittgenstein's theory of *Abbildung*, which would have linguistic propositions as icons of the state of things to which they refer (the later Wittgenstein was far more prudent with regard to this). Considering only the musical example, it seems clear to me that we are faced with two different phenomena.[49]

We have the iconic relation between sound waves and the grooves in the vinyl of the disc or the sequences of discrete signals in the CD. We are certainly dealing with cast relations, with a primary iconism like that discussed in 2.8, a relation that would establish itself even in the absence of any mind to interpret it and that continues to subsist both when the sound waves are recorded analogically and when they are translated digitally.

There is a different relation between the physical phenomenon and its transcription on the stave, on the one hand, and between it and the "musical idea," on the other. Transcription to the stave certainly represents a (highly conventional) way of rendering the musical idea public. That the procedure is conventional (highly codified) does not eliminate the fact that the sequence of the written notes is motivated by the sequence of the sounds imagined or tried out on an instrument by the composer. We are faced with one of those cases that in *A Theory of Semiotics* I defined as *ratio difficilis*, in which the form of the expression is motivated by the form of the content.

The problem arises when we wish to define the form of the content, which seems to correspond to what Wittgenstein called the musical idea, which is that ideal of "good form" upon which the performer is trying to confer substance while interpreting the notes on the stave. What does musical idea mean? Whatever it means, it is certainly that formal individuality that I must identify in order to recognize SC2 as such. But is it also that sequence of notes that Bach imagined, a Dynamical Object whose whereabouts (ontologically speaking) we no longer know, in the same sense that we do not know the whereabouts of the Square Triangle? One would have to say that the Immediate Object should be the physiognomic type of this Dynamical Object, otherwise how could we clone it in an intersubjectively acceptable way and recognize each of its clones? Nonetheless in my mental experiment the matter gets more complicated, because Bach conceived his suite *for the cello* (not for the recorder), and therefore his first musical idea also included features of timbre that were changed in the transcription. But I have not chosen such a damned complex situation by chance. The fact is that when people who know SC2 only in the transcription for recorder hear the piece performed for the first time by the cello, they have a moment of puzzlement, but usually by the end they will have recognized with surprise that it is the same composition. On the other hand we recognize any given song whether it is performed on the guitar or the piano, and it is therefore worth sticking to a physiognomic type so schematic that it can do without parameters such as timbre, which is no small matter.[50]

It is clear that, if the relation between the sound waves and the grooves of the disc is a case of primary iconism—and if the relation between Brüggen's execution and the notes of the score is already substantiated by multiple interpretative inferences, choices, and accentuations of pertinency—we have now arrived, with the physiognomic type, at an extremely complex process that seems very difficult to take account of. What is the musical idea I am considering? Must it correspond to Brüggen's? Certainly not. My physiognomic type might be different from Robert's. I can sight-read the score of the transcription for recorder of SC2, and if I try to play from memory, I can continue for a minute or two, then I stop and can no longer remember how it goes, while Robert, who can also play the recorder a bit, has listened to the piece thousands of times and can recognize it, but could not play it if he tried.

Therefore Brüggen, Robert, and I can recognize SC2, but we refer to (or bring into play) three different (different, that is, in terms of complexity and refinement or definition) physiognomic types. Can we speak of three "acoustic images" that are equivalent for the purposes of simple recognition? What is an acoustic image? It is not enough to say that I recognize Johann Sebastian on the basis of visual features and SC2 on the basis of acoustic features? The fact is that Johann Sebastian's physiognomic features are presented to me all together (even though inspecting them may sometimes take time), while the acoustic features of the musical composition are presented to me distributed over time. But our problem, in the dark room, is not a matter of recognizing SC2 after having listened to the whole record. That would be like recognizing Johann Sebastian only after having spent a long time making him walk backward and forward, smile, speak, and after a police-style interrogation regarding his past (something that happens only in exceptional circumstances). In order to satisfy my request, Robert must recognize SC2 in a fairly short time (perhaps on the basis of a few random selections). This is a problem we come across very often, for example, when we switch on the radio and listen to a piece that we certainly know but cannot identify straight off the bat. If Robert needs to listen to the whole composition before recognizing SC2, he has lost even before he has begun, so let him bring me *The Well-Tempered Clavier,* and I'll be just as happy, because I'm not hard to please.

Can we say that the physiognomic schema of SC2 is no different from that of the Mona Lisa? I should say not. If I can recognize the Mona Lisa, it is because I have seen it before; if I have seen it, I would know how to interpret it verbally (a half-length portrait of a smiling woman, seen against a landscape...), and even though I am only a very poor drawer, I could make a sketch of it that, no matter how rough the sketch was, would still be enough to make the *Mona Lisa* distinguishable from Botticelli's *Venus.* But I can recognize SC2 even without being able to play so much as the first few notes. And let it not be said that this is due solely to my or Robert's incapacity. If we know Traviata, all of us are perfectly capable of humming a few notes of "Sempre libera degg'io" or "Libiam nei lieti calici." But you can know Don Giovanni like the back of your hand, and nevertheless I challenge anyone who is not a professional singer to hum "Non si pasce di cibo mortale." Yet as soon as we hear it, we know instantly that it is the Commendatore who is singing.

We might be tempted to say that one recognizes a "style." But apart from the difficulty experienced in trying to define a stylistic schema (a musicologist can easily tell us what characteristics we seize on when we identify a piece as Bach and not Beethoven, but the trouble is that, in identifying the piece, we do not know what we are identifying), our problem is how we distinguish the second suite without confusing it with the first. Here I think that even the musicologist, so good at analyzing the melodic, rhythmic, and harmonic devices proper to Bach's style, could do no more than refer us to the stave: SC2 is that musical individual composed of this and that set of notes, and if the notes are different, then we are dealing with another composition.

What Robert should instinctively prepare to search for after my mentioning SC2 is something of which he possesses not a highly complex cognitive type (like that of Brüggen) but a partial physiognomic type, like a clue that encourages him with regard to the possibility, if necessary, of executing a more complex combination of "pattern recognition skills" (Ellis 1995: 87) and that curiously enough can also imply the capacity to recognize acoustic features he was unaware of when he associated a partial type with the name.

Ellis (1995: 95 ff.) suggests that we have memorized a simple melodic-rhythmic pattern, the first five notes, for example. I would say more, that we recognize some compositions not at the beginning but at a certain point, and therefore these five (or twenty) crucial notes could be anywhere, according to the physiognomic type that each of us has elaborated. In any event we would still be dealing with a *truncated* response: those few notes "give me the feeling of confidence that I could execute the piece."[51]

But what happens to people who cannot "carry a tune"? We must be careful here: I am talking not about clinical cases of tone deafness but of those people who can recognize a tune but are moderately "off key," and so when they try to hum a few bars, any listeners ask them to stop. People of this type would have in mind (or in any mnemonic recording apparatus standing in for mind), in some mysterious way, the first five or twenty notes, even though they would not be able to reproduce them (either with their voice or on the ocarina). The case is not unlike that of the lover constantly seeking to call up the image of his beloved; he is never satisfied with his evocation, would be absolutely unable to draw her portrait, and yet as soon as he meets her, he recognizes her. Faced with the greed of their own desire, all lovers are imaginatively off key.

The person who cannot carry a tune possesses a minimal schema of recognition, a feebler version of the one that would allow a great number of people to draw the silhouette of a mouse, or the outline of the Italian peninsula, and yet when he is subjected to the stimulus, he recognizes the configuration. Such a person has no idea what a musical fifth is, nor could he reproduce one with his voice, but he could recognize one (even without being able to name it as such) as a known configuration when he hears it.

And so we recognize SC2 by features that are sometimes melodic, sometimes rhythmic, and sometimes having to do with timbre, and on the basis of a "truncated" physiognomic type, in which pertinency has perhaps been assigned to features wholly absent from other people's physiognomic type. While a compendious set of encyclopedic facts (such as knowing that SC2 is a composition structured in such and such a way, written by Bach on such and such a date, etc.) may be of no use for purposes of recognition, truncated and often entirely idiosyncratic types may be sufficient.

The fact that we often proceed by truncated cognitive types reminds one of Peirce's pragmatic maxim (CP 5.9): "In order to ascertain the meaning of an intellectual conception one should consider what practical consequences might conceivably result by necessity from the truth of that conception; and the sum of these consequences will constitute the entire meaning of the conception." In fact, in order to know whether to agree with another person's perceptual judgment *This is an execution of SC2* or in order to verify my own (hazarded after not very many notes of the Prelude), I would have to know all its remote illative consequences: including the fact that the piece must continue in a certain way, recognizable when I listen to the notes. But as far as SC2 is concerned, it is also possible that I have always listened only to the "Allemande" and the "Courante" and that therefore I have no idea (and never will have one) of what the closing "Gigue" is like. In recognizing, we simply guess that in all probability the end will be as it should. In short, we maneuver vague but optative physiognomic schemata.

In these cases the only guarantee is the consensus of the Community—and too bad if the Community in my mental experiment was reduced to only two individuals. The series of interpretants will see to the rest: when the power comes back on, we shall both be able to read the title of the piece on the record sleeve, and only then, via interpretants publicly registered in the encyclopedia, will the Community tell us that we did not make a mistake.

3.7.10 Some open problems

We have admitted that, for all that it is truncated, I possess a cognitive type of SC2. Is it identical to the nuclear content? I should say not, because, however rough the nuclear content may be, it should be possible to interpret it, while we have ascertained that someone can recognize SC2 without being able to hum so much as a note or to write the first notes on the stave. Therefore the only interpretation that this person could provide of the name SC2 would be "composition written by Johann Sebastian Bach at first for cello, on such and such a date...," and we would be dealing with a verbal interpretation. Or else one could show the corresponding score, and we would be dealing with interpretation by ostension of the graphical interpretation of a sound event. Therefore truncated CTs have the characteristic of being wholly detached from the content, be it nuclear or otherwise.[52]

Are there other objects of knowledge that reveal the same phenomenon of detachment?

A case very similar to that of SC2 regards CTs of places, private, sufficient for subjective recognition, hard to interpret publicly, wholly detached from the NC. If I were blindfolded and taken to my hometown, and then left at the corner of a road, with the blindfold removed, I would recognize instantly—or fairly quickly—where I was. I could say the same thing if I were left in Milan, Bologna, Paris, New York, Chicago, San Francisco, London, Jerusalem, or Rio de Janeiro, cities I would recognize by the skyline if nothing else (see Lynch 1966). This eminently visual knowledge of mine is still private, because it would be hard for me to give someone a description of my hometown that would enable him to recognize it in analogous circumstances. What would I say? That it is a city whose streets are usually parallel, that there is a very high bell tower in the shape of a pencil and a river that separates the tower from a citadel? Not enough; the description would not be sufficient to identify the place. Sometimes these private CTs are most vivid; we can tell ourselves what our town is like, without being able to tell anybody else. It seems that visual experiences are easier to put into words than musical ones, but while I (if not Robert) could always interpret SC2 by whistling the first notes, I would not be able to interpret for anybody else the shape (unmistakable for me) of via Dante in Alessandria (a task that could be carried out, laboriously, by an architect, a painter, or a photographer; however, in that case we would be talking not about CT but MC).

In addition my cognitive type would have nothing to do with the NC that I have corresponded to the name of the city (which would be reduced to "Alessandria is a city in Piedmont"). Even in cases in which the NC includes some curious particular, such as the fact that in Rome there are the ruins of a great amphitheater or that New York is a city with lots of skyscrapers, the information would not make it possible to distinguish Rome from Nîmes or New York from Chicago—nor would it allow me to recognize the fact that I was in Rome, if I were deposited in a street in the vicinity of Piazza Navona (something that in reality I could do perfectly well).

One could continue with this typology of dubious cases. I can easily recognize Sharon Stone when I see her in a film, but I cannot explain to others how to recognize her (over and beyond saying that she is a glamorous blonde, but that's not much to go on), and yet I associate her name with an NC (human being of the female sex, American actress, starred in *Basic Instinct*). On the highway I can easily tell a Lancia from a Volvo, I have an NC associated with both makes, but I cannot tell anyone how to distinguish them, except in a vague fashion.

It is clear that with regard to our way of approaching the objects of the world (and of talking about them to others), all is not crystal clear, and not everything goes smoothly. When things do not go at all, there is no problem, it simply means that someone does not know something, just as one does not know the meanings of many words or cannot recognize unfamiliar objects. The problem arises when things should *not* work and yet in some way they *do,* as in the case of the recognition of SC2.

I think we have to stick to a fairly liberal view: for many of our cognitive experiences, CT and NC coincide; for others, they do not. I do not think this admission is a surrender. It is only a philosophical contribution to an ongoing debate. Let us content ourselves for the time being with clear-cut cases (the mouse, the chair), and let us ascribe the ambiguous cases to the list of phenomena of which we still know very little.

3.7.11 From the public CT to that of the artist

A CT is always a private matter, but it becomes public when it is interpreted as an NC, while a public NC can provide instructions for the formation of CTs. In a certain sense, therefore, although CTs are private, they are continuously subjected to public control, and the Community educates us step by step to match our own to those of others. The same thing happens with the control of CTs, as with hasty off-the-cuff assertions. If I say it is raining when my epidermis is struck by imperceptible particles of humidity, but water is not in fact falling from the sky, people will tell me that what I have perceived is mist and not rain, and how to apply the two terms correctly when I put my perceptual judgment into words. CTs become public, because in the course of our education they are taught us, reviewed, corrected, and enhanced according to the state of the art as sanctioned by the Community. Our introduction to the dog begins with someone's having us note that it has four legs and not two like a hen, and we are encouraged to see its friendly nature as pertinent; we are invited not to be afraid, to caress it, and we are warned that it will yelp if we tread on its tail. We are told very early on that the sun is in reality far bigger than it seems to the naked eye, and far bigger than we could imagine.

It has been said that the physiognomic types of individuals can be very private. And yet in communicational interaction even physiognomic types are, so to speak, brought together by chains of interpretations: it is possible that Mark and I have a different CT of Johnny, but we usually exchange descriptions of Johnny with other friends, we remark on his way of laughing, we say that he is stouter than Robert, we see photographs that we deem a better or worse likeness of him… In short, we establish (at least with regard to our private circle of acquaintances or to many public figures) sets of what we might call iconographic conventions, and the extent to which these count in the case of public figures emerges from the fact that we recognize them even in caricatures (the caricature being the art of accentuating, or even of discovering, the most salient typical features of a face).

Very private types could belong to artists. A painter has a perception of the difference between colors that is much more refined than that of an ordinary person, and Michelangelo certainly had a cognitive type of the human body more complex than a 3-D model. But this does not at all imply that his type was destined to remain private and idiolectic. On the contrary, a 3-D model is clearly the elementary type on which we generally agree when we perceive a human body; but the continuous interpretation of anatomists, painters, sculptors, or photographers serves to modify and enrich it. Only for some, obviously: there is a division of cognitive labor as there is of linguistic labor, and as there are elaborated and restricted codes, in the same sense in which a chemist has a more extensive notion of water than ordinary people. Just as in linguistic communication transactions between more or less restricted or broadened competences are always being made, so it also happens in the "trade" in CTs.

This is why it is said that artists enhance our capacity to perceive the environment. An artist (and this is what the Russian formalists meant by their concept of defamiliarization) continuously tries to revise current CTs, as if everything were perceived as a hitherto unknown object. Cézanne or Renoir trained us to look in a different way, in certain circumstances of particular felicitousness or perceptual freshness, at foliage, fruit, or the complexion of a young girl.

There are lines of resistance in the stimulating field that oppose uncontrolled artistic invention (or that oblige the artist to portray objects not of our world but of a possible world). This is why the artist's suggestions are not always completely absorbed by the Community. It would be hard for us to conceive a CT of the female body inspired by Duchamp's *Mariée mise à nu*, and yet the work of artists always tries to call our perceptual schemata into question, if in no other way than by inviting us to recognize that in certain circumstances things could also appear to us differently, or that there are alternative possibilities of schematization, which make some features of the object pertinent in a provocatively abnormal way (the skeletal lankiness of bodies, for Giacometti; the uncontrollable tendencies of the flesh and muscle, for Botero).

I recall an evening in which people were playing parlor games, including a variant of "statues," in which the onlookers had to guess which work of art the players were miming. At a certain point a (well-composed) group of girls presented themselves with their limbs and faces twisted into distorted positions. Almost everybody recognized the reference to *Demoiselles d'Avignon*. If the human body can interpret Picasso's representation of it, then that representation had caught certain possibilities of the human body.

Chapter Four

———◦◉◦———

THE PLATYPUS BETWEEN DICTIONARY
AND ENCYCLOPEDIA

4.1 MOUNTAINS AND MOUNTAINS

As usual, let us imagine a situation. When Sandra tells me she is going to cross Australia from north to south by car, I tell her that she must not forget to visit Ayers Rock, which stands in the center of the continent and is one of the world's many Eighth Wonders. I add that if, en route between Darwin and Adelaide, she passes through Alice Springs, she should then head southwest into the desert until she sees a mountain, hard to miss because it rises in the center of the plain like Chartres cathedral in the middle of the Beauce: this is Ayers Rock, a fabulous orographic formation that changes color according to the time of day and is stunning at sunset.

I have given her instructions not only for finding but also for identifying Ayers Rock, and yet I feel slightly ill at ease, as if I were deceiving her. And therefore I tell her that while I was telling the truth when I told her that (ia) *Ayers Rock is a mountain*, I am nonetheless also telling the truth if at the same time I state that (iia) *Ayers Rock is not a mountain*. Obviously, Sandra reacts by reminding me that a minimum of truth-functional good breeding requires that if (ia) is true, then (iia) must be false, and vice versa.

So I reiterate the difference between NC and MC (in this story, Sandra has already read this book, apart from this paragraph), and I explain to her that Ayers Rock displays all the characteristics that we attribute to mountains, and that if we were asked to divide the objects we know into mountains and nonmountains, then we should certainly put Ayers Rock in the first category. It is true that we are accustomed to recognize a mountain as something that rises to a great height after being preceded by hilly slopes that get steadily steeper and steeper, while Ayers Rock rises solitary and precipitous from the middle of the plain; but the fact that we are dealing with a curious, atypical mountain should not worry us more than the fact that the ostrich, insofar as it is a bird, is equally curious and atypical, without its being perceived as less of a bird for this reason. Nevertheless, from a scientific point of view, Ayers Rock is not a mountain, it is a *stone:* it is a single stone—in other words, a monolith planted in the ground as if a giant had hurled it down from the sky. Ayers Rock is a mountain from the point of view of the CT, but it is not from the point of view of the MC, i.e., of a competence definable as petrological or lithological or what have you.

Sandra understands very well why I did not tell her to proceed southwest until she saw a stone—because in that case she would have gone on with her gaze fixed on the ground without looking up. However, she might say that, as I am in the mood to play with logical paradoxes, I would do better to rewrite (ia) and (iia) in this way: (ib) *Ayers Rock is a mountain* and (iib) *Ayers Rock is not a* MOUNTAIN. In this way it would be clear that (ib) asserts that Ayers Rock has the perceptual qualities of a mountain, while (iib) would assert that it is not a MOUNTAIN in a categorial system. Naturally Sandra would use her voice to emphasize, with suprasegmental features, the use of small capitals, precisely to show that terms written in such characters stand for what compositional semantics calls dictionary properties, which are semantic primitives for some, and which in any case imply a categorial organization, in the sense of the expression as used in the preceding chapter.

But at that point she would have me notice a curious paradox.

The supporters of a dictionary representation maintain that such representations take account of relations within the language, leaving aside elements of knowledge of the world, while knowledge in an encyclopedic format presupposes extralinguistic knowledge. In order to provide a rigorous explanation of the functioning of language, the supporters of a dictionary representation maintain that we must turn to a package of semantic categories that are organized hierarchically (such as OBJECT, ANIMAL VS. VEGETABLE, MAMMAL VS. REPTILE) and that are of such a kind that—even when we have no knowledge of the world—various inferences can be made, of the type *If mammal, then animal; If this is a mammal, then it is not a reptile; It is impossible for something to be at once a reptile and not an animal; If this is a reptile, then it is not a vegetable;* and many other pleasant apothegms that, according to the experts, we habitually utter when, for example, we realize we have picked up a viper instead of an asparagus spear.

Encyclopedic knowledge, on the other hand, would be uncoordinated by nature, with an uncontrollable format, and the encyclopedic content of *dog* would have to include practically all that is and could be known about dogs, even details such as the fact that my sister has a bitch called Best—in short, a knowledge that would be too much even for Borges's Funes el Memorioso. Naturally it is not quite like this, because we can consider as encyclopedic knowledge only those items that the Community has in some way registered publicly (and moreover it is maintained that encyclopedic competence is shared across sectors, according to a sort of linguistic division of labor, or activated in different ways and formats according to the context). But there is no doubt that, with regard to the events and objects of this world, not to mention those of other worlds, there are always new facts to learn, and therefore those who find the encyclopedic format hard to handle are not wrong.

Nonetheless the curious accident has occurred whereby, given that the repertoires that succinctly record the properties of terms are called "dictionaries" while those that indulge in complex descriptions are called "encyclopedias," everybody thinks that dictionary competence is the indispensable one for the use of language.

Instead, what the story of Ayers Rock tells us is that, in order to recognize that object and to be able to talk about it every day, the perceptual (not linguistic) characteristic of appearing like a mountain (on the basis of many factual properties) counts for a very great deal, while the fact that it is not a MOUNTAIN but a STONE is a datum reserved only for an elite that shares a vast encyclopedic competence. Therefore Sandra would point out to me that people, when speaking plainly, run on encyclopedia mode, while only the learned turn to the dictionary. Nor would she be wrong.

The whole business could be confirmed in historic terms too. If we take a look at Hellenistic and medieval encyclopedias, we find only descriptions that either tell us what something looks like (for Alexander Neckham, the crocodile was a *serpens aquaticus bubalis infestus, magnae quantitatis*) or how something can be found (the instructions for capturing a basilisk). In general there is an accumulation of largely anecdotal features, such as in the *Cambridge Bestiary:* "The cat is called *musio* because it is traditionally the enemy of mice. The more common *catus* derives from *capturare,* or—according to others—because *captat,* i.e., it sees. It has in fact such acute sight as to be able to pierce the shadows of the night with flashing eyes."[1] When we get to dictionaries such as the one published by the Italian Accademia della Crusca in 1612, we find the definition of *cat* (entered, with admirable political correctness, in the feminine form *gatta*, even though the rest is then written using the masculine pronoun): "Known animal, kept in houses, owing to its particular enmity for mice, which it kills." And that's that.

As can be seen, once upon a time there were no dictionary-type definitions (except for the traditional "rational mortal animal"). The first attempts in this regard are found in the dictionaries of the perfect languages, such as in the *Essay toward a Real Character* by John Wilkins (1668), who attempted to define the furnishings of the entire universe by genus and *differentia*, basing himself on the first attempts at scientific taxonomy. But, after having worked out a table of 40 major Genera, subdivided into 251 peculiar Differences, from which he derived 2,030 Species, Wilkins (if we take, for example, the classification of "viviparous clawed beasts") managed to distinguish the fox from the dog but not the dog from the wolf (see Eco 1993: 242, fig. 12.2). And then if we want to know what a dog is and what it does, we have to go to consult the Differences, which are not presented as dictionary-type primitives but are authentic encyclopedic descriptions of empirical properties (e.g., rapacious viviparous animals generally have six short, pointed incisors and two long fangs; the "dog-kind" have an oblong head that distinguishes them from the "cat-kind," which have a round head; and the dog is differentiated from the wolf, because the former "is noted for tameness" and the latter for "wildness and enmity to sheep"). The dictionary schema is an instrument of classification, not an instrument of definition; it is like the Dewey method of librarianship, which allows us to identify a given book from among the thousands of shelves in a library, and to infer its subject matter (if we know the code) but not the specific content.[2]

Given therefore that scientific taxonomies took on a rough shape in the seventeenth century and were established organically only starting from the eighteenth century, we would seem to be led to the paradoxical conclusion that before then (in the absence of dictionary structures), from the appearance of *Homo sapiens* up to at least the seventeenth century, since a dictionary competence did not exist, no one managed to use his own language decently (Aristotle and Plato or Descartes and Pascal spoke, but they could not understand each other) and no one managed to translate from one language to another. Since historical experience contradicts this inference, one must conclude that, while the absence of a dictionary competence did not prevent humanity from speaking and understanding for millennia, that absence is, if not irrelevant, certainly not decisive for the purposes of linguistic competence.

Perhaps it would be sufficient to state that the NC is mostly composed of features of an encyclopedic nature, often disorganized, while forms of dictionary competence appear only in representations of MC. But it's not that simple. The authors of the medieval bestiaries would perhaps fail a zoology exam, but it cannot be denied that in their own way they were trying to constitute categories when they defined the crocodile (in terms of NC) as a water snake, evidently by taking for granted that this category was opposed to that of land snakes.

In addition, if there are semiosic primitives, precategorial distinctions such as that of "animal" (in the sense of animated beings), when we decide to perceive a mosquito as an animal, we collocate it (in a rather confused way) in a categorial order, just as we would put a chicken and an edible mushroom together among "comestible things," thereby opposing them to a rhinoceros or a poisonous mushroom (dangerous things).

4.2 FILES AND DIRECTORIES

Let us try therefore to compare our cognitive processes, from the first perceptions to the constitution of any knowledge, not necessarily scientific, to the organization of our computer.

We perceive things as sets of properties (a dog is a hairy animal that has four legs, a tongue that hangs out, and barks, etc.). In order to recognize or identify things, we construct *files* (which may be private or public: a file can be our own work, or it may have been communicated to us by the Community). As the file is gradually defined, by our judging similarities or differences, we decide to insert it (or the Community presents it to us as already inserted) in a given directory. Sometimes, when we need to look something up, we call the tree of directories up on the screen and, if we have a vague idea of how the tree is organized, we know that files of a certain type must be in a given directory. As we continue to gather data, we can decide to shift a file from one directory to another. But as the task gets more complex, it becomes necessary to split certain directories up into subdirectories, and at a certain point we may decide to restructure the entire tree of directories. A scientific taxonomy is no more than a tree of directories and subdirectories, and the only difference between the taxonomies of the seventeenth century and those of the nineteenth was that the tree of directories was simply (simply?) restructured on a series of occasions.

But this computer-inspired example conceals a trap. The files in a computer are full (in the sense that they are collections of information), while the directories are empty—in other words, they can be collections of files but, if there are no files, they contain no other information. In a scientific taxonomy, on the other hand (as has already been pointed out in Eco 1984, 2.3), when, let's say, the CANIDS are inserted among the MAMMALS, saying that dogs and wolves are mammals does not mean only that they are housed in the directory called MAMMALS: the scientist also knows that MAMMALS (be they CANIDS or FELIDS) usually reproduce in a similar manner. This means that the taxonomist cannot open a directory headed, let's say, CRYPTOTHERIA, and decide to put any old files in there should the need arise: he must have decided what the characteristics (perhaps brand-new) of the CRYPTOTHERIA are, so that—on the basis of the presence of these characteristics in a given animal—he can justify the insertion of the animal's file in that directory. This ensures that when the taxonomist says that a certain animal is a MAMMAL, he knows what general characteristics it possesses, even though he does not yet know if it looks more like an ox or a dolphin.

Therefore every directory ought to contain a "label" with a series of data on the common characteristics of the objects described in its files. (All we need do is think that it is possible, as is already the case with the files in certain operating systems, to register the name of a directory not as a simple cipher but as a *text:* in such a case, the MAMMALS directory would be registered as MAMMALS (POSSESSING SUCH AND SUCH REPRODUCTIVE PROPERTIES). As a matter of fact, taxonomic terms such as MAMMAL, OVIPAROUS, FISSIPED, or UNGULATE express a great number of qualities. In the Linnaean system, names such as *Poa bulbata* contain all the information that Pitton de Tournefort was still obliged to list as "Gramen Xerampelinum, miliacea, praetenui, ramosaque, sparsa canicula, sive xerampelinum congener, arvense, aestivum, gravem minutissimo semine" (see Rossi 1997: 274).

Such a condition is not at all indispensable for a dictionary semantics: if the species of the PRISSIDS were put in the subdirectory of the family of the PROSIDS, let's say, and if the PROSIDS belonged to the order of the PROCEIDS, it would not be necessary to know the properties possessed by a proceid or a prosid to be able to make (highly accurate) inferences of the type *If this is a prissid, then it is definitely a prosid, and it is not possible for something to be a prissid and not a proceid*. Unfortunately, while this is the way we reason when performing exercises in logic (laudable activity), and the way in which a zoology student who has memorized the book without understanding the argument (deplorable activity) attempts to answer an examination question, it is not the way we reason in order to understand either the words we use or the concepts that correspond to them, so it would not be unlikely that, on hearing it said that all prissids are prosids, somebody might just ask for some supplementary information.

But even if the dialectic between directory and files can be compared to that between Dictionary and Encyclopedia, or between categorial knowledge and knowledge by properties, this division is not homologous with that between NC and MC. We do in fact also organize directories at the level of NC (by putting cats among the animals and stones among inanimate objects), but the organizational criteria are less strict, and so it is all right, and it has been all right by us for a long time, to put the files on whales in the directory marked "fish," and when we recognize that Ayers Rock has many of the properties of mountains, we unthinkingly store it in the untidy file of mountainous objects, without putting too fine a point on things.

Therefore by dictionary competence I mean something that limits itself to registering (both in terms of NC and MC) that a given concept belongs on a certain node in the tree of directories. Encyclopedic competence, on the other hand, involves both a knowledge of the names of the directories and the files and a knowledge of their contents. The totality of files and directories (those currently registered and even those that have been deleted and reordered or rewritten in the course of time) represents what on various occasions I have called Encyclopedia as a regulative idea—the Library of Libraries, a postulate of a globality of knowledge that cannot be realized by any single speaker, a perpetually increasing treasure most of which has not been explored by the Community.

4.3 WILD CATEGORIZATION

At the level of NC there is a continuous organizing and reordering of "wild" categories, most of which spring from the recognition of constant precategorial features. For example, in the Western world the chicken is considered one of the edible animals while the dog is not, but in some Asiatic regions the dog is a fully fledged member of the edible category and is kept around the house much like a turkey or a pig in the West, in the knowledge that at a certain point it will have to be eaten.[3] But it is in the specialized sector of the MC that negotiations become more punctilious.

Just think of the notions of mineral, vegetable, or insect. Many speakers, who would hesitate about recognizing that a certain animal (the porpoise, for example) is a mammal, would cheerfully admit that the fly or the flea is an insect. Could it be said that we are dealing with a zoological category, at first proper to an MC, which in the course of time has been captured, so to speak, by the NC? I should say not: this would happen if we noticed that common competence has accepted the idea that cows are mammals (a notion learned at school), but there is no doubt that people were recognizing insects before taxonomists decided to label a certain class ARTHROPODS.

This happens because MAMMAL was coined in 1791 as a technical term, preceded by MAMMALIA (extended for the first time to include the CETACEANS), in Linnaeus's *Systema Naturae* of 1758, and it depends on a certain functional criterion that takes the reproductive system into account. On the contrary, *insectus,* a Latin calque from the Greek *entoma zoa,* meant a "cut" animal: this is an interpretation of a morphological feature that takes into account the typical form of these little animals (from the instinctive feeling that those bodies might be cut and divided where they are joined in a bottleneck shape or by rings). The "wild" category of insects still has

such strength that we commonly give the name insect to many animals that zoologists do not recognize as such, such as spiders
(which are ARTHROPODS but ARACHNIDS instead of INSECTS).[4] In this
way, on the level of NC we might find it odd if someone said that a
spider is not an insect, while on the level of MC the spider is *not* an
INSECT.

Therefore "insect" is either a semiosic primitive, of a precategorial type, which ordinary speech has presented to naturalists (while
the mammals are a category that, if anything, has been given to ordinary speech by naturalists), or it is a wild category in any case. In
categorizing wildly, we group objects by what use they have for us,
by their relation to our survival, by formal analogies, et cetera. Our
indifference in retaining the fact that an animal is a mammal is due
to the fact that the scientific category MAMMAL includes animals
that are not only very different to look at but also very different to
deal with (e.g., there are mammals that we eat and mammals that
eat us), while insects strike us as being more or less morphologically alike, and all equally noisome.

For the speaker, these wild categories usually sum up, almost
stenographically, a large number of features and also implicitly
contain instructions for identification or retrieval. When Marconi
(1977: 64–65) suggests that, even if we do not know what uranium
is or looks like but are told that it is a mineral, we could probably
identify it when it was showed to us together with an unknown
fruit and an unknown animal, he is referring to the wild category
of minerals, not to MINERALS. In fact, if we asked someone devoid
of any scientific knowledge to tell an ARTHROPOD from a spider, a
millipede, and an orthopedic prosthesis, he would not know what
to do. But when we know (roughly) that uranium is a mineral, we
go to look in the wild directory of minerals, just as when we are
told that Ayers Rock is a mountain, we go to look in the wild directory of mountains (and if they had told us that it was a stone, we
would have gone to look in a directory where we would not have
found good instructions for its identification).

Now, if we consider categorial (or dictionary) competence by referring to its scientific model, we have been told that one of the

characteristics of that competence is that it is composed of *indelible* features: if we know that a porpoise is a CETACEAN, a CETACEAN is a MAMMAL, and a MAMMAL is an ANIMAL, it cannot be said that something is a porpoise but not an ANIMAL, and if (just to avoid always using canonical examples) on a certain planet all the porpoises were robots, the fact that they were not ANIMALS would prevent us from saying they were porpoises: you can have toy porpoises, pseudoporpoises, virtual porpoises, but not *porpoises*. On the other hand, a folk competence tells us that a porpoise is like a dolphin with a rounded nose and a triangular dorsal fin (and so on, with regard to the habitat, habits, intelligence, and edibility of the porpoise), but any feature could be legitimately deleted, because the cognitive type does not organize the features hierarchically, nor does it rigidly fix number (of features) or precedence. We can recognize porpoises with prognathous or malformed or *retroussé* snouts and serrated dorsal fins, porpoises that would not win any porpoise beauty prizes but are porpoises for all that, just as much as their better-looking kin.

The features of a scientific taxonomy cannot be deleted, because they are organized into a series of embedded hyperonyms and hyponyms: if a spider is an ARACHNID, it cannot not be an ARTHROPOD, otherwise the entire categorial system would collapse; but precisely because a spider is an ARACHNID, it cannot be an INSECT at the same time.

Also on the level of NC our knowledge is organized into files and directories, but the organization is not hierarchical. Let us look over some features of the definition of mouse examined in 3.4.3:

People think that they are all of the same kind.
People think they live in or near places where people live.
A person could hold one easily in one hand (most people wouldn't want to hold them).

This means that the mouse file can be put both in the "animals that live in the home" category (which includes the cat file) and in the "repugnant animals" category, together with flies and cockroaches (which can also infest the home) as well as caterpillars and snakes. The same file, depending on the occasion, can be put in several directories simultaneously and taken from one to the other according to the context. And in fact, Lévi-Strauss reminds us that the Savage Mind proceeds by *bricolage*, which is a form of patchwork that does not envisage any hierarchical organization.[5]

But if this is the case, the file does not necessarily imply the directory, as in scientific taxonomies; in other words, it is very easy to deny entailment when entailment is not convenient. Those who breed charming white mice do not put them in the category of repugnant animals. In Australia, the rabbit is considered a harmful pest. In certain Chinese markets, people display cages containing things that they consider delicacies but we perceive as loathsome rats, and if they were to appear in our lofts, we would be terrified. On the other hand, chickens have been listed among farmyard animals for millennia, while that directory (if not already for us, at least for our descendants) will sooner or later contain only one species of chicken, known as free-range, while all its kin will be classified as factory-farmed animals. On the level of MC, a chicken is a BIRD and cannot not be one, while on the level of NC, a chicken (a bird up to a point, but certainly less so than an eagle) may or may not be classified among the farmyard animals.

4.4 INDELIBLE PROPERTIES

Does the wild nature of nonscientific categorizations therefore prevent there being features that cannot be deleted? It does not seem so, since it has been rightly observed (Violi 1997: 2.2.2.3) that some features appear more *resistant* than others, and that these indelible features are not merely categorial labels such as ANIMAL and PHYSICAL OBJECT. In the life of semiosis, we notice that we are also wary of deleting some "factual" properties that seem more salient and characterizing than others. A great many people would accept the idea that a porpoise is not a MAMMAL (we have seen that mammalness is not a feature that belongs to the CT of the porpoise; for centuries it was thought to be a fish) but no matter how little a person knows about porpoises, he would find it hard to accept the idea that porpoises live in trees. How to explain why certain negations seem more resistant than others?

Violi (1997, 7.2) distinguishes between *essential* and *typical* properties: it is essential that the cat is an animal; it is typical for it to meow. The second property can be deleted, but the first cannot. But in that case we are back at the old difference between dictionary and encyclopedic properties. On the contrary, Violi (7.3.1.3) holds that even functional properties (closely connected to the CT by virtue of an *affordance* typical of the object) are indelible, and so it is hard to say that something is a box while denying that it can contain objects (if it could not, it would be a *fake* box).[6]

Let us examine the following sentences:

(1) *Mice are not MAMMALS*. This is what in Eco 1976 (3.1.2) I defined as a semiotic judgment, that is, an assertion that confirms or challenges encyclopedic or dictionary conventions existing within the bounds of a given language or, better still, an assertion on the current taxonomic paradigm. Within the bounds of the paradigm this assertion is certainly false, but many people would be able to recognize and name a mouse without knowing that (1) is false. It could be that (1) should be understood as "I assert on the basis of new factual evidence regarding their reproductive process that mice can no longer be classed as MAMMALS." As will be seen in 4.5, assertions of this kind were in circulation for eighty years regarding the platypus. The proof of their truth was in the first instance up to the researchers who were carrying out an empirical examination of the animal's physiology and anatomy. But naturally it would be enough to change the taxonomic criterion to assert that the platypus is not a MAMMAL. In any case the assertion (1) does not refer either to the CT or the NC of the mouse; it is not a part of that area of common competence of which we spoke in 3.5.2. If anything, it is part of the MC: let the zoologists decide what is more or less worthy of deletion as far as they are concerned.

(2) *Mice do not have tails*. If the assertion were understood as being supported by a universal quantifier referring to all the mice in existence, it would be sufficient to provide at least one mouse with

a tail to falsify it. However, in everyday life, I think it unlikely that anyone would make such an assertion, which would presuppose that the speaker had made a previous inspection of all mice (billions of them) one by one. This utterance should simply be transcribed as "The property of having a tail is not part of the CT of the mouse or of the NC of *mouse*." We have seen that NCs are publicly verifiable, and I would say that it would be easy to challenge assertion (2). Those things we call mice (usually) have a tail; the stereotype of the mouse has one, as does its prototype, if the prototype exists somewhere or other. It seems improbable that someone would say (2), but it was possible, as we shall see, for someone to say that the female platypus has no mammae (it was a case of a CT-in-process). Now, is the property of having a tail cancelable or not? I think the question is badly put: when a CT is interpreted, all the properties have the same value at first, also because we still have to know to what extent the type is really wholly shared by all speakers. The acid test is when a *token* is recognized. Which brings us to the next example.

(3) *This is a mouse, but it has no tail.* It is possible to find a dead mouse and recognize it despite its mutilation. Our CT of the mouse also envisages the characteristic tail, and yet this is a *cancelable* property.

(4) *This is a mouse, but it is not an animal.* Here we must refer back to what has already been said: the attribution of animality has nothing to do with ascription to a category; we are dealing with a perceptual primitive, a precategorial experience. If this is not an animal, it cannot be a mouse (it must be the usual robot mouse that is chased through many pages of the philosophy of language by a robot cat). The property of being an animal is *indelible*.

(5) *This is a mouse, but it has the sinuously cylindrical shape, tapered at the extremities, of an eel.* Granted that someone, without having to take a philosophy of language exam, were so foolish as to utter (5) seriously, we would be unlikely to agree. An almost oval shape slightly tapering toward the nose is part of the indispensable (and indelible) conditions for recognizing a mouse. The importance of this gestalt is such that we can be flexible about the tail, and

flexible even with regard to the presence of the paws. The gestalt of the mouse, once it is perceived, allows us to *deduce* the paws and the tail (*if* mouse, *then* tail).[7] The presence on the ground of four little paws or a tail, on the other hand, allows us to infer the mouse that is not there only by *abduction*. In this case, we behave like the paleontologist who takes a jawbone and reconstructs a cranium, but precisely because he is referring to a CT, albeit a hypothetical one, of that prehistoric being. This amounts to saying that, if a 3-D model is part of a CT, it plays a role so important for recognition and identification, that it cannot be deleted.

(6) *This is a mouse, but it is eighty meters long and weighs eight hundred kilograms.* No one can exclude that, after some tinkering with the genetic code, this assertion might one day be utterable. But in such a case I would say we would be talking about the appearance of a new species (we shall call them mice$_2$ as opposed to normal mice$_1$). It should suffice to think of the different tone with which the assertion *There is a mouse in the kitchen* would be uttered depending on whether the reference was to a mouse$_1$ or a mouse$_2$. This means that the CT of the mouse also includes standard dimensions that, no matter how negotiable, may not go beyond a certain threshold. Let us recall the question put by Searle (1979), i.e., why is it that when we go into a restaurant and ask for a hamburger, we do not expect the waiter to serve a hamburger a mile long enveloped in a plastic cube? It is curious that not long after the formulation of this example, an American restaurant chain prepared a manual for its chefs containing specifications regarding the size, weight, cooking times, and condiments required for a standard hamburger; this was not in reply to Searle but because it was economically and industrially important to make public the standard concept of hamburger. Naturally this manual was the elaboration not only of a CT but of an MC of the term *hamburger:* however, it established the nuclear conditions for recognizing something as a hamburger, if not with regard to specifications of weight and cooking times at least with regard to its dimensions and approximate consistency. This is therefore why a property such as standard size seems, if not indelible, at least hard to delete. Of

course, saying that there is an eight-hundred-kilogram mouse is less of a problem than saying there is a mouse that is not an animal, but while in order to justify the first statement, it has to be admitted that we are dealing with a *fake* mouse, to justify the second, it is necessary at the very least to postulate a wholly improbable world, and so this mouse, if it is not fake, must be at least *fictional* or *fictitious*.

(7) *This is an elephant, but it has no trunk*. Here we have to distinguish between the proposition *This is an elephant, but it no longer has a trunk* (similar to the case of the mouse without a tail) and the assertion that a given animal is an elephant that nonetheless has no trunk but a snout made in some other way (like the snout of a kangaroo or the beak of an albatross, let's say). I think that each of us would react by maintaining that in such a case we are dealing no longer with an elephant but with some other animal. We can imagine a breed of mouse without a tail, but the idea of a breed of elephant without a trunk is unconvincing. This case is in fact similar to (5). The trunk is part of the characteristic gestalt of the elephant (more so than the tusks; don't ask me why, but try to draw an elephant with its trunk and no tusks, and other people will usually recognize it; but if you draw a beast with tusks and the round snout of the porpoise, no one will say you have drawn an elephant). At best we can say that the presence of the trunk is not sufficient for the recognition of an elephant, because the trunk could also belong to a mammoth, but there is no doubt that its absence eliminates the elephant. It is an *indelible* property.

This example suggests that cancelable properties are *sufficient* conditions for recognition (such as scratching a match to produce combustion), while indelible properties are seen as *necessary* conditions (there can be no combustion in the absence of oxygen). The difference is that in physics or chemistry we can ascertain experimentally which conditions are really necessary, while in our case the necessity of these conditions depends on many perceptual and cultural factors. It seems intuitive that an animal designed by nature without a trunk is no longer what we have decided to call an elephant. And what if nature had designed a rhinoceros without horns? I think we would have to assign it to another species and call it by another name, for the sake of etymology if nothing else. And yet I suspect that we would be more indulgent and flexible over the matter of the rhinoceros than that of the elephant. So much so, that while the Indian rhinoceros (*Rhinoceros unicornis,* probably the species Marco Polo saw) has only one horn, the African rhino (*Diceros bicornis,* in fact) has two. And yet, for anybody who is not a zoologist or a hunter, while the elephant's trunk is crucial, the rhinoceros's horns count for much less.

The recognition of a property as indelible depends on the history of our perceptual experiences. The zebra's stripes strike us as indelible properties, but it would be sufficient if evolution had produced breeds of horse or ass with striped coats; the stripes would become all too cancelable, because we would have shifted our attention to some other characterizing feature. And perhaps the same thing would happen in a universe in which all quadrupeds had trunks. In that case—perhaps—the elephant's tusks would become indelible.

An entire iconography in the cinema and in books convinced us that feather headdresses were an indelible property for the recognition of an American Indian; and then along came John Ford, who in *Stagecoach* had the iconographic courage to have Geronimo and his braves suddenly appear on the heights of the bluff without feathers, and the entire cinema audience was on the edge of their seats waiting for the attack on the stagecoach after having recognized the redskins (in a black-and-white film) perfectly well. We might say that Ford had probably identified other indelible features that basically determined our CT: painted cheeks, that gritty impassiveness, the gaze, who knows.[8] However, he managed to convince us by constructing a context (a network of intertextual references and a system of expectations capable of rendering some physiognomic features, and the position on the heights, and the presence of a certain type of weapons and clothing) that was more relevant than the presence of the feathers. That it is the context that establishes the relevant properties has already been pointed out in Eco (1979 and 1994). I therefore agree with Violi (1997, 9.2.1. and 10.3.3.) when in the end she assigns the function of selecting the indelible properties to the contexts. The essential properties therefore become the ones that we must know about if, in a certain context, we wish to keep the discourse open, and that can be denied only on pain of renegotiating the meaning of the terms we are using.

On occasion the context can be common to an epoch and a culture, and it is only in such cases that dictionary properties, which refer to the way in which that culture has classified the objects it knows, seem indelible. But even then things often proceed in a complex way, accompanied by many *coups de théâtre*. Which is all reconfirmed for us by what the reader has probably been waiting for for some time, and that is the real story of the platypus.

4.5 THE REAL STORY OF THE PLATYPUS[9]

4.5.1 Water mole or duck-billed platypus

In 1798, a naturalist called Dobson sent the British Museum a stuffed animal that the Australian colonists called the "water mole" or "duck-billed platypus." From an account published by Collins in 1802,[10] a similar animal had been found in November 1797 on the shores of a lake near Hawkesbury. It was the size of a mole, with little eyes; the front feet had four claws and were united by a membrane larger than the one that united the claws of the hind feet. It had a tail and the beak of a duck; it swam with its feet, which it also used to dig out its lair. It was certainly an amphibian type. Collins's text was accompanied by a most inaccurate drawing: the animal looks more like a seal, a whale, or a dolphin, as if, knowing that it swam, the artist had applied the generic CT of a marine animal to it at first sight. Or perhaps the source is another. According to Gould (1991: 19), in the course of a voyage to Australia in 1793, Captain Bligh (of *Bounty* fame) had discovered (and eaten, roasted, with gusto) an echidna. Now we know that the echidna is cousin germane to the platypus, with whom it shares the privilege of being a MONOTREME. Bligh drew it with great care, and the drawing was published in 1802. It looks very like Collins's platypus. I don't know if Collins had seen Bligh's drawing or not, but if he had seen it, so much the better. The conclusion would seem to be that both artists caught some common generic features of two different animals at the expense of specific features (Collins's platypus does not have a convincing beak and seems more suited for eating ants, like the echidna).

Let's get back to the stuffed platypus, which reached London and was described in 1799 by George Shaw as *Platypus anatinus*.[11] Shaw (who was able to examine only the skin, not the internal organs) betrayed various signs of amazement and puzzlement: at first he thought a duck's beak had been grafted onto the head of a quadruped. The use of "graft" was no accident. The skin had arrived after crossing the Indian Ocean, and it was known at the time that certain diabolical Chinese taxidermists were extremely good at grafting, for example, fish tails onto monkeys' bodies in order to create mermaidlike monsters. Shaw therefore had some reason to opine at first that he was faced with a bogus creature made by artificial means, but he later admitted he could find no sign of fraud. His reaction is interesting: the animal was unknown; he had no way of recognizing it, and he would have preferred to believe it did not exist. But since he was a man of science, he went on. And right from the start he swithered between Dictionary and Encyclopedia.

In order to understand what was before his eyes, he tried right away to classify it: the platypus seemed to him to represent a new and singular genus that, in the Linnaean organization of the QUADRUPEDS, should be placed in the order of the BRUTA alongside the order of the MYRMECOPHAGA. After that, he left the categories and moved on to properties. He described the shape of the body, the fur, tail, beak, spur, color, size (13 inches), feet, jaw, and nostrils. He found no teeth and noted that the tongue of his exemplar was missing. He saw something that seemed like eyes to him, but they were too small, and there was too much fur over them to make for good vision, which was why he thought they were like a mole's eyes. He said they might have been suited to aquatic life and surmised that the creature fed on water plants and animals. He quoted Buffon: Everything that is possible for Nature to produce, has in fact been produced.

In 1800, Shaw again took up the description, with renewed doubts and hesitation, as he did not dare include the animal among the QUADRUPEDS.[12] He said he had news of another two specimens sent by the governor of New Holland, Hunter, to Joseph Banks, which ought to have dispelled all suspicion of fraud. These specimens (and it seems that Hunter had sent another to the Newcastle Literary and Philosophical Society) were later described by Bewick in an addendum to the fourth edition of his *General History of Quadrupeds* (Newcastle: Berwick, 1824) as a unique animal with the triple nature of a fish, a bird, and a quadruped... Bewick's view was that it ought not to be collocated according to the standard methods of classification, but that it was sufficient to provide a description of these curious animals exactly as they were when he received them. And although this is followed by a picture entitled "An amphibious animal," we can see that Bewick refused to classify it as FISH, BIRD, or QUADRUPED, although he identified morphological features of fish, birds, and quadrupeds.

Finally exemplars complete with internal organs began to arrive preserved in alcohol. But still in 1800 the German Blumenbach received another stuffed specimen (he was to have two in alcohol only the following year), and he named it *Ornithorhynchus paradoxus*. The choice of adjective is curious; it does not correspond to taxonomic usage; it tells us that Blumenbach was trying to categorize something as uncategorizable. After him the name *Ornithorhynchus anatinus* was to prevail (and we should note that this is a dictionary name, but one that depends on an encyclopedic description, since it means "with a bird's beak similar to that of a duck").

In 1802, the specimens in alcohol (male and female) that Blumenbach had also seen were described by Home,[13] who also said that the animal did not swim on the surface but came up for air, like the turtle. Since he was faced with a furry quadruped, Home immediately thought of a MAMMAL. But a MAMMAL must have mammary glands with nipples. Now, not only does the female platypus not possess this property, but also, instead of forming a uterus, the oviduct opens out into a cloaca, as in BIRDS and REPTILES, that is, it serves as urinary tract and rectum as well as for reproductive purposes. Home was an anatomist, not a taxonomist, and therefore he did not bother overmuch about classifying, limiting himself to describing what he saw. But the analogy with the reproductive organs of BIRDS and REPTILES could hardly fail to make him think the platypus was OVIPAROUS, or perhaps merely oviparous (as we now know, it is oviparous, but it is not OVIPAROUS), and he decided that it might be ovi-viviparous: the eggs were formed inside the mother's body but then dissolved. Home found a supporter for his hypothesis in the anatomist Richard Owen, but by 1819 he was inclined toward viviparity (and this hypothesis usually crops up every time people reflect on the paradox of a furry animal born from an egg).

Home also found that the platypus resembled the echidna, already described by Shaw in 1792. But two similar animals ought to refer back to a common genus, and he guessed it might be that of *Ornithorhynchus hystrix*. Apart from that he expatiated at some length on the spur on the hind foot of the male, on the smooth beak and the rest of the body covered with fur, on the wrinkly tongue that served in lieu of teeth, on the penis suited for the passage of sperm, on the external orifice of the penis subdivided into various apertures, so that the sperm might be spread over a wide area, et cetera. At the end he spoke of a "tribe" that was certainly related to BIRDS and AMPHIBIANS, thereby putting forward, before Darwin, an idea very close to that of the evolutionary relation.

4.5.2 Mammae without nipples

In 1803, the protoevolutionist Etienne Geoffroy de Saint-Hilaire created the category of the MONOTREMES (and here too the term expresses a property: "with a single orifice"). He did not know yet where to put these animals, but assumed they were oviparous. Six years later, Lamarck created a new class, the PROTOTHERIA, saying they were not MAMMALS, because they had no mammary glands, and were probably oviparous; they were not birds, because they had no wings, and they were not reptiles, because they had a heart with four chambers.[14] If a class were to define an essence, we would have here two fine cases of pure nominalism. But at this point the need to categorize gave free play to the imagination of men of science: in 1811, Illiger was talking of REPTANTIA, intermediates between REPTILES and MAMMALS; in 1812, Blainville was talking of MAMMALS in the order of the ORNITHODELPHIA.

It is clear that it is the properties that decide whether the animal is assigned to one class or the other, and some people were already arguing that as a newborn creature with a beak cannot suckle milk, we ought to forget about MAMMALS. But the fact is that even a hypothesis about the class drives one to seek out or overlook some properties, or even to disregard them.

A case in point would be the business of the mammary glands, which were discovered in 1824 by the German anatomist Meckel. They are very large, practically covering the whole body from the front to the hind limbs, but they are visible only when the creature is nursing its young, after which their size is reduced, and this explains why they had not been previously identified.

Is an animal with mammae a MAMMAL? Yes, if it also has nipples, but the female platypus does not have these, not to mention the male. Instead it has porelike glands on the surface, rather like sweat glands that secrete milk. Today we know that this is how it is, and that the young take milk by licking, but Saint-Hilaire was not all wrong in refusing to see these organs as mammae, also because he was firmly convinced that the MONOTREMES were OVIPAROUS and could therefore not be MAMMALS. He considered the glands seen by Meckel as something like the glands on the flanks of the shrew, which secrete a substance for attracting a partner during the mating season. Perhaps they were glands that secreted a perfume, or a substance that made the fur waterproof, or something like the so-called mammary glands of seals and whales, which secrete not milk but a mucus that clots in the water and serves as food for their young.

But Owen, a supporter of the ovoviviparous hypothesis, suspended that secretion in alcohol and obtained something that seemed milk and not mucus. Saint-Hilaire did not give in. The reproductive apparatus was that of an OVIPAROUS animal; an OVIPAROUS animal can only produce an egg; an animal born from an egg is not breast-fed. In 1829, given that the MONOTREMES could not be MAMMALS; could not be birds, because they had neither wings nor feathers; could not be REPTILES, because they were warm-blooded; and, with their lungs sheathed in a pleura and separated from the abdomen by a diaphragm, could not even be FISH, Saint-Hilaire decided that it was necessary to invent for them a fifth category of VERTEBRATES (note that in those days AMPHIBIANS did not yet constitute a class in themselves and were normally classified among the REPTILES).

In doing this, Saint-Hilaire was appealing to a principle that strikes me as very important. Taxonomies, he said, are not just ways of ordering, they are guides to action. If we put the MONOTREMES among the MAMMALS, the question may be considered settled, while if we put them to one side, we are obliged to go in search of new properties. In a certain sense Saint-Hilaire was proposing the creation of an "open" genus, so as to avoid making a clumsy classification of the unknown object, a type that must stand as a stimulus to conjecture. And therefore he stubbornly waited for those eggs that had not yet been discovered but that sooner or later had to appear.

4.5.3 A la recherche de l'oeuf perdu

As we now know, Saint-Hilaire lost the battle of the mammae (and therefore the platypus was to be a MAMMAL, although it seems ill-at-ease sitting there all alone with only the echidna for company in the jump seat reserved for the monotremes), but he won the battle of the eggs.

As early as 1817, John Jameson had made mention of the eggs in a letter from Sydney. The datum was not certain, but in 1824 Saint-Hilaire took it as proven. It is not easy to see a platypus while it is laying eggs (one supposes it does so in private, in the depths of a burrow inaccessible to human explorers), and so one puts one's trust in those who ought to know more about it, in natives. Patrick Hill wrote in 1882 that "Cookoogong, a native, chief of the Boorah-Boorah tribe, says that they all know that this animal lays two eggs, of the size, color and shape of hen's eggs." Today we know that the eggs are tiny, one third of an inch long: either Cookoogong was wrong about the size, or he expressed himself badly in English, or Hill did not understand his language. Nor can we exclude the possibility that the aborigine chief had lied in order to please the explorer.

In 1829, new information reached Saint-Hilaire: someone had seen some eggs, laid in a hole in the sand, this time shaped like the eggs of a bird, snake, or lizard. He also received a drawing, and therefore his informers might really have seen the eggs. Unfortunately it is now thought that these were probably the eggs of a turtle, *Chelodina longicollis*. But Saint-Hilaire maintained that eggs of that size could not pass through the birth canal of a female platypus—and he was right, but for the wrong reasons, because he did not take into account that the eggs found in the sand had probably been in an advanced phase of development.

In 1831, Lieutenant Maule opened some burrows and found eggshells. The opponents of oviparity said the shells were excrement covered with urinary salts such that occur in birds, seeing that both urine and feces are expelled through the same orifice. In 1834, Doctor George Bennet, a supporter of viviparity, led some native informers into making contradictions on the subject of the eggs: he drew an oval egg, and they told him it was a Mullagong egg, then he drew a round one, and they repeated that it was the *cabango* (egg) of the Mullagong. However, they then said that the newborn animal "tumbled down." You don't tumble down out of an egg, but from the womb. Bennett admitted that the natives could not speak English well, but who knows what he asked them and what they understood, who knows what his ovals and circles were like. Better a *Gavagai* than a *Mullagong*.

In 1865, Richard Owen (of the anti-egg party) received a letter from a certain Nicholson sent in September 1864, which said how ten months previously a female had been captured and given to the district Gold-receiver. This person had put the animal in a cage, where on the following morning he found two eggs, this time about the size of a crow's egg, soft and without a calcareous shell. Nicholson said he had seen them, but two days later someone threw them away and killed the animal (finding in the belly many of what his informers called "eggs" but may have been ova). A subsequent letter from the Gold-receiver seems to confirm this account. Owen published the two letters but wondered what the two alleged eggs contained. If they had been opened and an embryo or at least a yolk had been seen, if someone had put them in a bottle of alcohol... But alas, nothing more was known about this matter. Perhaps it was all the effect of a miscarriage brought on by fright. Burrell (1927: 44) had to admit that Owen—whose behavior was that of a prudent scientist—was right; Burrell moreover reasoned that the eggs could not have been the size of any bird definable as a crow, and suggested that it might have been a prank on the part of some wag who had slipped bird eggs into the cage.

The debate continued in the scientific journals for many years after that, and it was only in 1884 (about eighty-six years after the discovery of the animal) that W. H. Caldwell, who had gone to Australia to carry out research on the spot, was to send a celebrated telegram to the University of Sydney: "Monotremes oviparous, ovum meroblastic" (where the second datum establishes that the cells of the embryo divide in a way typical of reptiles and birds).

End of argument. The MONOTREMES were MAMMALS and oviparous.

4.6 CONTRACTING

4.6.1. Eighty years of negotiations

What is the moral of the story? In the first instance, we might say that this is a splendid example of how observation sentences can be made only in the light of a conceptual framework or of a theory that gives them a sense, in other words, that the first attempt to understand what is seen is to consider the experience in relation to a previous categorial system (as in the case of Marco Polo and the rhinoceros). But at the same time we would have to say, again as in the case of Marco Polo, that when observations challenge the categorial framework, attempts are made to adjust the framework. In this way we progress on a parallel course, readjusting the categorial framework according to the new observation sentences and recognizing as real those observation sentences that are in accordance with the assumed categorial framework. As we gradually categorize, we await the identification of new properties (no doubt in the form of a disordered encyclopedia); as properties are gradually found, we attempt to reestablish the categorial structure. But every hypothesis regarding the categorial framework to be assumed influences the way we make observation sentences and acknowledge them to be valid (with the result that those who would have the platypus a mammal do not search for its eggs, or they refuse to recognize eggs when they appear, while those who would have the platypus oviparous refuse to acknowledge either the mammae or the milk). This is the dialectic both of cognition and understanding, that is, of understanding and knowledge.

But is this conclusion sufficient? In point of fact, someone finally showed that there were both mammae and eggs. We might say that, given two competing theories, both won the day, obliging researchers in the field to look for something that the theory required to be there, and that if one academic faction had prevailed over another (because this is the mechanism that comes into play even when scientific theories are compared), perhaps neither the mammae nor the eggs would ever have been seen. But the fact remains that in the end both mammae and eggs were seen, so that today it seems hard to deny that the platypus nurses its young and, notwithstanding this, also lays eggs.

The story of the platypus therefore serves to demonstrate that in the final instance facts prevail over theories (and, as Peirce wished, the Torch of Truth will in any case be passed on from hand to hand despite the difficulties). But, judging by the literature on the argument in question, we still have not stopped discovering many unsuspected properties of the platypus, and one might say that this happens because the winning theory required that the animal be grouped with the mammals. Peirce would put our minds at rest: all we need do is wait, and in the end the Community will find a point of consensus.

But remember Shaw's decision of 1799: it might be possible to assign the unknown animal to some class, but for the moment let us describe what can be seen. And what naturalists knew about the platypus, even before deciding on what class to put it in and, we note, as the debate about this wore on, was that it was a strange thing, certainly an animal, which could be recognized according to some instructions for its identification (beak, beaver tail, webbed feet, etc.).

For over eighty years, the naturalists could agree on nothing, except that they were talking about *that* creature made in such and such a fashion, specimens of which were gradually identified. That creature might or might not be MAMMAL, BIRD, or REPTILE, without its ever ceasing to be that double-damned beast that, as Lesson observed in 1839, had set itself athwart the path of taxonomy to prove its fallaciousness.

The story of the platypus is the story of a long negotiation, and in this sense it is an exemplary tale. But the negotiation had a basis, and this was that the platypus seemed similar to a beaver, a duck, and a mole, but not to a cat, an elephant, or an ostrich. If it is necessary to yield to the evidence that perception has an iconic content, the story of the platypus tells us so. Anyone who saw one, or a drawing of one, or a stuffed specimen, or one preserved in spirit, would refer back to a common CT.

There were eighty-odd years of negotiation, but the negotiations always revolved around resistances and the grain of the *continuum*. Given these resistances, the decision, certainly contractual in nature, to acknowledge that certain features were undeniable, was obligatory. At first, and for some decades after, people were prepared to delete everything about the platypus: that it was a MAMMAL or OVIPAROUS, that it had mammae or not, but certainly not the property of being the animal that was made in such and such a fashion and that someone found in Australia. And, while they were arguing, everybody knew they were referring to the same CT. Proposals regarding the MC were different, but negotiations were underpinned by an NC.

That the beak could not be deleted (first and foremost because it should not have been there) is revealed by the names with which the animal was indicated, both in ordinary and scientific language, from the beginning and throughout the course of the debate: *Duck-billed platypus, Schnabeltier, Ornitorinco*.

4.6.2 Hjelmslev vs. Peirce

I have long feared that the semiotic approach adopted in my *Theory of Semiotics* suffered from syncretism. What did it mean to try, as I did, to combine the structuralist perspective of Hjelmslev with the cognitive-interpretative semiotics of Peirce? The former shows us how our semantic (and therefore conceptual) competence is of a categorial type, based on a segmentation of the *continuum* by virtue of which the form of the content presents itself structured in the form of opposition and difference. We tell a sheep from a horse by the presence or absence of some dictionary markers, such as OVINE or EQUINE, and Hjelmslev suggests that this organization of content imposes a vision of the world.

But such an organization of content either assumes these markers as primitives not open to further interpretation (and therefore it does not tell us the properties of an equid or an ovine), or it demands that these components be interpreted in their turn. Alas, when we enter the phase of interpretation, the rigid structural organization dissolves in the network of encyclopedic properties, arranged along the potentially infinite thread of unlimited semiosis. How is it possible for the two points of view to coexist?

The result of the preceding reflections is that they *must* coexist, because if we choose one of them only, we cannot account for our way of knowing and expressing what we know. It is indispensable to make them coexist on a theoretical level, because, effectively speaking, on the level of our cognitive experiences we proceed so that we run—if the expression does not seem too reductive—with the hare and hunt with the hounds. The unstable equilibrium of this coexistence is not (theoretically) syncretistic, because it is on the basis of this happily unstable equilibrium that our understanding proceeds.

And this is why the categorial moment and the observational moment do not oppose each other as irreconcilable ways of understanding, nor are they juxtaposed through syncretism: they are two complementary ways of considering our competence, precisely because, at least at the "auroral" moment of understanding (when the Dynamical Object is a *terminus a quo*), they imply each other reciprocally.

Now I shall consider a possible objection. We consider *taxa* (let's say MAMMALS, or BIRDS) as cultural constructs insofar as they sum up observation sentences like "this animal nurses its young" or "this animal lays eggs." But why do we consider the presence or absence of mammal or eggs as facts to be simply observed? As if recognizing something as an egg rather than as an ovum, or deciding whether something is milk or mucus, does not depend on a structured system of concepts, only within which something is or is not an egg. In structural semantics, do we not have the oppositional analysis of properties, such as hard/soft, to distinguish a chair from an armchair?

The fact is that the constitution of a system of *taxa* is based precisely on the abstractive capacity to group as far as possible according to highly comprehensive classifications (and this is precisely why it is hard on a folk level of experience to decide that a giraffe and a whale are both mammals), while no structural semantics has ever managed to constitute a total system of opposites, one that accounts for all our knowledge and all the uses of language, a system within which there is a precise place for the egg and the spinal column, the scent of violets and climbing. On the contrary, for illustrative purposes we are always limited to highly restricted fields, such as furniture to sit down on or parental relationships. This does not exclude the possibility of our constructing one day (in theory) a global system of content (nor does it exclude the existence of such a system in the Divine Mind). All it tells us is that (precisely because, as Kant used to say, empirical concepts can never exhaust all their determinations) we can proceed only by temporary settlements and successive corrections.

Even the observation sentence *This is an egg* depends on cultural conventions. But, though egg and mammal are both concepts that spring from a cultural segmentation of the content, and though the very concept of mammal also takes account of experiential data, there is a difference in the proximity of the construction of the concept and perceptual experience (and it is on this that the difference between NC and MC is based).

When we say that, in order to decide whether an animal is a MAMMAL or not, we have to fall back on a system of cultural conventions (or, as we have seen, reconstruct one), while, in order to decide if something is an egg, we intuitively put our faith in perception and an elementary knowledge of the language being used, we are saying something that goes beyond intuitive obviousness. Of course if someone has not been trained to apply the word *egg* to a certain CT (which already considers the form, the presence of yolk and albumen, the presupposition that if this object is sat on for the right amount of time, then a living creature might be hatched from it), there will be no agreement on the recognition of an egg. Therefore perceptual consensus too always springs from a prior cultural agreement, no matter how vague or folk it might be.[15] And this confirms what I was trying to say shortly before, that in the process of understanding, the structural moment and the interpretative moment alternate and complement each other step by step. Nevertheless it cannot be denied that, in defining an egg as such, the testimony of the senses prevails, while in order to define a mammal as such, what prevails is a knowledge of classifications and our agreement on a given taxonomic system.

When we go on to refine perceptual judgments, and there is a clash about whether something is milk or mucus, it is necessary to treat the perceptual experience in cultural terms too and to decide which criteria and chemical classifications allow us to distinguish milk from mucus. But yet again we have evidence of an oscillation and a constant complementarity of our two ways of understanding the world. At a given moment even the common CT that would have allowed Saint-Hilaire to recognize something as milk had to give way to an MC already imbued with structured oppositions, on the basis of which it was inevitable that Meckel and Owen would emerge victorious.

4.6.3 Where does the amorphous *continuum* lie?

All this brings us back to the opposition between the systematic, or *holistic*, pressure of a system of propositions and the possibility of *observation sentences* dependent on perceptual experience.

The postulating of a perceptual semiotics ought to give rise again to the rift between those who maintain that we give form to an amorphous *continuum*, and that this form is a cultural *construct*, and those who maintain, on the other hand, that what we know about the environment is determined by characteristics of the environment itself, from which we take the *salient* information it offers us *sponte propria*.

It seems obvious that even an observation sentence such as *It's raining* cannot be understood, and judged true or false, if not within a system of linguistic conventions on the basis of which we distinguish the meaning of *rain* from that of *mist* and *dew*, and that therefore the concept of "rain" depends not only on some lexical conventions but also on a coherent system of propositions regarding atmospheric phenomena. To use a formula that Putnam attributes to West Churchman, who attributed it to A. E. Singer, Jr., who in his turn meant it to be an efficacious condensation of James's thought (Putnam 1992: 20), "knowledge of facts presupposes knowledge of theories, knowledge of theories presupposes knowledge of facts." However, the meaning of *rain* does not depend on the chemical notion of water; otherwise the unlearned could not assert that it is raining, and each one of us would assert this falsely in the case of "acid rain," in which God only knows what is falling from the sky. In the same way, in order to observe that it is sunny, or that there is a full moon, it is certainly necessary to share a sort of segmentation, albeit an ingenuous one, of the astronomic *continuum*, but it is not indispensable to know the astrophysical distinction between star and planet.

An ingenuous segmentation of the *continuum* can also survive within a system of interconnected notions that actually denies it: this is why we have no problem in asserting that the sun rises, when in the light of the system of notions upon which our knowledge is based, we ought to know that the sun does not move in that way.

Let us try to imagine an imaginary debate between Galileo, one of his Ptolemaic adversaries, and someone who prefers to keep one foot in both camps, such as Tycho Brahe, Kepler, or Newton. I don't think we need an enormous amount of imagination to assume that all the participants will agree on the fact that at a given moment they can see the sun or the moon in the sky, that both bodies seem circular in shape and not square, and that they illuminate over Arcetri something that everyone can recognize as trees. Nonetheless, within diverse systems of propositions, movement, distances, functions of the sun and the moon, notions such as mass, epicycle, deferent, gravity, or gravitation not only assume a different value but also can be acknowledged or refuted. However, even if each debater has a different conceptual frame of reference, all of them perceive some objects and phenomena in the same way.

For the heliocentrists the sun's movement is apparent, whereas for their opponents it is real. But this difference is relevant with respect to a coherent system of propositions regarding the universe, not with respect to the observation sentence upon which both parties have agreed.

It is one thing to ask whether everybody sees an eclipse of the moon and another to talk about the movement of the heavenly bodies that produce the perception of the eclipse. The first problem concerns the way in which we form a perceptual judgment (which despite its being dependent on the structure of our cognitive apparatus must nonetheless account for the manifold of sensation), while the second concerns a system of propositions (for Kant, a system of judgments based on experience) that is certainly influenced by internal structural relations. When we talk of holism, we mean the solidarity of a system of propositions; when instead we talk of perception, even though we can presume that it is influenced by a system of propositions that create a series of expectations, we are talking about *observation sentences* that must in some way take account of what the environment is proposing to us in an immediate sense.

I am well aware that advocating the existence of observation sentences independent of a general system of propositions was said by Davidson to be the third dogma of empiricism; but we cannot ignore the evidence that it is easier to negotiate (in a very short time) our assent to the sentence *Watch out, because there is a step* than to the sentence that expresses the second law of thermodynamics. The difference is that in the first case I immediately run a check on perceptual bases (the concept of step is an "empirical concept"). Thus in the story I told in 3.5.1, Gabriel and Belphagor might have had very different notions regarding virtue, but both were able to tell the sexual difference between Joseph and Mary.

Therefore, even if we admit that every cultural system and every linguistic system upon which it rests segments the *continuum* of experience in its own way (Davidson would talk of a "conceptual schema"), this does not alter the fact that the *continuum* organized by systems of propositions already offers itself according to a *grain* that provides directives for intersubjectively homogeneous perception, even between subjects that refer to different systems of propositions. The segmentation of the *continuum* brought into being by a system of propositions and categories in some way takes into account the fact that that *continuum* is no longer entirely amorphous; in other words, while it is *propositionally amorphous,* it is not entirely *perceptually chaotic,* because within it, objects interpreted and constituted as such on a perceptual level have already been carved out: as if the *continuum* in which a system of propositions carves out its own configurations has already been tilled by a "wild" and as yet nonsystematic semiosis. Before deciding whether the sun is a star, planet, immaterial body that revolves around the earth, or a body that lies at the center of the orbit of our planet, we perceive that a circular luminous object moves in the sky, and this object was familiar also to our remote ancestors, who probably had not yet so much as elaborated a name with which to designate it.[16]

4.6.4 Vanville

All this obliges us to offer some reflections on the concept of truth. Is there a difference between saying it is true that something is an egg and saying it is true that something is a mammal? Or between saying it is true that something is a mountain and saying it is true that something is a MOUNTAIN? If the continuous oscillation (between structural organization and interpretation in terms of experience) I was talking about before did not exist, the answer would be easy: to say that something is a MAMMAL or a MOUNTAIN can only be true within a language L, while saying that something is an egg or a mountain is true in terms of experience. Yet we have seen that even in order to recognize an egg, we cannot elude the restraints imposed by a language L, the same one by virtue of which it is decided that BIRDS are such insofar as they lay eggs (but not all animals that lay eggs are BIRDS).

There is a definition of truth in the *Dictionnaire* by Greimas-Courtés (1979) that seems tailor-made to irritate any upholder of a truth-functional semantics, not to mention every supporter of a correspondence theory of truth:

> Truth designates the complex term which subsumes the terms *being* and *seeming* situated on the axis of contraries within the semiotic square of veridictory modalities. It might be helpful to point out that the "true" is situated within the discourse, for it is the fruit of the veridiction operations; this thus excludes any relation (or any homologation) with an external referent.

Perhaps the *Dictionnaire* has discovered the most complicated way to say something that is by no means simple but has nonetheless been said before: and that is that the concept of truth should be seen within the context of a system of content; that the propositions that the receiver already deems guaranteed within the framework of his own cultural model are "true"; and that the interest of the analysis has shifted from the protocols for defining an assertion as a true one (the logical neopositivist stance, and that of the young Wittgenstein) to the analysis of the discursive strategies that present something as true.

This position was less scandalous and less impermeable to the (apparently opposite) discourses of analytic philosophy. Greimas's position is based on a Hjelmslevian version of the structuralist paradigm, and the Hjelmslevian version anticipated (and when it was not anticipating, it was on a parallel course: the dates speak volumes)[17] the development of that internal criticism of logical neopositivism and analytic philosophy that goes by the name of *holism,* the challenging of the difference between analytic and synthetic, the principle of warranted assertion, internal realism, and the individuation of scientific paradigms as incommensurable structures (or, in any event, as structures that do not admit of simple translation from one to the other). Even though indirectly, Hjelmslev's version also influenced, rather than anticipated, the criticism of knowledge as Mirror of Nature, and Rorty's (1979) idea that every representation is a mediation and that we must drop the notion of correspondence and see propositions connected with other propositions rather than with the world.

The only difference is that from what is known as the holistic standpoint there is in any case a tendency to define in what sense something can be assumed as true, albeit in terms of "warranted assertion," while in the semio-structuralist school, of which Greimas perhaps represents the most radical wing, the thrust of research was directed at understanding how a discourse *makes one believe* that something is true.

The limitations of the semio-structural approach lie in the fact that, to be able to say whether and how people accept something as true, and to make them believe it is true, we must also assume that there is a naïve concept of truth, the same one that authorizes us to say that the sentence *It's raining today* is empirically true—within the context in which it is uttered. I do not think that this criterion exists within the structuralist paradigm.

The trouble is that it does not exist within the truth-functionalist paradigm either. In any event, it is not provided for in Tarski's criterion of truth, which concerns the way in which the truth conditions of a proposition are defined but not how to establish whether or not the proposition is true. And to say that understanding the meaning of a sentence means knowing its truth conditions (that is to say, understanding under what conditions it would be true) does not amount to proving whether or not the sentence is true.

Agreed, the paradigm is by no means so homogeneous as it is usually held to be, and some also tend to interpret Tarski's criterion in accordance with a correspondence theory of truth. But, whatever Tarski thought,[18] it is hard to read in a correspondentist sense the canonical definition:

(i) "Snow is white"
is true if and only if
(ii) snow is white.

We are able to say which type of logical and linguistic entity (i) is —it is a statement, or a sentence in a language L, which conveys a proposition—but we still have no idea of what (ii) is. If it were a state of affairs (or a perceptual experience), we would be extremely puzzled: a state of affairs is a state of affairs, and a perceptual experience is a perceptual experience, not a statement. If anything, a sentence is produced to express a state of affairs or a perceptual experience. But if what appears in (ii) is a sentence regarding a state of affairs or a perceptual experience, it cannot be a sentence expressed in L, given that it must guarantee the truth of the proposition expressed by the sentence (i). It must therefore be a sentence expressed in a metalanguage L_2. But then Tarski's formula must be translated as

(i) The proposition "snow is white," conveyed by the sentence (in L) *Snow is white,*
is true if and only if
(ii) the proposition "snow is white," conveyed by the sentence (in L_2) *Snow is white*, is true.

This solution is clearly destined to produce a series of infinite sentences, each expressed in a new metalanguage.[19]

Unless we understand the definition in a strictly behaviorist sense: snow is white if—when confronted with the stimulus of snow—each of the speakers reacts by saying that it is white. Apart from the fact that we would find ourselves up to our necks in the difficulties of radical translation, I don't think this was what Tarski thought, and even if it were, this would still not be a way of deciding whether a statement is true, because it would simply tell us that all speakers make the same perceptual error, just as the fact that for thousands of years all speakers said that in the evening the sun fell in the sea is not proof that their statement was true.

It seems more convincing to admit that, in Tarski's formula, (ii) conventionally stands for *the assignation of a truth value to* (i). The Tarskian state of affairs is not something we can check in order to acknowledge that the proposition it expresses is true; on the contrary, it is that thing to which a true proposition corresponds, or everything that is expressed by a true proposition (see McCawley 1981: 161), in other words, its truth value. In this sense the Tarskian notion does not tell us if it is truer to say that a cat is a cat or that a cat is a mammal.

Which brings us back once more to the question of whether there are truth criteria for observation sentences that are different for nonobservation sentences.

Since such questions were debated in exemplary fashion in Quine's "Two Dogmas of Empiricism," I shall recycle a story I recounted in 1990 in the course of a conference on Quine himself.[20] I specify this, because otherwise it would not be possible to understand the names of the streets and the localities I use (all refer to famous examples taken from Quine's works)—neither the name Vanville attributed to the city (Van is how Willard Van Orman Quine was known to close friends) nor the passing reference to a brick-built house on Elm Street, a typical example of an observation sentence used in Quine 1951.

Figure 4.1 shows the map of Vanville, a little town that first grew up north of the river Gavagai in the days of the first pioneers.

Vanville is made entirely of wooden buildings, including the Presbyterian church, with the exception of the Civic Center, where at the beginning of the century they constructed three masonry buildings with cast-iron columns. The map also shows a house made of bricks on Elm Street, but this was built in 1951, and we shall have more to say about it later.

As can be seen, Tegucigalpa Street, Pegasus Street, and Giorgione Street run perpendicular to Elm, Orman, and Willard streets as well as to Riverside Drive. A sort of Broadway, called Tully Road, tells us that Vanville is not necessarily a Roman *castrum*, but that its development was inspired by a certain Anglo-Saxon empiricism. Then there are Midtown Place and Uptown Square, and between Midtown Square and Elm there are some hills that still have not been built on. At the corner of Pegasus and Willard, we find the three masonry buildings: the First Vanville City Bank, the Delmonico Hotel, and the Town Hall. The citizens of Vanville call it the Pegwill Center, which means "the center on the corner of Pegasus and Willard" (which is not very different from giving the name duck-billed platypus to a creature with a bird's beak).

The map is an interpretation of the expression *Vanville*, but only under a certain profile: it says nothing about the shape of the houses or the beauty of the river. Since the citizens know their way around town perfectly well, we can assume that each one has a certain knowledge of where the places are and that therefore the diagram that is the map is part of their CT and of the publicly shared NC.[21]

Let us now suppose that a tourist arrives in Vanville and asks for the Pegwill Center. Depending on the direction from which he enters the town, he will receive instructions of this type:

(1) The Pegwill Center is the place with three large buildings that can be reached by starting off from the corner of Tegucigalpa and Elm and then heading east across Elm before turning at the corner of Pegasus and Elm to take Pegasus in a southerly direction as far as the corner of Pegasus and Willard.

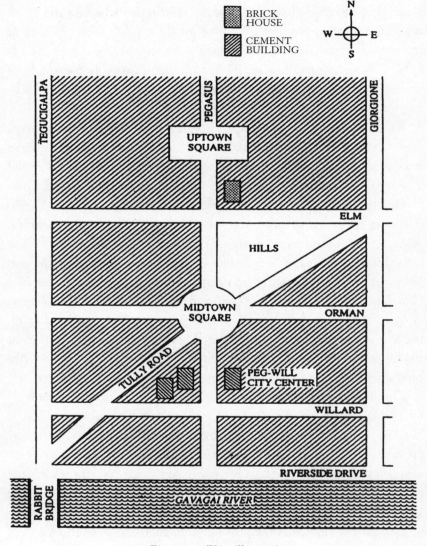

Figure 4.1 (Vanville 1951)

(2) The Pegwill Center is the place with three large buildings that can be reached by starting off from the corner of Tully and Willard and then heading east along Willard as far as the corner between Pegasus and Willard.

(3) The Pegwill Center is the place with three large buildings that can be reached by heading south along Giorgione as far as the

corner of Giorgione and Orman, then turning west onto Orman and proceeding to the corner of Orman and Tegucigalpa before turning north and proceeding along Tegucigalpa until the corner of Tegucigalpa and Elm, where you turn east and proceed along Elm before turning southwest at the corner of Elm and Tully and heading along Tully, where you have to cross Riverside and the Rabbit Bridge and then dive into the river Gavagai and swim eastward as far as the corner of Riverside and Giorgione before going north along Giorgione until the corner of Giorgione and Willard, where you go west along Willard until you come to the corner of Pegasus and Willard.

(1), (2), and (3) are all interpretations of the term Pegwill City Center. As such, they are a part of the NC of Pegwill Center, i.e., they are instructions for its retrieval (and, all things considered, for its identification, since there are no other large buildings in the town).

At first sight, instruction (3) may seem bizarre, but it would not be, if it were given to someone who wanted to reach the Pegwill Center after having acquired a sufficient knowledge of Vanville. Given that a characteristic of interpretations is that through them we always learn something more about the Immediate Object interpreted, interpretation (3) makes it possible to know something more about the Pegwill Center with regard to its relations with the rest of the town.

Insofar as they are statements, (1), (2), and (3) are all true, at least within the framework of the map (and the structure of the town). In our case (in which we are simply imagining Vanville and its map) it is clear that they are true only within the bounds of a system of assumptions (the only experience we have is that of the map), but the map is a drawing of a possible world, not a state of the real world). But if Vanville really existed and a real tourist found the Pegwill Center by following these instructions, he could truthfully say *I reached the Pegwill Center by following the route described in instruction x.*

One fine day, however, around 1953, someone built a house made of bricks on Elm Street, right at the corner of Pegasus.

Anyone passing there would now be entitled to say that there is a house made of bricks on Elm Street. This would be an observation sentence, which springs from a perceptual experience (and is probably taken as true by others who put their faith in credible testimony). As such, this sentence does not upset all the other assertions that could have been made previously about Vanville, and it does not make the definitions (1), (2), and (3) any less true. But we cannot say that it is independent of Vanville's general situation. If someone were to characterize that house as *the brick house on Elm Street,* at the very least it would have to be the only one of its kind on Elm Street. In a city full of brick houses, it would still be a true observation sentence to say that there is a brick house on Elm Street, but it would not be a description capable of providing instructions for the identification of the referent.

Suppose, however, that the house on Elm Street is the only brick structure in Vanville. As soon as its existence is registered by the citizens, the possible interpretations of the Pegwill Center will be increased. Without dragging in Ockham (*Quodl. Septem, 8*), who used to say that you cannot raise a finger without creating an infinity of new entities, because with this movement all relations of position between the finger and all the entities of the universe will be changed, it cannot be denied that one of the new possible interpretations of the Pegwill Center becomes "the group of buildings south of the brick house on Elm Street" or "the group of buildings that can be reached by starting from the brick house on Elm Street and then heading south along Pegasus."

What will happen if a second brick house is built in Vanville? If the citizens are used to calling the house on Elm *the brick house,* with the appearance of a second the name of the first will have to be changed. And one of the definitions of Elm Street will also have to change, if someone defines it as *that street in which stands the only house made of bricks in the city.*

How many new facts, with the observation sentences they involve, are necessary to make a radical change in a system of interconnected definitions? The question recalls the paradox of the heap. But between a heap and a single grain of sand there are many intermediate degrees, and by removing many grains of sand from a heap it is legitimate at least to assert that at a moment t the heap is smaller than it was in the moment t_{-1}.

Let us therefore leap from Vanville 1951 to the present day and see in figure 4.2 how, through a series of transformations, it has become Vanville 1997.

Around the famous brick house skyscrapers have gradually sprung up, and the new Civic Center (to which the Bank, the Town Hall, and the Museum have been transferred, while a new Hilton hotel has been built) has been created. Owing to the northerly expansion of the town, the old Uptown Square has become Midtown Square. As it now stands on the corner of Pegasus and Elm, it is curious that the new Civic Center is still called Pegwill: there are inertial phenomena in language (in the same way as today we still apply the name atom to something that has been shown to be divisible). Midtown is now occupied by the artificial Lake Barbarelli, to the delight of the wealthy inhabitants of the new Gaurisander Heights (a series of residential villas that have sprung up on what had previously been open hills). Tully Road stops at the lake, beyond which it appears again as Cicero Road. The old Civic Center now houses the Paradox Arcades: shops and amusements. The new brick houses built along Riverside Drive constitute Venus Village, which for a while was an area whose picturesque bars were frequented by artists, but then was gradually transformed into a red-light district with porn shops and strip clubs. It is now dangerous to walk alone at night in downtown Vanville.

Obviously, the previous interpretations of the Pegwill Center no longer work. Number (2) now defines the Paradox Arcades, while (1) and (3) no longer mean anything.

The two Vanvilles seem to constitute two mutually incommensurable systems, just as is said of languages when the notion of mutual translatability is called into question. How can we translate the sentences pronounced on Vanville 1951 to make them comprehensible (and true) with regard to Vanville 1997? The answer is that we cannot. We are faced with two systems in which the same names refer to different streets (in Vanville 1997, Tully Road means something different from what it meant in Vanville 1951).

The single facts and observation sentences that used to express these names and streets have gradually generated a new system, the Vanville 1997 system, incommensurable with the Vanville 1951 system. We can no longer even consider as equally true the sentence *There is a brick house on Elm Street,* because, if anything, there is a brick house on East Elm. Besides, that house is no longer close to Uptown Square but to Midtown Square; it is not north of the Pegwill Center but *in* the Pegwill Center, et cetera, et cetera.

Yet even though the entire system that once defined that brick house has changed, the brick house is still there; anyone can see it, and anyone who saw it in 1951 can recognize it in 1997 as the same house.

A curious situation, but not that dissimilar to the one in which I had put Galileo and Tycho Brahe, intent on looking at the same sun, acknowledging they were seeing the same thing and nevertheless obliged, in terms of the MC they attributed to the term *sun,* to define it in different ways within the framework of a different system of assumptions.

But although they recognize the brick house as the same one as before, do the citizens really perceive it in the same way? In New York today, dwarfed by the skyscrapers on Fifth Avenue, the neo-Gothic churches with their tall spires that once seemed towering affairs now strike us as minuscule, almost miniaturized. In the same way, how will this handsome and majestic house, so imposing when it was built, appear now, set against the skyscrapers of the new center that have sprung up around it? And that's how, on the one hand, an object does not change and is always perceived as such, and how, on the other hand, by virtue of the town plan system of which it is a part, is seen differently.[22]

The principle is also taken up again in Quine (1995: 43 ff.): although they are dependent on perceptual stimuli, observation sentences "change and develop with the growth of scientific knowledge." The parameter of an observation sentence is given, as well as experience, by the "pertinent linguistic community." It is "public

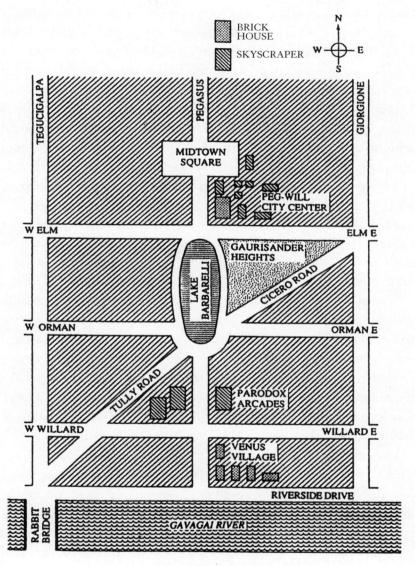

Figure 4.2 (Vanville 1997)

pressure" that obliges the subject to correct the observation sentence *Look at the fish* when faced with a whale.

Let us try to reformulate the question in the terms used by Putnam (1987: 33): "There are 'external facts,' and we can say *what they are*. What we *cannot* say—because it makes no sense—is what the facts are *independent of all conceptual choices*." Let there be three spatiotemporal points x1, x2, and x3: how many "objects" are there? In a world à la Carnap there would be three objects (x1, x2, and x3); in a world according to the Polish logicians, there would be seven objects (x1, x2, x3, x1 + x2, x1 + x3, x2 + x3, x1 + x2 + x3). The number of identifiable objects changes according to the conceptual framework. Yet (and I stress this) we recognize as an initial stimulus three spatiotemporal points, and in the absence of that agreement on the initial stimulus the debate on identifiable objects could not even get started. Not only that, the two universes would not be comparable.

That two systems are structurally *incommensurable* does not mean that their two structures cannot be *compared*, and the two maps of Vanville we have been playing with until now demonstrate this.

We are able to understand the two systems, and we are able to understand what it means when both cities contain the same brick house. On this basis we can certainly understand that the instructions (1)–(3) that held good for Vanville 1951 no longer hold good for Vanville 1997. Yet by taking the first map and checking the meaning of the expression *Tully Road*, we are able to establish from the second map that that content now corresponds to two different urban entities, nameable as Tully Road and Cicero Road.

This allows us to say that, if we found a treasure map from Vanville 1951, which said that starting from the corner of Elm and Giorgione, before turning southwest along Tully Road, three meters before the corner of Midtown Square, on the right we would find a buried chest of Spanish doubloons. In Vanville 1997, this sentence would translate as "Starting from the corner of East Elm and Giorgione, before turning southwest along Cicero, three meters before the area occupied by Lake Barbarelli, on the right, we will find a chest of Spanish doubloons." The interesting aspect of the business is that, by negotiating the criteria of reference and the criteria of translation between two systems considered incommensurable, we might really find those doubloons.

One of the more diverting problems to be found in old (and sometimes new) Italian translations of hard-boiled American crime fiction is that the detective often gets into a cab and says "Portami nella città bassa" (literally, "Take me to the lower city"). Sometimes he asks to be taken to the "upper city." The Italian reader immediately thinks that all American cities are like Bergamo (which is divided into upper Bergamo and lower Bergamo) or like Turin, Florence, Budapest, or Tbilisi, with one part of town on the plain and, across the river, another part on the hills. Obviously it is not like that. In the English text the detective asks to be taken *downtown* (or *uptown*).

But let's put ourselves in the translator's shoes, remembering that often he or she has never set foot in the United States. How must these terms be translated? If the translator asked a native for an explanation, the native would tell him that "uptown" and "downtown" are concepts that change from city to city: sometimes they mean the business center, sometimes the red-light district and therefore the oldest part of the city, sometimes the area along the river, according to how the city developed (in New York these concepts are occasionally absolute—and so Wall Street is certainly *downtown*—and occasionally relative, so if you want to go to the Village from Central Park you tell the driver to go *downtown,* while if you wanted to go there from Wall Street, you would tell him to go *uptown*).

Solutions? There is no rule, but the translator would need to know in which city the story is set. Then he would have to look at the map (and consult a good guidebook), understand what the detective is going to do (visit a gambling house, a five-star hotel, a seedy dive, or to find a ship), and then have him tell the cab driver each time to take him to the center, to the business quarter, to the old town, to the port, or wherever the devil it is he wants to go. The referent for *downtown* is to be negotiated, to the extent in which the meaning is negotiable, according to the city (to the system).

The chance of an observation sentence's being true is also a matter for negotiation. But this does not alter the fact that the observation sentence is based on perceptual evidence, on the fact that that brick house was built after all, and that in some way it is perceived even by a dog who knows nothing about the Vanville town plan. You can avoid noting its presence, but you cannot deny that it is there. However, the moment its presence is noted, it must be named and defined, and this cannot be done except within the context of the city as a system.

4.7 CONTRACT AND MEANING

By now I think it is clear that all this presupposes a *contractual* notion both of CTs and of NCs and MCs. I dealt elsewhere (Eco 1993) with the various attempts made over the centuries to construct (or rediscover) a Perfect Language. Most of these attempts were based on the assumption that it is possible to identify a series of primitive notions, common to the whole species, and arrange them in an elementary grammar, so as to construct a metalanguage in which the notions and propositions expressed in any natural language are entirely translatable, under all circumstances, and in a way devoid of that ambiguity proper to our mother tongues. Why, given that I have mentioned semiosic primitives and CTs connected with perceptual experience, might it not be possible to construct such a perfect language on this basis, which today might even assume the form of a mentalese that explains the way in which the human mind works and the way in which a silicon-based mind might humanly work?

Because, I think, it's one thing to proceed in the course of our experience by elaborating CTs and NCs, but it is another thing to say that these entities of ours are really universal and metahistoric in their format. You cannot construct a Perfect Language, because it would exclude that moment of negotiation that makes our languages efficacious.

Everybody finds himself more or less agreed regarding to the recognition of a rat, but not only is the zoologist's competence different from mine, the zoologist must also continually check to see whether his NC has the same format as mine. Is the fact that rats are carriers of disease a part of the NC of rat? It depends on the culture, the circumstances, and naturally the age. In the seventeenth century, people had still not associated rats with plagues, but they do today, and when pestilence strikes now, anyone, before perceiving the rat as a quadruped, would perceive it as a threat.

The CT and NC are always negotiable; they are sort of "chewing-gum" notions that assume configurations that vary according to circumstances and cultures. Things are there, with their invasive presence; I don't think there is a culture that can induce one to perceive dogs as bipeds or feathered creatures, and this is a *very strong* bond indeed. But apart from that, meanings scatter, dissociate themselves, and reorganize. Even the so-called "dispositional" properties give us serious reasons for doubting whether the proposition *Sugar is soluble* (in whatever language it is uttered) is the same when it is expressed in Latin America (with reference to brown cane sugar) or in Europe (with reference to white beet sugar). This "solubility" requires different times.

The same negotiability, as has been demonstrated by the story of the platypus, regulates the construction of scientific paradigms, even though in such cases the restructuring of the directories takes more time and is negotiated on the basis of rigorous and not wild criteria.

4.7.1 The meaning of terms and the sense of texts

Some have concluded that, if meaning is negotiable, then it is no longer of any use in explaining the way we understand one another.

There are two ways to avoid talking of meaning. The first consists in stating (e.g., as in Marconi 1997: 4) that we cannot talk of meaning, because it is an entity whose whereabouts is unknown, whereas we can talk about the various kinds of lexical competence, which are "families of skills." But in such a case, it seems to me, in order to establish that such competence exists, all we can do is try a behavioral test: that the speakers share the same degree of competence would be proved by the fact that they understand one another, making the same inferences from the same premises, or in referring to something, and making what I have called acts of felicitous reference. Now, in what way does this proof of the existence of shared competence differ from what I understand as proof by interpretation of the public existence of a content (or meaning) that in its turn proves the private existence of cognitive types? Let us remember that for Peirce even certain ongoing behavior can be seen as a *dynamic interpretant* (the fact that at the command *Attention!* all soldiers assume a determined position is a possible interpretant of the verbal command). Therefore to speak of meanings as content does not lead to any hypostatization of elusive entities, or no more at least than it does with concepts of competence or lexical abilities.

The second way consists in saying that the understanding of language happens simply by attributing *beliefs* to our interlocutor that may coincide more or less with our own. But I have the impression that the introduction of belief does not exorcise the ghost of meaning (and of the CT it expresses), at least not in the sense of content I have been using so far. To take an example from Davidson (1984: 279), if a boat sails past rigged as a ketch, and someone beside me says, *Look at that fine yawl!*, I assume (i) he perceived the rigging of the boat as I did and erred only in using the linguistic term that belongs to a simple slip; (ii) he does not know the content of the word *yawl;* or (iii) he has committed a perceptual error. But in all these cases I must postulate that he may know various types of boat just as I do and that he associates a term with these types that expresses their NC, otherwise I could not even suppose that he has (i) simply confused the use of the words, (ii) confused the meaning of words, or (iii) erred in associating a given token with an idea of boat that he is conceiving somewhere. Without the assumption that the two interlocutors must in some way share a system, no matter how asystematic, of directories and files, interaction is not possible. I might be moved by a principle of charity so generous as to attribute to the other person directories organized differently from my own, and try to adapt myself to them. If this means comparing "beliefs," well and good. But then we are dealing with a purely terminological issue. The tree of directories, and that which ought to be registered, is postulated as that organization of content, no matter how idiosyncratic, which others call "meaning."

I maintain that these discussions lack a distinction that many theories of semiotics have been making for a long time, even though I admit that it is difficult to come to an agreement regarding the sense to be assigned to the terms. The notion of *meaning* is internal to a semiotic system: it has to be admitted that in a given semiotic system there exists a meaning assigned to a term. The notion of *sense,* on the other hand, is internal to utterances or, rather, to texts. I do not think anybody would refuse to admit that there exists a fairly stable meaning of the word *dog* (to the point that we can even—an extreme act of semiotic imprudence—assume that it is the synonym of *cane, chien, perro,* and *Hund*) and that nevertheless the same word can assume different *senses* within different utterances (we need only think of metaphorical cases).[23]

Readers are enjoined not to think in terms of a total parallelism with the difference as posited by Frege between *Sinn* and *Bedeutung.* In any case it seems clear to me that the dictionary can assign a meaning to term X, and nonetheless within different utterances the same term can assume different senses (if nothing else, in the most trivial sense of the term, and so the expression *This pope is corrupt,* pronounced by an anticlerical with reference to Alexander VI, may have a sense that is different from that pronounced with reference to John XXIII by a traditionalist prelate).

Now, it is evident that in order to determine the *sense* of an utterance, it is necessary to have frequent recourse to the principle of charity. But the same rule does not hold good with regard to the *meaning* of a term.

To say that understanding one another is the effect of infinite negotiations (and acts of charity in order to be able to understand the beliefs of others, or the format of their competence) regards the understanding of utterances, i.e., of texts.[24] But it does not mean we can eliminate the notion of *meaning* by dissolving an old and venerable semantics in syntax, on the one hand, and in pragmatics, on the other. To say that meaning is negotiated does not mean that the contract springs from nothing. On the contrary, also from a juridical point of view, contracts are possible precisely because contractual *rules* are already in existence. A sale is a contract: if A sells a house to B, after the contract the house will be defined as the property of B, and it would never have been such had it not been for the sales agreement; but for the contract to be made, it was necessary for A and B to agree on the NC of *sale*. A and B can even negotiate the content of *house* (B could say to A that what he is trying to sell him is not a house but a farmhouse, a shanty, a cow shed, a skyscraper, a lake dwelling, or a ruin unfit for human habitation). But even in such a case they would start off from a shared notion of artifact originally intended to shelter living creatures or things, and if they were unable to have a *regulated* notion that at least allowed them to distinguish what *could* be defined as a house from what *could* be defined as a tree, they would not be able even to begin negotiating.[25]

Defining the meaning of the term *sale* is not the same as saying in what sense I must interpret the expression *You sold yourself to the enemy*.

It is one thing to say that we cannot formulate precise rules for the disambiguation of a concept (because it all depends on each individual's beliefs), and another to say that the meanings of terms in a given language, which to some extent must be public, are nonetheless always negotiable, and not only in the shift from language to language but also within the same language, according to different pertinences.

Insofar as they are contents, meanings can always be identified even though they fluctuate and coagulate, and for some speakers shrivel until they all but prevent them from speaking appropriately or from recognizing something. But I see no reason why a *contractual* view of the sense of utterances must rule out, on the one hand, the existence of a grain that binds our cognitive types and, on the other, the linguistic conventions that register these bonds and supply the basis for successive interpretations and negotiations.[26]

There is no doubt that if I, sitting in a car beside the driver, urge her on, saying, *You can go, the traffic light is blue*, she will instantly understand that I meant to say *green* (or she will think that I am color-blind, or that it was merely a slip on my part). Perhaps this happens because the meaning of the words does not count and she understands me only because she attributes to me a belief similar to her own? And what would have happened if in that moment I had said *You can go, because 7 is a prime number*? Would she have thought that, as I am like her, I could only have been referring to the green light? Or would not the strength of the words, independently of the situation, have obliged her to try to understand what I meant to communicate, perhaps implicitly, because my observation was certainly mathematical and had nothing to do with traffic circulation?

4.7.2 Meaning and the text

I have said that certain surprises regarding the flexibility of our semiotic instruments spring from the fact that, in almost all discourses on the elusive nature of meaning, there is confusion over the *meaning* of the terms and the *sense* of the utterance. But there is more to the problem than this. There is also confusion with regard to *elementary utterances* and *texts*.

In the traffic-light example, the dialogue cannot stop at that point. The driver has to ask me for extra information; I have to tell her what I meant by that mathematical allusion. Textual semiotics has acknowledged for some time that we can recognize systems of conventions on a *grammatical* level and nevertheless admit that negotiation occurs on a *textual* level. It is the text that negotiates the rules. All things considered, giving a book the title *Pride and Prejudice* also means to say that, at the end of the novel, our idea of those two sentiments, or of that social behavior, must emerge modified. But this on condition that right from the start we have a vague notion of what those two words mean.

As for isolated utterances, these highly improbable affairs (pronounced only in language laboratories) allow for no negotiation; only autistic subjects exchange fragments of their extremely private idiolect, asserting that men can be unmarried without being bachelors, that elephants can or cannot have trunks. But to negotiate with my patient readers that it is possible to say truthfully that *Ayers Rock is a mountain* and at the same time that *Ayers Rock is not a* MOUNTAIN, I had need of lengthy argumentation in textual form, and I could not rely on my interlocutor's goodwill, or on her charity—to be hoped for—toward me.

This brings me handily to some thoughts on the cartoonist Peyo's little blue gnomes, known in English as the Smurfs, which were originally called Les Schtroumpfs.[27] The characteristic of the Schtroumpf language is that in it, as often as possible, proper and common nouns, verbs, and adverbs are replaced by conjugations and declinations of the word *schtroumpf*.

For example, in one of the stories a Schtroumpf decides to rise to power and launches a political campaign. His speech sounds like this:

> Demain, vous schtroumpferez aux urnes pour schtroumpfer celui qui sera votre schtroumpf! Et à qui allez-vous schtroumpfer votre voix? A un quelconque Schtroumpf qui ne schtroumpfe pas plus loin que le bout de son schtroumpf? Non! Il vous faut un Schtroumpf fort sur qui vous puissiez schtroumpfer! Et je suis ce Schtroumpf! Certains—que je ne schtroumpferez pas ici— schtroumpferont que je ne schtroumpfe que les honneurs! Ce n'est pas schtroumpf!... C'est votre schtroumpf à tous que je veux et je me schtroumpferai jusqu'à la schtroumpf s'il faut pour que la schtroumpf règne dans nos schtroumpfs! Et ce que je schtroumpfe, je schtroumpferai, voilà ma devise! C'est pourquoi tous ensemble, la schtroumpf dans la schtroumpf, vous voterez pour moi! Vive le pays Schtroumpf!

The Schtroumpf language seems to lack all the requisites of a working language. It is a language devoid of synonyms and full of homonyms, more than a normal language could handle. But not only do the Schtroumpfs understand one another perfectly well, the reader does too, and that is what counts.

This would seem to work in favor of Davidson's position. The Schtroumpfs do not speak in a void (they do not utter sentences outside any given situation) but in the context of a comic strip, and therefore in a multimedial context, where we not only read (or hear) what they are saying but also see what they are doing. But this is the situation in which we usually interpret other people's words—and it is because we speak within a situation that we are able to apply the deictics, such as *this* or *that*. Therefore it might be said that, on hearing that burst of homonyms in a given situation, we attribute the speaker with the same beliefs we would cleave to in the same situation, and by the principle of charity we lend him those terms he has not uttered but which he could or should have uttered.

Or we might say (as Wittgenstein might have said) that in the Schtroumpf language the real meaning of the term is its use (obviously I am referring not so much to the *Schtroumpfus Schtroumpfico-Schtroumpficus* as to the *Schtroumpfische Unter-schtroumpfungen*).

But here two objections arise. The first is that we "lend" or attribute to the speaker the terms he has not uttered precisely because these terms (with their conventional meaning) *preexist* in our lexicon. If readers understand my joke about the Schtroumpf and Wittgenstein, it is because they have already heard the original titles mentioned. We can negotiate a contract only because a predefined semiotic (intertextual) system already exists, in which the various expressions have a content.

In the second place, the electioneering speech quoted earlier does not refer to the perceivable situation (i.e., to what the picture shows). It refers to the "political speech" scenario and its rhetoric. It refers to a large quantity of utterances we have heard in analogous situations and therefore to the universe of *intertextuality*. An expression like *Un quelconque Schtroumpf qui ne schtroumpfe pas plus loin que le bout de son schtroumpf* is understandable, because we know the stock phrase *He cannot see any farther than his own nose.* An utterance like *Je me schtroumpferai jusqu'à la schtroumpf* can be decoded, because we have heard on an infinity of occasions *I will fight to the death,* and we have heard it within the context of the rhetoric of deliberative speech. *La Schtroumpf dans la schtroumpf* is understandable, because we have heard *hand in hand* thousands of times.

This means that the Schtroumpf language responds to the rules of a linguistics of the text, where the sense depends on the identification of the textual topic. It is true that (see Eco 1979) every text is a *lazy machine* that requires active interpretative cooperation on the part of its receiver, and this laziness seems to invite us to make texts in Schtroumpf. Our collaboration is possible, because we appeal to the universe of intertextuality, and we can understand Schtroumpf, because all speakers use the term *schtroumpf* and its derivatives always and solely in those contexts in which a phrase of that kind has already been pronounced.

The Schtroumpf language is a parasitic language, because, although nouns, verbs, and adjectives are replaced with the all-purpose homonym, it would not be understood if it were not backed up by the syntax (and the various lexical contributions) of the base language (be it the original French or its translations). Now, in one of the stories we meet the enemy of the Schtroumpf, the wicked wizard Gargamel. He speaks the same French on which Schtroumpf is based, but normally. Gargamel casts a spell to change himself into a Schtroumpf and goes to the village of his little enemies. But he has to restrict himself to sidling along walls without replying to those who ask him why (we are told) he does not know the Schtroumpf language. How is this possible, if we have seen that the base language is the same as his, and he could interpret what the Schtroumpf say to him if only he applied the principle of charity? The fundamental rule of Schtroumpf is: Replace every term of the common language with *schtroumpf* as often as you can without excessive ambiguity. But Gargamel's problem is clearly that he finds all contexts ambiguous, or incomprehensible, for the simple reason that he has no intertextual information.

Let us suppose that an English speaker of average culture hears a Schtroumpf poet reciting *I schtroumpfed lonely as a schtroumpf*. He would certainly grasp the reference to Wordsworth. Obviously he would also grasp the reference to Shakespeare in *To schtroumpf or not to schtroumpf.* But he might well be stuck on hearing *Schtroumpf is the schtroumpfest schtroumpf,* because he may never have read T. S. Eliot before and may not know that some months are crueler than others. He would find himself in the same situation as Gargamel.[28]

Every application of the principle of charity to what someone is about to say is based on a modicum of lexical information but, above all, on a vast amount of information about what has already been said.

Chapter Five

Notes on Referring as Contract

After having spoken of meaning as contract, one is tempted to see if the notion of contract/negotiation might not also apply to the phenomenon of referring, and if so, to what extent.

It is no accident that the paragraphs of this essay are not numbered: this is precisely to exclude even the slightest suspicion that my discourse harbors any systematic ambitions. The question of referring, in all its ramifications, is one that would put the fear of God into even the strongest among us. Here I have restricted myself to a series of problematic observations, which throw light on some reasons why it is convenient to think that operations involving referring have a contractual nature—or at least a strong contractual component.

In Eco (1976: 163) I accepted Strawson's (1950) proposal, whereby mentioning or referring is not something an expression does but something that someone can use an expression *to do*. Strawson went on to say, "[To] give the meaning of an expression... is to give *general directions* for its use to refer to or mention particular objects and persons" and, "[To] give the meaning of a sentence is to give general directions for its use in making true or false assertions." I still think that this is a satisfactory arrangement and that referring is a *linguistic act.* Which does not alter the fact that it is very tricky to say what kind of linguistic act it may be and what are its conditions of felicitousness.

Between the meaning of an expression, which also provides instructions for the identification or retrieval of the referent, and the meaning of the sentence, which also ought to regard the expression's truth value, what remains empty is precisely the space for referring.

Can we refer to all cats?

First of all, so that these most partial notes may be understood, I must clarify what I mean by the term *referring.*

I intend to exclude a "broad" use of the term,[1] and I think it would be appropriate (also in the light of the previous essays) to limit the notion of referring to what is perhaps more properly describable as cases of *designation,* that is, to utterances that mention particular individuals, groups of individuals, specific facts or sequences of facts, in specific times and places. From now on I shall also be using the generic notion of "individual" for identifiable spatiotemporal segments, such as 25 April 1945, and I shall hold to the golden decision by which *nominantur singularia sed universalia significantur.*

I refer the reader to Eco (1989) for the extremely tortuous story of terms such as *denotatio* and *designatio,* which have taken on different senses in the course of the centuries, but I think we can accept what has now become the established custom whereby general terms "denote" properties of class or genera, while singular terms or expressions that circumscribe precise portions of space-time "designate" individuals (see, e.g., Quine 1955: 32–33).

I maintain therefore that we perform acts of reference by using designative sentences like *Look at that platypus, Go fetch me the stuffed platypus I left on the table, The platypus in Sydney Zoo is dead,* while I maintain that sentences like *Platypuses are mammals* or *Platypuses lay eggs* do not refer to individuals but assert some properties that are attributed to genera, species, or classes of individuals.

To return to the computer example I gave in 4.2, I am talking not so much about platypuses as about the way in which our directory tree (or that of the zoologist) is organized. We are not referring to any individual or group of individuals but reasserting a *cultural rule,* making a semiotic and nonfactual judgment,[2] reiterating the way in which our culture has defined a concept. Defining a concept means elaborating a unit of content, which corresponds in fact to the meaning, or to part of the meaning, of the corresponding term. Saying that "one refers" to meanings is at best a bizarre way of using the word *referring.*

If instead I say *In 1884, Caldwell saw a platypus while it was laying eggs,* I am referring to an individual x (Caldwell), who at the time y (1884) examined an individual platypus (which one I don't know, but he did, and it was certainly that platypus and not another, and I imagine it was a female) to discover that it laid ovoidal objects s_1, $s_2...s_n$ (I don't know how many, but he certainly knew, and the assertion refers to those objects and not to others).

While some authors hold that there are cases of reference to essences, which I shall call *quidditates,* here I should like to deal only with the designation of *haecceitates.* Naturally I mean *quidditas* in its Scholastic sense, as the essence itself seen as knowable and definable. To quote Aquinas, who however was referring in his turn to the words of Averroës (*De ente et essentia* III), "Socrates nihil aliud est quam animalitas et rationalitas, quae sunt quidditas ejus." In this context I am insisting on the fact that one can *designate* Socrates but not his quiddity, and I harbor doubts regarding the legitimacy of saying that *we refer* to the quiddity of Socrates. By bringing into play the concept of *haecceitas* (Scotist and not Thomist), I am calling into question the notion that Socrates is *nihil aliud* than his *quidditas.* And as a matter of fact Aquinas was well aware that, to talk of Socrates as an individual, it was necessary to appeal to a *principium individuationis,* which was the matter *signata quantitate.* Since my purpose here is neither to teach the history of medieval philosophy nor to profess neo-Thomism or neo-Scotism, I shall make free use of the notion of *haecceitas* as an unrepeatable characteristic of individuals (whether it depends on

the matter *signata quantitate* or any other principle of individuation—as, for example, a genetic inheritance, or registry office
records).

I assume the notion of individual in its most intuitive sense, the
way we use it in everyday speech. Usually we think not only that
there are unrepeatable objects of which no replica or double is conceivable (such as my daughter or the city of Grenoble) but that even
in the case of groups of objects in which each is the double of the
other (such as the sheets in a ream of paper) it is always possible to
choose one of those sheets and decide that, although it has all the
properties of the others, it is nonetheless *that* sheet, even though the
only mark of individuality I can allow it is that it is the sheet I am
holding in that moment. But that sheet is so individual that, if I
burn it, I have burned *that* one and not another.

It seems to me that the medieval notion of *materia signata quantitate is* no different from the idea of the principle of individuation
expressed, for example, by Kripke (1972: 350): "If a material object
has its origin in a certain hunk of matter, then it could not have its
origin in any other matter." This idea that the individual possesses
a *haecceitas* still has nothing to do with the idea that man or water
(in general) has an essence, even though in current causal theories
of reference these two problems often appear together. Which is a
good reason, in itself, for distinguishing between designation (of
individuals) and denotation (of genera).

However, I did specify that I intend to use referring not only for
the designation of individuals (in the broadest sense of the term,
and so even 25 April 1945 is an individuable segment of space-time,
and *the assassination of Julius Caesar* is an individually punctual fact)
but also for groups of individuals. By "groups of individuals to
which we can refer" (also including generic spatiotemporal segments, such as *the thirties*) we must understand a set of individuals
that has either been counted, or was countable, or might one day be
countable (so that every single individual could be individuated).

References to *the first victim of the Second World War* or to *the first
men to settle in Australia* are certainly very vague: but in using them,
we nevertheless presume that it may be theoretically possible one

day (or that it may have been possible in the past) to ascertain who the individuals in question were, if nothing else because of the fact that they certainly existed.

Deciding whether a sentence designates individuals or classes depends not on its grammatical form (on the basis of which one can construct an infinite number of bold examples and counterexamples without ever solving the problem definitively) but on the intention of the senders and on the assumptions of the receivers. Therefore a first contract is necessary to decide whether the sentence has a referential function or not.

Sometimes discriminating is very simple: *This stick is one meter long* certainly designates a certain individual stick, while *One meter equals 3.2802 feet* expresses a law or a convention. But other cases require more thought. If Herod, before the birth of Jesus, had said to Herodias that he hated all babies, she probably would have agreed about the fact that Herod was not referring to some particular babies but expressing his dislike of babies in general. But when Herod ordered his cutthroats to kill all the babies in Galilee, by his order he intended to designate *all* the babies born that year in a precise place, *one by one* (apart from anything else, they were identifiable thanks precisely to the census that had just been made).[3]

But there is a point that needs to be made clear, even though it should have been clear since the days of Plato and Aristotle. Isolated terms assert nothing (at best, they have a meaning): what is true and false is said only in the sentence, or in the corresponding proposition. Now, I am not saying that referring is the same thing as saying what is true and false (we shall see that acts of reference can be made even when we have not decided if what we are referring to is in fact the case or not), but without a doubt, if we always refer only to individuals, we refer to states of a world (any world). And to do this we need to articulate a sentence. If I say *cat,* I am not referring to anything. I can refer to *one* cat only, or to *some* cats localized or localizable in time and space. On the other hand, when people say we can refer to *generalia,* they are suggesting that referring is something we do with isolated terms. I often happen to hear otherwise entirely respectable persons stating that the word *cat* refers to cats, or to the essence of cats. For the reasons given previously, this strikes me as misleading, so I shall refrain from putting the problem that way.

The word *cat* always means or denotes, if you will, the essence of cat (or the NC, or the corresponding MC) in all circumstances, outside all contexts, and therefore its signifying or denotative power belongs to the lexical *type*. The same word designates a given cat only in the context of a sentence that has been uttered and that contains specifications of time and place, and therefore the function of designation is performed by the *token*. The sentence type *Cats are mammals* expresses a thought, in whatever context it appears, even if it is found in a bottle (and in any case one can decide whether it is true or false), while the sentence *There is a cat in the kitchen* refers to an X located in space-time and, if found written in a message in a bottle, it loses all referential efficacy. Even though we may suspect it to be an act of reference, we can no longer prove whether it was true or false at the time and place it was uttered (see Ducrot 1995: 303–05).

Having clarified the conditions under which the following discourse may be followed, follow me.

Referring to horses

If we return to the story of Montezuma related in 3.3, we see that (i) his messengers transmitted the NC of horse to him by interpretants; (ii) they were obviously referring to something they had seen in the course of the Spaniards' landing; (iii) Montezuma understood they were referring to something even before he understood what it actually was; (iv) on the basis of their interpretation, he constructed a CT of the horse, thanks to which, presumably, he was able to recognize the referent when he came across it; (v) it seems that after having received the message, he kept silent for a long time, and we may suppose that he never referred to horses until the moment came when he recognized one; and (vi) at the right time, he might have recognized the mysterious *maçatl* his messengers had told him about, yet, continuing to brood, he might have refrained from talking about and therefore referring to horses.

Therefore we can link an NC to a term, and this NC (which should have a corresponding CT) contains instructions for the recognition of the referent, but the instructions for the recognition of the referent and recognition itself have nothing immediately to do with the act of reference to something.

Now let's make our story a little more complex. The Spaniards arrive in Montezuma's palace. He thinks he recognizes a *maçatl* in the palace courtyard and dashes off to his courtiers (whose number include his messengers), saying that there is a *maçatl* in the courtyard. In that case he would certainly be referring to a horse, and this is what his messengers would understand, given that they are the ones who told him the meaning of the word. But one of the messengers might harbor a doubt: is it certain that Montezuma is using the word *maçatl* in the sense they use it? This is no small problem: if Montezuma is right, and a horse really has appeared in the courtyard, this means that the Spaniards have already arrived in the capital.

And what if, on listening to their description, Montezuma has misunderstood, and thinks he has seen a horse when in fact he has seen something else? Even though some otherwise respectable people will insist that the word *horse* always refers to horses and to horses only (to horsehood) independently of the intentions or lexical competence of the speaker, I don't think the messengers can content themselves with this comforting certainty, because their problem is to know what Montezuma has seen, and what he is referring to, even though he has got the name wrong.

The messengers' problem is the same as the one facing many philosophers today: how to "fix the reference." But their problem is not how to identify the referent of the word *maçatl,* about whose NC they have already agreed upon. They would be almost in agreement with those who define the extension of a term as the set of all the things for which the term is true (except that, aware they were still talking of terms and not sentences, they would have made a suitable correction: "the set of things to which one may correctly apply the term when wishing to utter true propositions"). But they must decide whether Montezuma is applying the name properly (and the criterion of correctness is the one they—the Nomothetes—fixed on the day the Spaniards landed), and only after having made this decision will they be able to *fix* the reference *understood* by Montezuma by the sentence *There is a maçatl in the palace courtyard*. Note that by speaking, Montezuma presumably intends to use the word *maçatl* in the same sense as his messengers use it, but this is hardly a guarantee for us, and even less so for them. They could, out of the principle of charity, assume that Montezuma is using it in the same sense as they are, but they cannot be sure.

The messengers are sure that Montezuma is referring to something, and what he is putting into effect is an act of reference, but they are not sure that it "points" to the referent they mean.

What are they to do? There is only one solution: to question Montezuma, to know if by the word *maçatl* he intends to refer to animals made in such and such a way. But even this is not enough. Certainty will be attained only when Montezuma points out a certain animal to them while uttering the appropriate term, but until that time it is necessary to stimulate Montezuma's interpretations with a view to making the NC of *maçatl* as public as possible.

Long negotiations must therefore follow, at the end of which both parties are holding a sequence of words, gestures, and drawings *made public,* like an affidavit or a sort of notarized deed. Only through that express contract can the messengers be reasonably sure that Montezuma is referring to the same thing they intend to refer to when they say *maçatl*. Fixing the reference of the sentence again means (as it does for the interpretation of the CT through an NC) making explicit a chain of intersubjectively verifiable interpretants.

At this point the messengers might be sure that Montezuma is referring to something and that what he is referring to is something they are prepared to recognize as a horse, yet they still cannot be sure that there really is a horse in the palace courtyard. Which tells us that referring to, intending (by referring) to use the language the way one's interlocutors do, and possessing the same instructions for recognizing the referent still have nothing to do with the question of whether a linguistic act of reference expresses a true proposition.

I think these differences should be borne in mind when it is admitted that semiotics of a structuralist stamp has ignored referring. I don't think anyone has ever denied that we use language for acts of reference; perhaps it has never been stated with sufficient forcefulness that the meaning of a term also includes a series of instructions for identifying the referent of this term (when it is used in a sentence with referential functions),[4] but neither has it ever been denied that there should be something in the meaning of *cat* (even if it is "meowing feline quadruped animal") that allows us to distinguish between a cat and a mat when necessary.

Instead, given that the problem facing structuralist semiotics was how to define the functioning of systems of signs (or of texts), the emphasis was placed, independently of the world to which they might refer, eminently on the relation between signifier and signified, or between expression and content.[5] Certainly no one was doubting that any system of signs could be used to refer to objects and states of the world; but, in extremely simple terms, it was held that, to be able to use the word *cat* to refer to a cat, the speakers had to agree on the meaning of "cat" beforehand.[6] Which was another way of putting, in a different context, Wittgenstein's later assertion (1953 §40) that one must not confuse the meaning of a name and the bearer of a name: "When Mr. N. N. dies, one says that the bearer of the name dies, not that the meaning dies. And it would be nonsensical to say that, for if the name ceased to have meaning, it would make no sense to say 'Mr. N. N. is dead.' "

Structuralist semiotics started from the principle that acts of reference are possible only insofar as we know the meaning of the terms used for referring—an idea with its supporters within the analytic paradigm; see Frege, for example. But unlike Frege, structuralist semiotics did not feel it worth going any deeper into the phenomenon of referring, considering it an extralinguistic accident. My suspicion is that the problem has also remained obscure for truth-functional semantics, and for obvious reasons: the problem of referring cannot be solved in formal terms, because it has to do with the intentions of the person speaking and is therefore a pragmatic problem. As such it has eluded the grasp of both structural semiotics and model-theoretic semantics. The provocative notion we owe to the theory of rigid designation (even though, as we shall see, I do not find it convincing)[7] is that there can be acts of reference that, at first sight at least, do not presuppose an understanding of the meaning of the terms used for referring.

The true story of the sarkiapone

This is the story of the *sarkiapone,* a famous humorous sketch from the Italy of the fifties, performed by the actors Walter Chiari and Carlo Campanini. For the purposes of my analysis, I have condensed the sketch into six phases.

Phase 1. Chiari enters the compartment of a railway train and greets Campanini and the other travelers. At a certain point Campanini gets to his feet and reaches up to the luggage rack, where there is a basket covered with a cloth. He withdraws his hand suddenly, as if he has been bitten. He asks the others not to make a noise, so that the sarkiapone, known for its irritability, will not be disturbed. Chiari, a vainglorious braggart, does not want people to know that he has no idea what a sarkiapone is; he sets to chatting about the animal like someone who has been dealing with sarkiapones all his life.

Phase 2. Not knowing what the sarkiapone is, Chiari opts for trial and error. For example, having learned from Campanini that his is an American sarkiapone, Chiari says he has only seen Asiatic sarkiapones. This allows him to hazard the enunciation of properties that Campanini's American sarkiapone does not have, but he soon runs into problems. He hints, using gestures, at the typical "snout" of the sarkiapone, but Campanini stares at him with a quizzical air and asks what he means by saying that the sarkiapone has a snout. Chiari adjusts his sights, declaring that in alluding to the beak, he expressed himself poorly, metaphorically. But no sooner has he said the word *beak* than he notes an amazed expression on Campanini's face. Chiari hastens to make amends by referring to the creature's nose.

Phase 3. From this point on, we have a crescendo of variations that follow one another thick and fast, in the course of which Chiari gets more and more stubborn and agitated. Defeated also on the nose, he turns to the eyes, then immediately after talks about a single eye. Defeated also on the eyes, he attempts to talk about the ears. Faced with the flat denial that the sarkiapone has ears, he immediately talks about its fins, then falls back on the chin, the fur, the wool, the feathers. He makes a tentative attempt to describe the way the animal walks, only to check himself immediately, saying that he meant its typical hopping gait. He guesses at the paws, progressively corrects himself about their number, tries to mention the wings, has a stab at scales, hints without success at the color (yellow? blue? red?), uses more and more half words and interrogative syllables in an attempt to "second guess" Campanini's (inevitably negative) reaction.[8]

Phase 4, the climax of the sketch. Exasperated, Chiari bursts into a violent and cathartic tirade against that "disgusting" beast, that impossible animal, which has no snout, no beak, no paws, hooves, claws, fingers, feet, nails, feathers, scales, mane, wattles, eyes, crest, tongue—he has by now given up trying to figure out what on earth it is.

Phase 5. Chiari demands that Campanini show the sarkiapone, the other passengers draw back terrified, and, as Campanini makes to open the basket, even Chiari is frightened. But then Campanini seraphically reveals that the sarkiapone does not exist. He shows Chiari that the basket is empty and confides that he often uses this trick to fend off the importunate and to keep the compartment to himself.

Phase 6. There follows a coda in which Chiari (cocky as ever) tries to have everybody believe that he knew all along it was a joke.

Are there closed white boxes?

I think the story of the sarkiapone is exemplary. In phase 1, the first interlocutor posits a term in the discourse, while the other (keeping to the rules of conversation) *presumes*—until the emergence of proof to the contrary—the existence of the corresponding object.[9] Given that at first Chiari does not know what properties a sarkiapone possesses, except for that of being presumably an animal, he negotiates the corresponding term *on trust.*

Perhaps I ought to clarify what I mean by "on trust." Although it has little to do with peering into that "black box," whose contents I have repeatedly stated I do not wish to inspect, we might nonetheless understand trust as a kind of "white box." A black box is something that by definition one cannot open, while a white box, even if closed, might be subsequently opened. We accept white boxes, especially when they are presented to us adorned with a handsome ribbon at Christmastime or on a birthday: before opening such a box, we already guess that it contains a present, and we begin to thank the donor. We put our faith in this person, presuming that he or she is not an oafish prankster bent on surprising us with an empty box. In the same way, buying something on trust means having faith in the seller, presuming that the box will effectively hold the guaranteed contents.

In day-to-day communicative interaction, we accept a great number of references on trust. If someone tells us he must take urgent leave of absence because Virginia is ill, we accept that somewhere or other there is a Virginia, even if we have never heard of her before. If instead our interlocutor says that we must apply to Virginia if we wish to be reimbursed for our traveling expenses to the Chipping Norton conference, we hasten to ask him if by that name he means the American state or the woman clerk in Chipping Norton, and we want to know right away how to identify or find out which is which. But this is an extreme case. Usually, unless we have some reason to harbor misgivings, if the speaker *posits* someone or something in the discourse, we accept that the someone or something exists somewhere. We collaborate in the act of reference, even when we know nothing of the referent and even when we do not know the meaning of the term used by the speaker.

In 3.7.1, I related how even though I too am incapable of telling an elm from a beech, I can easily recognize mangroves (which I was able to identify one day thanks to having read about them in many travel books) and banyan trees, about which I had received plentiful instructions in Emilio Salgari's adventure books. But I was convinced I knew nothing about the *paletuviere* (mentioned equally frequently in Salgari's books), until on reading an encyclopedia one day I discovered that, in Italian, *paletuviere* is simply another word for *mangrovia*. Now I could reread Salgari, imagining mangroves every time he mentioned *paletuvieri*. But what did I do for years and years, from childhood on, reading about these *paletuvieri* without knowing what they were? From the context I had deduced that they were plants, something like trees or bushes, but this was the only property I could manage to associate with the name. Nevertheless, I was able to read on by *pretending* to know what they were. I used my imagination to integrate what little I had been able to glimpse within the half-open box, but in fact I was taking something on trust. I knew that Salgari was referring to something, and I kept the communicative interaction open, to be able to understand the rest of the story, assuming (on trust) that *paletuvieri* existed somewhere or other and that they were plants.

Acceptance on trust might be understood as a case of *rigid designation*. According to the theory of rigid designators, in a counterfactual conditional that abstracted every known property from Aristotle we would still have to consider him the man who was baptized Aristotle at a determined moment, and by so doing we would accept on trust that a sort of unbroken bond connected the current utterance of the name to the individual thus baptized. But there is one ambiguity (and perhaps more than one) in the theory of rigid designation. On the one hand, we are supposed to assume—through an unbroken chain that binds the object that receives the name in the moment of its baptism to the name used by whoever refers to it—that the object is what *causes* the appropriateness of the reference (Kripke 1972: 298–99). On the other hand, Kripke maintains that the receiver of the name must intend to use it with the same reference as the person from whom he has learned it (Kripke 1972: 302). This is not the same thing.

Given that the sarkiapone does not exist, no object exists that could have caused the use of the name. Nonetheless there is no doubt that Chiari agrees to use the name *sarkiapone* in the same way Campanini presumably uses it: on trust. If there has been a causal chain, it therefore runs not from the object to the use of the name but from (Campanini's) decision to use the name to (Chiari's) decision to use it as Campanini uses it. We are faced not with a causality "object → name" but with a causality "use$_1$ of the name → use$_2$ of the name." I have no intention of solving this problem from the point of view of a causal theory of reference, since I do not agree with such theories. We might say that if the sarkiapone existed and had an essence, we would have "rigid" designation, while if it was imagined by someone who used that name to baptize a figment of the imagination, we would have "soft" designation. But I really do not know what either rigid or soft designation mean, because while this difference perhaps has ontological importance, it does not have semiosic importance: the act of reference set in motion by Campanini and accepted by Chiari would work the same way in both cases.

The problem seems to me to be different. And it is that the metaphor of the white box is imprecise. White boxes (just to spin out the metaphor a little longer) always tell us something about what is inside, because they inevitably have a label. If I use a proper noun such as Gideon, I am automatically stating that the bearer of the name is a human being of the male sex; if I use Dorothy, I am stating that she is of the female sex; if I insert my brother James into the discourse, James is already a human being who has the property of being my brother. Salgari had labeled the *paletuvieri* as plants, and—to conclude—if I mention Giuseppe Rossi, there is a strong possibility that the person designated is an Italian male, and if I mention Jean Dupont, there is a strong possibility that he is French, and if I mention Paolo Sisto Leone Pio Odescalchi Rospigliosi Colonna, there is a strong possibility that he belongs to the Roman aristocracy, apart from the fact that (at least originally) if someone was called Smith, he was described as the son of a blacksmith, and if he was called Miller, he was the son of a miller. Too little to be able to identify Peter Smith or Frank Miller as such, but enough to say that even proper names are not entirely devoid of content.

Note too that if proper names did not have a content (but only a *designatum*), there could not be such a thing as this second type of antonomasia, which is not the figure in which a general term par excellence is applied to an individual ("the Emperor" for Napoleon, "the Voice" for Frank Sinatra) but the figure in which the name of an individual is used, par excellence, as the sum of properties (he is a Rambo, Hercules, or Judas; she is a Messalina or Venus).

At first the story of the sarkiapone seems to be that of an unwary purchase made on trust, but in reality, by saying that the sarkiapone must not be disturbed because it is irritable, Campanini is already attaching a label to our white box (or basket): the sarkiapone is a living creature. Chiari takes it from there, and instantly uses the term as a "peg upon which to hang descriptions." His attempts in phase 3 are aimed at ascertaining the properties of the animal and therefore at obtaining instructions for the identification and recognition of the referent. Note that this sketch also exemplifies the difference between speaking-of and referring-to. Campanini refers to an individual sarkiapone (in the basket). Chiari accepts the reference, and it is to that sarkiapone that he refers. But, in order to establish what it is like, he appeals to the universal, or to general objects: he asserts that he has come across other sarkiapones and, in trying to define their properties, he talks of sarkiapones in general, in other words he is trying to acquire information with which to construct at least tentatively the NC of *sarkiapone* and to form its

CT, i.e., to have a chance to recognize the sarkiapone type. To do this, he always refers to the animal in the basket as if to a token that ought to exhibit all the properties of the type. You do not negotiate the reference without bringing content into play.

The dialogue in phase 3 can be understood as a process of "successive emptying" of all possible properties, so that the peg for hanging descriptions on remains exposed. When Campanini denies all possible properties for the sarkiapone, Chiari is left with little alternative, apparently, but to accept the name in a rigid manner. And he seems to do this, when in phase 4 he insults the mysterious beast, accusing it of not corresponding to any possible description. But he does not stop referring to that cursed being as a "beast."

When Campanini, in phase 5, reveals that the sarkiapone does not exist, Chiari realizes that he has been talking of a nonexistent creature, in other words, of a figment of Campanini's imagination, a fictitious individual that existed only in the possible world of someone else's tall story. But in phase 6, even after the trick has been revealed, Chiari still refers to the sarkiapone. Except now he refers to it not as an element of the real world but as an element of a world invented by Campanini. We might argue that in phases 1–5 Chiari is talking of a sarkiapone$_1$, which he thought existed, while in phase 6 he is referring to a sarkiapone$_2$, which he now knows exists only in a fictitious world. Yet he is still referring to the sarkiapone that Campanini was talking about, except for the fact that, before, he attributed it with the property of existing in the real world and, after, he attributed it with the property of not existing.[10] The two have reached perfect agreement and know exactly what they are talking about.

The moral of the story is that (i) referring is an action that speakers perform on the basis of a negotiation; (ii) in principle the act of reference effected by using a term might have nothing to do with the knowledge of the meaning of the term or even with the existence of the referent—with which it has no causal relationship; (iii) nevertheless, there is no designation definable as rigid that does not rest on an initial description ("label"), albeit a highly generic one; (iv) therefore, even apparent cases of absolutely rigid designation constitute the start of the referential contract, or the auroral moment of the relation, but never the final moment.

One might object that we are dealing with a comic sketch. Would the same thing happen if the dialogue were between two scientists, one of whom began to talk of a substance X, which she had discovered, and it was made clear at the end that that substance did not exist or had none of the properties that the discoverer attributed to it? In a similar situation a scientist would behave differently *from the scientific and moral point of view,* publicly discrediting whoever had lied to her, but from a semiosic point of view things would go no differently. In the course of a subsequent scientific conference the scientist would continue to cite substance X as an example of an imaginary substance, the subject of a scientific fraud (or of a major blunder), but she would continue to refer to it as the one she had spoken of when, before making the necessary checks, she had assumed, on trust, that it existed.[11]

I am well aware that there is another interpretation, if not of the story of the sarkiapone, at least of substance X. Some would say that, as the substance does not exist, the expression *substance X* has no referent, nor did it have one when the scientist thought, on trust, that it did. But to say that an expression cannot be applied to any referent does not mean to say that it cannot be used for an act of reference, and this is the point I wish to insist on. In this oscillation between the possible referent of the term and the use of the term in an act of reference there lurks an ambiguity that has been the cause of much debate on the ontology of reference.

The Divine Mind as e-mail

By an ontology of reference I mean above all the philosophical position according to which individuals (Saint Paul, Napoleon, Prague, or the Thames) can be defined *rigidly,* in the sense that, whatever description we assign to a name, it refers in any case to something or someone that has been thus baptized in a given moment of space-time, and—no matter how many properties may be denied it—it will always remain *that* someone or something (a *principium individuationis* based on a *materia signata quantitate*). However, the ontological theory of reference has also been extended to the *quidditates* (the essences, or general objects), which, even if we did not know them, would be natural constants with an objectivity of their own above and beyond both our mental acts and the way in which culture recognizes and organizes them. The extension of the hypothesis is not unjustified: if it is assumed that a name of a person can be connected directly to a *haecceitas* (even a past and therefore an immaterial one), why can a generic name not be linked directly to a *quidditas?* Which is more immaterial, horsehood or the *haecceitas* of Ashurbanipal, of whom I believe we no longer possess so much as a handful of dust? As we shall see, in both cases one cannot avoid assuming that the connection is provided by what Putnam (1981, III) calls *noetic rays* (which are merely a theoretical fiction).

From this point of view, for an ontological theory of reference, the term *water* would refer to H_2O in any possible world, just as the name Napoleon would always refer rigidly to that *unicum* of the history of the universe that occurred, genetically, physiologically, and biographically, once and once only (and would remain that way even if in some future world governed by radical feminists Napoleon were remembered only as the individual whose sole property was that of having been the husband of Josephine).

This would be a "strong" ontology, in which the reference to water would seem to be independent of all knowledge or intention or belief on the speaker's part. However, on the one hand this point of view does not exclude the question of what the reference is, while on the other hand it does not eliminate the notion of "cognition": it simply moves both from psychology to theology. What does it mean if we say that the word *water* always refers to H_2O regardless of all of the speakers' intentions? We would have to explain that species of ontological wire that binds that word to that essence, and, just to spin out the metaphor a little longer, we would have to think of the essence as a very bristly something from which protrude many wires, which connect it to *water, acqua, agua, eau, Wasser, voda, shui,* and even to the term (still nonexistent) that will be used in 4025 by visitors from Saturn to indicate the transparent liquid, unknown to them, that they will find on our planet. To exclude the intentions of the speakers, but to forge in some way the referential bond, a strong ontology would have to presuppose a Divine Mind, or an Infinite one, if you will. Taking for granted that the world exists independently of our knowledge of it, and that it exists as a population of essences reciprocally governed by laws, only a Mind that knows the world exactly as it is (and as It created it), and that indulgently accepts that the same essence can be referred to in different languages, can "fix" the referent in a stable manner.

To return to the well-known example from Putnam (1975: 223–27), if there existed on a twin Earth something that resembled the water of this planet in every way, something that looked the same, had the same flavor and biochemical effects, but nonetheless was not H_2O but XYZ, in order to say that whoever (on both planets) spoke of *water* would be referring to H_2O but not to XYZ, we would have to assume that some Infinite Mind sees things in exactly this way, because only its thought would guarantee the connection between names and essences. But it was Putnam himself (1981, III), in setting up an internal realism in opposition to the externalist point of view, who said that for the latter position to be tenable, we would need to presuppose a Divine Eye.

But postulating a Divine Mind poses an interesting problem in terms of intentionality. We must admit that the Divine Mind "knows" that every utterance of the term *water* refers to the essence of water, and that the nature of the intentional relation that binds the Divine Mind to the content of its "knowledge" eludes our understanding (and in fact we postulate that things happen this way, but we do not say how they happen). But what guarantees that all *our* utterances of the term *water* correspond to the intentionality of the Divine Mind? Clearly nothing, if not our good *intentions,* i.e., that when we speak of water, we intend to do, so to speak, the will of God and intend (voluntarily) to correspond to the intention of the Divine Mind.

Note that I say the "intention" and not the "intentionality" of a Divine Mind. Wondering about the intentionality of a Divine Mind goes beyond the limits of these humble reflections—and beyond those of far prouder reflections too. The problem is that it is also difficult to decide what corresponding to the intention of a Divine Mind means.

I admit that there is now a phenomenon that might serve as a model of a Divine Mind, and of an absolutely rigid designation. It is the phenomenon of the e-mail address. The "name" constituted by this address (let's say: adam@eden.being) corresponds to one entity and one alone (it is not necessarily a physical individual, it might be a company, but only that company and not another). We can be entirely ignorant of any properties the addressee might have (Adam might not be the first man, might not have eaten from the Tree of Knowledge, might not be the husband of Eve, etc.), but we know that that name (address) points to (via a chain of electrical phenomena that it is not worth analyzing in detail here but whose efficiency we witness daily) an individual entity distinguishable from all others, independently of our beliefs, opinions, lexical knowledge, and of the knowledge we have about the way in which it "points." In the course of time we could associate many properties with that name, but we do not need to: we know that if we type it into our mail program, we will reach *that* address and not another.[12] And we know that everything depends on a baptismal ceremony, and that the referential power of the address we use is *causally* due to that baptism.

But a phenomenon of this kind (so absolutely "pure" and beyond argument, independent of the intentions and the competence of all correspondents) exists only in e-mail. That the e-mail system may be a model of the Divine Mind may appear both reassuring and blasphemous, but there is no doubt that it is the only case in which we use an absolutely rigid designation in accordance with what is at least the model of a Divine Network, if not of a Divine Mind.

From the Divine Mind to the Intention of the Community

How do we withdraw from a strong ontology, guaranteeing at the same time a certain objectivity of the reference? By thinking up a weak ontology of the Mind of the Community (whose privileged representatives are, depending on the field, the Experts). In this sense referring correctly to water means referring to it in the same way as the community of experts—who agree that water is H_2O today but tomorrow, by taking the fallibilism of knowledge into due account, might opt for another definition. But in no way does this solve the problem posed by the hypothesis of the Divine Mind: what guarantee do we have that when we use the word *water* in an act of reference, we are using it as the Mind of the Community does? The answer lies simply in our (voluntaristic) decision to use that word in the same sense as the experts do.

Now, in the sketch about the sarkiapone, was Chiari doing anything different when he decided to use the word *sarkiapone* the same way Campanini used it? Chiari simply assumed that Campanini was an Expert. Is there is an ontological difference between Campanini's opinion and Einstein's? There is only our persuasion that, statistically speaking, our encyclopedias register Einstein as a qualified expert while they do not mention Campanini (and I grant there are good reasons for this preference). This means to say that, when we speak, we have an idea, sometimes vague and sometimes precise, about some matters covered by the consensus of the Community.

But while the terms describing so-called natural kinds (such as water and gold) suggest that there is an expert as a Privileged Interlocutor (an interpreter authorized by the Community), this is not the case with *my cousin Arthur, Mafalda's cat,* or *the first hominid to reach Australia*. Here there is ample possibility of a contract, because here Campanini's word is as good as Einstein's.

For example, faced with the sentence *Napoleon was born in Cambridge,* convinced as I am that *my* Napoleon was born in Ajaccio, by no means do I agree to use the name according to the intentions of the Community, because, out of the principle of charity at least, I immediately suspect that the speaker intends to refer to *another* Napoleon. Therefore I do my best to check the appropriateness of the reference, trying to induce my interlocutor to interpret the NC that he makes correspond to the name *Napoleon*, to discover perhaps that his Napoleon is a used car salesman born in this century, and so I find myself faced with a banal case of homonymy. Or I realize that my interlocutor intends to refer to my Napoleon, and therefore intends to make a historical proposition that defies current encyclopedic notions (and therefore the Mind of the Community). In such a case I would proceed to ask him for convincing proof of his proposition.

But now let us try to take seriously the decision to use a term according to the intention and the consensus of the Experts or the Community. Let us suppose that, faced with the threat of extinction of the African elephant, the ECO (Elephant Control Organization) realizes that (i) there are three thousand elephants in the Kwambia area, more than the number that the ecological balance can sustain (the elephants ruin the crops and therefore the population is led to slaughter them, whereas, if their number were lower, they might be tolerated); (ii) in the Bwana area, the elephants, slaughtered by ivory poachers, are on the verge of extinction (strict laws have been passed that might ensure their survival, but the number of them in circulation is too low to guarantee the continuity of the species); (iii) it is necessary to capture a thousand elephants in Kwambia and transfer them to Bwana; (iv) the confederation of African States and the World Wildlife Fund have approved the operation and have ordered the officers of the ECO to carry it out. In the course of these preliminaries, reference was made to Kwambia and Bwana, and the supposition is that there is an agreement regarding the referent of these territorial names. Now all the three thousand elephants in Kwambia are being *designated,* one by one, and the assertion is that one thousand of these will have to be transferred to Bwana. It is not yet known which animals the one thousand will be, but, just as we can designate a child about to be born, it is possible to designate a thousand elephants that, on the day of the transfer to Bwana, will be exactly those and not other individuals. The problem is ensuring that the officers of the ECO have an exact knowledge of the meaning of the term *elephant* and do not transfer rhinoceroses or hippopotamuses by mistake.

It is not enough to say that the officers of the ECO intend to use the term *elephant* to refer to the same genus of creatures that the Experts are referring to. This understanding, based on the Expert's goodwill, is good only for getting the discourse under way. The Experts want to be sure that there is no possibility of misunderstanding. Therefore they communicate to the officers in charge that by elephant they mean an animal that, according to official science, has the properties XYZ, and they also provide instructions for the recognition of animals with such properties. If the officers in charge agree and state they want to capture and transfer a thousand specimens of animal XYZ, the operation may begin.

At this point it is irrelevant to state that the officers of the ECO intend to use the term according to the Experts' intention. As a matter of fact, between them and the Experts there is the beneficial space of a series of interpretants (descriptions, photos, drawings) and it is on these that the agreement is based. If by chance there are some very rare white elephants in Kwambia, the contracting parties will have to agree on whether the term *elephant* includes or excludes white elephants, given that the correctness of the ecological operation depends on this agreement.

Yet again, rigid designation has had an introductory function, to get the contract under way, but it is not on this basis that the contract is concluded.

Quid pro quo and negotiations

Let us suppose that someone tells us a peace conference was held in Aix-la-Chapelle in 1748 and that we do not know that Aix-la-Chapelle is the other name for the city of Aachen. We find ourselves confronted with a "white box" that is still unopened and that is not the one in which we habitually collocate the city of Aachen. Perhaps the matter interests us so little that we drop all negotiations; perhaps we request further information, asking questions about that strange city, our curiosity aroused by the fact that another peace conference was held at the same time as the one held in Aachen; and finally perhaps, out of the principle of charity, we immediately suppose that by the name *Aix-la-Chapelle* the speaker meant to refer to the same city that we call *Aachen*. But in any case we would see how much our encyclopedic knowledge, and therefore our knowledge about content, conditions and directs our negotiations for the success of the reference.

Such knowledge also makes it possible to solve the apparent paradox (my example is a somewhat free elaboration of an idea taken from Kripke 1979) of a certain Pierre who had always heard tell in France of *Londres* and had conceived the idea that it was a most beautiful city, and so he wrote in his diary, *Londres est une ville merveilleuse;* and then he chanced to go to Great Britain to learn English from the source and visited a city called by its inhabitants *London*. He found it intolerable and wrote in his faithful diary (unfortunately for us a bilingual one), *London is an ugly city*. Hence the fears of his Italian translator, who would have to make him say (contradictorily) that *Londra* is both beautiful and ugly at one and the same time—not to mention the misgivings of logicians who would not know how to deal with two so shamelessly contradictory statements, et cetera.

All this amounts to an injustice with regard to translators, logicians, and normal people. The story offers two possibilities: after having visited the place and on the basis of some description Pierre received when someone told him about London (English city on a river, with a Tower), either Pierre realized that there was only one city where before he had believed there were two, or he is an imbecile who accepted the first reference to *Londres* on trust, without knowing anything other than that it was a city, and never understood that the names *Londres* and *London* refer to the same object. In the first case, let's give Pierre a chance to converse with other people and correct his beliefs, and perhaps to say that at first he thought (on the basis of unverified rumors) that London was beautiful, and later on he discovered it was ugly. In the second case,

Pierre remains locked in his cognitive and semantic confusion, and—apart from the fact that at this point one wonders why the diaries of an imbecile merit translation—the translator will have to insert some notes, to make it clear that we are dealing with an interesting semiotic and psychiatric document, because Pierre is one of those men who mistakes his wife for a hat or talks of Napoleon Bonaparte (as first consul and the loser of Waterloo) with the intention of referring to himself. All of which is of interest to psychiatry, not semantics.

Note that misunderstandings of this type are far commoner than suggested by the example—chosen with a taste for the improbable—that we have just examined. A collector of old books may see in a catalogue that the first (1662) edition of Gaspar Schott's *Physica Curiosa* was published in Würzburg. Then in another catalogue he finds that the first edition was published in the same year in Herbipolis. Therefore he notes in his diary that there are two editions of the same work from the same year, in two different cities—not an unusual phenomenon at that time. But a little extra information would enable him to verify that the pleasant Bavarian town of Würzburg includes among its encyclopedic properties the fact that it was previously designated as Herbipolis (and that the German name is simply a translation of the Latin name). End of the tragedy. All he had to do was ask. When they listen to acts of reference, people usually *ask lots of questions*. If our collector does not know enough to ask (or consult highly precise lexicons on such matters), then he simply becomes the subject of an amusing anecdote, like the student who (and this is apparently true) mentioned in a term paper essay the "well-known" debate between Voltaire and Arouet.

All in all, it seems to me that these contractual conditions, backed up by cognitive operations, provide a picture of what we effectively *do* when we refer to something that is more faithful than the one portrayed by ontological theories of reference. None of this amounts to a suggestion on my part that the question of ontological reference—or the treasures of subtlety that have been spent on settling it—is a trivial matter. And not just because the question is of particular importance in the universe of scientific discourse, where if two astronomers talk about the G14 nebula, they must be sure of what they are saying: even referring to the G14 nebula is a matter for negotiation, certainly more so than occurs in our day-to-day acts of reference (in which we often decide to "let it drop"), and certainly according to far stricter criteria. The problem lies rather in the fact that to be able to refer continuously and pragmatically, *we need the regulative idea of ontological reference.*

The strange case of Doctor Jekyll and the brothers Hyde

In London there are two brothers, John and Bob Hyde, identical twins and alike in every respect. The two (don't ask me why, but evidently they like it this way) decide to create a single public personality, Doctor Jekyll, and they prepare for this from earliest childhood. They study medicine together, begin their internship, become a doctor (Jekyll) of considerable renown, who is nominated director of the University Hospital. Right from the start, the brothers observe a rule: they impersonate Jekyll on alternate days. When John is Jekyll, Bob stays at home eating canned food and watching television, and vice versa the following day. In the evening, the one who comes home from work tells the other all about his day in meticulous detail, so that the next day the other can take his place and no one will notice the substitution.

One day, John, who is on duty, embarks on an affair with a colleague, Doctor Mary. Naturally the next day, Bob carries on the relationship, and so the affair continues, to the enormous satisfaction of the three protagonists: John and Bob in love with the same woman, Mary convinced that she loves one man.

Now if Mary tells her best friend, Ann, from whom she has no secrets, *Yesterday I went out with Jekyll,* and granting that Bob was on duty yesterday evening, who is Mary referring to? An ontological theory of reference would allow us to say that, even if Mary thinks that Bob's name is Jekyll, since she is referring to the person she went out with yesterday evening (who was christened Bob Hyde when he was a baby), she is referring to Bob. But if, this evening, she spends a night of passion with John, and the following day again tells Ann that she went out with Jekyll, to whom is Mary referring? Although she believes that John Hyde's name is Jekyll, from the point of view of a Divine Mind she is referring to John. Therefore she refers to different people on alternate days, through the same mistaken name, but she does not know it.

It is clear that from a pragmatic point of view this double reference is of minimal importance for us (as it is for her). A celestial accountant, who had to take into consideration the exactitude of all the acts of reference pronounced in the world, would probably have registered that on the fifth of December Jekyll was Bob, and on the sixth he was John. John and Bob might want to see themselves from the point of view of an Infinite Mind, because it might be very important for them to know if, in the course of her confidences with Ann, Mary judges one evening more satisfactory than the previous one. But John and Bob are indeed exceptional characters, whose function in this story of mine is that of the deus ex machina, and therefore we shall take no notice of their referential accounting (besides, I fancy that they too have lost count). The accounting that interests us is that of Mary and of all those in London who know Doctor Jekyll (and are unaware of the existence of the Hyde brothers).

For all these people, every reference to Doctor Jekyll is the reference not to an essence but to *an actor in the social comedy,* and in this sense any one of them knows one Doctor Jekyll and one only. They have a CT of him, they can list some of his properties, and they speak of him and no one else. Anyone who has been treated by Doctor Jekyll, has signed a contract with him, has received a good check from him, has told someone to find him Doctor Jekyll (and had his wish fulfilled), or says he has spoken with Doctor Jekyll and means to be believed, behaves as if there were one Doctor Jekyll and one only.

From an ontological point of view, we might say that Doctor Jekyll does not exist, that he is only a social figment, an aggregate of legal properties. But this social figment is sufficient to make every proposition concerning Doctor Jekyll socially true or false.

One day, while John is on duty, he trips on the stairs and breaks his ankle. He is immediately taken to the hospital orthopedist, Doctor Holmes, who takes an X-ray, puts the ankle in plaster, gives John two splendid aluminum crutches, and sends him home in a taxi. Fiendishly clever, the two brothers understand that it is not enough for Bob to put his foot in plaster: Doctor Holmes might want to replace the plaster, and would discover the deception. Heroically, Bob, after having made a careful study of his brother's X ray (we must remember they are both doctors), takes a hammer and with one precise blow breaks his ankle too, puts the foot in plaster, and shows up at the hospital the following morning.

The thing might work, but Holmes is highly meticulous. At the time of the accident, he ordered some blood tests on Jekyll-John; and a few days later, worried about an excess of triglycerides, he repeats the tests, but this time on Bob. And he notices that the results of the two tests do not coincide. Having no reason to suspect (so far) a deception, he presumes there has been an error and ingenuously speaks of the matter to Bob. That evening the two brothers put their heads together, scrutinize the results of the tests, and one of the two decides to go on a strict diet to bring his level of triglycerides to that of his brother. They do what they can, but it is not enough to fool Doctor Holmes, who—after the tests have been made again, and twice at that, and by a trick of fate on both John and Bob—still notices a discrepancy. Holmes begins to suspect the truth.

The two brothers engage in a deadly struggle with their enemy. In various ways they try to ensure that the fracture heals in the same time, they continue with their rigorous diet, but tiny details make Doctor Holmes more and more suspicious. He injects one of the two with an allergen that has an effect within twenty hours and lasts two days, and he notices that after injecting Jekyll with the substance on Tuesday at 5 P.M., on Wednesday at the same time the effects still have not manifested themselves. But on Thursday they appear. Holmes has grounds to conjecture that there are two people involved, but he has no convincing proof to show in public.

One way of ending the story would be that Doctor Holmes

manages to reveal the deception. From that moment (not considering all the legal, romantic, or social problems that would result) the social body would have to decide that the name *Jekyll* is a homonym indicating two different people. Among other things, even if they were sentenced to prison, the two brothers would be obliged by the judge to wear a lapel badge stating their blood group and other medical-biological data, so that they might be recognized. The other (more appealing) solution is that Doctor Holmes does not attain absolute certainty, nor does he manage to exhibit any decisive proof of the deception, because the two brothers are smarter than he is. The affair therefore continues ad infinitum, in a sort of hunt in which the prey always eludes the hunter but the hunter does not give up.

But in this case what interests us is: Why does the hunter not give up? Because Holmes, although used to pragmatic ways of referring like everybody else, has his own stubborn idea of ontological reference. He believes that, if Jekyll exists, there is an essence, a "Jekyll" *haecceitas* that represents the parameter of an ontologically true reference. Or he believes that, if two different people were to exist in place of Jekyll, as he suspects, at a certain point he ought to identify two different *haecceitates*. Remember that Holmes does not know which *principium individuationis* he is hunting for: it could be a particular composition of the blood, a minimal variation in two electrocardiograms, something that could be revealed by a scan or an intestinal exploration, the discovery of two different genetic makeups, a miraculous X ray of the soul... Holmes tries everything; he will always be defeated, but he will not stop searching, because he postulates the essence, that is, the Thing-in-Itself, which is not the Unknowable but the very postulate of infinite research.[13]

This persuasion that an ontological point of view may exist can be found in Peirce's notion of the final logical interpretant, the wholly ideal moment in which knowledge coincides with the totality of the thinkable. This is a regulative concept, which does not hinder the progress of semiosis but does not discourage it either, so to speak, and let it be understood that, even if it is infinite, the process of interpretation tends toward something. Like Peirce,

Holmes thinks that by continuing to search, he is carrying forward the Torch of Truth, and that in the long run the Community might agree to an incontestable final assertion. He knows that the long run could last for millennia, but Holmes has a philosophical and scientific mind, and he believes that those who come after him will arrive at the truth, perhaps through the examination of puzzling osteological evidence some hundreds of years later. He does not aspire to knowing: he aspires to carry on searching. Holmes could even be a relativist, who believes that we can provide infinite descriptions of the world as it is, and yet he is also a realist (in the sense of Searle 1995: 155) for whom a profession of realism does not mean to assert that we can know the way things are, and not even that we can say something definitively "true" about them. Realism means only to assume that *there is a way in which they are,* and that this way does not depend on us or on whether or not we will one day know it.[14]

Holmes has found a photo of Doctor Jekyll in the hospital archives. By now convinced of the existence of the two Hyde brothers (even though he perhaps does not call them this way), he knows with absolute certainty that, if the photo is a snapshot taken at a certain time on a certain day, it can be only *causally* connected to *one* of the two brothers (of whose existence, as Peirce would have put it, it is an index), and this is for him (as it is for us) an inconfutable certainty. But the photo is of no use to him at all, it is not even the proof that his hypothesis is right. It is the certainty alone that his hypothesis is right that drives him to think that the photo is causally connected to only one of the two individuals who impersonate Jekyll on alternate days. For anyone else the photo is causally linked to Doctor Jekyll, and social credence prevails over the ontological datum that is hidden, presumed, believed, but inaccessible.

What is the moral of our story? That in everyday life we always have to do with pragmatic acts of reference, and it would be our hard luck if we made too much of a problem of it. But to ensure the development of knowledge, we can invoke the ghost of ontological reference as a postulate that permits research in progress.

Is Jones mad?

Let's get back to negotiation. I apologize for reusing a decidedly overworked example, but after the impudence with which I have reflected on bachelors, nothing embarrasses me anymore. Let us return to the renowned example used by Donnellan (1966) to distinguish between the referential and attributive use of a sentence.[15] Used referentially, the sentence *Smith's murderer is mad* means that that description is intended to indicate a specific person, known both to the speaker and the listener; used attributively (to assess the brutality of the crime), it means to say that whoever has the property of being Smith's murderer also has the property of being mad.

Unfortunately, the matter is not that simple, and here is an (incomplete) list of the various situations in which the sentence could be uttered:

(i)   The speaker means to refer to Jones, who was caught as he was killing Smith with a power saw.

(ii)   The speaker means to refer to whoever murdered Smith with a power saw.

(iii) The speaker means (ii), but he does not know that in reality Smith is not dead (he was saved in extremis by Doctor Jekyll). In fact, there should not be a referent for the expression *Smith's murderer,* but the principle of charity prompts one to imagine that the speaker means to refer to the unsuccessful murderer (who would still be mad, and incompetent into the bargain).

(iv)   The speaker means (ii), but the speaker is probably mad, because no one has made an attempt on Smith's life. The listeners understand that the speaker is making a hallucinatory reference to an individual or a situation from the possible world of his beliefs.

(v)   The speaker believes (mistakenly) that Smith has been murdered, that the murderer is Jones, and that everybody knows this. If the listeners do not know that the speaker harbors these strange beliefs, we are in situation (iv). If the speaker goes on to make his beliefs explicit, the listeners will understand that he is referring to Jones. Now it will be necessary to decide whether the speaker thought Jones was mad because Jones was Smith's murderer or for other reasons (with the result that the speaker will still think Jones mad, even though Jones did not murder Smith).

(vi) Smith really has been murdered, and the speaker believes that the murderer is Jones (while everybody knows it was Donnellan). The interlocutors do not know the speaker's beliefs and think he means to say that Donnellan is mad (which is clearly false, because Donnellan has murdered Smith for scientific reasons, so as to be able to work on the difference between attributive and referential use). I imagine that, if the conversation went on for a little, it might be possible to clear up the misunderstanding but—as in (v)— extra information will be required to establish whether the speaker means to refer to Jones, though Jones is innocent, as a madman.

(vii) Smith really has been murdered, and the speaker believes that the murderer is Jones (while everybody knows it is Donnellan). But the listeners know that the speaker is biased against Jones and has repeatedly stated that he believes him to be Smith's murderer, and therefore they understand that the speaker means to refer to Jones.

(viii) The Smith murder trial is coming to an end, and in the dock Donnellan is listening to the sentence that officially defines his guilt. The speaker (a psychiatrist) has just entered the courtroom and thinks that Donnellan is a certain Jones he had known in the mental hospital. He is therefore referring to Jones and not Donnellan. Naturally the listeners believe he is referring to Donnellan. But I imagine that they will ask him to explain his judgment, and in the course of the conversation the referential misunderstanding might be cleared up.

This is a set of cases in which the reference is negotiated, and in which we cannot speak of an act of reference that is independent of the intentions and knowledge of the speaker and that points to a *haecceitas* of which the speaker knows nothing.

What does Nancy want?

But the same distinction between referential and attributive use leaves many borderline cases uncovered. Let's take a look at another famous example, reworked for the occasion.[16]

Let's suppose that I say, *Nancy wants to marry an analytic philosopher*. We can give two semantic interpretations, (i) and (ii), of this sentence that are possible even when the sentence is uttered out of context, and *at least* three pragmatic interpretations, (iii) through (v), that depend on some inferences regarding the speaker's intentions. Interpretations (iii) through (v) can be attempted only after a decision has been made between (i) and (ii):

(i)   Nancy wants to marry a determined individual X, who is an analytic philosopher.

(ii) Nancy wants to marry anybody, as long as he is an analytic philosopher.

(iii) Nancy wants to marry a determined individual, an analytic philosopher: she knows who he is, but the speaker doesn't, because Nancy has not told him the name.

(iv) Nancy wants to marry a determined individual X, an analytic philosopher: she has also given the speaker the name and introduced them to each other, but out of discretion the speaker has thought it more fitting to avoid going into details.

(v)   Nancy has taken a fancy to a fellow and wants to marry him; she has the told the speaker who he is; the speaker happens to know that the person in question is an analytic philosopher. At this point it is irrelevant whether or not Nancy knows that the fellow is an analytic philosopher, or whether or not the speaker has told her. The fact is that, as Nancy is doing her dissertation on Derrida, the speaker thinks that the two of them will never understand each other and that their marriage is doomed to fail. He tells his interlocutors (who know Nancy's ideas very well) of his perplexity.

Interpretations (iii) through (v) depend on interpretation (i), that is to say, on the decision, which has been made, to consider the sentence referential. The listeners will presumably ask for more information about this X, and in that case the speaker must either confess that he does not know him (case (iii), both he and the listeners must accept the reference on trust), or justify reticence (case (iv), only the listeners must accept the reference on trust), or provide instructions for X's identification or retrieval (by opening our "white box"). Or the listeners are uninterested in the identity of the speaker (this piece of gossip is juicy only because X is an analytic philosopher), and there the matter stops.

This leaves interpretation (ii), which at first sight would seem to point to an attributive use of the sentence. But, above all, we should note that attributive use (à la Donnellan) is also a case of referring. As a matter of fact, although the speaker did indeed define whoever killed Smith as a madman, in reality his supposition was that Smith was killed by a specific individual (albeit an unknown one as yet), and *that* was the individual he was referring to, even though on trust. Talking of Smith's murderer was like talking of the first victim of the Second World War. The unknown X who killed Smith was mad; that precise X who was killed before anyone else was unlucky. But madness and bad luck are predicated of an X, who, while remaining socially or historically or juridically indefinable, is ontologically defined.

But here we are talking not about *whom Nancy may marry* (in which case that man, even unknown, would still be one person and one only). Nor are we talking about *whomever Nancy will marry,* that is, her *possible* husband, in which case it would be as if a pregnant woman talked of the child to be born to her in a few months: whatever it may be, it will certainly be the son/daughter born of her womb at a fairly specific moment and equipped with a given genetic inheritance (or it might not be born, and this is precisely why it is *possible*). We are talking about *whom Nancy would like to marry*. The entity in question is not only possible but also *optative*.

The individual whom Nancy is said to want to marry is not only undefined as yet but also might never even come on the scene (and Nancy would remain single). To the extent that she is prepared to marry *whoever* has the property of being an analytic philosopher, she is in love with a property, as if she wishes to marry whoever has a mustache. Perhaps during her wildest erotic fantasies, Nancy has assigned a face to this imprecise X, imagining that he looks like Robert De Niro. She is prepared to compromise on looks, height, and age, as long as her X is an analytic philosopher, and therefore Kripke or Putnam would be equally good for her, but certainly not Robert De Niro.

Nancy (or whoever is talking about her intentions) is referring not to an individual but to a class of possible individuals, and therefore she is not performing an act of reference. Nancy's X is a general object, such as cats in general. And since I feel it is inopportune to talk of referring in the case of general objects, the sentence ought to be translated as *Nancy has the property of appreciating analytic philosophers (in general) and of desiring them as possible husbands,* or *Among their many properties, analytic philosophers also possess that of being desirable to Nancy.* Even though this would still be a reference to Nancy, it would not be a reference to any specific analytic philosopher.

We should also consider that it is by no means certain that Nancy wants to marry *whoever* is an analytic philosopher. It might mean that she intends to get married, has not yet decided with whom, but definitely wants the chosen one to be an analytic philosopher. Also, she does not intend to throw in her lot with just *any* analytic philosopher, only with an analytic philosopher she likes. If a marriage broker suggests she try Marco Santambrogio (who has the dual property of being an analytic philosopher and remarkably good-looking) Nancy might grumble, for example, because she does not appreciate his *vis polemica*.

Before saying that Nancy has a difficult character, let us acknowledge how difficult it is to negotiate referring, because this last case involved negotiating, beforehand, to see whether we were dealing with a case of referring or not.

On the other hand, who is Nancy? One presumes that the speakers are not fools: if there were many people with the same name in their circle, they would do well to ask for specifications. Unless they think it wiser to let the interlocutor, who is perhaps a little tipsy, to ramble on, that "white box" ought to be opened immediately.[17]

Nevertheless there *is* someone who has assumed the name *Nancy* in a highly rigid fashion, and that someone is we, I the writer and you the readers of these pages. We do not know who Nancy is (except that she is a girl with a weakness for analytic philosophers—a case of a labeled "white box"). But all things considered, we are not all that interested in knowing more about her. It was enough for us to know that she is the girl that the fellow in the example was talking about, and if someone will be so good as to talk to others about this book, Nancy will be the girl on whom I carried out this exercise in referring as contract. No one will be able to deny that for some pages we were referring precisely to her.[18]

Who died on the fifth of May?

A puzzling digression. Some people think that descriptions do not help to fix the reference. We have seen that there is no reference that does not acquire substance with some description. But there are cases in which it seems that the reference is fixed through descriptions only, leaving the name out of consideration.

The Italian writer Alessandro Manzoni wrote an ode called "5 maggio" (5 May) that deals with the death of Napoleon. However, those who go to read it again will notice that the name Napoleon is never mentioned. If we were to sum the ode up rather brutally in terms of macropropositions (and without any respect for its artistic value), we would say that the speaker is telling us:

(i) The person of whom I am speaking (to whom I am expressing my sentiments) is no more.

(ii) This person was characterized by a series of properties: he rose
to great heights, fell, rose again; he performed memorable
deeds from the Alps to the coasts of Africa, from the Iberian
peninsula to the borders of France and Germany; it is unsure
whether his was real glory, but there is no doubt that God saw
him as a sublime representative of the human species; he
tasted victory, power, and exile (and twice at that, as he knew
both triumph and defeat); he may be considered the arbiter of
two centuries; for a long time he planned to write his memoirs
recalling the events of his past, etc.

Those who do not know that the ode was written in 1821 and
that therefore the date 5 May refers implicitly to a precise day
in that year, and those who do not know that Napoleon died on
that day (which our encyclopedia has registered, by antonomasia
or metonymy, as the date of his death), would have no other instructions—apart from the rather vague description offered by
Manzoni—with which to identify the person designated. I have no
desire to attempt an inspection of universal history, but I am fairly
convinced we would find another historical figure to whom this
description could very well apply. With a little goodwill, and by
understanding some expressions as metaphors or hyperboles, someone might apply it to Nixon or to the great Italian cyclist Fausto
Coppi.

This is a very difficult case for many theories of reference, because we know that that text refers to Napoleon only on the basis
of much circumstantial and intertextual negotiation (and convention). Without these negotiations, the text would be most obscure,
referentially speaking.

But let's make things more complex. Let's suppose that Manzoni
(who luckily was not a wag of this type) wrote an ode very similar
to the sketch about the sarkiapone, which went roughly like this: "I
sing of the death of a Great man. All I will tell you of this man is
that he did *not* rise to great heights, did *not* fall, did *not* rise again;
he did *not* perform memorable deeds from the Alps to the coasts of

Africa, or from the Iberian peninsula to the borders of France and Germany; he was *by no means* the arbiter of two centuries, and, come to think of it, he is not even dead."

How could we understand his reference to *this man* (to whom he was evidently continuing to refer)? We would give him carte blanche, in the expectation that he would tell us something more about this person. We would still be unsure as to whether he meant to talk of Julius Caesar, Henry VIII, of his next-door neighbor, or of any other individual you care to choose from the billions who have populated the planet. Endorsing this carte blanche would be a form of acceptance of a really "soft" designation. It would have to be admitted, to keep the interaction going, that he was talking about someone who appeared somewhere or other, who was conceived with a certain genetic program, probably baptized in some way or other by his parents or by whoever saw him the first time, but what would not be known (for the moment) is who this person was. Nevertheless the designation would not be completely soft: the description given would lead us to exclude Napoleon at least.

Have I perhaps hypothesized an impossible communicative interaction? Of course not; things of this kind happen often, such as when someone says, *I met a fantastic girl at the disco yesterday evening, you can't even imagine what she's like!* And what do we do? We wait for the rest of the story. But we know that the reference is to a women and not to a man.

Impossible objects

According to one of its interpretations, the sentence about Nancy brings *optative possibilia* into play. Sentences such as *We will have a son and call him Louis,* or *I am certain I will find the man of my life in Hong Kong* are cases of reference to *optative possibilia.* The same holds for *I'm waiting for my croissants to arrive,* insofar as at the moment they were ordered, croissants in general were required, but at the moment they arrive, they are undoubtedly wholly individual croissants possessed by the speaker. As they are *optative possibilia,* these individual things might also (successively) not exist: but references to *possibilia* can be made. Is it possible to make references to *impossibilia* or, in any event, to inconceivable objects?

I should like to avoid the usual squared circle which is a general object like the unicorn (and at best a formal individual; see 3.7.7). But if I say *The highest prime number will be discovered in 2005,* I am referring not only to an *optative possibilium* but also to something inconceivable.

All impossible objects are inconceivable, but not all inconceivable objects are impossible. For example, a limitless universe is more than our imagination can handle, but it is not impossible in principle. On the other hand, becoming the son of our own son seems impossible as well as inconceivable (at least as long as we live in a universe with open causal chains and not loops). But what distinguishes both conceivable and inconceivable *possibilia* is the impossibility of constructing a CT and NC for them (I maintain that for inconceivable *possibilia* it is possible to construct an MC, but I'm not sure of what type).

Since it has been said that it is possible to refer (completely on trust) to objects whose NC is unknown, which would therefore be objects impossible to identify, recognize, retrieve, or even interpret, it seems clear that we can also refer to inconceivable objects. The fact that many novels or science-fiction movies talk of characters who travel backward in time and meet themselves as youngsters, or become their own fathers—and the fact that we are able to follow these stories (albeit with a certain sense of vertigo)—proves that we can nominate inconceivable objects and therefore (since referring is a use we put language to) refer to them.[19]

In Eco (1990, 3.5.6.) it was shown that not only can we name these objects but also, as a result of a cognitive illusion, we get the impression that we can conceive them. There are cognitive and referential ambiguities just as there are perceptual ambiguities. We have the impression not only that we can refer to these objects but also that we can, so to speak, open the "white box" that contains them, in the sense that if we examine them in toto, we can't manage to conceive them, but if we examine them *one piece at a time,*

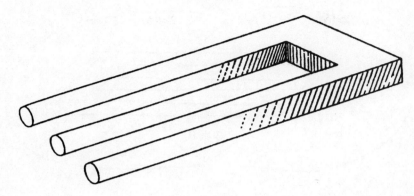

Figure 5.1

we have the impression that they *may have* a form, even though we are unable to describe it. Besides, if someone gives us what are recognizably bicycle parts but taken from bicycles of different makes, so that in the end we cannot manage to assemble them, it does not follow from this that we have failed to recognize them as the parts of a dismantled (possible and optative) bicycle.

A visual example of an impossible possible world is the famous drawing as shown in figure 5.1, an archetype of many visual *impossibilia*.

At first sight this figure seems to represent a "possible" object, but, if we follow its lines in accordance with their spatial orientation, we realize that an object of this kind cannot exist (in our universe, at least). However, and this is what I am doing at this moment (not only verbally but visually), I can refer to that figure (which, apart from anything else, is found in many psychology texts).[20] But that's not all; I can provide either a person or a computer with instructions for constructing it. The objection that, by so doing, one is referring to the expression (the graphic signifier) but not to the object, does not hold water. As I have already said, in Eco (1994: 100), the difficulty does not consist in conceiving this figure as a graphic expression; we can easily draw it, and therefore it is not geometrically impossible, at least in terms of plane geometry. The difficulty arises when we *cannot avoid* seeing the figure as a two-dimensional expression of a three-dimensional object. It would be

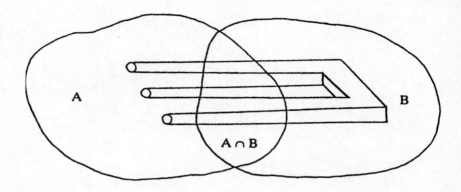

Figure 5.2

sufficient for us not to understand shading as a graphic sign that *stands for* the shadows of a three-dimensional object, and the figure would be easily perceivable. But we cannot manage to avoid the hypoiconic effect (see the discussion on "surrogate stimuli" in 6.7). And it is certainly the "interpreted" figure we are referring to.

A persuasive explanation of the cognitive illusion is supplied by Merrell (1981: 181), who offers us a segmented version of the image as shown in figure 5.2.

If we observe in isolation either zone A or zone B of the figure, each one presents itself as a possible three-dimensional object. It is simply that in zone A we see cylinders, while in zone B we see parallelepiped. The zone A∩B can be seen alternatively either as part of A or part of B (if focused on separately, it shows us only parallel lines). The difficulty arises only when we try to conceive the object as a whole. Likewise in Eco (1990, 3.5.6), I showed that even an inconceivable situation like that of an X_1 who meets himself as a younger man (X_2) can be sustained (by cognitive illusion), if the point of view is assigned consistently to the same entity (either always to X_1 or always to X_2). On the other hand, we shall see in 6.10 that we have no problem in imagining that we have a third eye on our index finger, with which we can observe the nape of our neck or see into cavities inaccessible to our normal eyes. The inconceivability arises when we try to imagine what would happen if we were to point the third eye toward our face. Would we see the index finger with the eyes in our head, or the eyes in our head with the index finger? Once more, either we go by zones of focus (we imagine, alternately closing the eyes in our head and the eye in our finger) or we slip into complete imaginative confusion.

Therefore I hold that when we refer to inconceivable entities, we behave as if, on being faced with our "white box," we were to peep into it by alternately lifting opposite sides of the lid for a few millimeters. Each time we would see something inconceivable, we would have problems in reconciling the various points of view, and we would concede that the box contained something whose properties strike us as obscure or incoherent. But this would not stop us from referring to that something.

The identity of the *Vasa*

With regard to pragmatic referring as a phenomenon of negotiating, there is always the venerable example of the ship of Theseus, which brings into play the problem of identity and any possibility of rigid designation. This is a well-known problem that has been treated of in various ways, from Hobbes to our own day, but for the sake of convenience, given that we know very little about Theseus's ship, let's talk of another ship, the *Vasa*.

In 1628, in Stockholm (more specifically in the Skeppengården shipyard), it was decided to build a formidable warship that was to be the royal flagship of the Swedish fleet: a ship constructed out of thousands of oak trees, fitted out with sixty-four heavy cannons, with masts over thirty meters tall, and several hundred painted and gilded sculptures. One Sunday morning, August 16, the ship was launched before cheering crowds. But, as we know from a letter from the Council of State to the King, "once it was out in the bay off Tegelviken, the ship took a little more wind and began to heel over downwind before righting itself a little; but when it reached Beckholmen, it heeled over completely to one side, the water came in through the gunports, and the ship slowly sank with all its complement of sails and flags."

A very sad business. We shall not wonder why the *Vasa* went down, nor shall we follow the numerous attempts made since that day to salvage her. The fact remains that the salvage operation was finally carried out, and today the *Vasa* is a poignant exhibit in the museum of the same name in Stockholm (from whose catalogues I have taken all the true information given here). Moreover I have seen the ship. She's not in perfect condition, of course, some parts are missing, but I know that what I saw is indeed the *Vasa* that sank like a stone on that morning in 1628.

Now let us imagine that the *Vasa* did not sink on the day of its launching but happily sailed the seas of the world. As happens with ships, especially after facing heavy seas and tempests, various components will have been replaced, on one occasion a part of the planking, on another a part of the masts, on another again some fixtures, often the cannons, until the moment in which our hypothetical *Vasa* on display in the Vasa Museum of Stockholm no longer had a single part of the original *Vasa*. Would we say that it was the original *Vasa*, in other words, would we rigidly designate as *Vasa* what no longer possessed any material part of the object that had been baptized as such?

One of the criteria for giving a positive answer is that three conditions must be observed: the replacement of the various parts must have taken place *gradually* and not all at once, so that the chain of perceptual experiences has not been interrupted, and the replaced parts must be morphologically the same as the ones that have been eliminated. Therefore we would say that the modern *Vasa* is identical to the *Vasa* of the past, because we would take as decisive parameters (i) *gradual continuity,* (ii) *uninterrupted legal recognition,* and (iii) *form.*[21]

Gradual continuity and legal recognition are the sole conditions that allow someone to recognize me as the same individual who was born in 1932. If one were to wax subtle about cells, God only knows what has changed between then and now. But the changes were gradual, and moreover the Registry Office has always defined me as the same person (at six, twenty, and sixty years of age).

I would not know what to say about my form (those who have not followed me year by year have trouble recognizing me in a

photo from the fifties), but it's all easier with the *Vasa*, as it was easier with Bach's Second Suite for Solo Cello (see 3.7.7), which we
recognize as the same even if played on different cellos and even in
a transcription for the recorder.

Therefore the modern *Vasa* would be the same as the old *Vasa*
not only because it has always been nominated that way in the
course of four centuries but also because—whatever alteration it
may have undergone in terms of materials—it still has the same
form as the original *Vasa*.

But for whom would it be the same? Certainly for a naval histo-
rian who wanted to examine it to understand how the vessels of the
seventeenth century were constructed. Would it be the same for a
conference on the physics of materials, interested in knowing how
wood and metal have reacted to the passage of time and the in-
clemency of the elements? Such scientists would have no use for
the modern *Vasa*, and they would say that it was not the original
Vasa.

I shall now list (without any pretensions to establishing a definitive typology) a series of cases in which the attribution of identity
(or authenticity) depends on different parameters, negotiable or negotiated from one time to the next.

(i)   The abbey of Saint Guinness was built in the twelfth century.
      Scrupulous abbots had it restored day by day, replacing stones
      and fixtures as they fell victim to wear and tear, and so from
      the point of view of materials the abbey we see today no
      longer has anything to do with the original, but from the
      point of view of architectonic design it is the same one. If we
      favor the criterion of the identity of form over that of identity
      of materials, and if moreover we introduce the criterion of
      "homolocality" (the modern abbey stands exactly in the same
      place as the original abbey), from a tourist's point of view
      (and to a certain extent from that of an art historian) we are
      led to say that this is the same abbey.

(ii) All that is left of the abbey of Saint-Pouilly Fouissé, never
      restored, is a lateral wall and the ruins of the transept. Why

do we consider it original? It is not enough to say that we consider original not the abbey but only its ruins. Many tourists go to visit the renowned abbey of Port Royal just outside Paris, and yet the abbey has disappeared, there is nothing left there anymore, not even a ruin: all that remains is a place. A place where something once stood but has subsequently disappeared. What is there that is original at Port Royal?

(iii) Citizen Kane, who dreams of building the perfect residence, finds it in Europe in the abbey of Cognac, which has remained intact since the time of its construction. He buys it, has it dismantled and the stones numbered before having it shipped to Xanadu and reconstructed. Is this the same abbey? He certainly thinks so, but certain supercilious European critics and historians think otherwise. Their preference is not for identity of materials or form but for homolocality. Would they therefore be obliged to say that Port Royal (which no longer exists) is more original than Cognac (which fundamentally exists, even though it is in the wrong place)?

(iv) The buildings in the Valley of Kings in Egypt risked being flooded when it was planned to build a new dam. UNESCO had those buildings dismantled stone by stone and then reconstructed in another valley. Are these the same buildings? UNESCO's assumption is that they are, what counts is the form and the identity of the materials, but those who contested the authenticity of Kane's reconstruction would have to disagree. Why should cases (iii) and (iv) be different? Why do we think that UNESCO has the moral and scientific right to do what Kane did arbitrarily and out of personal interest?

(v) The Parthenon in Nashville (Tennessee) was designed to resemble the formal structure of the original Parthenon in all respects, so much so that there was a rumor (how veracious, I do not know) to the effect that, after the last war, in order to restore parts of the Parthenon in Athens, experts went to gather evidence on the basis of the Nashville Parthenon.

Furthermore, the Nashville Parthenon is painted, as the original edifice is supposed to have been. Yet no one would dare to consider it original, even though the form is the same, simply because the stones are not the same ones, because it does not stand in the same place (among other things, it stands on a plain and not on an acropolis), and, above all, because the other one is still there.

(vi) Poland (as a political entity) has been one of the most tormented nations in history: all one has to do is glance at a historical atlas to see how its frontiers have expanded and contracted depending on the period; indeed, at a certain point it all but disappeared from the map. What does the name *Poland* refer to? It depends on the historical context in which it is used. Is the sentence *Bialystok belongs to Poland* true or false? It depends on when it was said.[22]

On Ahab's other leg

In the light of a contractual theory of reference, I think it may also be possible to solve the knotty problem of referring to fictitious characters, such as Sherlock Holmes or Pinocchio. If a strong ontological version of reference (from the standpoint of the eyes of a Divine Mind) is asserted, then all the arguments that have filled tens and hundreds of books can apply to fictitious characters.[23] If a weak ontological version (internal realism, reference in the eyes of a Community) is accepted, the discourse seems less dramatic, because we would refer to Hamlet every time we assumed we were dealing with the character described in Shakespeare's possible world and regarding whom all encyclopedias recognize some properties (though not others), just as the encyclopedias agree in saying that water is H_2O.

The interesting problem is not whether fictional characters exist in the same way as real people: in that case, the answer is "no," not even if one were to accept the realism of Lewis (1973: 85), for whom possible worlds are just as real as the one in which we live from day to day. The interesting problem is why we can refer to them in the same way in which we refer to real people, and we understand one another perfectly well both when we say that Napoleon was the husband of Josephine and when we say that Ulysses was the husband of Penelope. This happens because the encyclopedias agree in assigning to Josephine the property of having married Napoleon as her second husband and to Penelope that of having married Ulysses.

It has been said that narrative worlds are always *little worlds,* because they do not constitute a maximal and complete state of things (see Pavel 1986; Dolezel 1989: 233 ff.; Eco 1990, 4). In this sense narrative worlds are *parasitical,* because, if the alternative properties are not specified, we take for granted the properties that hold good in the real world. In *Moby-Dick* it is not expressly stated that all the sailors aboard the *Pequod* have two legs, but the reader ought to take it as implicit, given that the sailors are human beings. On the other hand, the account takes care to inform us that Ahab had only one leg, but, as far as I remember, it does not say which, leaving us free to use our imagination, because such a specification has no bearing on the story.

Once we have accepted the commitment to read a story, we are not only authorized but also invited—if we so wish—to make inferences both on the basis of events narrated and on those presupposed. In principle we could do the same thing with a sentence that refers to events that really happened and with a sentence from fiction. Given *Julius Caesar was assassinated in the Senate, in Rome, on the Ides of March, 44 B.C.,* we can infer in what year *ab urbe condita* the event took place (but we have to decide if it refers to the dating of Cato the Elder or to that of Varro). Given *D'Artagnan arrived in the city of Meung, on a sorrel nag at least fourteen years old, on the first Monday of the month of April 1625,* by consulting a universal calendar one might conclude that the first Monday of that April was the seventh.

But while it is of some interest to know in what year *ab urbe condita* Caesar died, it is not narratively of interest to know that d'Artagnan arrived in Meung on the seventh of April. It is of interest to establish that Hamlet was a bachelor, because the observation has some bearing on an understanding of his psychology and of the business with Ophelia. But when, at the end of chapter 35 of *The Red and the Black*, Stendhal, in recounting how Julien Sorel tries to kill Madame de Rênal, concludes, "Il tira sur elle un coup de pisto-let et la manqua; il tira un second coup, elle tomba." Is there any sense in wondering where the first bullet ended up?

As has already been stated in Eco (1979), fictional characters have different types of properties.

(i) We have, first and foremost, those properties that are not made explicit by the text but must be presupposed in the sense that they cannot be denied: a character's hair may not be described, but this is no reason for the reader to presume he is bald. The extent to which such properties may not be denied is seen in the processes of intersemiotic translation: if in a film version of the tale, Julien Sorel went off try to commit murder without his shoes (not mentioned in the story), the matter might appear curious.

(ii) Then there are those properties that in Eco 79 are called S-necessary (or structurally necessary), such as the property of maintaining, within the possible narrative world, reciprocally defining relationships with other characters. In the narrative world of *Madame Bovary*, there is no other way to identify Emma if not as the wife of Charles, who in his turn has been identified as the boy seen by the narrator at the beginning of the novel; any other narrative world in which Madame Bovary were to be the wife of Monsieur Homais would be another world, with its complement of different individuals (in other words, we would no longer be talking of Flaubert's novel but of a parody or remake of it).

(iii) The properties explicitly attributed to the characters in the course of the story are seen as particularly evident, such as having done this or that thing, being male or female, young or old. They do not all have the same narrative value: some have an important bearing on the story (e.g., the fact that Julien shot Madame de Rênal), others less (the fact that he

fired as the lady was at prayer with her head lowered, and
that he fired two shots instead of one only). We can make a
distinction between *essential* and *accidental* properties.

(iv) Finally there are the properties that the reader infers from the
story, which are sometimes crucial for its interpretation. In
order to make inferences, accidental properties are sometimes
transformed into essential ones: for example, the fact that
Julien's first shot missed can allow us to infer that he was
particularly nervous at that moment (in point of fact, a few
lines before, it says that his arm was trembling), and this
changes the nature of his deed, no longer due to cold
determination but to a disordered passionate impulse. Just to
stay with Stendhal, with regard to *Armance* there is critical
debate as to whether Octave de Malivert was really impotent,
since the text does not state this clearly.[24]

In general, however, when we refer to fictional characters, we do
it on the basis of the properties most commonly registered by the
encyclopedias, and the encyclopedias usually register properties of
the type (ii) and (iii), because those are the ones made explicit in the
texts and not the ones they presuppose or lead one to conjecture. To
talk of properties made explicit means thinking of a fictional text as
a musical score: just as a score prescribes the pitch, duration, and
often the timbre of sounds, so a story establishes the S-properties
and the essential properties of the characters. The fact that a story
also supplies accidental properties (the majority of which may be
deleted without losing the identity of the character) could be similar to the fact that in order to identify a musical composition, it is
not strictly essential for, let's say, certain differences between *forte*
and *fortissimo* to be respected, and a given melody can be recognized even though it is not executed con brio, as called for in the
score.

I have returned to the analogy with the musical score because I
intend to refer to the discussion (in 3.7.7) on *formal individuals*. On
that occasion both a musical composition and a painting or a novel
were considered as formal individuals. Now I intend to suggest

that fictional characters (inasmuch as they are intersubjectively and encyclopedically identifiable through the S-necessary and essential properties that a text has attributed to them) may be referred to just as one refers to Bach's *Second Suite for Solo Cello*. We have said that (above and beyond the practical and theoretical difficulties involved in its recognition on the basis of two or three notes) whoever talks of SC2 intends to refer to that formal individual that, in the impossibility of ascertaining the musical thought in Bach's head when he composed it, is represented by its score or an execution of it held to be correct and faithful.

In this sense fictional characters are formal individuals to whom we can refer correctly as long as all the properties made explicit by the original text are attributed to them, and on such a basis we can establish that anyone who asserts that Hamlet married Ophelia or that Sherlock Holmes was German is stating a falsehood (or is referring to some other individual who by chance bears the same name).

However, what I have said may be applied to fictional characters insofar as they are recounted by a specific work, which constitutes their score. What can we say about mythical or legendary characters who migrate across various works, occasionally performing different actions, or who simply survive in the mythic imagination without being bound to any one work? One typical example is Little Red Riding Hood, where the variations between the popular tradition and the literary versions are extremely numerous and also involve marginal details (see Pisanty 1993: 4). Let us limit ourselves to dealing with a fundamental difference between Perrault's version and that of the Brothers Grimm: in the first, the story ends when the wolf, after having devoured the grandmother, devours the little girl too, and the tale ends with a moralizing warning for rash and imprudent young ladies; in the second, the hunter comes on the scene and opens up the beast's belly to release both the little girl and her grandmother. To whom are we referring when we speak of Little Red Riding Hood? To a little girl who dies or to a little girl who emerges from the belly of a wolf?

I would say that the cases here are two. If someone talks of the resurrection of Little Red Riding Hood (reference to the Grimm score) and the interlocutor has in mind the Perrault score instead, then the interlocutor will ask for extra information; negotiations will continue until an agreement is reached regarding which score is being referred to. Or else the interlocutors are thinking of the popular score, the one that showed itself the stronger in the end, which is less complex than that of the various written versions and which circulates in a given culture as a basic *fabula*. This *fabula* is substantially the Grimms' version, and it is to this popular score that we usually refer (namely, the girl goes into the woods, encounters the wolf, the wolf devours the grandmother, takes on her appearance, devours the child, the hunter frees them both), while details that are important in the cultivated versions (e.g., whether the little girl undresses and gets into bed with her grandmother) or are only marginal (e.g., whether the girl took her grandmother cakes and wine or cakes and butter) are dropped. On this popular basis therefore we refer to Little Red Riding Hood in a contractual way that is defined independently of the detail of whether she took her grandmother wine or butter.

It likewise happens that certain characters from novels, once they are famous, come to be a part of—as they say—the collective imagination, and in terms of the basic *fabula* they become known even to those who have never read the work in the first place. I think that *The Three Musketeers* is a typical case. Only those who have read Dumas can take part in trivia games knowing that the nag on which d'Artagnan appears in the first chapter is from Béarn, is thirteen to fourteen years old, and was a present from his father. Most of the time, the three musketeers are referred to in terms of a basic *fabula* (they are daring, they duel with Richelieu's guards, they perform swashbuckling deeds in order to recover the Queen's diamonds, etc.). In this basic *fabula* not much distinction is usually made between their actions in *The Three Musketeers* and the actions they perform in *Twenty Years After* (while I would say that the popular *fabula* pays no attention to what happens in the less famous *The Vicomte de Bragelonne*—proof of this being that the infinite series of film versions ignore it). Thus we recognize d'Artagnan or Porthos even in film versions where events occur that do not happen in the novels of Dumas, and we are not disturbed by this, as we would be if someone were to tell us that Madame Bovary cheerfully divorced Charles and lived happily ever after.

In all these cases it is a matter of negotiating the score to be referred to (a specific work or a *fabula* deposited in the collective imagination), and, afterward, the reference occurs without ambiguity. So much so that, in the case of trivia games, one may hear protests of the type: "Look here, the *daughter* of Milady that you are referring to appears in the film! In *Twenty Years After* she is Milady's son!"

Ultimately, in such cases, the possible world in question is negotiated. And that agreement is not always reached may be because of the number of possible worlds at issue, not because it is impossible to fix the reference in a possible world negotiated with precision.[25]

Ich liebe Dich

Anyone who maintains that a pronoun in the first person singular is identified with the person speaking—without the mediation of an agreement regarding its own content—ought to explain what happens when a foreigner, whose language is unknown, says *Ich liebe Dich*. The objection that this is not a case of failed reference but simply of linguistic incompetence, is self-defeating: in point of fact I am saying that in order to understand the reference I must know not only the meaning of a verb such as *liebe* but also the meaning of the two pronouns—otherwise that declaration of love will end up as a case of infelicitous reference (and never was adjective more appropriate).

We had begun by taking as implicit and almost obvious the fact that, in order to use terms in acts of reference, it was first necessary to know their meaning. As we went on, we realized that, at least in part, we can understand acts of reference even without knowing the meaning of the term. Then we had to conclude that there are no "white boxes" without at least a label, that meaning creeps back in everywhere, and that finally we cannot have a reference crowned by success unless we first agree on the meaning of the terms, and only at that point can we proceed to negotiate with regard to the individual we intend to refer to. Let us conclude with some observations regarding the importance of a NC and of a successive negotiation, even for those terms that seem, so to speak, to acquire life, to make sense only when directly attached to an individual—and, when detached from them, to float in a fog of nonsense.

I am always puzzled by the fact that some people maintain that the indexical terms (the ones usually accompanied by a gesture, such as *this* or *that*), the deictics (relative in the context to the speaker and his spatiotemporal position, such as *yesterday, now, soon, not far from here*), not to mention the personal pronouns, designate directly without any mediation on the part of any possible meaning they might have. I tried to show in Eco (1975, 2.11.5) how even these types of signs must be contained in their meaning if they are to be applied in acts of reference; but I always find someone who denies this because of the simple fact that the instructions for understanding how one can use *cat* to refer to cats are different from the instructions for understanding how one can use *I* or *this* to refer to either the person who emitted the sentence or to the thing that is being indicated with a finger. It is certainly true that what I have called the NC of a term can suggest very different instructions for identifying the referent of *cat* and *cousin*. But saying that the instructions take on different formats does not mean that they are not there.[26]

Bertuccelli Papi (1993: 197) gives the example of these two sentences: (i) *Alice left yesterday and Sylvia three days ago* and (ii) *Alice left yesterday and Sylvia two days before*. If the two sentences are uttered on Saturday, in both cases Alice must have left on Friday and Sylvia on Wednesday. But in (i) the expression *ago* refers to the day of the utterance (Saturday) while in (ii) the adverb *before* is anchored to the point of temporal reference contained in the sentence itself (yesterday). If we were to replace *before* with *ago* in (ii), Sylvia's departure date would be shifted to Thursday. The authoress suggests that *ago* is therefore "intrinsically deictic," while *before* changes its value according to the temporal point of reference it stands in relation to. In any case it is clear that the use of the two expressions to designate a precise day depends on highly complex rules of textual linguistics, and I do not see why this set of rules cannot be understood as the content of the respective expressions—if by NC we do not mean a simple definition but also, or sometimes only, a complex set of instructions for identifying the referent.[27]

It has been said that "*I* denotes the one who utters the sentence" is an insufficient instruction for identifying the referent, given that the referent changes according to the context and the circumstances and therefore does not represent the content of the pronoun *I*. Yet again we are confusing instructions for the identification of the referent with a way of fixing the reference. The instruction for identifying the referent of *I* is as generic as that for identifying the referent of *interlocutor* (a term that identifies different persons according to the situation of linguistic exchange), of *assassin* (given that *Caesar's assassin* and *Kennedy's assassin* refer to two different people) or even of *cat* (given that the instructions for identifying cats are certainly not sufficient to fix the reference of *the cat I gave to Louis yesterday*). To give instructions for identifying, in a variety of circumstances, the possible referent of a generic term is not the same as deciding, by pragmatic negotiation, how to fix the referent when referring to individuals.

Putnam (1981, II) admits that a pronoun such as *I* has no extension but a *function of extension* that determines extension according to context. I would agree to consider this function of extension as part of the NC of the pronoun, and we might admit that it is a matter of an instruction for identifying the referent in an act of reference. Putnam also says he would rather not identify this function of extension (which would be an intension in Carnap's sense) along with meaning. But here (and I refer the reader to the discussion in 3.3.2, on the difficulties that can sometimes be caused by the term "meaning") he simply means to say, on the one hand, that this rule is an abstract function and, on the other, that it does not include all that we understand by the meaning of an expression, in the sense that both *cube* and *regular polyhedron with six square faces*—says Putnam—have the same intension and extension in all possible worlds but retain a difference of meaning.

In point of fact, the NC of a pronoun *includes* an instruction for identifying the referent (as an ability to apply a function of extension in a concrete fashion), and yet there is more to the content than that. I shall give a series of examples, which apart from anything else ought to provide grist for my contractual mill.

Let us suppose that someone says, *I'm sorry, we can't come tonight.* If the content of *we* were wholly identified with an instruction for identifying the referent, we would be up against a tricky problem, because it would oblige us to identify a community of authors of the utterance, whereas we can identify only a single individual. But we also possess a pragmatic rule whereby someone may speak on behalf of the group for which he is, let's say, the spokesman. And thus we go to search in the dialogical context to see whether a group had been designated previously. Finding that the speaker was invited to dinner along with his family, we know that the plural pronoun refers to the members of that family.

But there are also semantic-pragmatic rules. For example, the rule of the royal "we." In such cases we know that a single person has the constitutional right to use the first person plural instead of the first person singular of the personal pronoun. But even when we know this, other contractual elements come into play. If a monarch today says, *We feel tired,* we know right away that he is using the royal "we" as a matter of etiquette, and therefore the *we* refers to him individually and the sentence is intended to express an inner state of his. If, on the other hand, the same monarch says, *We confer upon you the Order of the Golden Fleece* or *Today we have declared war on Ruritania,* he is expressing something that was not the general will until that moment but becomes it as soon as the sentence is uttered. Therefore in some way that *we* refers (willy-nilly) also to the subjects listening to him. According to the context, the receivers fix the reference of the pronoun in different ways.

Now let us suppose that a scientist writes, *We cannot reasonably admit that the hole in the ozone layer has a decisive influence on the world's climate.* To whom does that *we* refer? Not to the members of her family, not to the subjects she does not have. However, for the meaning of *we,* an ideal dictionary ought to provide the contextual selection "can be understood as the *authoritative* plural, thanks to which a single speaker presents himself or herself as an interpreter of the scientific community, of sound reasoning or common sense." At this point we can identify the referent in various ways: (i) there is a first reading that I would define as "rhetorical charity," by which we recognize linguistic use as a stylistic mannerism, and we refer the *we* to the writer (we translate *we* as *I,* as if the writer was expressing herself in another language); (ii) there is a "fiduciary" reading, whereby we refer the pronoun to the scientific community (what the writer is saying is Gospel); (iii) there is a reading "of persuasion," whereby we feel involved and think that in fact we, the readers, are obliged to be subjects who think that way about things.

There is finally a reading in terms of textual semiotics (not available to just any receiver), which leads us to reflect on what the writer—in using the authoritative plural—wanted to have us believe about her: not only has she made an explicit statement regarding a physical phenomenon, she has also implicitly presented herself as a subject entitled to speak in our name too, or in the name of a superior cognitive authority. I admit that this reading should have nothing to do with the phenomenon of referring: we are still referring to the author of the written text, even though we now see her in a different psychological light. Yet it cannot be denied that a bias with regard to the writer (she wants to convince us by claiming an authority to which she has no right) can determine the way we referentially interpret that *we.* We can decide that she did not intend to use a stylistic mannerism with which to say *I,* that she in fact wanted us to understand that she intended to refer to the scientific community. This decision would involve an alethic judgment regarding the proposition she has expressed. Supposing we are convinced that the hole in the ozone layer does in fact influence the climate of the planet, and that every reliable scientist today has stated this. If this person meant *I,* then she said something false about a physical fact; if she meant *we,* she said something false about the opinions already expressed by the scientific community—or perhaps she wanted to deceive us on both counts.

Whatever the reading, the sense of the sentence changes as well as the lexical content of that *we,* which therefore does not boil down to the instruction for identifying the referent. Without a first tentative application of the instruction, it would not be possible to decide whether it was necessary to interpret the pronoun as an authoritative plural; but without the knowledge of that aspect of the content, it would still not be possible to apply the instruction, in any of the senses considered above.

Chapter Six

Iconism and Hypoicon

It may be that the moon, and likewise the rest of the universe, does not exist; or the Moon may be an image projected by some Berkeleyan divinity. But, even so, it would still count for something for us, and for the dogs who bay at it by night (Berkeley's god has a thought for them too). We therefore possess a cognitive type of the Moon, and it must be a very complex one. We recognize it in the sky whether it appears full or only as a sickle, whether it looks red or as yellow as custard. Even when it is obscured by clouds, we guess its presence thanks to its diffused glow; we know we have to look for it in the sky in positions that vary in the course of the night and the month. Our cognitive type of the Moon (and the corresponding nuclear content) also includes the information that it is in the sky, and this is what allows us to understand that the Moon in the well is only a reflection.

The fact that it is spherical and, even though we can see only one side of it, that it has another side that we do not see and have never seen, is part of a more elaborate, and historically variable, molar content: for example, both Epicurus and Lucretius were convinced that the Moon (and the Sun too) was exactly as large as it appears to us.

In short, I should like to make it clear that I believe in the existence of the Moon, at least to the same degree as I believe in the existence of everything else, my own body included. I am stressing this point because once I was accused of not believing in the Moon. It all came about in the course of what has been defined as "the debate on iconism."

6.1 THE DEBATE ON ICONISM

"In their obstinate idealism, they [the "semiolinguists"] dispute everything that, one way or another, might oblige them to admit that reality—in this case, the moon—exists." This was how, in 1974, Tomás Maldonado, with regard to what I had written on iconic signs, reminded me of my Galilean duty to look through the telescope, thus opening the final phase of the debate on iconism that was in progress during the sixties and seventies.[1] To this accusation of idealism—definitely something to worry about in those days—I replied (Eco 1975b) with an equally polemical essay, entitled, "Chi ha paura del cannochiale?" (Who's afraid of the telescope?). It is an essay I have never since republished, because I was beginning to realize that the debate had assumed, in public, heated tones that it did not have at all in private. Almost twenty years later, Maldonado republished his article, but minus the pages that concerned me, because, he stated, some of my criticisms of his critique "have contributed—I'll admit this willingly—to modify in part the presuppositions of my analysis" (1992: 59n). May this example of intellectual honesty inspire me now, as I review some of the positions I held at the time.

The debate came about at the wrong time, because, while Maldonado was publishing his essay, my *A Theory of Semiotics* (which he could not have seen) was already in print, with a chapter on sign production that would have perhaps proved to him that we were in agreement on more points than he thought. In any case it is singular that, after the row exploded, the general discussion reached an impasse, as if it had become a dead letter. There was a hiatus, I should say, of a decade: and then it flared up again, in the hands of others, who had taken a second look at the whole business.[2]

The progress of the debate between *iconists* and *iconoclasts*[3] seems linked to a ten-year cycle: this is not a symptom to be taken lightly, in the sense that perhaps everything should be reconsidered by bringing the zeitgeist onto the stage every so often. Groupe μ observes (1992: 125) that two works dealing with images appeared in 1968: *Languages of Art*, by Nelson Goodman, and my *La struttura assente*, and that these two books, written at the same time by two authors from two completely different cultural areas, contain some very similar examples and observations. As if, by way of a confutation of all idealism, the moment two persons distant from each other set to "looking at the figures," they noticed some common reactions.

When I reread the debate of 1974–75, it emerged clearly that the discussion hinged on three problems: (i) the iconic nature of perception, (ii) the fundamentally iconic nature of knowledge in general, and (iii) the nature of so-called iconic signs, in other words, of those signs that Peirce called (and which we shall be referring to exclusively as such, from now on) *hypoicons*. In my answer to Maldonado it seems that I take point (i) for granted without discussing it, I do not compromise myself over point (ii), while I discuss point (iii) at length. I made the mistake of separating the three problems, but perhaps Maldonado erred in keeping them bound together too tightly. From his convictions regarding the motivated nature of perception, Maldonado derived (on the basis of the early Wittgenstein) a definition of knowledge in terms of *Abbildungstheorie*, and consequently of the cognitive value of hypoiconic signs. From convictions regarding the highly conventional and cultural nature of hypoicons, I raised doubts regarding the motivation of cognitive processes. With hindsight it seems like a comic-strip version of the *Cratylus*: is it by law or by nature that the image of Mickey Mouse reminds us of a mouse?

Points (i) and (ii) have already been dealt with in 2.8. I don't think that people (whether they stood for an epistemology of specular reflection or a constructivist epistemology) had any doubts about point (i), even back in the seventies. However, I must admit that, in order to discuss the problem of the hypoicon, I relegated the problem of perceptual iconism to an area of scant semiotic pertinence.[4] On the other hand, many philoiconists (not only Maldonado) have identified the iconism of perception with the iconism of so-called iconic signs, attributing to the second the virtues of the first.

Finally, for a series of reasons we shall be dealing with later, the debate led people to identify both icons and hypoicons with visual entities, both mental images and those signs that (to avoid using a term overburdened with meanings, such as "image") we shall call *pictures*. Once more this sent the discussion partly off the track, whereas it should have been clear to everybody that both the concept of icon and that of hypoicon concern nonvisual experiences too.[5]

6.2 NOT A DEBATE BETWEEN MADMEN

Now let us try to consider the matter calmly. On the one side were people who questioned the vagueness of a concept such as "likeness" and who wanted to demonstrate how impressions of likeness caused by hypoicons were the effect of *rules for the production of likeness* (see Volli 1972). Is it possible that these people were denying that most of our everyday life is based on relations that, for want of a better term, are of likeness; that it is for reasons of likeness that we recognize people; that it is on the basis of likeness between tokens that we are able to use general terms; that the constancy of perception itself is ensured by the recognition of shapes; that it is for formal reasons that we can tell a square from a triangle? And even if we move on to hypoicons, is it possible that these people were denying the evidence—for example, that a photograph by Penn or Avedon looks more like the person portrayed than does a figure by Giacometti, and that even a person from a non-Occidental culture, if shown a group of statues from Ancient Rome, ought to recognize them as human bodies?[6]

Evidently not, and it is almost pathetic to see how, in the second phase of the debate (from the eighties until now), many illustrious iconoclasts hastened to make professions of faith in the iconic nature of perception—like the accused in a Stalinist or McCarthyite show trial, obliged above all to reiterate their loyalty to the system. See, for example, Gombrich 1975.

On the other hand, could it be that people so profoundly convinced of the iconic motivation of perception could at the same time deny that graphic conventions, proportional rules, and techniques of projection all come into play in the production and recognition of hypoicons? It seems improbable. This was not a debate between madmen.[7]

6.3 THE ARGUMENTS OF THE SIXTIES

As Sonesson also recalls in many of his writings, in the field of semiotics it all began when Barthes (1964), in his famous essay on pasta Panzani, stated that visual language was a language without a code. This was a way of suggesting that semiotics takes images exactly as they are and appear to us, and tries if anything to find the rhetorical rules for their concatenation, or to define their relations with the verbal information that makes up for their vagueness and polyvocity, thus contributing to establishing their sense.

In the same number of *Communications* 4, Metz launched what was to become the semiotics of the cinema. And he too assumed the cinematographic image as an image without a code, pure *analogon,* reserving semiotic studies (or, as they put it in *Communications*, semiological studies) for the great syntagmatics of film.

This happened at a time when semiotics was proposing itself as a *clavis universalis* capable of reducing all communicational phenomena to analyzable cultural conventions; at a time when people were adopting Saussure's principle, according to which the purpose of semiotics was to study "the life of signs within the framework of social life"; at a time when semiostructuralism was in the process of deciding to tackle not so much the study of laboratory-type expressions, linguistic or otherwise, like *John eats apples* or *The present king of France is bald,* as complex texts (even before there was any talk of textual semiotics). Most of these texts were taken from the world of mass communications (advertising announcements, photographs, images of television transmissions), and even when not a matter of mass communications, they were still narrative texts, persuasive arguments, and rhetorical strategies.

The new discipline was interested not so much in the good formation of a sentence (a study it delegated to linguistics) or in the relation between sentences and facts (which was unfortunately left in obscurity) as in enunciative strategies for making something "appear to be true." And therefore interest was focused not on what happens when someone says *It's raining today* and it really is (or isn't) but on the mechanism according to which, by talking, one can induce someone to believe that it is raining today, and the sociocultural impact of that disposition to believe.

Consequently, when someone was confronted with an advertisement showing a glass of ice-cold beer, the problem was not so much to explain whether and why the image corresponded to the object (and we shall see later that the problem would not go away) as to explain what universe of cultural assumptions was brought into play by that image and how the image aimed at reiterating or modifying that universe.[8]

One invitation to consider the phenomenon of iconism should have come from the encounter with Peirce—and it should be said that most of the demand for a rereading of Peirce as a semiologist came precisely from within the semiostructuralist paradigm.[9] But with regard to Peirce's work there is no doubt that more attention has been paid to the aspect of unlimited semiosis, the growth of interpretations within the cultural Community (certainly a fundamental and indispensable aspect), than to the more properly cognitive moment of the impact with the Dynamical Object.

These were the reasons for the polemic against so-called naïve iconism, which is based on an intuitive notion of likeness. The polemic was directed not so much at Peirce as at those who had simply confused iconism (as a perceptual moment) with hypoicons. If by icon one meant an "iconic sign" (and therefore, in Peirce's view, a hypoicon, whose "symbolic" or broadly conventional content he never denied), then saying that it possessed the properties of the object represented looked like a way of placing signs in a direct (and naïve) relation with the objects to which they referred, thus losing sight of the cultural mediation to which they were subjected (in short, treating phenomena of Thirdness as Firstness). I think (and the reader is referred to 2.8) I have made amends for those past simplifications, but it is also necessary to understand the reasons why people reacted the way they did at the time.

The virtually incontrovertible presupposition that hypoicons referred to their object by natural and immediate likeness, without the mediation of a content, was a way of reintroducing into visual semiotics that direct line between sign and referent that, with quasi surgical brutality, had been expunged from the semiotics of verbal language.[10]

It was a matter not of denying the existence of signs motivated in some way by something (and in fact I devoted to this problem the whole section on *ratio difficilis* in *A Theory of Semiotics*) but of making careful distinctions among motivation, naturalness, analogy, noncoding, "weak" coding, and unsayability. This attempt took various paths, some of which proved to be dead ends, but others led somewhere.

6.4. Dead ends

As an example of an absolute dead end I would cite the attempt to examine not only hypoicons but also semiotic systems such as architecture through linguistic categories—for example, minimal distinctive units, double articulation, paradigm and syntagm, et cetera. This attempt could not have led very far, but historic reasons applied in this case too. Consider the debate with Pasolini (1967a), when he maintained that the cinema is based on a "language of reality," an innate language of human action, in which the elementary signs of cinematographic language are said to be the real objects reproduced on the screen. Although Pasolini was later to moderate the radicalism of those early statements in an essay

that ought to be reflected upon anew today from a Peircean standpoint (1967b), his reaction was due to the fact that "hard-line"
semiologists were interested in demythologizing—as they used to
say then—all productions of realistic illusion and in revealing all
that was artifice, montage, and pretense in the cinema.[11] And that
is why we had come to individuate at all costs the presence of analyzable "linguistic" entities in films too, and I cite my own pages
(1968: B4, 1.5–1.9)[12] on triple articulation in the cinema, pages unfortunately still translated and republished in various anthologies
but not worth rereading, unless for documentary purposes.

By way of an example of a path that certainly led somewhere but
not in the direction intended, I would mention the attempt to reduce the analogical to the digital, i.e., to demonstrate that those hypoiconic signs that appeared to be visually analogous to their
objects could also be broken down into digitalized units and were
therefore translatable into (and producible by means of) algorithms. I am proud to have posed a problem that might have
seemed an irrelevant technicality in the sixties but—in the light of
computational theories of the image—is of the maximum importance today. But at the time the observation had rhetorical value
only, because it suggested that the aura of "unsayability" surrounding hypoicons could be reduced. From a semiotic point of view this
did not solve anything, because to assert the digital translatability
of the image to the expression plane does not eliminate the question
of how an effect of likeness comes about on a cognitive level.

6.5 LIKENESS AND SIMILARITY

The other path was to prove more productive. Since the notion of
likeness seemed vague and in any case circular (that which looks-
like is iconic, and that which is iconic looks-like), it had to be dissolved in a network of procedures to produce similarity.[13] What the
rules of similarity were was revealed to us by projective geometries,
the Peircean theory of graphs, and the elementary concept of proportion itself. But this did not eliminate the problem of perceptual
iconism, and of how an element of primary iconism—"likeness" in

the sense of Peircean Likeness, the very basis of perceptual constancy—can survive even in the perception of hypoicons (based on
criteria of similarity).

Taking their cue from Palmer (1978), May and Stjernfelt (1996:
195) propose the example as shown in figure 6.1:

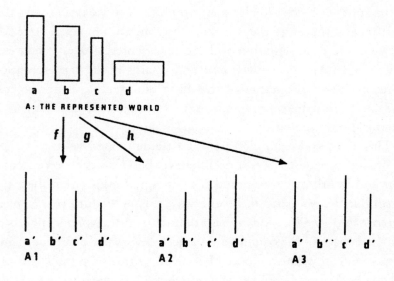

Figure 6.1

Imagine a world represented only by the objects a–d (it is not
necessary to establish whether this is a real universe or a possible
world inhabited by abstract entities). Consider A1, A2, and A3 as
three different "iconic" representations of this world (incidentally,
these would have every right to be considered as three interpretations of the world, just like those discussed in 1.8). Each of these
three representations adopts a single criterion for establishing similarity: by expressing the property of being "higher than," the criterion *f* (applied to A1) pertinentizes only the relations in terms of
height between the four figures in the world, and this is why *d* is
represented in *d'* by a vertical line, abstracting from the undoubted
property of breadth or horizontality that *d* shows in relation to the
other three figures. The criterion *g* (in A2) again pertinentizes relations of height, but by representing the property of being "shorter

than" (thus creating a visible relation of inverse symmetry between A1 and A2). The criterion h (in A3) is more complex: it pertinentizes the extent of area, but expresses the property "bigger than" through the mapping mechanisms employed in A2. In other words, the bigger an object, the shorter the vertical line that represents it. The three representations are certainly motivated by the nature of the objects (the length of the lines cannot be chosen arbitrarily), and therefore they certainly establish a hypoiconic relation between the representation and the represented. But this relation, which is defined as *homomorphic* and retains in the representation some structural properties of the thing represented, is not *isomorphic*, insofar as the representation does not have the same form as the thing represented.

This is a good example of similarity, motivated yet established according to rules. A certain "likeness" between each representation and the thing represented is maintained even when the rules of similarity are changed. By the way, this procedure corresponds to what in *A Theory of Semiotics* I defined as *ratio difficilis* (points of a virtual space of the content are projected onto the expression) and corresponds to what the post-Hjelmslevian tradition (and, most of all, the school of Greimas) has called the *semisymbolic:* where we have systems characterized not by the *conformity* between the expression plane and the content plane (as in a picture of a chessboard at a certain point in the game, or in a portrait) but through a correlation of two relevant categories of different planes (Greimas and Courtés 1979). In more comprehensible terms, in Jakobson (1970) the motor gestures for yes and no are not motivated by an object (which?) that they "would resemble," but they correlate, according to a nonarbitrary relation, a motor-spatial configuration (the movement of the head) with a categorial pair (affirmation and negation)—and even when in some cultures they seem conventionally different from ours, they nevertheless have a relation of motivation with the content they express.

Nevertheless, an understanding of these three representations is based on a perception of the difference in the length of the lines (not to mention the different format of the rectangles): now, this property of being longer or shorter is not established by the rule of similarity but is *its requirement on the basis of the natural iconism of perception*.

When I perceive a ball as such, I react to a circular structure. I cannot say to what extent my initiative contributes to my perceiving the ball as spherical too, but it is certainly on the basis of a pre-formed cognitive type that I also know that the ball ought to be made of rubber, be resilient, and therefore be capable both of rolling and bouncing according to how it moves or is thrown. To know that the statement *This is a ball* (which crowns the perceptual judgment) is true, I would have to grasp it and throw it (the prag-matic maxim holds here). But there is no doubt that what launched the perceptual judgment is the phenomenon of primary iconism, on the basis of which I immediately grasped a likeness with other objects of the same kind, which I had already had experience of (or of which a cognitive type had been transmitted to me in a very pre-cise fashion). To our distant ancestors, who saw the Moon without being provided with elaborate cognitive types, the Moon probably did not appear as spherical at first, but certainly (when it was full) as round.

This primary iconism is an indefinable parameter: it is, to repeat a question posed by Wittgenstein (1953 §50), like asking the length of the standard meter bar in Paris. Obviously the bar is exactly one meter long, since it represents the parameter on the basis of which we establish lengths according to the metric decimal system. Natu-rally, in the case of the standard meter bar we can elude this self-predication by applying another parameter and measuring it in feet and inches. But in the case of primary icons it is not possible to shift to another system of qualitative measurement, because even though there is another one, it does not exist on a perceptual level, as when we interpret colors according to wavelength. On a percep-tual level you cannot predicate anything of a Likeness other than the recognition that it is that Likeness. We may later say we were mistaken; the perceptual impact of a color can be modified by set-ting it alongside another color, but in that case we would simply be choosing one Likeness in place of another. Therefore this innate experience of likeness cannot be used to judge similarities, and rules of similarity cannot be used to define primary iconic likeness.

But we must get back to the old dispute, and to the reason why attempts were made to shift likeness wholly onto similarity. There was a tendency to favor iconographic techniques, whereby (to return to the classic example in Gombrich 1956) Dürer's rhinoceros had scales in accordance with a cultural type, while little attention was paid to the fact that, while today it strikes us as a quasi rhinoceros, we are nevertheless unlikely to take it for a crocodile.

6.6 OUTLINES

One example of iconoclast vehemence was the polemic about outlines. I am going to quote myself again, because it is not a good idea to reprove others for carelessness or errors that we may have committed along with them. In *La struttura assente,* I held that we cannot say that hypoicons have the properties of the objects represented, because if I take a sheet of paper and draw the profile of a horse, the only property that the pictured horse has (the continuous black line) is the only property that the real horse does not have. Therefore I would not have reproduced so much as the conditions of the perception.

The problem of outlines was taken up again by Hochberg (1972), Kennedy (1974), and Gombrich, who had become critical of his original conventionalism (1975). While it was usually held that there are no lines in nature and that outlines are therefore a human artifice, observed Gombrich, psychologists now tend to deny that their comprehension must be learned just like any other code. Outlines are a perceptual surrogate and serve as indicators of discontinuity. He notes that outlines can serve as an anticipation of the parallax effect of movement, because the objects within our reach will always detach themselves from the background but maintain an intrinsic coherence even if we move our head slightly (1975). In other words, if, on looking at a horse standing against a landscape, I move my head or change my position, I see other aspects of the landscape that I did not see before, while the horse is still the same:

and therefore the drawn outline accounts for this perceptual "boundary."[14]

Already in *A Theory of Semiotics* (3.5.2), taking my cue from some observations made by Kalkhofen 1972, I returned to the topic of outlines (this time of a hand). Again it was denied that the hand possessed the property of having a black outline, but it was granted that, if the hand were placed on a clear surface, the contrast between the edges of the body that absorbs more light and what reflects the light can generate the impression of a continuous line. I was picking up the idea of *surrogate stimuli,* already proposed, as we shall see, in *La struttura assente*.[15]

But before we move on to surrogate stimuli, it is worth reflecting a little more on what it means to say that outlines are given in nature.

Let us consider the "ecological" version of Gibson's psychology, according to which the object seems to have some privileged features, which directly excite our nerve cells, with the result that what we grasp of the object is exactly what the object preferentially offers us. In this regard, Gregory (1981: 376) observes polemically that to assert that all the information necessary for perceiving the environment—without the intervention of any interpretative mechanism—reaches us in the form of light stimuli that are already objectively organized would mean returning to the theories of perception prior to Alhazen's and Alkindi's observations on light rays, in other words, to the notion of "simulacra" coming from the object. We would still be adhering to a medieval idea of an intellect that grasps of the object precisely what counts for most in the object, its essential skeleton, its *quidditas*. But the lmitted seductiveness of Gregory's argument is no proof that it is correct. As a matter of fact, nothing forbids us (in principle) from thinking that the ancients were right and that Gibson is right in returning to them.

I think there is a difference between saying that outlines are already offered by the stimulating field and saying that the stimulating field offers the object in a definitive way, already wrapped to determine our completed perception, which simply recognizes and accepts what has been offered to it through the senses. This difference concerns the moment Peirce thought of as that of primary iconism, or of what he called the percept, and the completed perceptual judgment.

Hubel and Wiesel (1959) and Hubel (1982) tell us that in perceiving a stimulus, our nerve cells respond to an optimal orientation that already exists in the stimulus. After inserting tungsten microelectrodes in the brain of a cat, Hubel and Wiesel were able to ascertain which cells reacted to what stimuli, and proved that the animal, when shown a blot moving across a screen, reacted more to movement in one direction than to movement in the other. But that's not all. At a certain point, while a slide was being placed in the ophthalmoscope, the cat reacted with a sort of instantaneous cellular explosion: it was ascertained that the reaction had nothing to do with the images on the slide but with the fact that, on entering the machine, the slide had impressed the shadow of its own border on the cat's retina, and that was exactly "what the cell wanted."

Now, these data tell us how *sensations* are received, but it is doubtful whether they can tell us how *perception* works. They tell us that cats (which cannot have been infected by iconoclastic idealism) do not receive an uncoordinated mass of sensations but are led to focalize certain features of the stimulating field at the expense of others. But is this due to the way the object is made or to how the cat is made? Psychologists are very cautious about drawing conclusions from these experiments. We can easily accept that when a cat sees a table, it is struck more by the luminous incidence at its edges than by other aspects of the surface, and that it is the same for us: but from this to go on to state that the same process is prolonged (in us and in cats), always through the initiative of the object, all the way to the higher levels of perception, is another kettle of fish altogether.

True, Hubel maintains that our cortical cells respond poorly to diffuse light, with the result that, when I look at an egg against a dark background, the cells concerned with the central area of the egg are not stimulated, while those stimulated by the borders of the egg respond. But right after that, Hubel concludes: "How the information from such sets of cells is assembled at subsequent stages in the path to build up what we call percepts of lines or curves (if indeed anything like this happens at all) is still a complete mystery" (1982: 519). Quite rightly, conclusions on the level of a theory of perception are not drawn from data on the modalities of sensation, and the experimenter does not risk stating that therefore knowledge is a mirrorlike correspondence and not also a construction.

In referring to the research carried out by Hubel and Wiesel, Johnson-Laird reminds us that "trying to understand vision by studying only nerve cells, as Marr remarked, is like trying to understand bird flight by studying only feathers" (1988: 72). All this research says nothing about the differences between what is calculated, how our perceptual system elaborates that computation, and how our cerebral hardware functions in this computational process. Independently of the mechanism by which our retina receives stimuli from the environment, the problem of how our mental mechanism elaborates this input concerns our system of expectations.

> No matter how much information is in the light falling on the retinae, there must be a mental mechanism for recovering the identities of the things in a scene and those of their properties that vision makes explicit to consciousness. Without such mechanisms, retinal images would be no more use than the images produced by a television camera and, contrary to the naïve view, *they* cannot see anything...These processes must rely on certain assumptions about the world. (Johnson-Laird 1988: 61)

Moreover, maintaining that the process from sensation to perception involves unvarying privileged patterns to which the brain (human and animal) responds in a constant fashion, and even fully accepting an ecological theory of perception (in its most brutal form: we see what is there, and that's all), still tells us nothing about the hypoiconic modalities with which we artificially represent those same objects of perception.

The real crux of the misunderstanding yet again lies in the

immediate passage from the primary iconism of perception (that is, from the evidence that relations of likeness exist perceptually) to an established theory of similarity, in other words, of the creation of the effect of likeness. Anyone who has ever visited a perfume factory will have come up against a curious olfactory experience. We can all easily recognize (on the level of perceptual experience) the difference between the scent of violets and that of lavender. But when we want to produce industrial quantities of essences of violet or lavender (which must produce the same sensation, albeit a little enhanced, stimulated by these plants), the visitor to the factory is assailed by intolerable stenches and foul odors. This means that in order to produce the impression of the scent of violets or lavender, one must mix chemical substances that are most disagreeable to the olfactory sense (even though the result is pleasant). I am not sure if nature works like this, but what seems evident is that it is one thing to receive the sensation (fundamental iconism) of the scent of violets and another thing to produce the same impression. This second operation requires the application of various techniques with a view to producing surrogate stimuli.

Think, for example, of two schematic figures (in some perspective) of a cylinder and a cube.[16] A naïve iconist would say that they represent a cylinder and a cube exactly as they are; a supporter of the cognitive value of iconism would say (and we cannot disagree) that under normal circumstances—when the cultural inheritance is equal—the figures would allow a subject to identify a cylinder and a cube and to distinguish between them; the supporters of the natural nature of outlines (whose number I have decided to join) would say that the lines of the two drawings exactly circumscribe the profile by means of which the object presents itself to us.

But the representation is "good" *from a certain point of view,* and such is the function of all representations in perspective, whatever the projective rule applied. Perspective is a phenomenon that brings into play both the object and the position of the observer, and that position also has a role to play when a three-dimensional object is being observed. Therefore the hypoicon in some way transcribes these conditions of observation. But now let's reflect on the fact that the straight lines that circumscribe the contours of the cylinder do not have the same semiosic function as those that circumscribe the surfaces of the cube. The parallel lines that circumscribe the contours of the cylinder are surrogate stimuli that represent the way in which, from whatever direction we look at it, we will see the cylinder stand out against its background (the number of these lines, if we were to rotate the cylinder, would be infinite, and Zeno would admit that we would never stop seeing the cylinder's infinity of outlines). The lines of the cube, on the other hand, represent not only the profile of that object seen from *that* point of view but also, at the same time, the edges of the solid, which remain as such, even though their perspectival relation changes, depending on the point of view we look at or represent the cube. In both cases, we are dealing with surrogate stimuli, but (again in both cases) these stimuli "surrogate" different phenomena, which depend partly on the form of the object and partly on the way in which we decide to look at it.

6.7 SURROGATE STIMULI

It is not true that the iconoclasts took into consideration only the profiles of horses or fanciful rhinoceroses, without posing the problem of the immediate impression of likeness experienced by the observer when in the presence of a realistic or hyperrealistic image. In *La struttura assente* (1968: 110 ff.), I examined an advertisement showing a foaming glass of beer, which evoked a sense of pronounced coolness, because on the glass you could see a film of icy vapor. Clearly the image contained neither glass nor beer nor icy vapor: therefore it was suggested that the image reproduced *some of the conditions of the perception of the object:* where, on perceiving the object, I would have been struck by the incidence of light rays on a surface, in the image there were certain chromatic contrasts that *produced the same effect,* or an effect that was satisfactorily equivalent.

Therefore, even though I realize that what I see is not a glass but the image of a glass (but there are cases of trompe l'oeil where I do not realize the image is an image), the perceptual inferences I bring into play to perceive something (and certainly on the basis of previous cognitive types) are the same ones I would bring into play to perceive the real object. From the relatively satisfactory way in which these surrogate stimuli stand in for the effective stimuli, I will take the image either as a good approximation or as a miracle of realism.

Now, this idea of surrogate stimuli has frequently been asserted by various psychologists. For example, Gibson (1971, 1978) has spoken in these cases of "indirect perception" or "secondhand perception." Hochberg (1972: 58) says on several occasions that the scene represented by a picture is a surrogate, because it acts on the eye of the observer in a way "similar" to the real scene; that an outline is "a stimulus that is equivalent in some way to the features by which the visual system normally encodes the images of objects in the visual field" (1972: 82); that when a border between two surfaces appears in the visual field, it is usually accompanied by a difference in luminosity, and therefore an outline provides an *index of depth* insofar as it makes us perceive (in a *vicarious* fashion) the very border where the luminous difference is found (1972: 84).

Research by Marr and Nishishara (e.g., 1978: 6) on computer simulations of perceptual processes tells us that a scene and the drawing of a scene look similar to us, because "the artist's symbols correspond in some way to natural symbols that are computed out of the image during the normal course of its interpretation."

But there is no doubt about the vagueness of all these definitions (in which we frequently come across expressions such as "in some way"). More than explain how surrogate stimuli work, these definitions acknowledge the fact that they exist and function. We have to do with surrogate stimuli in all those cases in which the same receptors react as they would in the presence of the real stimulus, just as birds respond to decoy whistles or as a sound-effects expert in the radio or the cinema supplies us (through the use of strange instruments) with the same acoustic sensations we would experience on hearing the gallop of a horse or the roar of a racing car. The mechanics of surrogate stimuli remain obscure, also because these "surrogations" range from the highest of high fidelity, as we shall see, to a simple invitation to behave as if we were receiving a nonexistent stimulus.

The fact that—even though we do not know exactly how they work—there are surrogate stimuli is exemplified splendidly in Diderot's pages on Chardin (the 1763 Salon):

> The artist has placed on a table an old porcelain china vase, two biscuits, a jug full of olives, a basket of fruit, two half-full glasses of wine, a Seville orange and some pâté. To look at the pictures of others it seems that I need to have new eyes made; to look at Chardin's, all I need do is keep the eyes nature gave me, and use them well... The thing is that the porcelain vase is porcelain; these olives are really separated by the eye from the water in which they float; should I wish to eat the biscuits all I need do is reach out and take them; all I need do is peel this orange and squeeze it, take this glass of wine and drink it, peel these fruits, take this pâté and sink my knife into it...O Chardin, it is not white, red, or black that you spread on your palette; it is the very substance of the objects, it is the air and the light that you gather with the tip of your brush and put on the canvas.

At first sight Diderot's praise expresses the delight of a spectator who, believing that there cannot be absolutely realistic painting, finds himself in the presence of a masterpiece of realism, in which there is no gap between the stimulus that may come from the real object and the "surrogate" stimulus. But Diderot is not so naïve. The first effect having worn off, and well aware that what he can see is not real fruit and biscuits, he seems to get closer to the painting, where he finds out he is longsighted:

> One cannot understand this magic. The color is applied in thick layers, one on top of the other, whose effect transpires to the surface from below. Sometimes one would say that it is a vapor that has been puffed onto the canvas, sometimes it seems that it has been

smeared with a light froth…You get closer, all is confused, flattens and disappears. Move further away, all is recreated and reproduced.

That is the point. The stimuli aroused by real objects, with variations that are negligible from the point of view of perceptual recognition, act at different distances. Surrogate stimuli, when examined from too close up, betray their illusory nature, their substance of the expression, which is not that of the objects they suggest; and to obtain their iconic effect they require a calculated distance. This is the principle behind the trompe l'oeil, the epiphany of the surrogate stimulus. Chardin's magic is due to the fact that the stimuli he provides for the spectator are *not* the ones that would be provided by the object. Diderot confesses he cannot understand how the painter manages to do this, but he has to admit that he does it. In his own way, in celebrating the miracles of iconism, Diderot is stating the *nonnatural* nature of hypoicons.

I should like to elaborate upon an observation made by Merleau-Ponty with regard to a die (1945: 2, III). The die is there, visible from different points of view. It may be that those beside me do not see it, and therefore it is part of my personal history. As I look at it, it loses its materiality and reduces itself to visual structure, form and color, light and shade. I note that not all aspects of the die can fall within my perceptual field, the Thing-in-Itself can be seen only from my personal point of view. I grasp not the thing but my experience oriented by the thing, my way of experiencing the thing (the rest, we might say, is inference, a hypothesis as to how the thing might be if others could see it too). I perceive the die with my body, including the point of view from which I look at it. If my body (or my point of view) were to move, I would see something else. Thanks to long perceptual experience, I know all this. But in the presence of the surrogate stimulus (the representation of a die, regarding which, were I to shift my point of view, I could not perceive anything that might be behind it), I have already accepted that someone has *seen for me*.

Therefore a good rule for detecting surrogate stimuli would

seem to be the following: if I change my point of view, do I see something new? If the answer is no, the stimulus is surrogate.[17] The surrogate stimulus tries to impose upon me the sensation I would have were I to observe matters from the point of view of the Surrogator. In front of me there is the outline of a house (and we have seen that outlines are founded in nature); if I move, can I see the tree behind the house? If I cannot see it, the stimulus is surrogate. Only by usurping the point of view of someone who has seen before me can I define if a stimulus is surrogate or not. The surrogate stimulus prevents me from seeing (or hearing) from the point of view of my subjectivity, understood as my corporeality; it gives me only one profile of things, not the multiplicity of profiles that real perception would offer me. In order to decide whether a stimulus is surrogate or not, all you have to do is move your head.

6.8 BACK TO THE DISCOURSE

My review of the historical reasons for the debate on iconism has perhaps already suggested some of the reasons why it can now be resumed *sine ira et studio*. The idea of a semiotics that has to study the workings of signs in social and cultural life no longer requires the polemic energies of apologist fathers: it is a matter of fact. Semiotic studies have been developed at a subcultural level (from zoosemiotics to the problems in cellular communication that I mentioned in 2.8.2), where concepts such as primary iconism reemerge on the scene without their being dissolved in a broth of cultural stipulations. Many have gradually been converting from the semiostructuralist paradigm to the Peircean one (at least with attempts to blend the most interesting aspects of both). Faith in what interpretation posits and constructs with respect to any datum has led (certainly in the field of texts, with Derrida, but also with regard to the world, at least in the case of the latest Rorty) to the triumph of deconstructionist drift. For those who thought that we needed to regulate this in some way, it was necessary to tackle the problem of *the limits of interpretation*. This was precisely the expression I used for Eco 1990, apropos of textual interpretation, but already on that occasion the essay on drift and unlimited semiosis posed the problem of the limits of the interpretation of the world; and, as far as the world is concerned, I have dealt with this with greater resolution in 1.8–11.

And so we can now return to the discourse of hypoicons. By so doing, I do not think I have succumbed to the temptation of having my own personal *Kehre*. More modestly, all I think I am doing is bringing to the forefront what, without rejecting it, I had previously left in the background, but in such a way that both the "figures" remain legible.

6.9 Seeing and drawing Saturn

My discussion with Maldonado sprang from an objection he made in favor of iconism: that the image of the Moon that Galileo saw in his telescope was an icon and as such possessed an innate likeness with the Moon itself. I objected that the image in the eyepiece of the telescope was not an icon—at least not in the sense of an iconic sign. The iconic sign, or hypoicon of the Moon, emerged when, after having looked in the telescope, Galileo drew the Moon. And since Galileo already knew a lot about the Moon, as a result of his having observed it like everybody else with the naked eye, I chose to discuss a more original and more "unheard-of" situation: that of Galileo looking at Saturn through his telescope for the first time and then—as can be seen, for example, in *Sidereus Nuncius*, making drawings of it.

In such a case there are four elements in play: (i) Saturn as Thing-in-Itself, as Dynamical Object (even when not an object, it would be a set of stimuli); (ii) the luminous stimuli that Galileo received when he put his eye to the telescope (and it's up to optics to study what happens when the rays reflected by the planet travel through space, through the concave eyepiece, and through the double-convex lens); (iii) the conceptual type that Galileo reconstructed of Saturn, the Immediate Object (which will in some way be different from the one he had when struggling to observe it with the naked eye); (iv) the drawing (hypoicon) that Galileo made of Saturn.

Apparently the four stages come in this order:

Saturn-in-itself → Saturn on the lens → Cognitive type → Drawing

This is what I would do today if I wished to draw what I see in a telescope. But Galileo was looking for the first time. And, on looking, he saw something never seen before. There are various letters in which Galileo communicated his discoveries as they came along, and you can see the effort he made (as he looked) to *see*. For example, in three letters (to Benedetto Castelli, 1610; to Belisario Giunti, 1610; and to Giuliano de' Medici, 1611), he says he saw not one star but three joined together in a straight line parallel to the equinoctial, and he represented what he saw like this (fig. 6.2):

But in other letters (e.g., to Giuliano de' Medici, 1610; and to

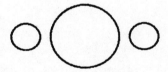

Figure 6.2

Marco Velseri, 1612) he admits that owing to the "imperfection of the instrument and the eye of the observer," Saturn might also appear like this ("in the shape of an olive," fig. 6.3):

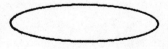

Figure 6.3

The figure clearly reveals that, since it is wholly unexpected for a planet to be surrounded by a ring (which apart from anything else clashed with every notion held at the time with regard to heavenly bodies), Galileo was trying to understand what he could see, in other words, he was laboriously trying to construct a (new) cognitive type of Saturn.

After looking and looking again (see his letter to Federigo Borromeo in 1610), Galileo finally decided that it was a matter no longer of two small round bodies but of larger bodies "and of a shape no longer round, but as can be seen in the enclosed figure, two semi-ellipses with two very obscure little triangles in the middle of the said figures, and contiguous to Saturn's middle globe." This consideration led Galileo to a third representation (fig. 6.4):

Figure 6.4

If we look at the drawing, we recognize Saturn and its rings, but simply because we have already seen other elaborated representations, of which this sketch anticipates a few pertinent features (a globe with an ellipse around it—and it's up to us to see perspective in a sketch that does very little to suggest it). Note that Galileo did not see this perspective, otherwise he would have spoken not of two semiellipses but of an elliptical band.[18] Galileo still saw a kind of Mickey Mouse, a face with two large ears. But it cannot be denied that this third drawing is more like successive images, even photographic ones, of Saturn at its point of maximum inclination. In any case, on a morphological level it corresponds to the cognitive type of Saturn possessed by a person with average knowledge. Note that (due to the claimed coincidence between cognitive type and nuclear content or Immediate Object) if asked to represent Saturn, a person without particular graphic talents would today make a drawing fairly similar to Galileo's, probably completing the lower part of the two ellipses so that the ring passes in front of the globe.

In the light of Galileo's efforts, one is led to think that it is not the construction of the cognitive type that precedes the drawing; if anything, it follows it:

Saturn-in-itself → Saturn on the lens → Drawing → Cognitive Type

It is only by trying to fix on paper the essential features of what was being received (in this stage, clots of Firstness, an uncoordinated sequence of stimuli) that Galileo gradually began to "see," to perceive Saturn and to construct a first hypothetical cognitive type. Which is also what I was trying to say in *A Theory of Semiotics* with regard to radical inventions.[19]

Having said all this, we have still said nothing about the second element of the chain, Saturn on the lens. From a semiotic point of view, it would seem to be a negligible phenomenon: the telescope constitutes a channel through which Galileo received a series of stimuli, as he would have received them had he boarded a spaceship and traveled to a point sufficiently close to Saturn.

But it is precisely this "as if" that demands some additional reflection (and never was metaphor so literal). Not so much to gain a better understanding of perception as to return yet again to the phenomenon of hypoicons.

6.10 PROSTHESES

Normally we give the name prosthesis to any apparatus that *substitutes* a missing organ, but in a broad sense prostheses are all apparatuses that extend the range of action of an organ. When people are asked where they would like to have a third eye, were this possible, they usually provide rather uneconomical responses: some would like one on the nape of the neck, others on the back, without taking into account that whereas this would certainly allow them to see what is going on behind them, it would not help with regard to an infinity of other places into which they often wish they could see: the top of the head, behind the ears, on the other side of a door, or inside the hole into which their key has fallen. The correct answer, in the sense that it is the most reasonable one, would be: on the tip of the index finger. It is obvious that in this way we might extend the range of our vision to the maximum, within the limits of our bodily range of action.[20] Well, if we had an artificial eye that was as maneuverable as our index finger, we would have an excellent *extensive* prosthesis with an *intrusive* function into the bargain (in the sense that it would go see not just in places where the eyes could look if we turned our head or moved but also into places where the eyes cannot penetrate).

Substitutive prostheses do what the body used to do but for one accidental reason or another no longer does: such devices include artificial limbs, walking sticks, spectacles, pacemakers, and hearing aids. Extensive prostheses, on the other hand, extend the natural action of the body: such devices include megaphones, stilts, and magnifying glasses, but also certain objects that we do not habitually consider extensions of our body, such as chopsticks or pliers (which extend the action of our fingers), shoes (which strengthen the action and resistance of the feet), clothes in general (which enhance the protective action of the skin and hair), and ladles and spoons (which substitute for and improve the action of the hand seeking to collect a liquid and bring it to the mouth).

Another device that might be considered an extensive prosthesis is the lever, which in principle works like the arm but better; but the lever does this so well, and with such results, that it probably ushers in a third category, that of *magnifying* prostheses. These do something that our body had perhaps dreamed of doing but without ever succeeding: telescopes and microscopes, but also vases and bottles, baskets and bags, the spindle, and certainly the sledge and the wheel.

Both extensive and magnifying prostheses can also be specified as *intrusive*. Among the *extensive-intrusive* prostheses, we would mention the periscope or certain medical instruments that make it possible to explore immediately accessible cavities such as the ear or throat, while the *magnifying-intrusive* prostheses include scanners, gamma-ray measuring devices in nuclear medicine, or certain probes equipped with miniature television cameras that explore the entire intestines and project what they "see" onto a screen.[21]

I have made use of this attempt at classification only to be able to talk of that original and special type of prosthesis, which is the mirror.

6.11 MORE ON MIRRORS[22]

What is a mirror, in the current sense of the term? It is a regular plane or curved surface capable of reflecting rays of incident light. A plane mirror forms a virtual, upright, reversed (or symmetrical), specular (of the same size as the object reflected) image devoid of so-called chromatic aberration. A convex mirror forms virtual, upright, reversed, and reduced images. A concave mirror is a surface of a type that (a) when the object is between the focus and the spectator, it forms virtual, upright, reversed, enlarged images; (b) when the object's position varies, from infinity to coincidence with the focal point, it forms images that are real, reversed, enlarged, or reduced, depending on circumstances, at different points in space, which can be observed by the human eye and collected on a screen. Paraboloidal, ellipsoidal, spherical, or cylindrical mirrors are not in common use and, if anything, are used for deforming images and in catoptric theaters.[23]

In Eco (1985) I was struck by the oddity and the quasi "idealistic" nature of the idea—established in optical studies—that the mirror image is *reversed* or, rather, "inversely symmetrical." The naïve opinion that the mirror puts the right in place of the left and vice versa is so deeply rooted that some people are surprised by the notion that mirrors reverse left to right but not up to down. Now let's reason for a moment: if in front of the mirror I have the impression that it reverses right and left, because in the image it seems that my watch is on my right wrist, for the same reason, if I look into a mirror on the ceiling, I ought to think that it has changed up to down, because I see my head where my feet ought to be.

But the point is that not even vertical mirrors reverse things or turn them upside down. If we make a diagram of the specular phenomenon, we realize that *camera oscura*–type phenomena do not occur in it (see fig. 6.5): there are no intersecting rays in specular reflection (see fig. 6.6).

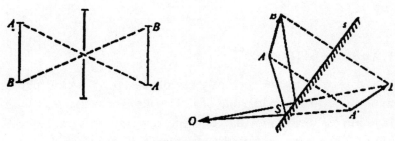

Figures 6.5 and 6.6

The mirror reflects our right exactly where our right is, and the same holds for the left. It is we who identify ourselves with the person we see in the mirror, or think that it is another person standing in front of us, and we are surprised at his wearing a watch on the right wrist (or his gripping a sword with the left hand). But we are not that virtual person in the mirror. All we have to do is avoid "entering" the mirror, and this illusion will no longer trouble us. In fact, we can all manage to comb our hair in the mirror in the morning without acting as if we had cerebral palsy. We know how to use the mirror, and we know that the lock of hair over our right ear is on our right (even though for the person in the mirror, were he there, it would be on the left). On the perceptual and motor plane, we correctly interpret the mirror image for what it is, but on the plane of conceptual reflection we still cannot entirely manage to separate the physical phenomenon from the illusions it encourages, in a sort of hiatus between perception and judgment. We use the mirror image the right way, but we talk about it the wrong way (whereas in astronomy we talk correctly about the relation between the Earth and the Sun, even though we perceive it wrongly, as if it were the Sun that moved).

This is certainly a very curious point: that mirrors reverse left and right is an ancient belief, from Lucretius to Kant, and some cling to it to this day.[24] If things were like this, we would have to think about the fact that, when someone stands behind me, his right is on my right and his left is on my left; but if he turns around and stands in front of me, his right is where I have my left and vice versa (and he wears his watch on the opposite side to me). And so we would have to conclude that *it is people who reverse*, not mirror images, and this ancestral habit of seeing people reversed is what invites us to see mirror images as reversed (if we consider them as persons).

This much, simply to say that mirrors make us lose our head. But if instead we would keep our head, we must conclude from this that mirrors do not provide reversal but perfect congruency, as when I press blotting paper on a sheet of paper. The fact that I cannot read what remains impressed on the blotting paper has to do with my reading habits, not with specularity (Leonardo da Vinci, who had other reading and writing habits, would not have had this problem). However, I could read what remains impressed on the blotting paper by using a mirror, that is to say, by having recourse to a mirror image of a mirror image. The same thing happens to me if I stand in front of the mirror holding the dust jacket of a book. I can't manage to read the title in the mirror; but if I have two angulated mirrors, as people often have in their bathrooms, I can see reflected in one of the two mirrors (more easily in one than the other, depending on the angulation) a third image in which the letters on the dust jacket appear as they do when I look at the book directly (moreover, I really would see myself with my watch on the left wrist). Now, this third image really is a reverse of the mirror image (which in itself reverses nothing).

We use mirrors well, because we have introjected the rules of catoptric refraction. We use them well, when we know that we are dealing with a mirror. When we do not know this, misunderstandings or deceptions may arise. But, when we do know, we always start from the principle that the mirror is telling the truth. It neither "translates" nor interprets but registers what strikes it exactly as it strikes it. And so we trust mirrors, just as we trust, under normal conditions, our own organs of perception. We trust mirrors just as we trust spectacles and telescopes, because, like spectacles and telescopes, mirrors are prostheses.

There is no doubt that mirrors are extensive and intrusive prosthetics par excellence, for example, in that they allow us to look where the eye cannot reach: they allow us to look at our face and eyes, they allow us to see what is happening behind our back. Starting from this principle, we can use mirrors to obtain some very sophisticated intrusive effects: think of angulated dressing table mirrors that allow us to see ourselves in profile, or of barbers' mirrors arranged *en abîme*. Some mirrors are also magnifying prostheses, because they reproduce an enlarged image of our face; others are deforming prostheses. With complex theaters of mirrors we can create illusions, right up to the disquieting catoptric theater in Orson Welles's *The Lady from Shanghai*. With series of mirrors arranged at suitable angles we can extend our intrusive powers (I can construct systems of mirrors that allow me to see what is happening in the next room, even if I am not looking toward the door); we can use mirrors as channels for transporting or projecting luminous stimuli (think of the various possible signaling systems that use light reflected by mirrors)... But for the moment what interests us here are simple everyday mirrors, which I am going to consider as presemiosic phenomena.

Of course if I "interpret" my image in the mirror and draw conclusions about my aging (or my unfading beauty), I am already in a more complicated phase of semiosis. And this can also be said of that "mirror stage" in which Lacan saw the moment in which the symbolic was established. But the fact that children must learn to use mirrors does not mean (as some people think) that the mirror is not a primary experience. Children have to learn everything, even to use their hands and eyes; let's give them time. But the magic of mirrors is such that it is hard for many people to accept the extremely banal experience that I stubbornly insist on proposing: I intend to speak of the mirror image in terms of the way I use the dressing-table mirror every day, perhaps to adjust my tie, and in this phase there is no longer any interpretation, apart from that perceptual interpretation that also comes into play when I look at someone in front of me.

The normal mirror is a prosthesis that does not deceive. All the other prostheses, insofar as they interpose something between the organ whose powers they extend or magnify and what they "touch," can deceive our perceptions: walking with shoes on leads us into making a poor judgment of the terrain; clothes give us poor information about the external temperature; pliers can give us the impression we have gripped something that then eludes us. But with mirrors we can be sure that we see things the way they are, even when we look in the mirror and wish we were not as we see ourselves.

Naturally we must exclude mirrors that have misted over, cases in which we are deceived by our own mistake (such as when we think we see someone coming toward us, and it is our reflected image instead), misunderstandings in which we take for a mirror an empty frame on the other side of which there is someone who imitates our every movement (as in the Marx Brothers film). In normal circumstances we use mirrors armed with the certainty that they do not lie.

We do it because we have learned that the specular prosthesis provides the eye with the same stimuli that the eye would receive were the prosthesis in front of us (perhaps on the tip of an index finger that we point toward our face). We are sure that the mirror provides us with the absolute double of the stimulating field. If an iconic sign (in the sense of hypoicon) really were an image that has all the properties (visual, at least) of the object represented, the mirror image would be the iconic sign par excellence, or it would be the only icon external to our mind of which we really have experience. But this pure icon stands only for itself.

However, it is not even a Firstness in the Peircean sense, because what we see is already interwoven with an awareness of a relation to a fact: if anything, the mirror image is a Firstness already anchored to a Secondness, insofar as it establishes a necessary and direct relation between the mirroring and the thing mirrored. *But it is not yet a sign*. This statement holds as long as we assume that in order to define a sign as such, the following criteria must be respected:

(i)   The sign is something that stands for something else *in its absence*. The mirror image, on the other hand, stands *in the presence* of the object it reflects.

(ii) The sign is materially distinct from the thing of which it is the sign, otherwise one might say that I am a sign of myself. The mirror image, on the other hand, is, as we have seen, an absolute double of the same stimuli that our eye would receive were it in front of the reflecting object.

(iii) In the sign the expression plane is distinguished by substance and form, and the form itself could be transposed into another substance. But with a mirror, at most I transfer (by reversing it) the same luminous substance onto an opposed specular surface.

(iv) For there to be a sign, it must be possible to relate a sign token to a type. In the mirror image, on the other hand, type and token coexist.

(v)   The sign can be used to lie or to state (erroneously, even though in good faith) that which is not the case. The mirror image, on the other hand, never lies. The sign can be used to lie, because I can produce the sign even though the object does not exist (I can name chimeras and portray unicorns), while the mirror image is produced only in the presence of the object.

The mirror image has no indexical value. It is not an index of the fact that we are in front of the mirror, because we would not need it (if anything, the absence of the image of the mirrored object could be a symptom, but only for the Invisible Man or for vampires). It is not an index of the fact that we have, for example, a mark on our nose: insofar as the mirror is a prosthesis, we see the mark as we would see it if the mark were on our hand.

The mirror image is not even an imprint (unless in the sense in which the sensation is a metaphorical "imprint" of what has been sensed): imprints are such, and tell us something, when they subsist as material traces in the absence of an imprinter, and only then do they become a semiosic phenomenon. For someone following me, the tracks left on the ground by my feet are imprints, but not for me, because I am not concerned about the fact that my feet make an impression as they touch the ground—unless (supposing I am drunk) I turn around to check my footprints to see if I have been walking in a straight line. If I had eyes in the soles of my feet, I would see my prints one by one as they were impressed in the ground, and I could interpret them in order to make inferences about the shape of my feet. But with mirrors, not even this happens: all I have to do is expose the soles of my feet to the reflecting surface, and I can see them as they are, without any need to infer anything.

Sonesson (1989: 63, referring to Maldonado 1974: 288 ff.) has suggested that the mirror image may be a "hard icon," as are the impressions on an X-ray plate or the mark left by a hand on the walls of a prehistoric cavern. But these are indeed imprints (see *A Theory of Semiotics* 3.6.2), in which the substance of the expression (stone, sand, film) has nothing to do with the material of which the imprinting object is constituted, and in which we can work up from a few features (generally profiles) to an inferential reconstruction of that possible object. Moreover, these imprints naturally subsist even after the object that made them, and therefore they can also be falsified, which does not happen with the mirror image.

Finally, the imprint is a sign, insofar as it is fundamentally an expression that refers to a content, and content is always general. When Robinson sees the footprint on the sand, he does not say, *Man Friday passed here,* but, *A human being passed here.* A hunter on the trail of a given deer, or a "tail" following the tracks left on the ground by Mr. X, initially sees the prints left by *a* deer and *a* person (or of a shoe), and it is only by inference that the hunter or "tail" is convinced he is dealing with *that* deer or *that* Mr. X.[25]

Naturally one might object that objects are used as ostensive signs (I show a mastiff or a telephone to say that mastiffs or telephones are made like this or like that; see *A Theory of Semiotics* 3.6.3). In processes of ostension, an object is chosen as an example that refers to all the objects in its category, but we use an object as an ostensive sign precisely because it is first and foremost an object. I can look at myself in the mirror to tell myself that human beings are like me in general, but in the same way I could look at my telephone on the table to tell myself that all telephones are like this in general. And therefore the mirror image is yet again a prosthesis that allows me or others to see an object that can be *chosen* as an ostensive sign.[26]

Therefore the image we see in the mirror is not a sign, any more than the enlarged image provided by a telescope or the one we can see through a periscope.[27]

If anything, the dream of a sign that has the same properties as the mirror image springs from the fascination that mirrors have held for humanity since Narcissus's day. The specular experience can explain the birth of a notion such as the (semiotic) one of the iconic sign (as hypoicon), but is not explained by it.

But then, if we take this path, it is from the timeless appeal of mirrors that springs the idea of an understanding that is a complete correspondence ("specular," in fact) between thing and intellect. The idea of indexes springs from such a specular experience: it says "this" and "here" and points to me looking at myself in the moment in which I look at myself. From it springs the idea of a sign that, devoid of meaning, refers directly to its referent: the mirror image is really the example of an "absolute proper noun"; it is really the most rigid of rigid designators; it resists all counterfactuals. I cannot suspect that, even were the mirror to lose all its properties, what I see in it would no longer be what I see in it. But these are metaphors—which, when said by the poets, can become sublime. The character proper to the mirror image is that it is only a mirror image, it is a *primum,* and in our universe, at least, there is nothing that may be compared to it.[28]

6.12 CHAINS OF MIRRORS AND TELEVISION

Let us suppose now that along a distance of some miles—from a point A, where there is an object or where an event is taking place, to a point B, where there is an observer—a continuous series of mirrors has been put in place and angled in such a way that thanks to a play of chain reflections the observer at B sees, in real time (as they say), what is or what is happening at A.

The only problem is whether we want the observer to receive a mirror image or the image he would see were he physically present at point A to observe the object or the event there. In the first case, the number of mirrors must be odd; in the second, it must be even. Since we presume that the observer wants to see what is at A as if he were a direct witness to it, an even number of mirrors is needed. In that case, the final result will not be what a simple mirror produces but will correspond to the image produced by angulated mirrors.

If the observer knew that what he sees is transmitted to him by a chain of an even number of angulated mirrors, he would be convinced he was seeing what was effectively happening at A—and he would be right.

Now let us imagine that the observer knows that the light signals reflected by the mirror can in some way be "dematerialized" (or *translated* or *transcribed* into impulses of another nature) and then recomposed at their destination. Confronted with the final image, the spectator would behave as if it were a mirror image— even accepting that in the process of codification and decodification something was lost in terms of the definition of the image (his behavior with regard to the received image would be similar to our behavior when faced with a mirror that is a little misted over, or when we see something in a dimly lit room; in other words, when we integrate the stimuli with what we know already or with some inference).

This is what happens with the television image. The television can be seen as an electronic mirror that shows us what is happening at distances that our sight could not otherwise reach. Like the telescope or microscope, it is an excellent example of a magnifying prosthesis (and an abundantly intrusive one at times).

Naturally we have to think of television in its purest state, which would be a *closed-circuit* apparatus with a fixed television camera filming everything that happens in a given place. Otherwise television, like the cinema and the theater, is something that shows us a mise-en-scène (Bettetini 1975) set up beforehand with the aid of lighting effects, a play of field and counterfield, montage, Kuleshov effects, et cetera, and with this we enter the universe of signification or communication.

But if we consider "pure" television, we are dealing with a prosthesis, albeit a "foggy" one, not a phenomenon of signification. Certain perceptual stimuli, however weakened, suitably translated into electronic signals, reach (decoded by a machine) the receiver's organs of perception. Everything that the receiver can do with those stimuli (reject them, interpret them, or whatever) is the same as would happen if the receiver were watching what was happening directly.

In order to provide a more sharply defined picture of this equivalence between the television and the mirror, let us imagine that the closed-circuit television camera is in our home environment, and that it transmits what it films to a monitor in the same environment. We would have mirror-type experiences, in the sense that we would see ourselves from in front or from behind (as happens with opposed mirrors), and we would see what we were doing in that moment on the screen. What would be the difference? That we would not have the experience provided us by a simple mirror; instead, but we would see a third image produced by two angulated mirrors, and therefore we would have to be careful when we used the image on the screen to comb our hair, shave, or put on makeup. This is the same embarrassing situation that occurs when you are interviewed in a television studio where you can see yourself at the same time on a monitor in front of you. But if the closed-circuit apparatus were to provide me with a reversed (it does this time) image, then I could use the monitor as a normal dressing-table mirror.

I leave it to the experts on vision to establish to what extent the television image is optically different from the mirror image, and the same holds for the various cerebral processes that the television image may bring into play. Here I am interested in the pragmatic role of the television image, the way in which it is received, and the truth value accorded to it. Certainly, also from the point of view of conscious reception, there are differences between the mirror and the television image: television images (i) are reversed, (ii) have poorer definition, (iii) are usually smaller in size than the object or scene, and (iv) are such that we cannot peek sideways into the screen as we do with the mirror, to see what it is not showing us. As a consequence we shall describe such images as *paraspecular*.

Let us suppose, however, that the television has been perfected to the point that we can have three-dimensional images large enough to correspond with the dimensions of my field of vision, and even (as suggested in Ransdell 1979: 58) that the screen has been eliminated and there is some apparatus that transmits the stimuli directly to the optic nerve. In such a case, we would really find ourselves in the same circumstances as someone looking into a telescope or standing in front of a mirror, and this would do away with most of the differences between what Ransdell calls a "self-representing iconic sign" (as happens in the perception of objects or in mirror images) and an "other-representing iconic sign" (as in photographs or hypoicons in general).

The fact is that there are no theoretical limits to high definition. Today it is possible to follow on a screen what is seen by an intestinal probe fitted with a built-in television camera as it travels through our insides (an experience now accessible to anyone, and one that we are the first creatures of our species to be able to have). It is clear that the probe is a magnifying prosthesis par excellence, allowing us to see with a clarity and precision that is certainly greater than we would enjoy if we were lucky enough to be able to wander about inside our own body. Not only that but, as the probe moves about, we can also see obliquely, as happens when we move our head to look beyond the physical confines of the mirror.[29]

However the technology of image definition may develop, and

even if one day it might be possible to have virtual gastronomic or sexual experiences (which also involve thermic and tactile sensations, taste and odor), all this will not alter the definition of such stimuli as stimuli received through a prosthesis—and therefore, from a semiotic point of view, just as relevant as the normal perception of the real object. If these virtual stimuli then provide us with something *less defined* than the real stimulus (and I think that this is the present status of virtual reality, which has to be made up for with a surplus of interpretation, albeit unconsciously), then we will have entered the category of surrogate stimuli, which we shall be discussing shortly.

In this sense, television is a very different phenomenon from cinema or photography, even though the television may occasionally transmit filmed images or photographs, just as it is a different phenomenon from the theater, even though the television may occasionally transmit shows performed on a stage (of which it offers the paraspecular image). We can put our trust in cinematographic and photographic images insofar as they are an indication that something, which was there, has left an impression on a film. Even if we know or suspect them to be images of a prophotographic or profilmic mise-en-scène, in any case we hold them to be indications of the fact that that mise-en-scène really took place. But we also know that such images are and always have been subject to elaboration, filtering, and photomontage; we are aware that, from the moment of impression to the moment in which the images reach us, some time has passed; we consider the photo and the film as material objects that are not identified with the object portrayed, and therefore we know that the object at hand stands for something else. This is why it is easy for us to treat photographic and cinematographic images as signs.

Things are different with the television image, in which the materiality of the screen functions as a channel in the same way as the layer of glass that serves us as a mirror functions as a channel. Under ideal circumstances, i.e., filming live within a closed circuit, the image is a paraspecular phenomenon that gives us exactly what happens the moment it happens (even if what happens is a pretense), and it vanishes when the event comes to a conclusion. Someone eludes the grasp of the mirror, and vanishes; someone eludes the eye of the television camera, and vanishes.

Therefore, still from a theoretical point of view, what appears on the television screen is not a sign of anything: it is a paraspecular image, which is received by the observer with the same trust accorded to the mirror image.

The fundamental concept of TV that most people have introjected is that of closed-circuit live broadcasting (otherwise the concept of television would not be "thinkable," insofar as it is opposed to that of the cinema or the theater). And this explains the trusting attitude we have toward television, as well as our tendency to receive most programs as if they were closed-circuit live broadcasts.

In short: we take the television image the same way as we take the telescopic image, with the result that when we look at the Moon through a telescope, we think that those blotches are really there. Even the most credulous among us distrust signs (when someone tells us it is raining, we always think that in reality it may not be raining), but (almost always) we do not distrust our perceptions. We do not distrust TV, because we know that, like all extensive and intrusive prostheses, in the first instance it provides us not with signs but only with perceptual stimuli.

Let us now try another experiment. By means of some procedure (be it technical or magical) we "freeze" a paraspecular image. We can freeze it altogether, by printing it on paper, or we can freeze a sequence of actions on a film that can later be reprojected so we can see the objects move through time again. We have "invented" both photography and the cinema. That is, even though historically they come first, from a theoretical point of view photographic and cinematographic images are an impoverished version of television images, clumsy inventions, so to speak, attempts to reach an *optimum* that was still technically impossible.

And this is why these observations on mirrors lead us to rethink the semiotic status of photography and the cinema (and even of certain hyperrealistic painting techniques that seek to reproduce the effect of a photograph). We are thus led to redefine *hypoicons*.

6.13 RETHINKING PAINTING

Although they are frozen on an autonomous material (and without our considering the various possibilities of special effects and staging), photographic representations provide us with *surrogates of perceptual stimuli*.

Are these the only cases of such a procedure? Certainly not. We have come to photography and cinema by deducing them, so to speak, from mirrors, but all hyperrealistic representation conceals a specular dream.

The absolute maximum of identification between representative stimuli and real stimuli is to be found in the theater, where real human beings must be perceived as such, except for the added conventional fiction, as a result of which they must be seen as Hamlet or Lady Windermere. The example of the theater is an interesting one: to be able to accept (by suspending one's disbelief) that the woman acting on the stage is Ophelia, one must first of all perceive her as a female human being. Hence the puzzlement, or provocation, that would arise if an avant-garde director were to have Ophelia played by a man, or by a chimpanzee. Therefore the theater is an extreme example of a semiosic phenomenon in which, even before it is possible to understand the meaning of what is happening and to interpret gestures, words, and events, *it is necessary first of all to bring into play the normal mechanisms whereby we perceive real objects*. Then, on the basis of interpretations and expectations, on perceiving a human body, we participate in the semiosic process by applying all we know about that body and all we expect from it: hence the sense of wonder (pleasant or irritating, according to our disposition) if, by chance, in a theatrical fiction the human body is raised up into the air by some hidden contraption, or if a mime makes it move as if it were a marionette.

On the first level of partial surrogation of the stimuli, we find the figures in the waxworks, where the faces are made as if they were death masks, perfect congruencies, but the clothes of the characters portrayed, and the objects surrounding the characters (tables, chairs, inkwells) are real objects, and sometimes the hair is real too. These are hypoicons in which we find a balanced blend of surrogate stimuli, very highly defined (but still vicarious and indirect), and of real objects offered directly to the perception, as in the theater.

This means that the concept of the surrogate stimulus is a very hazy one, which can range from a minimum of identification with the real stimulus (in which it obtains an effect vaguely equivalent to that of the real stimulus) to a maximum. Which leads us to think that a sort of principle of charity holds when we are confronted by surrogate stimuli. The fact that animals too can react to surrogate stimuli ought to make us favor the possibility of a "natural" principle of charity. I do not think I am introducing a new category: at bottom, a principle of charity is at work in normal perceptual processes too, when in circumstances where the stimuli are hard to discern one tends to favor the most obvious interpretation—a rule broken by those who see flying saucers where others would interpret a bright spot that moves in the sky like an airplane in the process of landing.[30]

Without therefore detracting anything from the active moment in the perception and interpretation of hypoicons, we must admit that there are semiosic phenomena in which, even if we know that we are dealing with a sign, before perceiving it as a sign of something else we must first perceive it as a set of stimuli that creates the effect of our being in the presence of the object. In other words, we must to accept the idea that there is a perceptual basis even in the interpretation of the hypoicon (Sonesson 1989: 327) or that the visual image is first and foremost something that *offers itself to the perception* (Saint-Martin 1990).

If we get back to the waxwork figure, and admit that a good photograph poses the same problem, even though the stimuli it brings into play are "more" surrogate and vicarious, it must be admitted that the majority of attempts to analyze so-called iconic signs in morphological and grammatical terms—as if they could be subdivided in a way typical of other sign systems, starting from the principle that a photo, for example, can be broken down into the smallest elements of the screen upon which it is founded—have been largely frustrated. These minimum elements become grammatical entities when they are intentionally magnified as such, that is, when the screen does not tend to disappear to give the effect of a perceptual surrogate but instead is enlarged and highlighted with a view to constructing (if nothing else, an objet trouvé, in terms of aesthetic interpretation) abstract symmetries and oppositions.

In this case, in a picture, all we are doing is distinguishing the *figurative* elements from the *plastic* ones. Whereas a hypoicon refers (however it refers, and whatever the form of the expression) to a content (whether it be an element of the natural world or the cultural world, as in the case of the unicorn), in the perception of plastic elements one is essentially interested in the form of the expression. Therefore an enlargement of a photo that magnifies its screen would be a way of pertinentizing the plastic elements of the form of the expression, almost always at the expense of the figurative elements.[31] As has already been said, as long as the image is still perceivable, the fact that its digital nature has been made clear is no argument against its iconism. It is as if on the television screen we were to go to individuate, from close up, the lines traced by the electron beam. It would be an interesting plastic experiment, but usually the effect of those lines is comparable to the effect of a mirror that has been painted with opaque strips at regular intervals. If the strips are not too many, so that recognition of the image is rendered impossible (just as if on the television screen the lines are not too few), we treat the surface of the mirror as if it were misted over or marked (with reduced definition, as if the water in Narcissus's pool became cloudy, but not too much), and we do our best to integrate the stimuli and perceive a satisfactory image.

Yet the screen test is not a useless one. The fact is that, by working on enlarged screens, we measure the threshold beyond which the image is no longer perceivable and a purely plastic construction appears. What counts (see Maldonado 1974, plate 182) is the last stage of rarefaction at which the figure is still perceived: that stage represents the *minimum* of definition necessary for any stimulus to function as a surrogate stimulus (and not to function as a purely plastic stimulus). Naturally this threshold varies according to how well the object represented is already known. No matter how grainy the screen is, the faces of Napoleon or Marilyn Monroe will always be more recognizable than those of unknown persons: the lower the definition and the less known the object, the greater the inferential process required. But I think we can say that beyond this threshold we leave the territory of surrogate stimuli to enter that of the sign.

There is a passage in Ockham that has always perplexed and disquieted me, in which the philosopher states not only that if on coming across the statue of Hercules, I do not compare the statue to the original, I cannot say if it resembles him or not (an observation born of pure good sense) but also that the statue does not allow me to know what Hercules looks like if I have not met him before (i.e., if I do not have *notitia mentalis* regarding him). Yet, as the police forces of the world have shown us, on the basis of a passport photo one can (or one can try to) identify a wanted person.

One possible interpretation of this curious opinion is that Ockham was familiar with the Gothic and Romanesque statuary of the previous centuries, which portrayed human types, through highly regulated iconic schemata, rather than individuals, as was the case with Roman statuary and with the statuary of the centuries to come. Therefore he wanted to tell us that, in conditions of low definition, the hypoicon allows us to perceive generic but not individual features.

Let us think of a normal passport photograph, one of those taken in a hurry and badly in a photo booth. On the basis of such a document it would be very difficult for a policeman to identify the right person in a crowd without making a major blunder. The same thing happens with police sketches, on the basis of which many of us could be held responsible for horrendous crimes, because it frequently happens that the sketch does not resemble the wanted person and that many of us resemble the sketch.

Passport-size photos are imprecise, because both the pose and the lighting leave much to be desired. The police sketch is imprecise, because it represents an artist's interpretation of the verbal expressions a witness uses to make a schematic reconstruction of the features of an individual who in many cases was seen for only a few moments. In both instances, hypoicons refer to generic and not individual features. This does nothing to alter the fact that, in the presence of both the photo and the sketch, each of us is able to recognize these generic features (the person is a male, has a mustache and a low hairline, or the person is a woman, not that young, blond, with full lips). All the rest is inferred in order to pass from the generic to the individual. But that modicum of the generic that is grasped depends on the fact that a very poor portrait has provided us in an even poorer fashion with surrogates for perceptual stimuli, otherwise the photo on my driving license would be indistinguishable from that of a penguin.

6.14 RECOGNITION

Let us imagine that in a family the mother keeps on her desk a stack of rectangular filing cards, of various colors. She uses them for different kinds of notes: red cards for kitchen expenses, blue for travel and holidays, green for clothing, yellow for medical expenses, white for her work appointments, sky blue for noting down the passages that strike her most when she reads a book, et cetera. Every so often she adds these cards to the others in the filing cabinet, divided up by color, so she always knows where to find a certain piece of information. For her those rectangles are signs: not in the sense that they are the physical support for the graphic signs she has made on them but in the sense that, even before they are filed away, they already refer to their own particular topic—in accordance with the various colors; they are expressions of an elementary semiotic system, within which every color is correlated to a content.

But her little boy always tries to get hold of them to play—to build houses of cards, let's say. Naturally he distinguishes between their shapes and colors very well, but for him they are not expressions, they are objects and that's that.

We may say that the cognitive type that allows the mother to identify the cards is more complex than that of the child. She might feel a sense of disquiet on picking up a yellow card, blank or filled in as the case may be, because this would mean that she would have to deal with questions of health; whereas the child might be indifferent to the color and more interested in the consistency of the filing cards (or he might simply prefer his houses of cards to be red). But if mummy tells the little boy to go to fetch her a red card from the desk, and the act of reference is crowned with success, this means that the fundamental perceptual process for the recognition of the cards is the same for both mother and son. Before the upper levels of semiosis, where the cards become expressions, there is a level of stable perceptual semiosis for all the actors in this little domestic comedy.

We can now consider ways of recognition that concern pertinent nonvisual features, such as sound phenomena. The phenomenon of recognition is also at the root of a fundamental semiosic activity, such as verbal language.[32]

As is suggested in Gibson (1968: 93–93), phonemes are potential stimuli like natural sounds, but the characteristic thing about them is that for the listener they must be interpreted not just as pure stimuli but also as responses (for Gibson, in the sense that they have been deliberately produced by someone with a view to having that particular phoneme recognized). As Peirce would have put it, to recognize a sound made by the language as such, one must have already entered Thirdness. If I hear a sound on the street, I can always decide not to interpret it, to consider it a part of background noise. I can do the same with phonemes too, when I vaguely register that someone is talking in my vicinity but am uninterested in what he is saying, and therefore I put it all down to noise or chatter. But if someone speaks to me, I must decide both that he is talking and what he is saying.

Now, recognizing a phoneme certainly means identifying it as the token of a type. This recognition might be founded on a phenomenon of primary semiosis, that of "categorial perception" (see Petitot 1983, 1985a, 1985b). But what most interests me is that, above and beyond the laboratory experience, to perceive a phoneme as such amid the confusion of the sound environment I must make the interpretative decision that it is indeed a phoneme and not an interjection or groan or sound emitted by chance. It is a matter of starting from a sound *substance* in order to perceive it as the *form* of an expression. The phenomenon can be rapid, even unconscious, but this does not alter the fact that it is interpretative.

Moreover, we can categorize a phonation or a string of phonations as phonemes without having yet ascertained to which phonological system they belong. It is enough to think of international conferences: someone comes up and starts talking; she emits one or two introductory sounds, and we have to decide what language she is speaking. If she says [ma], we might be dealing with an adversative in Italian, or a possessive in French. Naturally people speak in an uninterrupted flow, so even before we make an interpretative decision about the first phoneme that someone has emitted, we are already in the context of the spoken string. We are of course guided by the accent, by a meaning that we attribute tentatively to the phonations. But what should be stressed here is that this is in fact a matter of interpretation, whereby we decide both about the material identity of the stimulus and about the *functional* identity of the stimulus.[33]

There is therefore a perceptual process both in the recognition of a dog and in the recognition of the word *dog* scribbled on a sheet of paper.

However, I do not think we can say that it is the same thing to perceive a photo of a dog as the hypoicon of a dog, and as a consequence to perceive the dog as the token of a perceptual type, and to perceive a scribble on the wall as a token of the word *dog*. In cases of trompe l'oeil, I might even think I am perceiving a real dog directly without realizing that it is a hypoicon; with the written word, I can perceive it as such only after I have decided that it is a sign.[34]

6.15 ALPHA AND BETA MODE: A CATASTROPHE POINT?

Having now established a few fixed points, let us try to take up the thread of our discourse. Basic semiosic processes take place in perception. We perceive fixed points because we construct cognitive types, interwoven no doubt with culture and convention but nonetheless largely dependent on determinations from the stimulating field. To understand a sign as such, we must first bring perceptual processes into play, that is to say, we must perceive substances as forms of expression.

But there are signs whose expression plane, in order to be recognized as such, must be perceived (even if by virtue of surrogate stimuli) through *basic semiosis,* so that we could perceive them as signs even if we decided we were not dealing with the expression of a sign function. In such cases I shall talk of alpha mode.[35]

On the other hand, there are cases where to perceive a substance as form I must first of all presume that it is an expression of a sign function, deliberately produced with a view to communicating. In such cases I shall talk of beta mode.

It is through alpha mode that we perceive pictures (or photos, or a film image: note the reaction of the first spectators at the Lumière brothers' projection of a train arriving at the station) as if they were the "scene" itself. It is only on subsequent reflection that we establish the fact that we are confronted with a sign function. It is thanks to beta mode that the word *house* is recognized without being confused with *hose:* we favor the assumption that this must be a linguistic expression, and that this linguistic expression must find itself in a rational context, which is why, on having to decide whether the speaker has said *The house in which I live is a hundred yards away* or *The hose in which I live is a hundred yards away,* we tend (under normal circumstances) to favor the first interpretation.

I define as alpha mode that mode in which, even before deciding we are confronted with the expression of a sign function, we perceive through surrogate stimuli a given object or scene which we then elect as the expression plane of a sign function.

I define as beta mode that mode in which, in order to perceive the expression plane of sign functions, it is necessary first to presume that we are in fact dealing with expressions, and the supposition that they are indeed expressions orients our perception.

The alpha/beta distinction does not correspond to that between motivated and conventional signs. The face of a clock is a motivated expression of planetary movement, or of what we know about it (we are dealing with a case of *ratio difficilis*), nevertheless we must first perceive that face as a sign (beta mode) before being able to read it as a motivated sign (and so the position x of the hands is in motivated correspondence with the position y of the sun in the sky, and vice versa). Alpha mode would let me perceive only a circular form across which two little rods move, and this is how a primitive who has never seen a clock would see one.

It is obvious that, whatever the circumstances, we must first perceive the substance of the expression, but in alpha mode a substance is perceived as form even before this form is recognized as the form of an expression. All that is recognized, as Greimas would put it, is a "figure of the world." In beta mode, on the other hand, a form must be interpreted as the form of an expression before it can be identified.

Just how fuzzy is the boundary between the two modes is revealed by the two drawings in figure 6.8 (Gentner and Markman 1995).

The first impact is perceptual. Confronted with the surrogate stimulus that offers me two basic parallelepiped structures set above two circular structures, I perceive a generic "land vehicle." Of course, in this phase too, if I have never had any experience of a vehicle, it would be hard for me to identify it as such. Montezuma, who had no knowledge of wheeled vehicles, might have "seen" something else in these drawings, for example, two eyes under a strange shape of helmet. But he would still have interpreted surrogate stimuli in the light of one of his own cognitive types.

When I move on from the perception of a vehicle to the interpretation of the various vehicles in play as motorcar, motorboat, and tow truck, much encyclopedic knowledge has already intervened. I have already entered Thirdness. Once I have perceived "vehicle," I must proceed from the recognition of the percept (owing to surrogate stimuli) to the interpretation of a scene. I then recognize it as the hypoiconic representation of a real scene, and I begin to use the image as an expression that refers me to a content.

Figure 6.8

Only at that point can I elaborate macropropositions that put the two scenes into words: I note an inverse symmetry between them (in the first drawing, the car is being towed by the truck; in the second it is the car that is towing the motorboat), and, if I possess an "Unlucky Weekend" script, I can also put the sequence back in order by putting the second drawing in place of the first.

But what interests us here is that only after having interpreted the two scenes as hypoicons can I understand the circle depicted in both images as a sun (otherwise it could have been any other circular object, or a circle, in the geometric sense of the term), and, above all, only then can I understand the two squiggles in the second image as birds (out of context, I might have understood them as hills or as a clumsy transcription of the number 33). This example strikes me as a very useful one for demonstrating the oscillations that continuously intervene, in our interpretation of hypoicons, between the alpha and beta modes. That sun and those birds were not perceivable the way the vehicles were. First I had to decide that they were *two signs that stood for something,* and only afterward did I try to understand them as if they were surrogate stimuli (very poorly defined). In a certain sense, in order to interpret those signs as signs of surrogate stimuli, I had to appeal to the principle of charity.

6.16 FROM PERCEPTUAL LIKENESS TO CONCEPTUAL SIMILARITIES

It seems clear to me that to speak of alpha and beta modes does not mean returning to the theory of "scales of iconicity." The scales established degrees of abstraction, while here we are talking about a *catastrophe point.* The classic scales of iconicity can at best establish the difference between a photo of a car and a schematic drawing of a car, and they discriminate among different levels of definition of the surrogate stimuli. But the possible responses with respect to the two drawings we have examined go beyond the scales of iconicity to bring categorial relations into play. Yet we talk of similarity or analogy even with respect to categorial relations, just as we are led to say that the motorboat is similar to the motorcar from the standpoint of vehicular function. We have entered a territory that seems totally propositional and categorial, which is that of so-called metaphorical similarity, with the result that we can call the camel "the ship of the desert" (above and beyond all possible morphological similarities, and on the basis of a purely functional analogy).

Let us examine a series of assertions (after Cacciari 1995):

(i)   He looks like Stephen to me.
(ii)   These flowers look real.
(iii)   I think someone's ringing the doorbell.
(iv)   That portrait looks like me.

(v)   He looks exactly like his father.

(vi)   Wittgenstein's rabbit looks like a duck (or vice versa).

(vii)   That cloud looks like a camel.

(viii) This music sounds like Mozart.

(ix)   When he smiles, he looks like a cat.

(x)   She looks ill.

(xi)   He looks angry.

(xi)   A camel is like a taxi.

(xiii) Conferences are like sleeping pills.

(xiv)   Sleeping pills are like conferences.

Certainly (i) and (iv) are based on primary iconism. We have already dealt with the recognition of faces, and there are some who persuasively maintain that this is an innate capacity, also found in animals. Artificial flowers, like waxwork figures, are an example of very high definition surrogate stimuli. As for the impression that we can hear the doorbell, it is like the impression of perceiving a certain phoneme. In the presence of imprecise stimuli, we relate the token to a type; but we could have decided that it was the telephone, or, as often happens, that the sound of a bell (very high definition surrogate stimulus) was coming from the television program we were watching. Finally, the impression of likeness generated by those hypoicons that are photographs and hyperrealist paintings (iv) has already been discussed.

A sentence such as (v) has to do with primary iconism (and with the recognition of faces), but on a more abstract level. Here we are not recognizing a face, we are selecting some features common to two faces, leaving the rest in obscurity. We are all well aware that, *from a certain point of view,* a person can resemble his father and mother both, and sometimes the impression is wholly subjective, and optative (the last resort of cuckolds).

Sentences (vi) and (vii) have to do with phenomena related to the perceptual ambiguity of hypoicons. As the drawing gradually becomes more abstract, we enter the *Droodle* zone (as in fig. 6.9), in which the iconic hook is minimal and the remainder is a system of expectations and propositional suggestion (key to interpretation).

Sentences (viii) and (ix) pose serious problems. A piece of music may resemble Mozart for reasons of timbre, melody, harmony, or rhythm, and it is hard to say on what bases (from which point of view) the judgment of likeness is made. Out of prudence I would consider the judgment of likeness as being akin to that of the likeness between father and son. In Malaparte's *La pelle,* there is a fine page in which it is related how, on listening to Addinsel's *Warsaw Concerto,* certain English officers say that it sounds like Chopin, while the author manifests doubts of an aesthetic nature. I would say that Malaparte is behaving like a cuckolded but aware husband, who rejects attributions of likeness between him and his presumed son (or, better, he is refusing to recognize Addinsel as the son of Chopin). For reasons that are still mysterious, I would put the sentence on the cat in the same category. The reasons for which someone's smile reminds me of that of a cat could be the same (*ceteris paribus*), and so Addinsel can seem to be Chopin, and they largely depend on what I think both Chopin and a cat are.

To say that someone looks ill probably has only rhetorical value. As a matter of fact, the term "to look" is used metaphorically to express a symptomatic inference, but a perceptive doctor might say that by certain physiognomic features he can immediately recognize someone suffering from a certain disease. In this sense, saying that someone looks ill to me would be like saying that someone looks angry to me. It would concern a capacity (I do not intend to state whether innate or based on cultural competence) whereby a passion can be recognized by the facial expression. There is a great deal of literature on this subject, and I think the question is still open to debate. There is no doubt that from the point of view of the polemic from the sixties it was not difficult for the iconoclasts to recognize the evident fact that Asians express their feelings differently from Europeans, but it must perforce be admitted that a smile (whatever feeling it expresses, be it embarrassment or good humor) is perceived on the basis of iconically universal physiognomic features.

It would be hard to say that (xii) through (xiv) are based on morphological similarities. We are completely on the categorial level.

Similarity is established from the point of view of certain properties that are propositionally attributed to the objects in play. To such a degree that, contrary to current opinion (see Kubovy 1995 and Tversky 1997), I think it can be said with equal efficacy both that conferences are like sleeping pills and that sleeping pills are like conferences. It is true that in the first case the salient feature of the predicate (sleeping pills induce sleep) is a peripheral feature of the subject, while in the second case it would seem that no salient feature of the predicate is a peripheral feature of the subject. But after years of frequenting seminars and conferences, I hold that one salient feature of conferences is their ability to induce sleep, and if I said to a colleague that sleeping pills are like conferences, my metaphor would be understood. Which confirms that on these conceptual levels similarity is only a question of cultural stipulation.

What is the threshold that separates these levels of so-called "similarity"? I think we can draw a line of demarcation between cases (i) through (xi) and cases (xii) through (xiv). In the first eleven cases, the judgment of likeness is pronounced on perceptual bases. In the other three cases, we apply successive levels of interpretation and greater knowledge, which is why the analogy can be established on purely propositional bases: I can say that a camel seems a taxi or a ship of the desert even if I have never seen a camel and possess a purely cultural knowledge of them (for example, they have been described to me as animals that are used as a means of transport in the desert). I can say that uranium is like dynamite even if I have never had any perceptual experience of a uranium sample, knowing only that it is an element used to trigger atomic bombs.

Yet even at these propositional levels there lingers, albeit in a most pallid form, a shade of primary iconism (in the same way as I would tend to say that cultural elements intervene even at levels on which the presence of primary iconism appears with greater clarity): as if to say that for different subjects the threshold between alpha and beta mode shifts in accordance with criteria that cannot be established a priori but depend on circumstances.

In the expression *The dog bites the cat,* it is beta mode that allows us to recognize *dog* and *cat* as words in the English language, but what has been called a phenomenon of syntactic iconism is recognized through alpha mode: in English syntax, the fact that the sequence is "A + verb + B" tells us, through a perception of vectoriality, that A performs the action and B undergoes it.

An interesting example of similarity at the limits of the categorial is given by Hofstadter (1979: 168–70) apropos of two different melodies, which he calls BACH and CAGE, taking advantage of the fact that musical notation also makes use of alphabetical letters. The two melodies are different but share a "skeleton" that is the same from the point of view of the intervals and the relations between them. The first, from the opening note, goes down one semitone, then goes up by three semitones, and finally goes down again by one semitone (-1, +3, -1). The second goes down three semitones, goes up by ten, and then goes down again by three (-3, +10, -3). It is therefore possible to obtain CAGE by starting from BACH and multiplying each interval by 31/2 and then rounding down to the smaller number.

I have tried playing the two melodies and would not say that a normal ear could perceive any likeness at all. Hofstadter has undoubtedly constituted a criterion of similarity on a conceptual level. Nonetheless, although we are a very long way from something that can be "perceived," the iconism of perception is implicit in the fact that if the similarity is to be established, we must assume the perception of the intervals, or at least of the single notes (and in this regard at least, Peirce would say that we are in the presence of pure icons).[36]

Again Hofstadter (1979: 723) lists a series of bizarre objects that nonetheless strike us as similar from some points of view or, rather, that share a common "conceptual skeleton": a tandem unicycle, a piano concerto for two left hands, a one-voice fugue, the art of clapping with one hand. In all these cases we would have "a plural thing made singular and repluralized wrongly." I would say: "We have a context that demands two actants, we isolate only one of them and put it back into the original context to perform the function of two actants." Here I think it can be said that no element of perceptual iconism subsists. The rule can be expressed in purely propositional terms; the sense of familiarity aroused by these strange objects springs from reflection and interpretation, it is not immediately given. We apply the rule, and we immediately find an example that Hofstadter did not make but could have made: we find an activity with two actants, for example, the snap of two fingers; we isolate one actant only, the thumb; we put it back into the original context to perform the function of both actants, and we have the snap of one thumb.

Naturally it might always be said that each of these "scenes" could be mentally visualized (in a way similar to the impression one receives when confronted with "impossible figures"). But I would say that this is a consequent and nonnecessary interpretative effect. I do not think anyone could visualize a biciphalus and a pentacalidus (because these are two objects that I have just invented), but I believe it is possible to identify a conceptual skeleton common to a monociphaloid biciphalus and a pentacalidus with two calids.

6.17 THE MEXICAN ON A BICYCLE

Along the scale that leads by degrees from a maximum of alpha mode to a maximum of beta mode, we pass through a maximum of extremely high definition surrogate stimuli (the waxwork figure) and a maximum of abstraction, where the stimuli (even if still visual) no longer have pictorial efficacy but only plastic value. Let us look at figure 6.9, which reproduces one of those very well-known visual "puns" called Droodles.

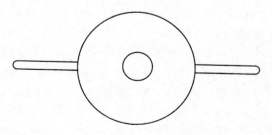

Figure 6.9

As some will know and others will not, the solution is "bird's-eye view of a Mexican on a bicycle," and once the key has been found, aided by a certain degree of goodwill, we can identify the sombrero and the external part of the two wheels. But with just as much goodwill we might also see a Mississippi paddle steamer or Cyrano and Pinocchio sitting back to back under a beach umbrella. This is why, during the polemic on iconism, the (perfectly correct and indispensable) principle was assumed that from a suitable point of view and in an appropriate context anything can resemble anything else, all the way to the equally famous black square that is to be read "black cat on a moonless night." What perception gives me, in the case of the "Mexican" droodle, is not much help when it comes to making an interpretative decision. I certainly perceive two concentric circles and two radically flattened semiellipses. Let us admit that we are instinctively led to identify only one flattened ellipse, partly hidden by the larger circle; a whole psychological tradition is there to confirm this, even if we failed to notice it ourselves, and this is always a good proof of the inferential nature of perception. But in order to decide that those forms represent a given object or a scene, I must possess or guess the key (a verbal one in this case, unhappily). Afterward, I can adapt what I perceive to what I know.

So, between the sixties and the seventies the polemic focused on a relaxed use of the notion of "likeness" (which exempted many people from the need to establish rules of "similarity"), and therefore there was more argument about those so-called iconic signs with "symbolic" characteristics (in the sense of Thirdness), such as the Mexican Droodle, than about photographs or hyperrealist representations. This also explains why opponents of iconism pointed out that the iconist position was weak with regard to iconography and diagrammatics in general.

Much emphasis was—very rightly—laid on beta mode, but alpha mode was left in obscurity. In the heat of the debate, which has never completely died down, we neglected, and perhaps still neglect, to identify (according to individuals, cultures, circumstances, and contexts) the threshold between the two modes and to recognize its "fuzzy" nature.[37]

Endnotes

Introduction

1 Domenico Porzio, "Introduzione," in J. L. Borges, *Tutte le opere*, vol. 2, Milan: Mondadori 1985: xv–xvi.

2 In order of appearance: Giovanni Manetti, Costantino Marmo, Giulio Blasi, Roberto Pellerey, Ugo Volli, Giampaolo Proni, Patrizia Violi, Giovanna Cosenza, Alessandro Zinna, Francesco Marsciani, Marco Santambrogio, Bruno Bassi, Paolo Fabbri, Marina Mizzau, Andrea Bernardelli, Massimo Bonfantini, Isabella Pezzini, Maria Pia Pozzato, Patrizia Magli, Claudia Miranda, Sandra Cavicchioli, Roberto Grandi, Mauro Wolf, Lucrecia Escudero, Daniele Barbieri, Luca Marconi, Marco De Marinis, Omar Calabrese, Giuseppina Bonerba, and Simona Bulgari.

3 In alphabetical order (except for the two organizers, Jean Petitot and Paolo Fabbri): Per-Aage Brandt, Michael Caesar, Mario Fusco, Enzo Golino, Moshe Idel, Burkhart Kroeber, Alexandre Laumonier, Jacques Le Goff, Helena Lozano Miralles, Patrizia Magli, Giovanni Manetti, Gianfranco Marrone, Ulla Musarra-Schroeder, Winfried Nöth, Maurice Olender, Pierre Ouellet, Hermann Parret, Roberto Pellerey, Isabella Pezzini, Maria Pia Pozzato, Marco Santambrogio, Thomas Stauder, Emilio Tadini, Patrizia Violi, Tadaiko Wada, Alessandro Zinna, and Ivailo Znepolski. But if I am to talk of critical contributions to my work, I feel must not omit other reflections—even though not immediately connected to the themes discussed in this book—that came to me only while I was putting the final touches to it. I want therefore to mention the contributors to the following anthologies: Rocco Capozzi, ed., *Eco: An Anthology* (Bloomington: Indiana UP, 1997); Peter Bondanella,

Umberto Eco: Signs for This Time (Cambridge: Cambridge UP, 1997); Norma Bouchard and Veronica Pravadelli, eds., *The Politics of Culture and the Ambiguities of Interpretation: Eco's Alternative* (New York: Peter Lang Publishers, 1999); Thomas Stauder, ed., *"Staunen über das Sein": Internationale Beiträge zu Umberto Ecos "Insel des vorigen Tages"* (Darmstadt: Wissenschaftliche Buchgesellschaft, 1997).

Chapter One / On Being

1 In difficulty, Seneca (*Ad Lucillum*, 58, 5–6) was to translate this *on* as *quod est.*

2 "Nominalism vs. Realism," 1868 (WR 2: 145). For analogous positions see also Hartmann (*Zur Grundlagung der Ontologie*, Berlin, 1935): the Aristotelian formula, inasmuch as it starts from the concrete entities but wishes to consider that which is common to all, expresses being, i.e., that for which the entity is an entity.

3 Gilson 1984. In scholastic language, at least, "existence is the condition of that which whose being develops from an origin... It is rightly said that if God is, he doesn't exist." Gilson's text contains a wealth of reflections on philosophical lexicography, of which I make free use also in the paragraphs that follow.

4 For these oscillations, cf. M.-D. Philippe 1975. For example, in the *De ente et essentia* we have the *quod quid erat esse,* the *esse actu simpliciter,* the *esse quid as esse substantiale,* the divine *esse tantum,* the *esse receptum per modum actus,* the *esse* as an effect of the form of matter, the *esse in hoc intellectu,* the *esse intelligibile in actu,* the *esse abstractum,* the *esse universale,* and the *esse commune*... The permanence of these ambiguities is also discussed in Heidegger 1973, iv B.

5 "One, Two, and Three," 1967, WR 2: 103.

6 I hope that one day this will be translated into German; that way, in Italy at least, philosophers will take it seriously.

7 "On a new list of categories," 1867 (WR 2).

8 "Of reality as pure reality it can neither be said that it is because it could be, nor that it is because it could not be: but solely that it is because it is. Reality is wholly gratuitous and unfounded: dependent wholly upon freedom, which is not a foundation, but an abyss, that is to say a foundation that always denies itself as a foundation" (Pareyson 1989: 12).

9 In *What is Metaphysics?*, Heidegger reminds us that it is different to grasp the totality of the entity in itself and the sensation of being at the center of the entity in its totality. The first thing is impossible, the second happens to us all the time. And as proof of this he cites the states of ennui (which are applied to the entity in its totality), but also the joy felt in the presence of the beloved being.

10 The problem is: Do I draw definitions from the evidence that gives me the sensation (and the subsequent abstraction of the phantasm) or is it the

precognition of the definition that allows me to abstract the essence? If the active intellect is not a repository of previous forms but the pure mechanism that allows me to identify forms under way in the *synolon,* what is this faculty? It is easy to fall into the Arab heresy and say that it is unique for everybody, but saying that it is unique does not mean that it is immutable and universal; it could be a cultural active intellect, it could be the faculty of identifying and carving out the forms of the content. In which case the code, supplied by the segmentation *brought about* by the active intellect, would determine the nature and the exactitude of the reference! In the *Poetics* 1456b 7 (notes Aubenque) it says: "What would discourse have to do if things already appeared by themselves and had no need of discourse?" Aubenque is quoting a page from *On Sophistical Refutations* (1962: 116). Since we cannot bring the things themselves into the discussion but must use their names by way of symbols, we suppose that what happens with names also happens with things; as when pebbles are used as counters. But there is not a complete resemblance between names and things; names are limited in number, as is the plurality of definitions, while things are infinite in number (as their accidents are infinite).

11 Gianni Vattimo argues that there is a Heideggerian right and a left (in the same sense as there is a right and a left among Hegelians). The right thinks we should pursue a return to being in the form of an apophatic, negative, and mystical reading; while the left holds that it is a matter of providing a quasi "historicist" interpretation of the weakening of being, and therefore of rediscovering the history of a "long goodbye," without attempting to lend it currency again, "not even as a term that is forever beyond all formulation" (1994: 18).

12 For a mental experiment in this sense, see my *On Truth: A Fiction*, in Eco et al. 1986 (now in Eco 1990).

Chapter Two / Kant, Peirce, and the Platypus

1 Sometimes Marco Polo adds to the zoological universe, and through firsthand experience (or by the reconstruction of faithful accounts) he tells us of a sort of cat (in the Italian version, or a gazelle in the original French) that from a "sore" below the navel secretes "musk" that has an exquisite perfume. Today we know the animal exists, and we have identified it as *Moschus moschiferus:* and while it is not a gazelle, it is not far from one, being a species of deer that, from a pod near the aperture of the prepuce, secretes a musk with a penetrating perfume.

2 See the IX Lowell Lecture, 1865 (WR 1: 471–87); "On a method of searching for the categories," 1886 (WR 1: 515–28); and "On a new list of categories," 1867 (WR 2: 49–58).

3 With regard to the sin of compulsive triadism, Peirce offers us a good example in the eleventh Lowell Lecture, where he dares to compare the

first triad with the Holy Trinity, and Ground is compared to the Holy Ghost. Which would authorize us to take the whole business less than seriously, were it not for the fact that in all that vagueness there lurks the search for something very important.

4 It is true that often ambiguous shadows gather around the Immediate Object, as when it is said that it too is an icon (CP 4.447), that it is an idea like the Ground and a quality of sensation identified at a perceptual level (8.183), that it is a percept (4.539), while elsewhere it is identified with meaning (2.293). But these oscillations are, if anything, indicators of the fact that in the formation of the Immediate Object there converge all the preliminary moments of a process that establishes itself in it.

5 See *Detached Ideas on Vitally Important Topics*, 1898 (CP 4.1–5). Even though in CP 7.540 Peirce is wrong about the date of Kant's death, which he gives as 1799.

6 In *Anthropology* (I, 38–39) we see how also in his later years Kant delineated (at least as a didactic service) a summary of a theory of signs—not original, with a debt to traditional doctrines, from Sextus Empiricus to Locke and perhaps to Lambert, but one that demonstrates a respectful interest in semiotic thematics. Semiotic interests are also present in such pre-*Critique* writings as *De mundi sensibilis atque intelligibilis forma et principiis* § 10. On Kant and semiotics, see Garroni (1972 and 1977), Albrecht (1975, IV), and Kelemen (1991).

7 See note 12 to the introduction by Diego Marconi and Gianni Vattimo to the Italian edition of Rorty 1979.

8 "Of course, in Kant's thinking, the logical categorial functions play a most remarkable role: but he does not arrive at the fundamental extension of the concepts of perception and intuition in the categorial field...That's why he does not even distinguish between concepts as general significations of words and concepts as species of *direct* general representation and finally as general objects, i.e., as intentional correlates of general representations. Right from the start Kant slips on the ground of a metaphysical theory of knowledge because he is preparing the critical 'rescue' of mathematics, natural science and metaphysics, even before having subjected knowledge as such, the overall sphere of the acts in which prelogical objectification and logical thought are accomplished, to essential analytical clarification and criticism, and before having brought back primitive logical concepts and laws to their phenomenological origin" (*Logical Investigations* VI § 66).

9 See Marconi-Vattimo's objection in the introduction to Rorty 1979: xix.

10 I owe this thought to Ugo Volli (personal communication). For taxonomies in the quest for universal languages, see Eco 1994. See also 3.4.2 and 4.2 in this book.

11 I use the following ciphers for Kant's works: *Critique of Pure Reason* (CPR/A and CPR/B, according to whether it is the first or second edi-

tion); *Critique of Judgement* (CJ); *Prolegomenon* (P); *Logic* (L). For the CPR, the references are to the pages of the Akademie edition.

12 Published as part of *Metaphysik L_1* in *Kants Gesammelte Schrift, Band XXVIII, Vierte Abteilung, Vorlesungen, Fünfter Band, Erste häfte.* Berlin: de Gruyter 1968, pp. 2212–2301.

13 In the *Prolegomena* (§18) there is also mention of a kind of superordinate genus of empirical judgments *(empirische Urteile),* which are founded in the perception of the senses, and with respect to which experiential judgments add the concepts that originate in the pure intellect. It does not seem clear to me how these empirical judgments differ from perceptual judgments, but I think (unless we want to indulge in Kantian philology) that here we might restrict the comparison to perceptual judgments and experiential judgments.

14 CPR/B: 107. Therefore, with regard to the difference between perceptual judgment and experiential judgment, "the problem has not by any means been solved" (Martinetti 1946: 65). Cassirer (1918) also realized this, but he only mentions it in note 20 to chapter III, 2: "It should be noted that a similar exposition of empirical knowledge…is not so much the description of a fact, as the construction of an extreme case…Kant's view was that there is no 'single judgment' that does not already claim some form of 'universality'; there is no 'empirical' proposition that does not include in itself some 'a priori' assertions: since the very form of the judgment contains this claim for 'universal objective validity.' " Why is such an important statement found only in the form of a footnote? Because Cassirer knew he was extrapolating according to common sense and systematic consistency what Kant should have spelled out clearly, by excluding all other ambiguous formulations. Which Kant did not do.

15 Here let us leave open the question as to whether he perceived the stones, but had just, so to speak, removed the percept, or whether he perceived only the moment in which he responded, interpreting memories of still disconnected visual sensations.

16 Marconi (1997) reached me when I had already finished this essay, but it seems to me that the pages he devotes to Kantian schematism (146 ff.) efficaciously emphasize its procedural nature.

17 For the puzzling story of the ruminants, see the *Posterior Analytics* (II, 98, 15 ff.) and *Parts of the Animals* (642b–644a 10 and 663 ff.); as well as my "Horns, Hooves, and Shoes: Three Types of Abduction," now in Eco 1990: 227–33)

18 On the other hand let's posit from the point of view of a hypothetical Adam who sees a cat for the first time without ever having seen another animal. For this Adam, the cat will be schematized as "thing that moves," and for the moment this quality it possesses will render it similar to water and clouds. But we can imagine that very soon this Adam will put the cat together with dogs and chickens, among the moving bodies that react

unpredictably to his stimulating them and fairly predictably to his calling them, distinguishing them from water and clouds, which indeed appear to move, but are insensible of his presence. Here some would talk of a form of *precategorial perception* that precedes conceptual categorization, and so the animality perceived on seeing a dog or a cat still has nothing to do with the genus ANIMAL, which has been exercising semioticians since the time at least of Porphyry and his Tree. Nonetheless for the present I do not intend to introduce this notion of the "precategorial," because, as we shall see in 3.4.2, with regard to the processes known as "categorization," this form of expression implies a notion of category that is not the Kantian one.

19 This is what in "Horns, Hooves, and Shoes" (now in Eco 1990) I defined as *creative abduction*. In this regard see Bonfantini and Proni 1980.

20 *Opus Postumum*: 231, note 1. In the Introduction, Mathieu observes that "even by retaining the necessary structure of the categories one can still take into consideration an *ulterior* spontaneous activity, which the intellect realizes *starting from* the categories, but without stopping at them... constructing not simply that which *derives* from them, but all that can be thought and without falling into contradiction" (p. 21). Perhaps in order to attain all this boldness Kant needed to pass through the aesthetic reflection of the third *Critique*; only then "is a new schematism born—a free schematism, without concepts, of the *imagination*—as the original capacity to organize the perceptions" (see Garroni 1986: 226)

21 V. Mathieu, Introduction to the *Opus Postumum* 41–42. The most interesting aspect of this *matter* is that, the more Kant assigns constructive power to the intellect, the more he does it because he seems persuaded that the *continuum* has (as we said in the first essay in this book) a grain; that is, he wants all the more to account for the fact (if I may express myself with a Peircean formula) that general laws are operative in nature, and naturally, therefore, that there is an objective reality of the species. It would also be interesting to show that the closer Peirce got to this realist conception, the farther he got from Kant's earlier work. In this regard see Hookway 1988: 103-12.

22 That is, as Paci (1957: 185) says, they are founded not on necessity but on *possibility*.

23 See Apel 1995. The transcendental subject of knowledge becomes the community, which in a quasi "evolutionist" sense approximates that which could become cognizable in the long run through processes of trial and error. See also Apel 1975. This induces us to reinterpret the anti-Cartesian polemic and the refusal to admit incognizable data, which could also be defined as a cautious and preventive disassociation from the Kantian idea of the thing-in-itself. The Dynamical Object starts off as a thing-in-itself, but in the process of interpretation it is adjusted more and more—even if only potentially.

24 In this sense Popper (1969, I, I, v) says that when Kant stated that our in-

tellect does not draw its own laws from nature but imposes them upon it, he was right; but he was wrong in maintaining that the said laws are necessarily true, or that we certainly succeed in imposing them on nature. Nature often obliges us to abandon our laws insofar as they have been confuted. And so Popper opts for a reformulation of the Kantian principle, namely, that the intellect does not draw its own laws from nature but seeks to impose them upon it—with a varying possibility of success.

25 Or again: "By a *feeling* I mean an instance of that type of consciousness which involves no analysis, comparison, or any process whatsoever, nor consists in whole or in part of any act by which one stretch of consciousness is distinguished from another, which has its own positive quality which consists in nothing else, and which is of itself all that it is..." (CP 1306).

26 Habermas (1995) stressed the criticism of the psychologism that Peirce embarked upon from the Harvard Lectures. The process of interpretation itself is "anonymized," "depersonalized": the mind can be seen as a relation between signs. This led Habermas to see in Peirce a lack of interest in the process of communication as an intersubjective event, which permitted Oehler (in Kettner 1995) to reply to him by emphasizing, on the contrary, the moments in which Peirce shows himself to be sensible of communication between subjects. But it's well known that you can make Peirce say anything you want, according to how you approach him. I think it is possible to explain the process of primary iconism without having recourse to mental events or representations—without betraying the spirit of Peirce.

27 Note that at this stage it cannot even be stated that the sensation presents some likeness with *something* that was in the object or the stimulating field (in the case of a sensation of red we know very well that there is no red in the object, there is at most a pigment, or a phenomenon of light, to which we respond with the sensation of red). We might even have two subjects, one color-blind (who mistakes green for red) and the other not, so that the sensation in the first subject is different from that in the second, but both still have a constant response to the stimulus, and both have been taught to reply *red* to that stimulus. What we mean to say is that for each there would always be a constant relation between stimulus and sensation (and by a cultural accident the two can easily interact by their both always calling fire red and grass green).

28 See Mameli (1997, 4): "Given that Peirce thinks and shows that intelligibility is not an accidental characteristic of the universe, that it is not a simple epiphenomenon of how things are, but is a characteristic that 'shapes' the universe, it follows that a theory of intelligibility is also a metaphysical theory of the structure of the universe."

29 In this regard, see Sebeok 1972, 1976, 1978, 1979, 1991, 1994.

30 In this sense Ransdell (1979: 61) can maintain that given the two theoretical possibilities of knowledge (knowledge is a representation of the

object, and knowledge is the immediate perception of that which the object is in itself), Peirce's proposal presents itself as a dynamic synthesis of the two positions.

31 Fumagalli (1995: 167) notes, "The theory of perceptual judgment is one of the last pieces of Peirce's philosophy to see the light," and he emphasizes all its novelty. He also makes it clear that Peirce's percept is not a *sense datum,* a *quale,* but "is already the result of a non conscious cognitive elaboration, which synthesizes the data in a structured form," or "a construct resulting from psychological operations on data from the pure senses, on nervous stimuli" (1995: 169).

32 It strikes me that one of the more fruitful attempts to interpret the shift from process to perceptual judgment is that made by Innis (1994: 2), where the author outlines convincing parallels between Peirce, Dewey, Bühler, Merleau-Ponty, and Polany.

33 For these suggestions I am grateful to Perri 1996 (I.II.3) and to Nesher 1984.

34 MS 410, quoted in Roberts (1973: 23–24). In CP 2.277, Peirce makes it clear that, given the category of icons, the ones that contain simple qualities are *images,* those that represent dyadic relations are *diagrams,* those that represent a parallelism between the characteristics of two objects are *metaphors* (and it seems to me that the term is used in the broad sense of "conceptual simile").

35 For a concept of the motivation of signs, which does not exclude their conventionality, and the presence of alternative representations both of which are *motivated,* see *A Theory of Semiotics* 3.5.

Chapter Three / Cognitive Types and Nuclear Content

1 Sometimes the connection is explicitly, albeit rapidly, cited (see, among many, Johnson 1989: 116) and sometimes discussed critically (see Marconi 1997: 145–48—but it is no accident that here we are dealing with an author who, despite everything, is "continental").

2 "Of course, in Kant's thinking, the logical categorial functions play a very important role but he does not arrive at the fundamental extension of concepts of perception and intuition to the categorial field... It is for this reason that he does not even distinguish between concepts as general meanings of words and concepts as a species of direct general representation and finally as general objects, i.e., as intentional correlates of general representations" (*Logical Investigations* VI, §66).

3 I would not have thought of asking myself many of these questions if I had not read Violi (1997) in the manuscript stage and—in what was by then the final stage of this work of mine—Marconi 1997, to whom I shall often refer the reader. I am almost completely in agreement with Violi; with regard to Marconi, when the case arises, I shall emphasize some points in which our approach strikes me as different.

4 In *A Theory of Semiotics* I stated that perceptual semiosis is a postulate of semiotics. In that book, and in the phase that semiotic debate had reached at that point, it seemed important to emphasize the sociocultural nature of systems of signs. The effort to find a definition of content in terms of interpretants, all publicly exhibited by the "public" repertory of the encyclopedia, was intended to prevent meaning from running aground on the shoals of mentalism, or at least to avoid having recourse to the subject that was then identified (in a risky fashion, according to me) in the depths of the unconscious. *A Theory of Semiotics* in fact wound up with the observation that the problem of the signifying subject (very important at that time in the Lacanian milieu of poststructuralist French semiology) was doubtless important, but for the moment it had to be excluded from semiotics understood as a logic of culture. I have always been embarrassed about this exclusion, and made amends for it by introducing into the part of the French version of *A Theory of Semiotics* that dealt with the production of signs: "Today I would correct the statement according to which our capacity to recognize an object as a *token*, or an occurrence of a general *type*, is a postulate of semiotics. If there is semiosis even in the perceptual processes, my capacity to consider the sheet of paper upon which I write as the double of other sheets of paper, and to recognize a word pronounced as the replica of a lexical type, or to identify in the Jean Dupont that I see today the same Jean Dupont I met a year ago are processes in which semiosis intervenes on an elementary level. And therefore the possibility to discriminate between token and type cannot be defined as a postulate if not within the framework of the present discourse on the production of signs, in the same sense in which in order to explain a nautical instrument that is used to measure latitude, it is taken as proven that the Earth revolves around the sun—while this 'postulate' once more becomes a scientific hypothesis to be proven or shown false within the framework of an astronomic discourse" (*La production des signes,* Paris: Livre de Poche, 1992). But the point is that, in *A Theory of Semiotics* too, the emphasis was placed on the social life of signs, not on epistemological problems, otherwise it would not have begun with a chapter dealing with a Logic of Culture (and not of nature). However, my exclusion was not as radical as it seemed, and I am grateful to Innis (1994, 1) for having highlighted all the points in *A Theory of Semiotics* in which (even though only "postulating it") I reiterate that perceptual semiosis is a central problem for semiotics, and that it is indispensable to think of a semiotic definition for percepts (e.g., 3.3.3). I could not be indifferent to the problem, given that in my presemiotic works such as *Opera Aperta*, I had been enormously inspired by phenomenology, from Husserl to Merleau-Ponty, and by the psychology of perception, from Piaget to transactional psychology. But evidently that "postulating" instead of dealing with (which was intended to be a simple limitation of my field of investigation at that time) presupposed and produced a fundamental

ambiguity: as a matter of fact I was not making it clear whether the inferential effort required to understand something was the object of a psychology of perception and cognition, and therefore a problem that was vestibular but not central for semiotics, or on the contrary whether intelligence and signification were a single process, and therefore of a sole subject of investigation, as required by the phenomenological tradition with which I identified myself. One of the reasons for that ambiguity has been explained in the preceding pages: *A Theory of Semiotics* was structured in such a way as to focus first and foremost on the Dynamical Object as a *terminus ad quem* of semiosis (and therefore it opened with a theory of sign systems insofar as they were already socially constituted). In order to posit the problem of perceptual semiosis in the first place, it was necessary to consider, as I do in this book, the Dynamical Object as a *terminus a quo* and therefore as that which comes before semiosis and from which we start off in order to elaborate perceptual judgments.

5 It is true that we can consider (according to Helmholtz's Empirical Theory of Vision) sensations as "signs" of objects or external states, from which by (unconscious) inference we begin to set an interpretative process in motion (we must learn to "read" these signs). Nevertheless while a word or an image, or a symptom, refers us to something that is not there as we perceive the sign, Helmholtz's signs refer us to something that is there, to the stimulating field from which we take or receive these sign-stimuli, and at the end of the perceptual inference these things that were there make what was already there comprehensible to us.

6 This is the difference between the Alpha and Beta modalities I discuss in 6.15.

7 I could say that in this case one sets in motion that process (described in Pareyson 1954) whereby the artist, starting from an as yet formless cue offered him by the material he is working with, draws from it, so to speak, a suggestion that affords a glimpse of the form that will give sense to the work as a whole upon its completion but that is not yet present at the beginning of the process so is only *heralded* by the cue.

8 The reader is referred to Ouellet (1992) for one of the most interesting attempts to blend Husserlian problematics with that of semiotics, by reviewing the relations between sensible knowledge and propositional knowledge, perception and meaning, and the opposition between a semiotics of the natural world and a semiotics of natural language (in Greimas and Courtés 1979: 233–34). For the problems of primary semiosis, see also Petitot 1995.

9 In 2.8.2 I admitted that it is possible to recognize organic phenomena such as steric "recognition" as presemiosic (and nevertheless at the roots of semiosis).

10 I have tried to make use of this episode without straying too far from the known facts, even though it is a mental experiment. All the philological information comes from Alfredo Tenoch Cid Jurado, who wrote a hith-

erto unpublished essay called "A Deer Called Horse" specifically for me
and to whom I am most grateful. See also the reflections on the semiotic
aspects of the conquest by Todorov (1982, II).

11 Cases of felicitous reference cause serious problems for theories that allow
of no "transcendental meaning." It may be that it is hard, and sometimes
impossible, to define the transcendental meaning of a text, or, of an articulated and complex system of propositions, and that at this point an interpretative drift comes into play. But when I say to someone *There's
somebody at the door, please go let him in,* and that person (if cooperative)
goes to open the door and not the window, it means that on a level of
everyday experience we tend not only to assign a literal meaning to utterances but also to associate certain names with certain objects in a consistent fashion.

12 Since I feel there is no need for me to go into the terms of the debate, I refer the reader to Gardner (1985, 11) for a fundamentally faithful account,
and to Johnson Laird (1983, 7) for a series of reasonable proposals. For
images, see also Varela 1992 and Dennet 1978.

13 Neisser (1976) would postulate even in the case of verbal instructions the
activation of "cognitive maps" that are of the same nature as the schemata
and that orient perception.

14 Felicitous reference, insofar as it is behavior that interprets the sign, is
also a form of interpretant. For the referent as implicit interpretant, see
Ponzio 1990, 1.2.

15 With regard to this vexed question Goodman (1990) suggests trying to
translate the noun with a verb: as if, instead of wondering about the concept of "responsibility," we were to ask ourselves what being or feeling
responsible for something means.

16 Marconi (1995, 1997) talks of a double lexical competence: the *inferential*
and the *referential* sort. It seems to me that this latter type of competence must divide into the three different phenomena of the instructions for
recognition, for identification, and for retrieval, and naturally must not
be identified with the execution of acts of reference (as we shall see in 5).

17 Some time ago I was amazed that in Paris many Vietnamese taxi drivers
had a very poor knowledge of the city, whereas one presumes that a taxi
driver must prove he has a remarkable knowledge of the local map if he
is to obtain a license. When I once questioned one of them about this, he
replied, evidently in an access of sincerity: "When one of us shows up
with his documents for the exam, would you be able to say whether the
photo on the document was really his?" Therefore, speculating on the
proverbial fact that for Westerners all Orientals are alike, and vice versa,
a sole competent candidate presented himself on several occasions for the
exam showing the identity documents of his incompetent fellow country-
men. The identity documents supplied the NC connected with his name
(with all the required accuracy), but the intercultural situation ensured
that the instructions for identification were very weak as far as the

examiners were concerned, inducing them to entertain a CT that was cognitively generic and nonindividual.

18 Bruner (1990: 72). But see also Piaget 1955, II, vi. At various stages in their development children initially apply the idea of life to everything that moves and then gradually only to animals and plants, but this idea of life precedes all categorial learning. When children perceive the sun as something living, they are activating a subdivision of the *continuum* that is still precategorial. See also Maldonado (1974: 273).

19 For a series of Thomist texts on this argument (*De ente et essentia* vi; *Summa Theologiae* I, 29, 2 ad 3; I, 77, 1 ad 7; I, 79, 8 co; *Contra Gentiles* III, 46), see the treatment in Eco 1984, 4.4.

20 For a view of classifications that are much closer to effective linguistic usage, see Rastier 1994: 161 ff.

21 By maintaining that the concept expressed by the pronoun *I* is one of her "primes"—and it strikes me as reasonable to admit that the sense of one's own subjectivity, insofar as it is opposed to the rest of the world is a "prime," but one understands how it is such only at a certain stage of ontogenesis—Wierzbicka (1996: 37) maintains that, insofar as it is a universal common to all cultures, this idea cannot be interpreted. Therefore, faced with the proposal that *I* may be interpreted as "the pronoun referring to, or in general denoting, the subject of the act of utterance," she comes up with, as a negative proof, the fact that, at this point, the sentence *I am not in agreement with the one who is speaking* should be translated as "The one who is speaking is not in agreement with the one who is speaking." The result would obviously be absurd, but it calls for a fundamentally stupid speaker. In point of fact the sentence should be interpreted as "The subject of this act of utterance is not in agreement with the subject of the act of utterance to which he is referring."

22 The perplexity connected with this identification between the signified and the proposition or verbally expressed marker is in evidence even when it is a matter of interpreting not visible objects, or real or presumed mental images, but also hypoicons, in other words pictures and drawings. See for example *Languages of Art* by Nelson Goodman (1968). The book exploits the experience of a philosopher of language in the search to legitimize the existence of visual languages, and tries to construct adequate semiotic categories, as happens in the pages on "exemplification and samples," or on the difference between autographic and allographic art. And yet Goodman remains bound to a propositional (and verbal) idea of denotation. When he wonders whether a picture that represents (and certainly denotes) a landscape in a tonality of gray denotes the property of grayness, or whether it is denoted by the predicate "gray," or whether a red object exemplifies the property of redness, or whether it exemplifies the predicate "red" (in which case the problem arises as to whether it exemplifies the predicate "rouge" for a French speaker), or whether it exemplifies the denotation of that same predicate, Goodman tries only to

render a phenomenon of visual communication that may be grasped in linguistic terms, but he says nothing about the signifying function that (let's say) in the course of a film a red object acquires for someone who has witnessed a bloody scene some moments before. He makes subtle distinctions between a "man-picture" and a "picture of a man," and sets himself multiple problems regarding the denotative modalities of a picture that represents the Duke and the Duchess of Wellington together. In his view, at one and the same time it denotes the couple while in part it denotes the Duke; as a whole it is a "two-person-picture" and in part it is a "man-picture," but it does not represent the Duke as two people, and so on. These are questions that can arise only if the picture is understood as the equivalent of a series of utterances. But anyone looking at the portrait (if not in the extreme case in which it might be used for historic-documentary purposes or for identification) does not translate his own experience in these terms. See, rather, how Calabrese (1981) identifies plastic signifiers of eminently visual signifieds. The categories in play, over and beyond the problematics of resemblance, are, for example, oppositions regarding the size of the picture, the position of the hands, the relation between figure and space-background, the direction of the gaze, and consequently the relation between a portrait that betrays the knowledge that it will be looked at by the spectator and another portrait in which the person depicted is looking at something but not at the spectator, and so on. A portrait does not just tell me that I am looking at a "man-picture," nor does it tell me that what I see is the Duke of Wellington (by the way, I get this information from the plaque on the frame, not from the image): but also whether that man is likable, in good health, sad, or disturbing. To say verbally that Mona Lisa's smile is "enigmatic" is a poor interpretation of what the image communicates to me. However, I could identify (by modifying Leonardo's image with a computer) the minimal features that make that smile enigmatic, and if I were to alter them, the smile would become a grin, or an inexpressive grimace. These eminently visual features are also crucial for interpreting the portrait as a reference to a person or a state of things.

23 The new cognitive approaches have certainly recovered this pre- or extralinguistic space, even though they sometimes appear reluctant to consider it a semiosic space. See, for example, the position of Jackendoff. The assumption is that thought is a mental function independent of language and that the inputs for the cerebral processes arrive not only by auditory means but also through other channels: visual, thermic, tactile, proprioceptive. It is worth observing that for each of these channels various specific semiotics have studied semiosic processes that develop precisely at these levels. But the problem of a semiotics of perception is not whether an image or a musical sequence can be analyzed in "grammatical" terms, a problem that appertains to a specific semiotics; it is whether the cognitive type also handles information arriving through these channels.

Jackendoff seems to have admitted the role of visual information, and for example he stresses that the representation of a word in the long term memory not only requires a partial combination of phonological, syntactical, and conceptual structures but also may contain a partial 3-D structure—in other words, knowing the meaning of a word that denotes a physical object implies in part a knowledge of the appearance of this object (1987, 10.4). The same thing would also happen with propositions that express complex scenes or situations. For example, in Jackendoff (1983, 9) the disambiguation of a phrase such as "The mouse went under the table" would require the visualization of two situations, one in which something *goes* to position itself under the table, and another in which something *passes* under the table. However, I do not think he went on to discuss other sensory channels, perhaps out of the difficulty of verbalizing such experiences.

24 As Violi (1997, 1.3.4) also points out, the fact that visual qualities are easier to interpret than the olfactory or tactile variety depends on our physiological structure and our evolutionary history: even medieval man knew that senses such as sight and hearing were *maxime cognoscitivi*. We are better at remembering and interpreting sensations we can reproduce: with a drawing, even a poor one, we can reproduce what we have seen, and we can reproduce a sound or a melody we have heard; we cannot reproduce, nor produce (voluntarily) a smell or a taste (except for particular cases such as perfumers and cooks: however, they do not do this with their own bodies but by blending substances). This incapacity to *make* with the body resolves into an incapacity (or reduced capacity) to interpret and even to remember (we remember a melody and we can reproduce it, but we do not recall with the same vividness the scent of a violet, which we tend to evoke by associating it with the image of the flower or a situation in which we perceived it). The tactile sense is a case apart: using our own or another person's body, or through our own body, we can reproduce many tactile sensations (many but not all, not that of velvet, for example). This mixed nature of the tactile sense explains why it can sometimes be used as a cognitive medium, for example in the Braille alphabet, not to mention many cases of the deliberate arousal of affections or disagreeable feelings, in erotic or conflictual relationships. As for the relation between reception and production in animals with other sensory resources, I cannot pass judgment.

25 For frames, see Minsky 1985. For scripts, see Schank and Abelson 1977. For a 3-D representation of behavior and corporeal actions, see Marr and Vaina 1982. For anger, see Greimas 1983.

26 Or by using 3-D models like those of Marr and Vaina 1982. Let us suppose there is a person (e.g., one of these severe scholars of whom it is said that they have been studying like university professors since they were small, i.e., they have never played) to whom it is explained during a de-

bate on translation how one *skips*. On such an occasion it would not be very dignified to explain this by ostension. So, trusting in his ability to understand and formulate propositions, one would translate the instructions contained in Nida's table into words for him, thus leaving him free to go back to his garden and enjoy the corresponding primary experience for the first time.

27 Gibson 1966: 285; Prieto 1975. See also Johnson-Laird (1983: 120): an artifact is seen as a member of a category not so much for morphological reasons as because it appears appropriate to a certain function. See also Vaina 1983: 19 ff.

28 On the relationship between cognitive types and corporeal and motor reactions, see Violi (1997, 5.2.4): "Whereas from a Whorfian standpoint we were accustomed to thinking of the language as the hinge linking thought and cultures, now the linguistic system has assumed a mediatory function between body and thought too."

29 To talk only of "figures in the mind" would postulate the traditional *homunculus* that perceives them, and the consequent regression of homunculi to infinity; for this argument, see also Edelman (1992: 79–80). However, one could say that the 3-D representation is not part of the semantic representation but, rather, serves to access the representation (Caramazza et al. 1990). For this, see also Job 1995. For the ensuing problem of double coding, see Benelli 1995.

30 In the morning we usually recall fairly vividly what we did or saw or said the evening before (and not only in visual but also in auditory terms, for example). However, when one awakes after an evening of copious libations, one recalls that something was done or said (and one is able to express this verbally to oneself or to others), but one cannot reconstruct "iconically" what happened. Let us say that a threshold has been created whereby one recalls in iconic terms what happened between nine and midnight (before the alcohol intake became excessive), while one conserves only a "propositional" memory of what happened after (and hence the scenes exploited in so many comedies, in which the character recalls having said or done something horrible the previous evening but can no longer reconstruct the scene).

31 See Fillmore 1982, Lakoff 1987, Wierzbicka 1996, Violi 1997, 2.2.2.1 and 3.4.3.1.

32 This discussion on bachelors exemplifies very well the difference between a formal and a cognitive semantics. It reminds one of the famous problem: If the village barber is the one who shaves all the men who do not shave themselves, then who shaves the village barber? In cognitive terms (and once I put the question to two little children) the answers are many and all reasonable: the barber is a woman, the barber never shaves and has a very long beard, the barber is a trained orangutan, the barber is a robot, the barber is a beardless youth, the barber does not shave but singes

off his beard (and so he is known as the Phantom of the Opera), and so on. But on a logical level, if the question is to make sense, we have to imagine a universe made up only of men who shave by definition.

33 On the other hand, and to leave mystic fiction for a moment: at a conference some astronomers are discussing the long defunct star N4, which winked out a million years ago and whose light can be detected only with the aid of a complex apparatus. The astronomers know well how to identify the star, and they associate its name with an MC made up of very sophisticated information. Nevertheless, while they are talking about it, each one has a relatively similar CT of N4 that includes the procedures they follow in order to identify it and the signals (of whatever kind they may be) that they receive when they focus on it.

34 Neisser (1987: 9) talks of cognitive schemata but makes it clear that they are neither categories nor models; in fact they appear as systems of expectations, based on previous experiences, which orient the construction of the perceptual judgment. He does admit, however, that "I cannot say what they are: we will not know how to characterize the structural prerequisites for perception until we are able to describe the information that perceivers pick up. There is little reason to believe that those 'prerequisite structures' have much in common with the cognitive models on which categorization depends; there is every reason to believe that they are exquisitely tuned to the ecologically relevant properties of the real world."

35 In what follows, I have taken into account Rosch 1978, Rosch and Mervis 1975, Rosch et al. 1976, Neisser 1987, Lakoff 1987, Reed 1988, and Violi 1997.

36 One might object that these texts are vitiated by the fact that the subject must respond verbally: I bet that perceptually and emotionally anyone can distinguish a pair of evening trousers from a pair of pink hot pants with the same immediacy with which he distinguishes trousers from a jacket. But I have certainly chosen a sly example, because it is evident that we distinguish a banana from an apple better than we distinguish a rennet from a Golden Delicious.

37 "Since the semantics of a language is not separable from a semantics of the natural world, the schemata that we use to understand the language are not different from those we use to understand the world. If the experience of the world may not be reduced to limited and preformed inventories, the same holds good for the linguistic sense" (Violi 1997, 11.1).

38 Violi (1997: 5.2.2) notes: "Let us think of manufactured objects: a chair, a bed, or a shirt are all objects whose function may be defined by an intensional act on the basis of which a defined motor program and one common to all the objects of that type will be developed. All chairs are objects on which I sit following the same sequence of actions, all glasses are objects from which I drink in the same way, and so on. When I move from

this level to the superordinate, the category of furniture for example, I can no longer identify a single motor program, because furniture does not give rise to a single common interaction, but to various different kinds of action." This insistence on the role of corporeality in determining both meaning and categorization brings us back to the theme of *affordances,* and constitutes one of the turning points in contemporary cognitivism with respect to traditional semantics.

39 Reed (1988: 197) wonders why, having elaborated a category of clothes, it is more difficult to recognize a bow tie as clothing than a shirt. It depends on the fact that clothes have been defined as something one puts on to keep warm, and in this case a bow tie would not even be clothing. However, the test would obtain different results if instead of the category of clothing we were to propose to the subject the category of items of dress. But I am afraid that in this case the category would be commercial rather than functional, and so the bow tie would go very well alongside shirts and belts because one buys them in the same shops, or one keeps them with trousers and handkerchiefs in the wardrobe or in the bedroom rather than on the bookshelf or in the kitchen. At a certain level of categorial ability, bicycle and motor car can be put together among the Vehicles, but if the category is objects suitable for birthday presents, the bicycle joins the watch or the scarf and the motor car risks exclusion from the group.

40 Some suggest that if we are asked to draw a triangle, we usually draw an equilateral triangle. I do not intend to discuss whether the matter is due to memories of school days or the fact that both in nature and in culture the triangular forms we see (such as mountains or Egyptian pyramids) are more easily comparable to the equilateral model than the right-angled one (even though in general mountains are somewhat scalene). What makes these experiments scarcely relevant to a discourse on cognitive types as prototypes is their statistical value. Let us suppose that 99% of the population of the world draws triangles as equilaterals. This would leave 1%, practically the entire population of the UK, which would behave differently. Now let us ask a representative of the 99% and a representative of the 1% to decide whether something is triangular rather than square or circular: I imagine there would be consensus. This would tell us that it is not necessary for the CT of the triangle to be identified with the statistically more widespread prototype.

41 Lakoff (1987: 49) distinguishes between categories as *kinds* and effects of classification, but makes no distinction between *kinds* and categories. On page 54 he calls *cause* a category in the sense that there is a prototype of how and why a thing must be considered a cause (an agent does something, a patient undergoes it, their interaction constitutes a single event, part of what the agent does changes the patient's state, there is a transfer of energy between the agent and the patient, et cetera—all features that

strike me as regarding only human causality). Therefore with regard to cause Lakoff talks of category in a Kantian sense; nevertheless the list of *frames* or grammatical cases supplied to define cause make one think (in Kantian terms) not of the category but of the schema. Once more an ambiguity has appeared that could have been reduced by considering the history of the concept of category with more care.

42 I find it strange that normal subjects did not also define it as something with the shape of a box, difficult to open when in movement or when it stops between one floor and another, seeing that it is precisely these two properties that explain the instinctive claustrophobia that this means of transport inspires in many. Perhaps the whole sample group was made up exclusively of agoraphobics.

43 Lakoff (1987: 66) notes that prototypical effects are real but superficial. They spring from a variety of sources. It is important not to confuse prototypical effects with the structure of the category as it is given by cognitive models. Note the meritorious confusion that Lakoff creates regarding common opinions on the content and possible uses of *mother* (and his pages seem particularly prophetic, or at least brilliantly pioneering, in the context of the current debates on cloning and artificial insemination).

44 The reader is referred to Violi (1997: 6.13.2) for the difference between categorial prototypicality and the typicality of meaning.

45 The situation is not different from that imagined by Locke for the sensations (*Essay* II, xxxii, 15): "Neither would it carry any imputation of falsehood to our simple ideas, if, by the different structure of our organs, it were so ordered that the same object should produce in several men's minds different ideas at the same time; *v.g.,* if the idea that a violet produced in one man's mind by his eyes were the same that a marigold produced in another man's, and vice versa. For since this could never be known; ...neither the ideas hereby nor the names would be at all confounded, or any falsehood be in either. For, all things that had the texture of a violet producing constantly the idea which he called "blue"; and those which had the texture of a marigold producing constantly the idea which he as constantly called "yellow"; whatever those appearances were in his mind, he would be able regularly to distinguish things for his use by those appearances, and understand and signify those distinctions, marked by the names "blue" and "yellow," as if the appearances, or ideas in his mind, received from those two flowers, were exactly the same with the ideas in other men's minds." Reformulated by Wittgenstein, the problem sounds like: "Suppose everyone had a box with something in it: we call it a 'beetle.' No one can look into anyone else's box, and everyone says he knows what a beetle is only by looking at *his* beetle. —Here it would be quite possible for everyone to have something different in his box. One might even imagine such a thing constantly changing. —But suppose the word 'beetle' had a use in these people's language? —If so it would not be used as the name of a thing. The thing in the box has no place in the lan-

guage game at all; not even as a *something:* for the box might even be empty. —No, one can 'divide through' by the thing in the box; it cancels out, whatever it is" (*Philosophical Investigations* I, 293).

46 A variant of this experience occurred in my department in the university. Unexpectedly glabrous, I entered a colleague's office, where she spoke with me for several minutes without showing any surprise. It was only when I had left, that a student present asked her if it had really been me. Faced with her amazement at such a question, he emphasized the fact that I did not have a beard. At that point my colleague understood. The explanation is that she had known me for a great many years, from the days in which I had no beard. But that same afternoon she had passed by my office and through the open door glimpsed an unauthorized person seated at my desk. She was puzzled for a moment and then obviously realized it was I without my beard. She knew me from my *pre*-beard days, but in that office (into which we had moved only a few years before) she had always seen me in *post*-beard mode. It would seem therefore that she had two different physiognomic types for me, let's say one private and one professional. Another experience that should be common to people who undergo weight swings punctuated by periodic diets is to meet other people who hasten to say how they find them fatter or slimmer than usual; the pronouncement never coincides with the subject's actual state; what happens is that the subject hears himself defined as fatter when he has lost at least eight kilos, and slimmer when he has put them back on again. What this means is that the issuer of the judgment relates the other person to a type constructed a long time before and that this is based on the state of the subject on the first, or most significant, encounter. In social relationships one is not fatter or slimmer in relation to what the scales say but in relation to other people's physiognomic types.

47 Note that, if a technique of total cloning were possible, in which the person cloned had not only the same body but also the same thoughts, the same memories, and the same genetic inheritance as the archetype, then even individuals like Johnny would become reproducible like a novel or a musical composition: there would be a "score" for producing Johnnies at will.

48 Obviously we must consider the case in which my interlocutor and I are both familiar with SC2. Otherwise we all have uncertainties. Some people, for example, can recognize the *Appassionata* (or "Michelle") at the first notes but not *Les Adieux* (or "Sergeant Pepper")—but this is the same as saying that we recognize Johann Sebastian because he works with us every day, while we find it hard to recognize Ludwig every time we meet him after a ten-year absence.

49 In this regard, see some interesting mentions in Merrell (1981: 165 ff.).

50 If the parameter of timbre counts for so little, could we say that Beethoven's *Fifth* played on the mandolin is still the same composition? Intuitively we could not—at best we would recognize the melody line.

Why then do we content ourselves with the transcription of SC2? Evidently because the latter is a composition for a solo instrument, while the former is a symphonic work, and in the execution on the mandolin of the former we do not simply pass from one timbre to another but also lose the overall complexity of timbre that is essential to the work. But this answer is not entirely satisfactory. What reductions in the number of orchestral instruments are we prepared to put up with in order to say that that execution is still the *Fifth*? Would SC2 transcribed for the ocarina still be SC2 as it remains transcribed for the recorder? If I whistle the beginning of SC2, am I "executing" SC2 or am I providing only a sort of paraphrasis, as if I were to say that *Ivanhoe* is a historical romance? Or by whistling am I only offering mnemonic backup with which to call up the type, as when I say that *Twelfth Night* is that play that begins "If music be the food of love, play on..." And what happens with *Ivanhoe* translated into French? Is it like SC2 transcribed for the recorder? I shall have to wait for another day to supply answers to these and other questions, of great moment for what is known as the intersemiotic theory of translation (and here the reader is referred to Nergaard 1995) but of lesser importance with regard to the problem I am discussing here.

51 I think this is getting closer to the second of the two cases considered by Marconi (1997: 3): intact inferential competence and poor referential competence versus good referential competence and poor inferential competence.

52 Brüggen would be capable of equating his CT with his MC, but in this case we would be dealing with the same competence that the zoologist has of the mouse, and we have seen that we are interested only in the competence that we share with the zoologist.

Chapter Four / The Platypus between Dictionary and Encyclopedia

1 Diego Marconi (1986, Appendix) examined a series of bilingual and monolingual dictionaries from the Middle Ages to the eighteenth century and found that definitions (or glosses) appear (when they appear and are not mere lists of permitted words): (i) as synonyms in another language; (ii) as instructions for the identification or production of the referent (see, e.g., Sextus Pompeius Festus, second century, *De verborum significatu,* in which *muries* (brine) is obtained by crushing coarse salt in a mortar, collecting it in an earthenware vase, etc.); (iii) as pure word lists of difficult words translated into simple words (but the problem of a dictionary-type competence is that of defining simple words!); (iv) through synonyms (*adulterate* = to counterfeit or to corrupt); (v) with the use of Latin as the lingua franca (*ambiguous* = "anceps," "obscurus").

2 The drawbacks with Wilkins's (1668) method are those I commented on in the definition of *bachelor* in Katz and Fodor (see Eco 1975: 2.10).

3 Even when cognitive psychologists talk of categorial activity, they refer mostly to a primary capacity to subsume experience under classifications that we can define as wild. For example, Bruner et al. (1956: 1) talk of classes of "dangerous situations" in which one is naturally induced to include an air-raid alarm, a python disturbed while we are climbing a tree, and a rebuke from a superior.

4 For this information, see Alan Rey, ed., *Le Robert Dictionnaire Historique de la Langue Française,* Paris: 1992.

5 In other words, we proceed in the way many of us organize our own library. While ten years ago Croce's *Aesthetics* was found in the division called "Aesthetics," the moment epistemological research begins, the book can be moved (until the research is completed) to the section "Knowledge." The criterion is personal but nonetheless pertinent, once the rules for retrieval are fixed.

6 This category of cancelable properties on the level of NC includes not only taxonomic properties. Marconi (1997: 43) offers the example of two assertions that, according to his point of view, are both necessary but not constitutive of common competence, although the first is universal and the second particular: (i) *the atomic number of gold is 79,* (ii) *37 is the thirteenth prime number*. Sentence (i) certainly does not reflect common competence, and I would accept that it is "necessary," that is to say indelible, within the bounds of scientific discourse. It might not be so in the future, when it is discovered that the present paradigm does not account adequately for the difference between the elements. A goldsmith can tell gold from pinchbeck on the basis of criteria (I don't care which) that I would define as empirical, and in any case people have a rather vague CT of gold, a fact that allows confidence men and forgers to pass off fake gold with ease. As for (ii), it could be more "cogent" than (i), if one accepted the Kantian distinction between analytic judgments and a priori synthetic judgments. Kant would have said that our knowledge regarding the number depends on transcendental schematism, while that of gold is an empirical concept (as a matter of fact, Kant presumed to know how the number 37 could be generated but not how one could determine what gold is). Between the two sentences there is a difference that I do not think has been completely captured by the universal and necessary opposition vs. the necessary particular. There is no doubt that (ii) does not belong to the NC: all we need to know is that 37 is a number less than 38 and greater than 36, and how we can generate it. If we were told to go buy as many peanuts as may be counted on the basis of the thirteenth prime number, I think we would return empty-handed. These observations allow us to say that denying that mice are MAMMALS, that the atomic number of gold is 79, and that 37 is the thirteenth prime number are all irrelevant statements from the standpoint of NC, precisely because they are important (and indelible) only for the purposes of a more elaborate sectorial knowledge.

7 What do we perceive when we see someone wearing a shirt under a jacket? We do not see but we know that the shirt also covers the back. We know this, because we have a CT of the shirt based on perceptive (and productive) experiences. Whether or not it has a collar and of what type, or whether it has long or short sleeves is optional, but if it has cuffs, then it has long sleeves. Now, in the film *Totò e la dolce vita,* the miserly wife obliges her husband Totò to wear a shirt made only of a collar, front, and cuffs. The rest was covered by his jacket, and so there was no need to waste cloth unnecessarily. Totò reasonably objects that, if by chance he were to feel unwell on the tram and they were to remove his jacket, everybody would discover the shameful deception: in point of fact, he is saying that in such as case the onlookers would realize that they had integrated incomplete stimuli with a strong CT, thus coming to pronounce a mistaken perceptive judgment. At that point the onlookers would decide that what they had perceived as a shirt was instead a *fake* shirt. But the wife (excluding the possibility of this incident) speculates on her own irrepressible faith in the existence of CTs that include indelible features.

8 On the other hand, Walt Disney managed to make us recognize as a mouse an animal that has the tail and the ears of a mouse but is bipedal with an anthropomorphic torso. It is legitimate to ask ourselves if we would have recognized him as a mouse if he had not been introduced to us right away as Mickey Mouse. In such a case we might say that the name, in suggesting a CT to us, has led us to apply the CT in an indulgent manner (while iconographic convention saw to the rest).

9 The story is so amazing and still controversial in many senses (some evidence or scientific articles from the period are hard to find, as historians admit), and the bibliography is so complex, that I will stick to what I have learned from Burrell (1927) and Gould (1991), referring the reader to them for more complete bibliographical references. Where Burrell's own references are incomplete, I have put "Burrell" in parentheses. I would also point out that on the Internet I found over 3,000 sites regarding the platypus, some of which were entirely accidental (persons or institutions that have decided to name clubs, bookshops, and the like after the platypus) but others worthy of interest, ranging from university centers to those who maintain that the platypus is the best proof of the existence of God, to fundamentalist groups that, having ascertained the paleontological seniority of the platypus with regard to other mammals, ask themselves how this little animal managed to migrate from Mount Ararat to Australia after the Flood. More or less at the same time as the Italian version of this book, Harriet Ritvo published her *The Platypus and the Mermaid*, Cambridge: Harvard UP, 1997, from which I have drawn some additional bibliographic information for this English translation.

10 *Account of the English Colony in the New South Wales*, 1802: 62 (Burrell).

11 *The Naturalist Miscellany*, Plate 385, 386 (Burrell).

12 *General Zoology*, London: Kearsley, 1800, vol. I (Burrell).

13 Everard Home, "A description of the anatomy of the *Ornithorhynchus Hystrix*," *Philosophical Transactions of the Royal Society* 92, 360.

14 For Home, see "A description of the anatomy of the *Ornithorhynchus paradoxus*," *Philosophical Transactions of the Royal Society*, part 1, no. 4, pp. 67–84. For Geoffroy de Saint-Hilaire, see "Extraits des observations anatomiques de M. Home, sur l'échidné," *Bulletin des Sciences par la Societé Philomatique*, 1803; "Sur les appareils sexuels et urinaires de l'Ornithorynque," *Memoires du Muséum d'Histoire Naturelle*, 1827. For Lamarck, *Philosophie zoologique*, Paris, 1809.

15 Unless it is manifested through behavior rather than language. Put ten men to march through the desert and, after days of thirst, have them come across three palm trees and a pool of water: all ten will throw themselves at the water and not the trees. Have they recognized the water? The problem is badly put, they have certainly recognized something that all of them desired equally, but we might say that they recognized it as water only after they had been led to interpret their behavior verbally, or only after two of them agreed to interpret it in such a way—and so we are back to square one.

16 Hjelmslev's analysis (1943), whereby the semantic space covered by the French term *bois* does not coincide with that covered by the Italian word *legno* ("wood"), tells us that the category "bois" for a French speaker can include both wood for burning, wood for building (which for an English speaker would be only *timber*), and the clump of trees that Italians would call *bosco* ("a wood"). This segmentation of the *continuum* can correspond to what Davidson, in refuting it, called a conceptual schema. But it is certain that a French speaker has a CT for the trees and another for the woods, even though his language obliges him to use a homonymous term. In the same way Italians can very easily tell the difference between the sons of their sons and the sons of their brothers or sisters, even though they (unlike the French) have only the homonymous term *nipote* with which to indicate both.

17 Hjelmslev's *Prolegomena* is from 1943. Quine's "Two Dogmas of Empiricism" is from 1951. Kuhn's *The Structure of Scientific Revolutions* is from 1962. That the two currents proceeded independently is another matter. Hjelmslev knew Carnap, and from personal knowledge I can testify that Kuhn did not know Hjelmslev but had decided to take a look at the structuralist tradition before writing the works he was unable to complete before his death. I do not know how much Quine knows about the structuralist tradition.

18 In any case here is what he thought in "The Semantic Conception of Truth and the Foundations of Semantics" (*Philosophy and Phenomenological Research* 1944). He said that we can accept the semantic conception of truth without abandoning whatever epistemological stance we may have;

we can continue to be naïve realists, critical realists or idealists, empiricists or metaphysicians—or whatever we were before. See Bonfantini 1976, III, 5, and Eco 1997.

19 If we assume Tarski's example in a naïve way, we find ourselves in the same situation as Saussure's publishers, who represented the relation between signifier and signified with an oval divided in two, whose lower part contained the word *arbre* and whose upper part contained a sketch of a tree. Now the signifier *arbre* is certainly a word, but the drawing of a tree is not and cannot be a signified or a mental image (because if anything, it is another, nonverbal, signifier that interprets the word below). Given that the drawing elaborated by Saussure's publishers had no formal ambitions, only a mnemonic function, we can forget about it. But in Tarski's case, the problem is more serious.

20 The conference, entitled "W. V. O. Quine's Contributions to Philosophy," took place in the International Center for Semiotic and Cognitive Studies of the University of San Marino in May 1990. The proceedings of the conference are now in P. Leonardi and M. Santambrogio, 1995.

21 I am talking of the map, not of the "physiognomy" of the place: for this problem the observations made in 3.7.9. hold good.

22 I should like to refer to an old piece of research done on the barking of dogs (which now appears in Eco and Marmo 1989). The idea for the research came about (during a seminar on medieval semiotics) when it was noticed that, in talking of various forms of expression as opposed to articulated human speech, different authors of the period always mentioned the *latratus canis* (together with the groaning of the sick and the cock's crowing). Since we were dealing with highly complex classifications, attempts were made to outline a sort of taxonomic tree for each author, and in doing this we realized that the dog's bark, the groaning of the sick, and the cock's crowing occupied, according to the authors, a different node of the tree (and sometimes they appeared as examples of the same semiosic behavior, sometimes as different cases). Medieval man was in the habit (I don't know how deprecable, but certainly opposed to modern habits) of saying new things while pretending to be repeating what had been said before by others, with the result that it is always difficult to understand to what extent he assumed positions contrary to earlier tradition. This experiment showed us clearly that apparently analogous discussions on communicational phenomena concealed profound systematic differences. In short, and without going further into the matter, the barking of a dog was one thing for a thinker and something else for another. In the light of the system, the same behavior assumed different meanings. Yet each author perceived the same phenomenon (the common experience of hearing dogs bark). This was a case of analogous observation sentences (*There is a dog barking*) or even of semiotic judgments (*Dogs are barking animals*) that were, all things considered, homologous, and so, even some centuries later, all gave the impression of having the same NC of *dog*. Yet, in the

light of each author's framework of assumptions, and therefore within the framework of different MCs, that dog who was barking represented a different phenomenon. The barking of the dog was like the brick house in Vanville.

23 In this regard, see Picardi in the introduction to the Italian version of Davidson 1984 and Picardi 1992. Picardi (1992: 253) wonders about the relation between the theories an interpreter must have at his disposal in order to understand a language and the theories the interpreter must construct every time for each individual interlocutor at each stage of the conversation. I don't think Davidson does anything to solve this problem, and this is precisely because, perhaps for linguistic reasons, he makes no distinction between *langue* and *parole,* in other words between the *meaning* of the terms of a language and the *sense* of utterances and texts.

24 For this, see the observations in Alac 1997.

25 For this, the reader is referred to the analysis made in Zijno 1996 on the positions of Davidson and Sperber-Wilson. It is clear that none of these authors maintains that there are no linguistic conventions, and that all of us follow determined rules, both for presupposing the interlocutor's beliefs and for negotiating pertinency and elaborating inferences regarding the communicative situation. Nevertheless, the emphasis is laid on the work for "minimizing disagreement," letting it be understood that, having a good theory of the speaker, one might do without a theory of language. Yet when it is said that "communicating means trying to modify the *cognitive environment* of another individual" (Zijno 1996, 2.1.2.) and that a cognitive environment for an individual is the set of facts manifest to him (Sperber and Wilson 1986: 65), this cognitive environment comes to look very like what I call a CT, and in order to presuppose it on the speaker's part, I too must have a representation in the form of NC. The inference and the contract regard the effort required to make our cognitive environments publicly compatible. This is the case with my Ayers Rock example. It is clear that if someone says to me that Ayers Rock is an animal, I infer from this that his cognitive environment is not only rather unlike mine but also unlike the publicly agreed one. Minimizing disagreement means leading the other to accept at least in part an NC that the Community finds passably acceptable. At most I can extend the principle of charity beyond normal limits, if I am talking with a primitive who really does see Ayers Rock as an animal. But I agree to adapt my cognitive environment to his only for the purposes of communicative interaction, which I feel ought to be safeguarded at all costs. Afterward, I still think that that mountain *is not* an animal. To put it brusquely, the popular principle whereby one always agrees with the insane does not mean that the Community accepts their viewpoint. It is another matter if the Community turns out to be wrong, and the one we thought a madman was right: history teaches us that this has often happened in the past, and the Community has taken a bit of time to modify what, by social

decree, everyone thought was right. In short, therefore, negotiation does not institute a cognitive environment, it takes account of previous cognitive environments, corrects them, and attempts to homogenize them.

26 To say that we negotiate from time to time does not mean to say that stronger and stabler conventions do not gradually sediment. See Dummett 1986: 447–58. A fine contractual view of meaning is to be found in Bruner, one of whose merits is having put the problem of *Meaning* at the center of the Cognitive Sciences. Not only does he state that culture makes meanings *public* and *shareable* (and he knows of the Peircean idea of the *public nature of* interpretants), but he also maintains that, although all our discourses are ambiguous and polysemic, we are always able to make their meaning public through *negotiation* (1990: 13).

27 Marconi 1997, 5, also contains reflections on the Schtroumpfs, quoting my article "Schtroumpf und Drang" in *Alfabeta*, 5 September 1979 (now in *Sette anni di desiderio*, Milan: Bompiani, 1983: 265-71).

28 What is the cognitive universe of the Schtroumpfs like? Given that they indiscriminately give the name *schtroumpf* to houses, cats, mice, and bachelors, does this perhaps mean that they do not possess these concepts and cannot distinguish between a cat and a bachelor? Or have they a system of expression (a lexicon, in particular) that is rather poor, but a system of content that is at least as vast and articulated as the experiences allowed by their environment? Or again, since the Schtroumpf language makes it as possible to say *Beethoven's Fifth Schtroumpf* as *Beethoven's Schtroumpf Symphony* or the *Fifth Symphony of Schtroumpf* (but never *Schtroumpf's Schtroumpf Schtroumpf!*), perhaps they have a lexicon as rich as ours and use the all-purpose homonym for reasons of laziness, aphasia, affectation, or secrecy. But does using only one word for many things not lead them to see all things united by some strange relation? If eggs, spades, and mushrooms are all *schtroumpfs,* do the Schtroumpfs not live in a world where the links between eggs, spades, and mushrooms are far fuzzier than they are in our or in Gargamel's world? And if this is the case, does this confer upon the Schtroumpfs a deeper and richer contact with the totality of things, or does it make them unable to make a correct analysis of reality, immuring them inside the imprecise universe of their pidgin? These are all questions I feel I cannot answer here, but I have listed them in order to say that Peyo's stories, even though conceived for children, pose some serious semiotic problems for adults.

Chapter Five / Notes on Referring as Contract

1 For example, the one used in Santambrogio (1992), which deals with reference to "general objects." Santambrogio intended to study how we can deal in terms of quantification with sentences about general objects. In a truth-functional semantics the problem is of some interest, but I hold that in such a case *referring to something* becomes a synonym for *talking about*

something. Every time we talk, we talk about something, but, then, I don't see what specific phenomenon is signified by the term *referring*.

2 For the difference between semiotic and factual judgments, see *A Theory of Semiotics*, 3.2. If I said that all platypuses lay eggs, and even if I quantified it, as I did for the properties of mammals, I would certainly not be referring to all the platypuses that exist or have ever existed, because the existence of barren platypuses cannot be excluded. Simply, I would once more be saying that, whatever the animal one wishes to apply the term *platypus* to, it would have to be an animal that has the property of laying eggs. One might argue that the state of being a mammal is not the same as nursing one's young: at first sight this would seem to be the case, because the fact that platypuses nurse their young has been proved by various observation sentences, while their status as mammals depends on taxonomic convenience. But since taxonomy registers as mammals those animals attributed with the property of nursing their young, and numerous observation sentences tell us that platypuses nurse their young, we can consider the two sentences as equivalent from our standpoint. Those who make such sentences refer to nothing but contribute to the reconfirmation of the social agreement regarding the MC to be assigned to the corresponding term, in other words, regarding the format of the categorial system assumed within a given conceptual schema.

3 The referential function is not necessarily expressed by the grammatical form. Let's take a sentence such as *Napoleon died on the fifth of May*. The sentence would be understood as referential if it was uttered in the same month by a courier arriving in London from Sant'Elena. If a scholar were to say, on the basis of newly discovered documents, that Napoleon did not die on the fifth of May, he would certainly still be referring to Napoleon as an individual, and if he said, *All the history books I have studied give erroneous information about Napoleon,* he would certainly be referring to all the single history books he had consulted. But if, in answering a question in a history exam, a student were to say *Napoleon died on the fifth of May,* I would doubt that this was still a sentence with a referential function. The student, completely uninterested in Napoleon, is merely citing an encyclopedic datum to please the teacher. In other words, the student is only trying to show that he knows the cultural convention whereby the notion of Napoleon is associated with the property of having died on the fifth of May 1821, exactly in the same way as if he had replied to the chemistry teacher that water is H_2O (where it is very clear that the reference is not to water but to what the current textbooks have to say about the matter). If the student were to say that Napoleon died on the eighteenth of June 1815, the teacher would tell him that he had a poor recollection of what the textbooks say, given that this is recorded as the date of the battle of Waterloo. If, however, the teacher observed sarcastically, *Look, on that date Napoleon was still alive and kicking,* in that case his intention would be to refer to Napoleon as an individual. I agree that this

example of mine could be challenged, and I would be glad if someone did so, because it would back up my conviction that deciding whether a sentence has a referential function or not is a matter for negotiation.

4 Why this was never said or admitted is explained very well by Ducrot. For Saussure and the structuralist school, signifieds were purely differential and were not defined by their content. The meaning of a sign registered only the features that distinguished it from the other signs in a language and not a description of its possible referents: To return to the Aristotelian example, the meaning of *homme* does not involve the feature "featherless," because as a matter of fact the natural classification incorporated in French does not oppose *homme* and *oiseau* within a category *bipède,* but *homme* and *animal* within a category *être animé* (Ducrot and Schefer 1995: 303).

5 I must admit that, in previous works, I gave rise to the misunderstanding that semiotics should not take any interest in processes of referring, and that it was possible to deal with both the problem of identifying the referent and the problem of acts of reference in a unitary fashion. But my polemic was due to the fact that in those works I wanted to emphasize how culture constituted a system of content, and how discourses produced an effect of truth, so it seemed less important to establish what individual or state of affairs was being referred to by saying that Dion runs. Naturally no one thought that language was not used for referring to something. The problem hinged on seeing reference as a function of meaning and not vice versa. The second half of *A Theory of Semiotics* treats of what happens when we express indexical judgments and of how, in referring to objects, perceptual data are compared with cultural data; while the chapters on sign production hinge largely on the tasks involved in the interpretation of symptoms, prints, clues, and toposensistive vectors in order to learn something about that which is the case, and about how we construct or take as signs examples, samples, or projections to refer, indicate, designate, or portray objects of the world. In conclusion, my preoccupation with abduction, and with regard not only to general laws but also to facts—as happens in the investigations of Sherlock Holmes (Eco and Sebeok 1983)—means that I was interested in the mental mechanisms by means of which we come to say something true or at least likely with reference to specific individuals and events. I am grateful to Augusto Ponzio (1993: 89) for having observed that in *A Theory of Semiotics* I moved from an apparently "antireferential" semiotics to a "non immediately referential semiotics." In other words, if at first it seemed as if I was stating that semiotics has nothing to do with our relation with reality, in the second phase I was saying that it is not possible to explain how we refer to reality if we do not first establish how we give meaning to the terms we use.

6 I am condensing an argument put forward by Bonomi (1994, 4). In 1934, Carlo Emilio Gadda wrote an article, "Morning in the Abattoir." This

was a description of the town abattoir in Milan. In Bonomi's mental experiment, the article remained unpublished, it never mentioned the city of Milan, and a researcher had found a manuscript copy among Gadda's papers, taking it for a piece of narrative fiction. If the researcher later discovered that the text was a newspaper piece, to be judged in terms of true/false, even though he changed his opinion about the nature of that text, he would have no need to reread it. The world described, the individuals who inhabit it, and their properties would all still be the same, and the researcher would then simply "project " that representation onto reality. Therefore "for the content of an account that describes a certain state of things to be understood, it is not necessary for the categories of true and false to be applied to that content."

7 For my objections with regard to rigid designation, see Eco 1984, 2.6.

8 In an atechnical way, Campanini proceeds much like the pseudointelligent computer involved in project Eliza. In this experiment, which obviously does not understand what its human interlocutors say, is instructed to take the subject of an interlocutor's sentence and use it for the construction of a question that seems intelligent. If the interlocutor confesses to having parental problems, then the computer responds by saying, "Tell me a bit about your parents." In the sarkiapone sketch, Campanini restricts himself to grasping the name of the property supposed by Chiari and in essence replies, "But the sarkiapone does not possess the property you have mentioned."

9 With regard to this type of existential presupposition, see Eco and Violi 1987 and Eco 1990, 4.4.

10 On this point we could dust off the old medieval argument as to whether existence is an accident of the essence (attributed to Avicenna) or an act of the essence (Aquinas). There is no doubt that it is necessary to distinguish between the predicative and existential use of the essence (for a crystal-clear synthesis, see Piattelli Palmarini 1995, 11). This makes it possible to clarify a point made in 2.8.3 in reference to the interpretation offered by Fumagalli (1995), who says that while in Peirce's early work the three categories of Firstness, Secondness, and Thirdness were elements of the proposition, in his later writings they were moments in experience. As a moment of experience, existence is not a predicate, it is the clash with something that stands against me, before me, anterior to all conceptual elaboration—and it is this immediate sensation of being that I was talking about in 1.3. It is a prepredicative existence. But when, on the other hand, I state that Paris has the property of existing in this world while Calvino's Invisible Cities do not have it, I have moved on to existence as predicate.

11 For the paradoxes of rigid designation in scientific contexts, see Dalla Chiara and Toraldo di Francia 1985.

12 One can object that the domain label (*uk.,* or *fr.,* or *it.*) can be a description, insofar as it defines at least the baptismal area. If it were true, the

description would be too vague and inscrutable. But a British citizen is free to subscribe to a French site: therefore the domain loses any descriptive value it may have had.

13 One might say that no one is really interested in the solution. But if the Jekyll-Mary relationship were to result in the birth of a son, Charles, who at the age of twenty discovers there are two Jekylls, then he might be seriously interested in knowing who his biological father is. But owing to the daily sexual relations between Jekyll and Mary, it would be impossible to determine the day on which Charles was conceived, so we would have someone who knows that his father was certainly *one* of the two Hyde brothers, but no amount of trying to find out would tell him which of the two it was.

14 Like Putnam (1992), Holmes thinks that the Thing-in-Itself is not so much an unknowable by definition as an ideal limit of knowledge. Therefore I agree also with Føllesdal (1997: 453): the rigidity of the designation is a regulative idea; in the Kantian sense of the term, a normative notion.

15 Among the infinite contributions to the debate on the murder of Smith, I will mention only the three texts I had in mind as I was writing this paragraph: Bonomi (1975: 4), Santambrogio (1992), and, above all, Berselli (1995 1.3).

16 In the original version, Nancy wanted to marry a Norwegian. To the best of my knowledge the example appears in McCawley 1971, but perhaps it was already in circulation. Interesting suggestions on Nancy's case were sent to me (in manuscript form) by Franz Guenthner in the course of a debate at the Centro di Semiotica in Urbino in the seventies.

17 I am always irritated when I receive a postcard, let's say, from Bali with "Greetings, John." Which John? Is it possible that this John does not know there are many other people in the world with the same name as his, and that I know at least a score of them? Can he possibly think he is the only John I know? I am citing a very common case. This means that people think of their names in terms of rigid designation. But the fact that people make this mistake (or fall victim to this weakness) is no reason for philosophers to make it too.

18 As was pointed out in note 16, I took the example of Nancy from McCawley. Are we dealing with the same Nancy? It is true that his Nancy wanted to marry a Norwegian and mine wanted an analytic philosopher, but the same Nancy might be very willful. Or she might harbor the strange notion that all analytic philosophers are Norwegian. When we talk about my Nancy, are we talking about McCawley's Nancy? As can be seen, negotiating a reference is a very complex operation.

19 Inconceivable worlds (in narrative and the figurative arts) are an example of *impossibilia,* i.e., worlds that the reader is led to conceive only as far as it is necessary to understand that it is impossible to conceive them. In this

regard Dolezel (1989: 238 ff.) talks of "self-voiding texts" and of "self-disclosing meta-fiction." In these cases, on the one hand, the possible entities seem to be brought into narrative existence, given that conventional procedures of validation are applied; on the other, the status of this existence is rendered uncertain, because the very foundations of the validation mechanism are undermined. These impossible narrative worlds include internal contradictions. Dolezel gives the example of *La maison de rendezvous* by Robbe-Grillet, in which the same event is introduced in different conflicting versions, the same place is and is not the setting of the novel, the events are organized in contradictory temporal sequences, and the same narrative entity is represented in different existential ways.

20 Here it is not enough to object that this is a matter of representation and not of referring. Apart from the fact that this would come to contradict the fairly established opinion that we can use an image of something to refer to something (think of a news photo that to all effects and purposes constitutes news), the paradoxes of inconceivability—craftily excluded from the phenomenology of reference—would resurface in the phenomenology of representation, and we would have gained nothing.

21 For a good compendium of the various arguments, see Salmon (1981, Appendix 1).

22 On the other hand, the same argument could also be applied to countries with a stabler history, France included, and it is not easy to say what the expression *United States of America* refers to if one asks oneself whether it was said before or after the purchase of Louisiana or Alaska.

23 The most recent is that put forward by Santambrogio 1992, for whom fictional characters are similar to "general objects."

24 While properties of type (iv) can seem of little importance for an encyclopedic definition of the fictional character, consider this curious news item I found in *La Repubblica* of 1 September 1985 (since the same piece of news appeared in what was only a slightly different version in the *Corriere della Sera* of the same day, it can be supposed that it came from a news agency): "The false death notice published by *The Times* was the revenge of a jealous woman and not a message in code for some spy, reveals *The Sun*. The death notice announced the sudden death in Cornwall of Mark, Timothy, and James, 'favourite sons' of a German countess. Rita Colman, a London magistrate, has admitted to having had the text published at the request of countess Margareth von Hessen, the mother of the three boys. The paper has now discovered that Rita Colman's present husband divorced from countess von Hessen five years ago, and is the father of Mark, Timothy, and James. The three boys are alive and kicking and one of them, Mark, is in fact holidaying in Cornwall, where he was contacted by *The Sun*. 'Whoever is behind this macabre joke is the same person who attempted to blacken my mother's name two years ago,' commented the young man. In 1983 an English newspaper had published a false news item according to which an Anglican minister, Robert Parker,

was on the point of abandoning wife and career to run off with the countess von Hessen. Since yesterday Rita Colman has been untraceable in London: she has left with her husband for a holiday in Devon." Note that this text specifically names those involved in the affair, it links them reciprocally through S-necessary relationships, and attributes to them both "Registry Office" properties and fairly precise actions. However, if we thought this was a story, we would fall prey to much puzzlement. There is certainly a Rita Colman who has admitted to having had the false news item p published, but why did she have it published? On the request of the countess von Hessen, her husband's ex-wife, we are told. But since the countess knows that the three boys are alive, why did she induce Colman to have the story published? To terrify her ex-husband? And why did Colman accept, given that the ex-husband is now hers, and that she clearly wants him in good spirits if they are to holiday together in Devon? To please the countess? But why, if, according to the insinuations of one of the sons, Colman bears no love for the countess and on the contrary had spread a false story about her alleged affair with an Anglican vicar, in order to blacken her name? If this news item were a story, we would not be able to paraphrase it in a sensible way, precisely because it confuses our ideas about properties of the type (iv). Or we might take it as the beginning of an affair whose mysteries will have to be cleared up later. Naturally the text is confusing as a news item too, but at this point it suffices to think that the agency editor was an incompetent bungler or that the Italian press had mistranslated an English text, and there's an end to it.

25 Semprini (1997) devotes a paragraph to the conditions for the recognition of legendary characters from the history of comics, and shows they are identifiable by name, by pronounced physiognomic features, by unmistakable clothing, by civil status, by a series of specific skills, and by various other details (typical phrases, sounds that constantly accompany some canonical gestures, etc.). Are there many real people for whom we have such detailed instructions for recognition?

26 An indexical or deictic term has a meaning independent of context and circumstances. But it is amid circumstances that the way it is to be used for referring must be negotiated. Ducrot (1995: 309) gives an example that reminds us of the uncertainties of Quine's explorer faced with the native's *gavagai*. "*This* or *that,* even taking the gesture of designation into account, are not enough to delimit an object. How can I know that what someone shows me on the table is the book in its entirety, or its dust jacket, or its colour, or the contrast between its colour and that of the table, or the particular impression it gives me in this moment? A noun, possibly implicit, is necessary to complete the act of reference."

27 See in Eco (1979, 1.3) the analysis of two contextual uses of *instead*.

Chapter Six / Iconism and Hypoicon

1 For a review of the debate, see Calabrese 1985; Fabbrichesi 1983; Bettetini 1996 (1.3 and II.1.1.)

2 Fabbrichesi (1983) puts forward the suggestion that that debate did not die a natural death, because semiotics refused to reflect "philosophically" on the concept of likeness, and this likeness to be explained was not the correspondence between two objects (let's say a drawing and its original) but Peircean Firstness, as an internal difference, which does not distinguish concrete objects but prepares their individuation and constitution (1983: 109).

3 This distinction is not homologous with that, to use the words of Dennet (1978, III, 10), between *iconophiles* and *iconophobes* in the cognitive sciences. I would say that having distinguished (i) the iconic value of knowledge and (ii) the nature of the hypoicon, Dennet's objection is internal to point (i). In any case, according to the various registers already mentioned, the number of the iconoclasts usually includes Goodman, Gombrich, most of the followers of Greimas, the Liège Group, and even psychologists such as Gregory, while among the iconists one might mention the early Barthes and the early Metz, Gibson, the early Wittgenstein, and Maldonado.

4 I am justly accused of this by Leo Fabbrichesi (1983: 3), even though he perhaps underestimates how the problem resurfaced in *A Theory of Semiotics* apropos of the "inventions," and does not consider (owing to the publication date) the way in which I partly tried to retable it in the essay on mirrors (1985).

5 Sonesson, for example, is one who reproves me for having treated only of visual iconism: but, in those very years, I published in *VS* two essays by Osmond Smith (1972, 1973) on musical iconism, and I mentioned for example the experience of syntactical iconism. However, it is also true that on at least two occasions I wrote that to talk of iconism for Peirce's existential graphs was pure metaphor, because they do not reproduce morphological and spatial relations. A sign that in that cultural climate, he who uttered the word "icon" was already naturally anchored to the pictorial universe.

6 There is an extremely wide-ranging debate on this subject. On the one hand, there are experiments that show how even animals recognize images (starting with the legend of Zeuxis); on the other, there are ethnographic reports that show us a "primitive" (in any case, someone who has no experience of photographic images or even portraits) toying with a photograph of a known person and manifesting perplexity, anxiety, or even an absolute lack of interest. These are almost always insufficiently tested experiments: in certain cases what strikes the primitive is the offer of a piece of paper, an object unknown to him, whereas if the image is printed on a piece of cloth, he will approach it with greater confidence. In

other cases, the problem is the poor quality of the image. In others, the fact that the primitive is still puzzled means not that he has not recognized the subject portrayed but that he simply cannot understand how the features of a known person can appear as if by magic on a piece of paper. In others again, it is evidently a matter of badly formulated questions, which recall the misunderstandings in Quine's radical translation.

7 Otherwise Maldonado himself, in reminding me of the need to consider the motivated relations between icon and reality, would not have insisted so much on the "optimization" of likeness, that is, on the study of techniques that might make it possible in future to "find, on a technical level, the best possible correspondence between the conventional requests that come from the observer and those nonconventional ones that spring from the observed object" (1974: 291).

8 This explains why Metz (1968b: 115n) was immediately prepared to accept my criticisms regarding an idea of the hypoicon as *analogon* and to take another look at its cultural components.

9 With regard to this line of thought, I like to cite the most recent contribution: Jean Fisette 1995.

10 It should be said that, rather than a surgical operation, this was a matter of preventive medicine, because it was carried out well before the appearance of a theory of rigid designation.

11 For a tempered view of the positions, see Bettetini 1971 and 1975.

12 For an English translation, see "Articulations of the Cinematic Code," in Bill Nichols, ed., *Movies and Methods*, Berkeley: University of California Press, 1976, 590-607).

13 Some today might propose defining likeness as a dyadic relation between something and itself, and similarity as a relation that is in any case triadic (see Goodman 1970): A is similar to B from the point of view C, and perhaps similarity is what has been defined as a "multiplace predicate" (see Medin and Goldstone 1995). However, see in 3.7. the discussion on the difference between recognizing an individual as the *same* individual and recognizing it as *similar* to others of its species. Given that the recognition of basic categories (such as a dog or a chair) is rooted in the perceptual process, in these cases too shouldn't we be talking about likeness rather than established similarity?

14 "The abrupt changes in intensity in the image reveal outlines and hence the shapes of objects in the visual world" (Vaina 1983: 11).

15 Once more the need prevailed to connect the hypoicon immediately to a meaning, to a cognitive type, and therefore I maintained that from the hypoiconic experience one immediately arrives at the "abstract representation of the hand." In other words, the problem was that of the (individual) Dynamical Object as the (ideal) *terminus ad quem* of a cognitive process, of which one could control only the (general) Immediate Object. And therefore one always risked not taking into consideration the object as a *terminus a quo,* i.e., the fact that in order to constitute any abstract

representation of the hand, we (or whoever had transmitted the type to us) had still started off from a perceptual experience.

16 I owe these observations to Paolo Fabbri, who was moreover referring to some discussions with Ruggero Pierantoni. Fabbri suggests that therefore a semiotics of perception should recover the concept of "enunciation," which implies the point of view of the subject. I find the suggestion a fecund source of developments, as I think I have mentioned in these essays. Fabbri's advice is to make the concept of enunciation central to all the paragraphs that follow, like the one on prostheses and the one on mirrors and imprints. I feel that the presence of the subject and his point of view is central—even though not expressed in terms of "enunciation"—to the other parts of this chapter, and in particular to the piece on mirrors.

17 If the answer is yes, it is not yet sure that the stimulus is natural: we could be faced with a hologram. I suspect that the question of holograms should be approached from the point of view of my further discussion on mirrors and TV images (see 6.10 ff).

18 He did not see it even though he lived in a culture that was by that time dominated by the pictorial theory of perspective. A curious phenomenon that seems to clash with two opposed positions, that perspectival relationships are given to us by the object and that they are imposed as an interpretative schema of cultural origins. Let's say then that, however things may be, the object did not supply him with a sufficient trace with which to grasp the perspective, and the culture had not yet supplied sufficient schemata with which to see it.

19 Except that there the type contemplated four stages: (i) stimuli (what I am presently calling the Moon-in-Itself); (ii) transformation (the labor carried out by drawing); (iii) perceptual model; (iv) semantic model. In the light of what has been said in this book, the cognitive type would now come to fulfill the dual function of the two "models," perceptual and semantic.

20 Valentina Pisanty (in a puzzled personal communication) asked me what I would see were I to point my index finger toward my eyes (the ones in my head). It would seem difficult to handle two images at the same time; perhaps it would be necessary to close the two normal eyes when the third is in use, but I'm not sure this would be enough. The most reasonable conclusion is that the innovation would make it necessary to redesign our brain. Perhaps it is because of this difficulty that no one has ever tried to graft a third eye onto the tip of the index finger. But the problem is not of my competence.

21 On the other hand, I would reserve the term *tool* for devices such as knives, scissors, flints, and hammers, which not only do what the body could never do but also, with regard to the prostheses that simply help us to interact better with what is there, produce something that was not there before. They crush, subdivide, and modify forms. An improvement on the tool is the *machine*. Machines work, but without any need to be

guided by the organ whose possibilities they magnify. Once started, they work by themselves. But one might ask whether locomotive machines such as the bicycle and even the motorcar, which still require the direct collaboration (together with the strength) of the hand and foot, are not at the same time magnifying prostheses (at their peak); and in such a case an early airplane would be a machine and a magnifying prosthesis at the same time, while a jumbo jet is pure machine, as much as the mechanical loom. But substitutive, extensive, and intrusive prostheses, tools and machines are abstract types to which the various objects can be variably related according to the use made of them and their degree of sophistication.

22 In the eighties I wrote an essay on mirrors (now in Eco 1985). In it, I developed some observations made in *A Theory of Semiotics*, but the thrust of the piece was directed at a profound revision of the concepts of icon and hypoicon, which is why I am reproducing the fundamental aspects here.

23 What is the meaning of "virtual," which seems opposed to "real"? Maltese (1976) "picked up on" an expression of mine (1975: 256), where I say that a virtual image is not a material expression (by which I obviously meant that it is not a drawing or a painting, and that it disappears when the mirrored object moves away) and accused me of idealist antimaterialism—never mind, the rhetoric of the time was like that. The distinction between real and virtual images is not mine, it comes from optics, according to which shadow-theater and cinematographic images (and even the images formed in concave mirrors, which can be collected on a screen) are real, while specular images are virtual (see Gibson 1966: 227). The virtual image of the mirror is so called, because the spectator perceives it as if it were inside the mirror, while the mirror has no "inside."

24 It is surprising to find a scientist remarkably familiar with the eye (Gregory 1986) who continues to wonder at this phenomenon (and on the fact that mirrors do not invert the up-down dimension). Gregory realizes that this must be a cognitive matter (we imagine ourselves, as I was saying, inside the mirror) but seems dissatisfied with the answer, maintaining that if things were really like this, we would have to have an "extraordinary" mental skill, as if we did not already possess others that seem even more extraordinary. Gregory also quotes Gardner (1964), who had also made the obvious observation that mirrors do not reverse anything at all. But not even this is enough for Gregory, and he adds another reason for surprise: that mirrors also reverse depth, and that is to say, if we walk away from a mirror, say, toward the north, the image moves away from us toward the south, and it gets smaller (I would add that it's hardly likely to come running straight at us). But, Gregory says, mirrors do not reverse concave and convex. All you have to do is think of the mirror as a prosthesis, or an eye on the index finger, and it will let me see what I would see if someone were standing in front of me: if that some-

one moves away, his image gets smaller, but if he has a potbelly, then it
will stay that way, nor will the pit of his stomach contract toward the inside.

25 Even if the "tail" had made identifying notches on Mr. X's shoes, he
would only have a *very strong* clue that those shoes are Mr. X's. In point of
fact, he would perceive only the imprint left by shoes (in general) that reveal the presence of notches (in general) similar to the ones he had made
on a particular sole.

26 From a practical point of view, it would be fairly exceptional were I to
show someone my jacket reflected in the mirror to tell him that by the
word *jacket* I mean something made in such and such a way, but let's
imagine that the jacket I am indicating is in the other room and my interlocutor can see it only thanks to the effect of intrusively opposed mirrors: the specular prosthesis allows him to perceive an object that, in the
second instance, shall be chosen as an ostensive sign.

27 Bacchini (1995) has written an ingenious essay in which, starting from my
texts, he intends to demonstrate that the mirror image is a sign. After
what I have been reiterating up to now, it ought to be clear that various
theses can be upheld as long as my premise is not accepted: I am talking
about the experience of a person when he looks at himself in a mirror,
knowing that it is a mirror. Bacchini's view is that this premise is "ideological" and deems it to be on "too low a level" (he prefers complex mises-
en-scène like the one staged by Orson Welles). But in my view this low
level is fundamental, and if this premise is ideological, it is so just like any
other premise. Once this low level has been overcome, all Bacchini's examples concern cases of lies, error, trickery, and catoptric theaters, which
I had already considered in Eco 1985. Bacchini says that we need to create
a *pragmatics* of mirrors (and I agree, if only because this was the title of a
paragraph of my essay) and that we need to consider various "epistemic
modalities." Agreed, and I think that this discourse can be linked to the
proposal made by Fabbri that I quoted previously, whereby a theory of
enunciation also becomes central to a visual semiotics, and to a semiotics
of perception in general. However, in this discourse I am considering
only one epistemic modality (that of the person aware he is standing in
front of a mirror); I am not interested in the others. I believe it is legitimate to make choices and to select obvious cases to show that they are not
obvious at all. And then I did not deal with the discourse on imprints,
which I have taken up again in these pages. Bacchini says that the imprint is temporally but not spatially separate from the imprinter, because
it is "contiguous" to the imprinter, to which it corresponds point by point.
Here I think there is some confusion between temporal copresence, spatial contiguity, and congruence (purely formal, which also subsists with
regard to the death mask of a person long dead).

28 "Probably we shall never succeed in knowing the phylogenetic itinerary
that has allowed us to pass from the perception of the reflected image to

the development of technologies aimed at the artificial production of images " (Maldonado 1992: 40).

29 I cannot but agree with Maldonado (1992: 59 ff.): a new typology of iconic constructs, all the way to virtual reality—and therefore not static but dynamic and interactive iconic constructs—sets new problems that require new conceptual instruments. Except for the fact that the growth of these instruments now finds itself at a vague crossroads somewhere between the various cognitive sciences. I think that a general semiotics must explain the fact that these phenomena *exist* (and question us), and not *how* they work in a cognitive sense.

30 One argument in favor of the power of surrogate stimuli could be that in general we have a (genuine) sexual reaction when confronted with *images* of human bodies, as happens with actors or with models for pornographic magazines. It is not valid to argue that should those who have fallen victim to the appeal of such images happen to meet the original, they often realize that he or she is far less seductive in the flesh: the photo was simply preceded by a mise-en-scène (makeup, cunning camera angles and lighting) or even skillfully retouched. This would simply prove that hypoicons can lead us, through surrogate stimuli, to perceive something that does not exist in nature. Nor is it valid to object that, over the centuries, various persons have excited themselves sexually by looking at images that we do not consider realistic at all, such as African Venuses, or poor-quality woodcuts depicting Eve in some *Biblia Pauperum*. It would be facile to say that the image plays a secondary role in such processes of excitement, while the primary role is reserved for the imagination and the strength of desire. If things were exclusively like this, it would still not explain why the hypoicon has always been used as an erotic stimulus—or why, even when desire is very strong, some might not find the image of a right triangle sufficient to their purposes. Therefore, despite the low definition of surrogate stimuli, in different ages and cultures hypoicons have provided erotic excitement. This leads us to think that the notion of "vicariousness" of a stimulus cannot be fixed on the basis of strict criteria but depends on the culture and disposition of the subjects.

31 From the point of view of the present discourse, it is irrelevant whether these procedures concern those processes of the further pertinentization of the substance of the content on which many artistic operations are based (see *A Theory of Semiotics*, 3.7.1).

32 Given that Sonesson (1989) says some things on what follows that I am in agreement with, I should like to specify that I dealt with precisely this problem in my speech to the annual conference of the Italian Association for Semiotic Studies, held at Vicenza in 1987 (Eco 1987).

33 See Simone 1995. For the recognition of phonemes, see also Innis (1994: 5), who takes up and develops the ideas of Bühler ("Phonetik und Phonologie," 1931): identifying a sound as a form (*Klanggestalt*) and recognizing an object (*Dinggestalt*) are said to be the same type of learning.

In reference to the typology of types of abduction (Eco 1983 and Bonfantini 1980, 1983, 1987), I could say that phonematic recognition represents
an abduction of the first type, where the rule is already known, and is in
fact a matter of recognizing the token—the result—as a case of that rule.
But the fact that the abduction is almost automatic does not mean that it
is not abduction 562 but hypothesis.

34 Cryptographers maintain that every coded message can be decoded, as
long as one knows that it is a message.

35 "What these sorts of iconic signs do have in common, though, is that the
use of them *as* iconic signs supposes that they have themselves immediately been perceived as sensory objects in their own right prior to their
use as representative of something else" (Ransdell 1979: 58). After almost
forty years of discussion, it is now necessary once more to give the rights
of the matter to Barthes (1964a), when apropos of photography (not
paintings) he spoke of a message without a code. What he was talking
about was none other than what I call alpha mode. In this sense he said
that the image simply denoted. For him, the shift to beta mode occurred
in the moment of connotation, when the image is seen as a text and interpreted (above and beyond that which may be called perceptual interpretation).

36 Beyond this threshold we move on to conceptual similarity. A relation of
perceptual similarity can be established between a man and a woman, but
the similarity between husband and wife, or between in-laws, is purely
conceptual.

37 At a certain point Peirce says: "Icons are so completely substituted for
their objects as hardly to be distinguished from them... So in contemplating a painting, there is a moment when we lose the consciousness that it is
not the thing, the distinction of the real and the copy disappears, and it is
for the moment a pure dream—not any particular existence and yet not
general. At that moment we are contemplating *an icon*" (CP 3.362). Shall
we grant that at a certain point our great and venerated master was
merely using a metaphor?

WORKS CITED

Translator's Note: As a general rule, even where English-language translations of foreign-language books already exist, I usually translated from the original with the help of the author.

ALAC, MORANA

1997   *Gli schemi concettuali nel pensiero di Donald Davidson*. Degree thesis in semiotics. University of Bologna. Faculty of Literature and Philosophy. A. Y. 1995–96.

ALBRECHT, ERHARD

1975   *Sprache und Philosophie*. Berlin: Deutscher Verlag der Wissenschaften.

APEL, KARL-OTTO

1972   "From Kant to Peirce: The Semiotical Transformation of Transcendental Logic." In Beck, L. W., ed. *Proceedings of the Third Kant Congress*. Dordrecht: Reidel: 90–105.

1975   *Der Denkweg von Charles S. Peirce*. Frankfurt: Suhrkamp.

1995   "Transcendental Semiotics and Hypothetical Metaphysics of Evolution: A Peircean or quasi-Peircean Answer to a Recurrent Problem of post-Kantian Philosophy." In Ketner 1995: 366–97.

ARNHEIM, RUDOLF

1969   *Visual Thinking*. Berkeley: University of California Press.

AUBENQUE, PIERRE
1962 *Le problème de l'être chez Aristote*. Paris: PUF.

BACCHINI, FABIO
1995 "Sugli specchi." *Il cannocchiale* 3: 211–24.

BARLOW, HORACE, COLIN BLAKEMORE, AND MIRANDA WESTON-SMITH, EDS.
1990 *Images and Understanding*. Cambridge: Cambridge UP.

BARTHES, ROLAND
1964a "Rhétorique de l'image." *Communications* 4: 40–51.
1964b "Eléments de sémiologie." *Communications* 4 (Eng. trans. *Elements of Semiology*. Noonday Press 1977).

BENELLI, BEATRICE
1991 "Categorizzazione, rappresentazione e linguaggio: Aspetti e tendenze dello sviluppo del pensiero concettuale." In Cacciari, ed. 1991: 5–46.

BERSELLI BERSANI, GABRIELE
1995 *Riferimento ed interpretazione nominale*. Milano: Angeli.

BERTUCCELLI PAPI, MARCELLA
1993 *Che cos'è la pragmatica*. Milano: Bompiani.

BETTETINI, GIANFRANCO
1971 *L'indice del realismo*. Milano: Bompiani.
1975 *Produzione del senso e messa in scena*. Milano: Bompiani.
1991 *La simulazione visiva*. Milano: Bompiani.
1996 *L'audiovisivo*. Milano: Bompiani.

BICKERTON, DEREK
1981 *The Roots of Language*. Ann Arbor: Karoma.

BONFANTINI, MASSIMO A.
1976 *L'esistenza della realtà*. Milano: Bompiani.
1987 *La semiosi e l'abduzione*. Milano: Bompiani.

BONFANTINI, MASSIMO A., AND ROBERTO GRAZIA
1976 "Teoria della conoscenza e funzione dell'icona in Peirce." *VS* 15: 1–15.

BONFANTINI, MASSIMO A., AND GIAMPAOLO PRONI
1983 "To Guess or Not to Guess." In Eco and Sebeok, eds., 1983: 119–34.

BONOMI, ANDREA
1975   *Le vie del riferimento.* Milano: Bompiani.
1994   *Lo spirito della narrazione.* Milano: Bompiani.

BONOMI, ANDREA, ED.
1973   *La struttura logica del linguaggio.* Milano: Bompiani.

BOUISSAC, PAUL, MICHAEL HERZFELD, AND ROLAND POSNER, EDS.
1986   *Iconicity.* Tübingen: Stauffenburg.

BRANDT, PER AAGE
1989   "The Dynamics of Modality." *Recherches sémiotiques / Semiotic Inquiry* 9.1/3: 3–16.

BRUNER, JEROME
1986   *Actual Minds and Possible Worlds.* Cambridge: Harvard UP.
1990   *Acts of Meaning.* Cambridge: Harvard UP.

BRUNER, JEROME, ET AL.
1956   *A Study of Thinking.* New York: Science Editions.

BURRELL, HARRY
1927   *The Platypus: Its Discovery, Zoological Position, Form and Characteristics, Habits, Life History, etc.* Sydney: Angus & Robertson.

CACCIARI, CRISTINA
1995   Preface to Cacciari, ed. 1995.

CACCIARI, CRISTINA, ED.
1991   *Esperienza percettiva e linguaggio: Numero speciale di VS* 59/60.
1995   *Similarity.* Sl.: Brepols.

CALABRESE, OMAR
1981   "La sintassi della vertigine: Sguardi, specchi, ritratti." *VS* 29: 3–32.
1985   *1 linguaggio dell'arte.* Milano: Bompiani.

CARAMAZZA, A., A. E. HILLIS, B. C. RAPP, AND C. ROMANI
1990   "The Multiple Semantic Hypothesis: Multiple Confusions, *Cognitive Neuropsychology* 7.

CARNAP, RUDOLF
1955   "Meaning and Synonymy in Natural Languages." *Philosophical Studies* 7: 33–47.

CASATI, ROBERTO AND ACHILE C. VARZI
1994   *Holes and Other Superficialities.* Cambridge: MIT Press.

CASSIRER, ERNST

1918   *Kants Leben und Lehre.* (Eng. trans. *Kant's Life and Thought,* Yale UP, 1986).

CHIARA, DALLA, MARIA LUISA, AND GIULIANO TORALDO DI FRANCIA

1985   "Individuals, Kinds and Names in Physics." *VS* 40: 29–50.

DAVIDSON, DONALD

1984   "On the Very Idea of Conceptual Scheme." In *Inquiries into Truth and Interpretation.* Oxford: Oxford UP: 183–98.

1986   "A Nice Derangement of Epitaphs." In Lepore, E. and B. McLaughlin, eds. *Actions and Events: Perspectives on the Philosophy of Donald Davidson.* Oxford: Blackwell: 433–46.

DELEUZE, GILLES

1963   *La philosophie critique de Kant.* Paris: PUF.

DE MAURO, TULLIO

1965   *Introduzione alla semantica.* Bari: Laterza.

DENNETT, DANIEL C.

1978   *Brainstorms.* Montgomery: Bradford Books.

1991   *Consciousness Explained.* New York: Little Brown.

DIONIGI, ROBERTO

1994   *Nomi forme cose.* Bologna: Fuori Thema.

DOLEZEL, LUBOMIR

1989   "Possible Worlds and Literary Fiction." In Allen, S., ed. *Possible Worlds in Humanities, Arts and Sciences.* Berlin: De Gruyter: 221–42.

DONNELLAN, KEITH

1966   "Reference and Definite Descriptions." *The Philosophical Review* 75: 281–304.

DUCROT, OSWALD, AND JEAN-LOUIS SCHEFER

1995   *Nouveau dictionnaire encyclopédique des sciences du langage.* Paris: Seuil.

DUMMETT, MICHAEL

1973   *Frege: Philosophy of Language.* London: Duckworth.

1986   "A Nice Derangement of Epitaphs: Some Comments on Davidson and Hacking." In Lepore, E., ed. *Truth and Interpretation: On the Philosophy of Donald Davidson.* Oxford: Blackwell.

Eco, Umberto

1968   *La struttura assente*. Milano: Bompiani (2nd ed. 1980).

1971   *Le forme del contenuto*. Milano: Bompiani.

1976   *A Theory of Semiotics*. Bloomington: Indiana UP.

1975b   "Chi ha paura del cannocchiale?" *Op. cit.* 32: 5–32.

1979   *The Role of the Reader*. Bloomington: Indiana UP.

1983   "Horns, Hooves, and Shoes." In Eco and Sebeok 1993: 228–55.

1984   *Semiotics and the Philosophy of Language*. Bloomington: Indiana UP.

1987   "Introduction" to the XV Conference of the A.I.S., Vicenza 1987, on "The Signifier." *Carte semiotiche* 7, 1990: 11–16.

1990   *The Limits of Interpretation*. Bloomington: Indiana UP.

1992   *Interpretation and Overinterpretation*. Cambridge: Cambridge UP.

1994   *Six Walks in the Fictional Woods*. Cambridge: Harvard UP.

1997   "On Meaning, Logic and Verbal Language." In Dalla Chiara, M. L., et al., eds. *Structures and Norms in Science*. Dordrecht: Kluver, 431–48.

Eco, Umberto, and Costantino Marmo, eds.

1989   *On the Medieval Theory of Signs*. Amsterdam: Benjamins.

Eco, Umberto, Marco Santambrogio, and Patrizia Violi, eds.

1986   *Meaning and Mental Representations: Special issue of VS* 44/45 (now Bloomington: Indiana UP, 1988).

Eco, Umberto, and Thomas A. Sebeok, eds.

1983   *The Sign of Three*. Bloomington: Indiana UP.

Eco, Umberto, and Patrizia Violi

1987   "Instructional Semantics for Presuppositions." *Semiotica* 64.1/2: 1–39 (new version in Eco 1990).

Edelman, Gerald M.

1992   "The Science of Recognition." In *Bright Air, Brilliant Fire*. New York: Basic Books, 73–80.

Eichmann, Klaus

1988   "The Control of T Lymphocyte Activity May Involve Elements of Semiosis." In Sercarz et al. 1988: 163–68.

Ellis, Ralph D.

1995   "The Imagist Approach to Inferential Thought Patterns: The Crucial Role of Rhythm Pattern Recognition." *Pragmatics & Cognition* 3.1: 75-109.

EVANS, GARETH
1982   *The Varieties of Reference*. Oxford: Clarendon.

FABBRICHESI LEO, ROSSELLA
1981   "L'iconismo e l'interpretazione fenomenologica del concetto di somiglianza in C. S. Peirce." *ACME, Annali della Facoltà di Lettere e Filosofia dell'Università degli Studi di Milano* 34.3: 467–98 (further developed in Fabbrichesi 1986).
1983   *La polemica sull'iconismo*. Napoli: Edizioni Scientifiche Italiane.
1986   *Sulle tracce del segno*. Firenze: Nuova Italia.

FILLMORE, CHARLES
1982   "Towards a Descriptive Framework for Spatial Deixis." In Jarvella, R. J. and W. Klein, eds., *Speech, Plan and Action*. London: Wiley: 31–59.

FISETTE, JEAN
1995   "A la recherche des limites de l'interprétation." *Recherches sémiotiques / Semiotic Inquiry* 15.1/2: 91–120.

FODOR, JERRY A.
1975   *The Language of Thought*. New York: Crowell.

FODOR, JERRY A., AND ERNEST LEPORE, EDS.
1992   *Holism*. Oxford: Blackwell.

FOLLESDAL, DAGFINN
1997   "Semantics and Semiotics." In Dalla Chiara, M. L., et al., eds. *Structures and Norms in Science*. Dordrecht: Muver: 431–48.

FUMAGALLI, ARMANDO
1995   *Il reale nel linguaggio: Indicalità e realismo nella semiotica di Peirce*. Milano: Vita e Pensiero.

GARDNER, HOWARD
1985   *The Mind's New Science*. New York: Basic Books.

GARDNER, MARTIN
1964   *The Ambidextrous Universe*. New York: Penguin.

GARRONI, EMILIO
1968   *Semiotica ed estetica*. Bari: Laterza.
1972   *Progetto di semiotica*. Bari: Laterza.
1977   *Ricognizione della semiotica*. Roma: Officina.
1986   *Senso e paradosso*. Bari: Laterza.

GENTNER, DEDRE, AND ARTHUR B. MARKMAN
1995   "Similarity Is Like Analogy: Structural Alignment in Comparison." In Cacciari, ed. 1995: 11–148.

GERLACH, PETER
1977   "Probleme einer semiotischen Kunstwissenschaft." In Posner, R., and H. P. Reinecke, eds. *Zeichenprozessen*. Wiesbaden: Athenaion, 262–92.

GIBSON, JAMES J.
1950   *The Perception of the Visual World*. Boston: Houghton Mifflin.
1966   *The Senses Considered as Perceptual Systems*. Boston: Houghton Mifflin (London: Allen and Unwin, 1968).
1971   "The Information Available in Pictures." *Leonardo* 4/2: 197–99.
1978   "The Ecological Approach to Visual Perception of Pictures." *Leonardo* 11/3: 227–35.

GILSON, ETIENNE
1948   *L'être et l'essence*. Paris: Vrin (enlarged 2nd ed. 1981).

GOMBRICH, ERNEST
1956   *Art and Illusion*. The A. W. Mellon Lectures in Fine Arts (now New York: Bollingen, 1961).
1975   *The Mirror and the Map: Philosophical Transactions of the Royal Society of London* 270: 119–49.
1990   "Pictorial Instructions." In Barlow et al. 1990: 26–45.

GOODMAN, NELSON
1951   *The Structure of Appearance*. Cambridge: Harvard UP.
1968   *Languages of Art*. Indianapolis: Bobbs-Merrill.
1970   "Seven Structures on Similarity." In Swanson, ed. *Experience and Theory*. Boston: U of Massachusetts P (now in Goodman, N. *Problems and Projects*. Indianapolis: Bobbs-Merrill, 1972).
1990   "Pictures in the Mind?" In Barlow et al. 1990: 358–64.

GOULD, STEPHEN JAY
1991   *Bully for Brontosaurus*. London: Hutchinson Radius.

GREGORY, RICHARD
1981   *Mind in Science*. Cambridge-London: Cambridge UP.
1986   *Old Perceptions*. London: Methuen.
1990   "How Do We Interpret Images?" In Barlow et al. 1990: 310–30.

GREIMAS, ALGIRDAS JULIEN
1983   "De la colère." *Du sens 2*. Paris: Seuil.
1984   "Sémiotique figurative et sémiotique plastique." *Actes sémiotiques* 6: 60.

GREIMAS, ALGIRDAS JULIEN, AND JOSEPH COURTÉS
1979   *Sémiotique: Dictionnaire raisonné de la théorie du langage*. Paris: Hachette. (Eng. trans. *Semiotics and Language: An Analytical Dictionary,* Indiana UP, 1983).

GROUPE μ
1992   *Traité du signe visuel*. Paris: Seuil.

HABERMAS, JURGEN
1995   "Peirce and Communication." In Ketner 1995: 243–66.

HAUSMAN, CARL R.
1990   "In and Out in Peirce's percepts." *Transactions of Charles Sanders Peirce Society* 6.3: 271–308.

HEIDEGGER, MARTIN
1915   "Die Kategorien und Bedeutungslehre des Duns Scotus." *Frühe Schriften*. Frankfurt/m: Klostermann, 1972.
1950   *Holzwege*. Frankfurt/m: Klostermann.
1929   *Was ist Metaphysik?* Bonn: Cohen.
1973   *Kant und das Problem der Metaphysik*. Frankfurt/m.: Klostermann, 4th ed. 1973. (Eng. trans. *Kant and the Problem of Metaphysics (Studies in Continental Thought)*, Indiana UP, 1997).

HILPINEN, RISTO
1995   "Peirce on Language and Reference." In Ketner 1995: 303.

HJELMSLEV, LOUIS
1943   *Prolegomena to a Theory of Language*. Madison: Wisconsin UP.

HOCHBERG, JULIAN
1972   "The Representation of Things and People." In Gombrich, E., et al. *Art, Perception, and Reality*. Baltimore: Johns Hopkins UP.

HOFSTADTER, DOUGLAS
1979   *Gödel, Escher, Bach*. New York: Basic Books.

HOGREBE, WOLFRAM
1974   *Kant und das Problem einer transzendentalen Semantik*. Freiburg-München: Alber.

HOOKWAY, CHRISTOPHER
1988 "Pragmaticism and 'Kantian Realism?'" *VS* 49: 103–12.

HOUSER, NATHAN
1992 Introduction. In Kloesel, C., and N. Houser, eds. *The Essential Peirce; Selected Philosophical Writings.* Bloomington: Indiana UP.

HUBEL, DAVID H.
1982 "Explorations of the Primary Visual Cortex, 1955-1978 (a review)." *Nature* 299: 515–24.

HUBEL, DAVID H., AND TORSTEN N. WIESEL
1959 "Receptive Fields of Single Neurons in the Cat's Striate Cortex." *Journal of Physiology* 148: 105–54.

HUMPHREYS, GLYN W., AND M. JANE RIDDOCH
1995 "The Old Town No Longer Looks the Same: Computation of Visual Similarity after Brain Damage." In Cacciari, ed. 1995: 15–40.

HUSSERL, EDMUND
1922 *Logische Untersuchungen* (3rd ed.). Halle: Niemayer. (Eng. trans. *Logical Investigations,* Prometheus Books, 1996).
1970 "Zur Logik der Zeichen (Semiotik)." In van Breda, H. L., ed. *Husserliana* XII. Den Haag: Nijhoff, 340–73.

INNIS, ROBERT E.
1994 *Consciousness and the Play of Signs.* Bloomington: Indiana UP.

JACKENDOFF, RAY
1983 *Semantics and Cognition.* Cambridge: MIT Press.
1987 *Consciousness and the Computational Mind.* Cambridge: MIT Press.

JAKOBSON, ROMAN
1970 "Da i net v mimike." Jazyk i čelovek (English trans. "Motor Signs for 'Yes' and 'No.'" *Language in Society* 1.

JOB, REMO
1991 "Relazione tra fattori visivi e fattori semantici nell'identificazione di oggetti: Alcuni dati neuropsicologici." In Cacciari, ed. 1991: 197–206.

JOHNSON, MARK
1989 "Image: Schematic Bases of Meaning." *Recherches sémiotiques / Semiotic Inquiry* 9.1/3: 109–18.

JOHNSON-LAIRD, PHILIP
1983   *Mental Models*. Cambridge: Cambridge UP.
1988   *The Computer and the Mind*. Cambridge: Harvard UP.

KALKHOFEN, HERMANN
1972   *"Pictorial* Stimuli Considered as *Iconic* Signs." Ulm: mimeo.

KANT, IMMANUEL
1781 – 87   *Kritik der reiner Vernunft: In Kants gesammelte Schriften*. III–IV.
         Berlin-Leipzig, 1903–04.
1783   *Prolegomena zu einer jeden künftigen Metaphysik*. In *Kants gesam-
         melte Schriften*. IX. Berlin-Leipzig, 1911.
1790   *Kritik der Urteilskraft*. In *Kants gesammelte Schriften*. V. Berlin-
         Leipzig, 1908–13.
1800   *Logik*. In *Kants gesammelte Schriften*. IX. Berlin-Leipzig, 1923.
1936–38 Opus Postumum. In *Kants gesammelte Schriften*. XXI, XXII.
         Berlin-Leipzig. 1936–38.

KATZ, J., AND J. FODOR
1963   "The Structure of a Semantic Theory." *Language* 39: 170–210.

KELEMEN, JÁNOS
1991   "La comunicazione estetica nella *Critica del Giudizio*. Appunti per
         la ricostruzione della semiotica di Kant." *Il cannocchiale* 3: 33–50.

KENNEDY, JOHN M.
1974   *A Psychology of Picture Perception*. San Francisco: Jossey-Bass.

KETNER, KENNETH L., ED.
1995   *Peirce and Contemporary Thought*. New York: Fordham UP.

KJØRUP, SØREN
1978   "Iconic Codes and Pictorial Speech Acts." *Orbis litterarum 4*.
         Copenhagen: Munksgaard: 101–22.

KOSSLYN, STEPHEN M.
1983   *Ghosts in the Mind's Machine: Creating and Using Images in the
         Brain*. New York: Norton.

KRAMPEN, MARTIN
1983   *Icons of the Road*. Special issue of *Semiotica* 43.1/2.

KRIPKE, SAUL
1971   "Identity and Necessity." In Munitz, M. K., ed. *Identity and Indi-
         viduation*. New York: New York UP.
1972   "Naming and Necessity." In Davidson, D., and G. Harman, eds.

Semantics of Natural Language. Dordrecht: Reidel; 2nd ed. Oxford: Blackwell.

1979   "A Puzzle about Belief." In Margalit, A., ed. *Meaning and Use*. Dordrecht: Reidel: 239–83.

KUBOVY, MICHAEL
1995   "Symmetry and Similarity." In Cacciari, ed. 1995: 41–60.

KUHN, THOMAS
1989   "Possible Worlds in History of Sciences." In Allen, S., ed. *Possible Worlds in Humanities, Arts and Sciences*. Berlin: De Gruyter, 9–31.

LAKOFF, GEORGE
1978   "Cognitive Models and Prototype Theory." In Neisser, ed. 1978: 63–99.
1987   *Women, Fire, and Dangerous Things*. Chicago: Chicago UP.

LEECH, G.
1974   *Semantics*. Harmondsworth: Penguin.

LEONARDI, PAOLO, AND MARCO SANTAMBROGIO, EDS.
1995   *On Quine: New Essays*. Cambridge. Cambridge UP.

LEWIS, DAVID K.
1973   *Counterfactuals*. Oxford: Blackwell.

LYNCH, KEVIN
1966   *A View from the Road*. Cambridge: MIT Press.

LYONS, JOHN
1968   *Introduction to Structural Linguistics*. Cambridge: Cambridge UP.
1977   *Semantics* I-II. Cambridge: Cambridge UP.

MALDONADO, TOMÁS
1974   "Appunti sull'iconicità." In *Avanguardia e razionalità*. Torino: Einaudi, 254–98.
1992   "Appunti sull'iconicità." In *Reale e virtuale*. Milano: Feltrinelli, 119–44.

MALTESE, CORRADO
1978   "Iconismo e esperienza." In *Aspetti dell'iconismo: Acts of the IV Conference of the A.I.S.S.* September 1976 (mimeo): 55–71.

MAMELI, MATTEO
1997   *Synechism: Aspetti del pensiero di C. S. Peirce*. Degree thesis in semiotics. U of Bologna, Faculty of Literature and Philosophy. A.Y. 1995–96.

Marconi, Diego

1995 "On the Structure of Lexical Competence." *Aristotelian Society Proceedings*: 131–150.

1986 *Dizionari e enciclopedie*. 2nd ed.: Torino: Giappichelli.

1997 *Lexical Competence*. Cambridge: MIT Press.

Marconi, Diego, and Gianni Vattimo

1986 "Introductory Note" to the Italian translation of Rorty 1979.

Marr, David

1987 "Understanding Vision from Images to Shapes." In Vaina, L., ed. *Matters of Intelligence*. Dordrecht: Reidel: 7–58.

Marr, David, and H. Keith Nishishara

1978a "Visual Information Processing: Artificial Intelligence and the Sensorium of Sight." *Technology Review* 81.1: 2–23.

1978b "Representation and Recognition of the Spatial Organization of Three-Dimensional Shapes." *Proceedings of the Royal Society of London* 200 (B): 269–94.

Marr, David, and Lucia Vaina

1982 "Representation and Recognition of the Movements of Shapes." *Proceedings of the Royal Society of London* 214 (B): 501–24.

Martinetti, Piero

1946 *Kant*. Milano: Bocca.

Mathieu, Vittorio

1984 *Introduzione a I. Kant: Opus Postumum*. Bari: Laterza.

Maturana, Humberto

1970 "Neurophysiology of Cognition." In Garvin, Paul, ed. *Cognition: A Multiple View*. New York: Spartan Books.

May, Michael, and Frederik Stjernfelt

1996 "Measurement, Diagram, Art." In Michelsen, A., and F. Stjernfelt, eds. *Billeder fra det fjerne / Images from Afar*. Sl: Kulturby (Universitetsforlaget i Oslo): 191–204.

McCawley, James D.

1971 "Where Do Noun Phrases Come From?" In Steinberg, D. D., and L. A. Jakobovits., eds. *Semantics*. London: Cambridge UP: 217–31.

1981 *Everything That Linguists Have Always Wanted to Know about Logic*. Chicago: U of Chicago P.

MEDIN, DOUGLAS L., AND ROBERT L. GOLDSTONE
1995 "The Predicates of Similarity." In Cacciari, ed. 1995: 83–110.

MERLEAU-PONTY, MAURICE
1945 *Phénomenologie de la perception*. Paris: Gallimard. (English translation *Phenomenology of Perception*, Routledge, 1992).

MERRELL, FLOYD
1981 "On Understanding the Logic of 'Understanding': A Reincarnation of Some Peircean Thought." *Ars Semeiotica* 4.2: 161–86.
1991 "The Tenuous 'Reality' of Signs." *Signs Becoming Signs*. Bloomington: Indiana UP.

METZ, CHRISTIAN
1964 "Le cinéma: Langue ou langage?" *Communications* 4: 52–90.
1968a "La grande syntagmatique du film narratif." *Communications* 8: 120–24.
1968b *Essais sur la signification au cinéma*. Paris: Klincksieck.

MINSKY, MARVIN
1985 *The Society of Mind*. New York: Simon & Schuster.

MORRIS, CHARLES
1946 *Signs, Language, and Behavior*. New York: Prentice Hall.

NEISSER, ULRICH
1976 *Cognition and Reality*. San Francisco: Freeman.
1978 "From Direct Perception to Conceptual Structure." In Neisser, ed. 1978: 11–24.

NEISSER, ULRICH, ED.
1987 *Concepts and Conceptual Development: Ecological and Intellectual Factors in Categorization*. Cambridge-London: Cambridge UP.

NERGAARD, SIRI, ED.
1995 *Teorie contemporanee della traduzione*. Milano: Bompiani.

NESHER, DAN
1984 "Are There Grounds for Identifying 'Ground' with 'Interpretant'?" In *Peirce's Theory of Meaning: Transactions of Charles Sanders Peirce Society* 20, 1984: 303–24.

NEUBAUER, FRITZ, AND JÁNOS S. PETÖFI
1981 "Word Semantics, Lexicon System and Text Interpretation." In Eikmeyer, H. J., and H. Rieser, eds. *Words, Worlds and Contexts*. Berlin: De Gruyter: 344–77.

Nida, Eugene
1975   *Componential Analysis of Meaning*. The Hague: Mouton.

Nietzsche, Friedrich
1873   "Ueber Wahrheit und Lüge im aussermoralischen Sinne." In *Grossoktav-Ausgabe*. Leipzig, 1895.

Oehler, Klaus
1979   "Peirce's Foundation of a Semiotic Theory of Cognition." *Peirce Studies* 1: 67–66.
1995   "A Response to Habermas." In Ketner 1995: 267–71.

Osmond-Smith, David
1972   "The Iconic Process in Musical Communication." *VS* 3: 31–42.
1973   "Formal Iconism in Music." *VS* 5: 43–54.

Ouellet, Pierre
1992   "Signification et sensation." *Nouveaux actes sémiotiques* 20. Limoges: Pulim.

Paci, Enzo
1957   "Relazionismo e schematismo trascendentale." In *Dall'esistenzialismo al relazionismo*. Messina: D'Anna.

Palmer, Stephen
1978   "Fundamental Aspects of Cognitive Representation." In Rosch and Lloyd, eds. 1978.

Pareyson, Luigi
1954   *Estetica*. Torino: Edizioni di "Filosofia." (Milano: Bompiani, 1988).
1989   *Filosofia della libertà*. Genova: Melangolo.

Pasolini, Pier Paolo
1966   "La lingua scritta della realtà." In *Empirismo eretico*. Milano: Garzanti, 1972: 198-226. (Eng. trans. *Heretical Empiricism*, Louise K. Barnett (ed.)).
1967a   "Discorso sul piano sequenza ovvero il cinema come semiologia della realtà." In *Linguaggio e ideologia nel film (Atti della Tavola Rotonda alla III Mostra Internazionale del Nuovo Cinema, Pesaro, maggio 1967)*. Novara: Cafieri, 1968: 135–50.
1967b   "Il codice dei codici." In *Empirismo eretico*. Milano: Garzanti, 1972: 277–84.

Peirce, Charles S.
1934–48 Collected Papers. Cambridge: Harvard UP.
1980   *Semiotica*. Torino: Einaudi.

1982–83 *Writings of Charles S. Peirce*. Bloomington: Indiana UP.

1984 *Le leggi dell'ipotesi*. Milano: Bompiani.

1992 *Categorie*. Bari: Laterza.

PÉREZ CARREFIO, FRANCISCA

1988 *Los placeres del parecido: Icono y representación*. Madrid: Visor.

PERRI, ANTONIO

1996a *Scrittura azteca, semiosi, interpretazione*. Ph.D. thesis in semiotics, U of Bologna (for a more succinct version, see Perri 1996b).

1996b "Verso una semiotica della scrittura azteca." In De Finis, G., J. Galarza, and A. Perri. *La parola fiorita: Per un'antropologia delle scritture mesoamericane*. Roma: Il Mondo 3 Edizioni: 141-286.

PETITOT-COCORDA, JEAN

1983 "Paradigme catastrophique et perception categorielle." *Recherches sémiotiques / Semiotic Inquiry* 3.3: 207–47.

1985a *Les catastrophes de la parole*. Paris: Maloine.

1985b *Morphogénèse du sens*. vol. l. Paris: PUF.

1989 "Modèles morphodinamiques pour la grammaire cognitive et sémiotique modale." *Recherches sémiotiques / Semiotic Inquiry* 9.1–3: 17–51.

1995 "La réorientation naturaliste de la phénomenologie." *Archives de philosophie* 58.4: 631–58.

PHILIPPE, M.-D.

1975 *Une philosophie de l'être est-elle encore possible?* III: *Le problème de* L'Ens *et de* L'Esse. Paris: Téqui.

PIAGET, JEAN

1955 *La représentation du monde chez l'enfant*. Paris: PUF.

PIATTELLI PALMARINI, MASSIMO

1995 *L'arte di persuadere*. Milano: Mondadori.

PICARDI, EVA

1992 *Linguaggio e analisi filosofica*. Bologna: Patron.

PIERANTONI, RUGGERO

1981 *Fisiologia e storia della visione*. Torino: Boringhieri.

PISANTY, VALENTINA

1993 *Leggere la fiaba*. Milano: Bompiani.

POPPER, KARL
1969   *Conjectures and Refutations*. London: Routledge.

POSNER, ROLAND
1986   "Iconicity in Syntax." In Bouissac et al., eds. 1986: 305–38.

PRIETO, LUIS
1975   *Pertinence et pratique*. Paris: Minuit.

PRODI, GIORGIO
1977   *Le basi materiali della significazione*. Milano: Bompiani.
1988   "Signs and Codes in Immunology." In Sercarz et al. 1988: 53–64.

PRONI, GIAMPAOLO
1990   *Introduzione a Peirce*. Milano: Bompiani.
1992   *La fondazione della semiotica in C. S. Peirce*. Ph.D. thesis in semiotics. U of Bologna, A. Y. 1991–92.

PUTNAM, HILARY
1975   "The Meaning of Meaning." In Gunderson, K., ed. *Language, Mind, and Knowledge*. U of Minnesota P. Now in Putnam, H. *Mind, Language and Reality*. London: Cambridge UP: 215–71.
1981   *Reason, Truth, and History*. Cambridge: Cambridge UP.
1987   *The Many Faces of Realism*. LaSalle: Open Court.
1992   *Il pragmatismo: Una questione aperta*. Bari: Laterza.

PYLYSHYN, ZENON W.
1973   "What the Mind's Eye Tells the Mind's Brain: A Critique of Mental Imagery." *Psychological Bulletin* 8: 1–14.

QUINE, WILLARD V. O.
1951   "Two Dogmas of Empiricism." In *From a Logical Point of View*. Cambridge: Harvard UP, 1953.
1960   *Word and Object*. Cambridge: MIT Press.
1995   *From Stimulus to Science*. Cambridge: Harvard UP.

RANSDELL, JOSEPH
1979   "The Epistemic Function of Iconicity in Perception." *Peirce Studies* 1, 1979: 51–66.

RASTIER, FRANCOIS
1994   "La microsémantique." In Rastier, F., et al. *Sémantique pour l'analyse*. Paris: Masson.

REED, STEPHEN K.
1988   *Cognition: Theory and Application*. Pacific Grove: Brooks-Cole.

ROBERTS, DON D.
1973   *The Existential Graphs of Charles S. Peirce.* The Hague: Mouton.

RORTY, RICHARD
1979   *Philosophy and the Mirror of Nature.* Princeton UP.

ROSCH, ELEANOR
1978   "Principles of Categorization." In Rosch and Lloyd, eds. *Conditioned Categorization.* Hillsdale: Erlbaum: 15–35.

ROSCH, ELEANOR, AND B. B. LLOYD, EDS.
1978   *Cognition and Categorization.* Hillsdale: Erlbaum.

ROSCH, ELEANOR, AND CAROLINE B. MERVIS
1975   "Family Resemblances: Studies in the Internal Structure of Categories." *Cognitive Psychology* 7: 573–605.

ROSCH, ELEÁNOR, ET AL.
1976   "Basic Objects in Natural Categories." *Cognitive Psychology* 8: 382–440.

ROSSI, PAOLO
1997   *La nascita della scienza moderna.* Bari: Laterza.

RUSSELL, BERTRAND
1905   "On denoting." *Mind* 14: 479–93.
1940   "The Object-Language." In *An Inquiry into Meaning and Truth.* London: Allen & Unwin.

SACKS, OLIVER
1985   *The Man Who Mistook His Wife for a Hat.* London: Duckworth.

SAINT-MARTIN, FERNANDE
1987a   "Pour une reformulation du modèle visuel de Umberto Eco." *Protée*, autumn: 104–14.
1987b   *Sémiologie du langage visuel.* Sillery: Québec UP.
1988   "De la fonction perceptive dans la constitution du champ visuel." *Protée* 16.1/2: 202–13.
1990   *Semiotics of Visual Language.* Bloomington: Indiana UP.

SALMON, NATHAN U.
1981   *Reference and Essence.* Princeton: Princeton UP.

SANTAMBROGIO, MARCO
1992   *Forma e oggetto.* Milano: Saggiatore.

SANTAMBROGIO, MARCO, ED.
1992   *Introduzione alla filosofia analitica del linguaggio*. Bari: Laterza.

SCHANK, ROGER, AND R. P. ABELSON
1977   *Scripts, Plans, Goals, and Understanding*. Hillsdale: Erlbaum.

SEARLE, JOHN
1979   "Literal Meaning." In *Expression and Meaning*. Cambridge: Cambridge UP: 116–36.
1985   *The Construction of Social Reality*. New York: Free Press.

SEBEOK, THOMAS A.
1972   *Perspectives in Zoosemiotics*. The Hague: Mouton.
1976   "Six Species of Signs." In *Contribution to the Doctrine of Signs*. Bloomington: Indiana U: 117–42.
1979   "Iconicity." In *The Sign and Its Masters*. Austin: U of Texas P: 107–27.
1991   *A Sign Is Just a Sign*. Bloomington: Indiana UP.
1994   *An Introduction to Semiotics*. Toronto: Toronto UP.

SEBEOK, THOMAS A., ED.
1978   *Animal Communication*. Bloomington: Indiana UP.

SELLARS, WILFRID
1978   "The Role of Imagination in Kant's Theory of Experience." In Johnston, Henry W., Jr., ed. *Categories: A Colloquium*. Pennsylvania State U.

SEMPRINI, VALENTINA
1997   *La rappresentazione del conflitto nella letteratura a fumetti*. Degree thesis in semiotics. U of Bologna, Faculty of Literature and Philosophy. A. Y,. 1995–96.

SERCARZ, ELI, FRANCO CELADA, AVRON MITCHISON, AND TOMIO TADO, EDS.
1988   *The Semiotics of Cellular Communication in the Immune System*. Berlin: Springer.

SHERZER, JOEL
1974   "L'indicazione tra i Cuna di San Blas." *VS* 7: 57–72.

SIMONE, RAFFAELE
1995   "The Search for Similarity in the Linguist's Cognition." In Cacciari, ed. 1995: 149–57.

SONESSON, GÖRAN
1989 *Pictorial Concepts*. Malmö: Lund UP.
1994 "Pictorial Semiotics, Gestalt Theory, and the Ecology of Perception." *Semiotica* 993/4: 319–400.

SPERBER, DAN, AND DEIRDRE WILSON
1986 *Relevance*. Cambridge: Harvard UP.

STRAWSON, PETER F.
1950 "On Referring." *Mind* 59: 320–44.

TARSKI, ALFRED
1944 "The Semantic Conception of Truth." *Philosophy and Phenomenological Research* 4: 341–76.

TODOROV, TZVETAN
1982 *La conquête de l'Amerique*. Paris: Seuil. (Eng. trans. *The Conquest of America: The Question of the Other*, U of Oklahoma P, 1999).

TVERSKY, AMOS
1977 "Features of Similarity." *Psychological Review* 81: 327–52.

VAINA, LUCIA
1983 "From Shapes and Movements to Objects and Actions." *Synthese* 54: 3–36.

VARELA, FRANCISCO, ET AL.
1992 *The Embodied Mind*. Cambridge: MIT Press.

VATTIMO, GIANNI
1980 *Le avventure della differenza*. Milano: Garzanti, 84. (Eng. trans. *The Adventures of Difference: Philosophy After Nietzsche and Heidegger (Parallax Re-visions of Cultures and Society)*, Johns Hopkins UP, 1993).
1983 "Dialettica, differenza, pensiero debole." In Vattimo, G., and P. A. Rovatti, eds. *Il pensiero debole*. Milano: Feltrinelli.
1994 *Oltre l'interpretazione*. Bari: Laterza.

VIOLI, PATRIZIA
1991 "Linguaggio percezione, esperienza: Il caso della spazialità." In Cacciari, ed. 1991: 59–106.
1997 *Significato ed esperienza*. Milano: Bompiani.

VOLLI, UGO
1972 "Some Possible Developments of the Concept of Iconism." *VS* 3: 14–29.

WIERZBICKA, ANNA

1990   *Semantics: Primes and Universals*. Oxford: Oxford UP.

WITTGENSTEIN, LUDWIG

1922   *Tractatus Logico-Philosophicus*. London: Routledge. (Eng. trans. *Tractatus Logico-Philosophicus,* Routledge, 1981).

1953   *Philosophische Untersuchungen*. Oxford: Blackwell. (Eng. trans. *Philosophical Investigations,* Prentice Hall, 1973).

ZIJNO, ALESSANDRO

1997   *Fortunatamente capita di fraintendersi: Intersezioni tra la concezione di lingua di Donald Davidson e la Teoria della Pertinenza*. Ph.D. thesis in semiotics. U of Bologna. A. Y., 1995–96.

INDEX

abduction, 60, 64, 92, 96, 98, 431*n*33
abstract semes, 170
affordances, 161–63, 184, 188, 236, 409*n*38
Alhazen, 349
Alkindi, 349
alpha mode, 383–86, 389–92
Aristotle: and Aristotelian classifications, 6, 87; and being, 10, 15–17, 21–28, 39–40, 394*n*2; and categories, 146–48; and form, 87; and knowledge, 70, 74; and schema, 66, 67, 89–90
Arnheim, Rudolf, 162, 167
attentionality, 14–15, 61
Aubenque, Pierre, 24, 395*n*10
Avicenna, 18–19

Banks, Joseph, 243
Bartezzaghi, Stefano, 6
Barthes, Roland, 341
being: and Aristotle, 10, 15–17, 21–28, 39–40, 394*n*2; and continuum, 52–55; duplication of, 26–31; and Gorgias, 9–10; and Heidegger, 11, 26–30, 34–35, 50, 394*n*9,

395*n*11; and interpretation, 4; and knowledge, 35–43, 45; and language, 22, 23–26, 27, 31–32, 44, 45, 47, 51, 52, 54, 55; and languages, 11, 12, 19, 27, 28, 36, 39–40, 43, 44, 52, 53, 54; and perspective, 42–50; and poetry, 31–35, 45, 46, 47, 49, 56; problem of, 15–17; and reality, 17–18, 29, 394*n*8; reason for, 17–20; resistances of, 50–52, 56; and semantics, 9; and semiotics, 12–15, 60–61
Bennet, George, 247
Berkeley, George, 18, 337
beta mode, 383–86, 389–92
Bewick, Thomas, 243
Bickerton, Derek, 159
Blainville, Henri-Marie Ducrotay de, 245
Bligh, William, 241–42
Blumenbach, Johann Friedrich, 243
Borges, Jorge Luis, 1, 6
Brahe, Tycho, 98, 255, 266
Braque, Georges, 162
British Empiricists, 67, 68, 69